# SCIENCE AND PHILOSOPHY

# SCIENCE
# AND PHILOSOPHY
## AND OTHER ESSAYS

## BERNARD BOSANQUET
FELLOW OF THE BRITISH ACADEMY

" Philosophy rests on the whole spectacle of the ordered universe, and on the judgments of value which are essentially and rationally implied in that vision."

*Essay Index Reprint Series*

## BOOKS FOR LIBRARIES PRESS, INC.
FREEPORT, NEW YORK

First Published 1927
Reprinted 1967

TO THE

MEMORY OF

HELEN BOSANQUET

# PREFACE

BERNARD BOSANQUET'S philosophical activity between 1884, the date of the publication of the translations from Lotze, which he edited, and 1923, the year of his death, is represented by some twenty volumes. Few, if any, of the philosophical writers of his time can show work of the same range and uniform distinction. But while engaged upon these books he was an indefatigable contributor to *Mind*, the *Proceedings of the Aristotelian Society*, the *International Journal of Ethics* and other periodicals, as well as to volumes of lectures and essays under his own or other editorship. No writer was less given to repeat himself, and all of these occasional writings add to what is contained in his more substantial works on the same subjects. Too many of them are now only with difficulty accessible, and it was the last labour of love, to which his wife, Helen Bosanquet, devoted herself, to collect the best of them with a view to republication. Her own sudden death last year prevented her from completing this task. We have tried to carry out her wishes so far as possible, merely adding one or two to the papers she had collected, and arranging them according to the subjects with which they dealt, without much regard to chronological order. For permission to reprint them we desire to thank the Editors and Committees responsible for the journals named above, the Council of the British Academy, and Messrs. Macmillan, who published the volume of essays, *Aspects of the Social Problem*.

Any lengthy Preface, biographical or other, is here unnecessary. What Helen Bosanquet desired that the world should know of her husband's personality will be found in the finely restrained " Short Account of his Life " which she published in 1924. Articles dealing with his position in philosophy will be found in vol. xxxii, No. 12, of *Mind*, and vol. xxxii, No. 6, of the *Philosophical Review*. But a few words of explanation seem called for by the title we have chosen for the volume.

We have taken it from the essay we have placed first, in spite of the apparent absence of any further discussion of scientific subjects in the narrower sense of that term in the subsequent essays. For there is a certain appropriateness in the title even as applied to them. Science and philosophy have drawn closer together in our time. Scientific writers have shown a keen interest in the philosophical investigation of the concepts and principles which underlie their methods. Philosophers, on their part, have recognized the great importance of the borderland between mathematics and logic on the one hand, physics and metaphysics on the other. While this has meant a certain *entente* between science and philosophy, it has also suggested a division. Kant himself raised the question whether problems of value in morals, æsthetics, and religion were properly a subject of scientific treatment, and attempts have recently been made to limit philosophy to the properties, categories and logical forms that are common to all departments of knowledge on the ground that, so soon as questions of value for life enter, it is impossible to exclude subjective preferences, which inevitably bias the thinker and vitiate the result.

Bosanquet had the liveliest sympathy with the new relations between science and philosophy, but he regarded the view that would rule out of the domain of either of them the great constructive work of philosophers from Plato and Aristotle to Spinoza and Hegel (not to speak of others nearer our time) in ethics and politics, æsthetics and religion, as entirely arbitrary and itself an instance of a narrow theoretic bias. A man may think that there is nothing like leather, but that does not justify him in denying that there is any other wear.

The first of the following articles deals with this question, and is a plea for the view that a theory of ethics, æsthetics, religion, or for the matter of that of logic (in so far as it deals with the criterion of truth), will be known, like other things, by its fruits. It cannot be ruled out on a priori grounds from the field of legitimate knowledge. Whether such knowledge should be called " scientific " or not is a matter of words. Science is what science does. If these subjects can be shown, after experiment, to be susceptible of systematic and, from the side of human life, fruitful treatment, they have all the justification that can reasonably be required for them. From this point of view the subsequent articles in the first part, and even more so those in the second and third parts, may be regarded as essays in support of the main contention with which the volume opens and as supplying what Coleridge in a similar connection calls " the link or mordant by which philosophy becomes scientific and the sciences philosophical."

We add references to the journals and books from which these papers have been taken.

I. *Proceedings of the Aristotelian Society*, N.S. xv (1915), pp. 1–21.

II. *Essays and Addresses* (1889, now published by George Allen and Unwin), pp. 162–180. Read before the Aristotelian Society. First printed in *Mind*, xiii (1888).

III. *Essays and Addresses*, pp. 181–198. An address given before the Edinburgh Philosophical Society.

IV. *Proceedings of the Aristotelian Society*, N.S. xi (1911), pp. 29–40.

V. *Mind*, N.S. xv (1906), No. 57, pp. 1–12.

VI. *Proceedings of the Aristotelian Society*, N.S. xviii (1918), pp. 479–506. Also published by the Society in a special volume, *Life and Finite Individuality* (1918), pp. 75–102.

VII. *Proceedings of the Aristotelian Society*, iii (1896), pp. 1–10.

VIII. *Proceedings of the Aristotelian Society*, ii (1894), pp. 44–50.

J. H. MUIRHEAD
R. C. BOSANQUET
*Editors*

# CONTENTS

## C.—ÆSTHETICS

# A.—LOGIC AND METAPHYSICS

# I

## SCIENCE AND PHILOSOPHY [1]

THE main subject with which I deal in this paper is the question in what way, if at all, philosophy is concerned with human interests and desires, and therefore with the world of concrete fact. The importance of this problem for our whole view of philosophy has been impressed on me anew by some expressions in Mr. Russell's recent lectures *On our Knowledge of an External World.* There is a great deal of matter in this book which I should have liked to discuss at length, little competent as I am in regard to certain aspects of it. But to do so would have required a treatise, and I shall do best to confine myself, in principle, to the subject which I have indicated. I should hope, by giving a fairly full consideration to this single point, and a single example of it, to make clear a view of the traditional philosophy differing in principle from that of the work referred to.

I will approach the subject in this way. There has been a growing desire, I think, of late, on the part of students of philosophy to claim for their subject the name of science and the reputation of scientific method. I have always regarded with some misgiving Kant's famous aspiration to " the sure march of a science," which I have held in my own mind to be responsible for a good deal of false route-making in modern philosophy. One simple test of the influence of this aspiration, and of the sense in which it is interpreted, is the prevalence of the opinion that philosophy should be, as I suppose exact science is in the main—I really do not know, in detail, how far this is true—cosmopolitan in character and free from special national qualities. Of course, all students can learn from each other, and can co-operate, in a general sense, for the advancement of knowledge. But I share the opinion of the late Professor

[1] From *Proceedings of the Aristotelian Society,* 1914–15.

Wallace [1] that philosophy, being, like language, art, and poetry, a product of the whole man, is a thing which would forfeit some of its essence if it were to lose its national quality. The technical reasons for this we shall see below. I take it to be a fundamental difference between philosophy and exact or mathematical science, which restricts itself to a more limited object and springs from a more specialized capacity.

But I must not give an impression that Mr. Russell holds philosophy either to be one with science or to be a summary of its results. On the contrary, philosophy, as he holds, must consist of propositions which could not occur in the other sciences ; propositions which, like those of mathematics, would be true of all abstractly possible worlds, and among which such a difference, for example, as that between a good and a bad world is not sufficiently abstract to appear. Indeed, all questions which have what is called a human interest—such as the question of a future life—belong, for him, in theory to special sciences and not to philosophy. Nevertheless, in respect of ethical neutrality and the philosophical temper of mind, it is the ideal of the special physical sciences which he holds before the philosopher. Ethical neutrality, in psychology as in physics, has been essential to scientific success ; and it is no less essential in philosophy. This principle, I must add, is insisted on more particularly in the critique of evolutionism, though it is taken as also constituting a censure upon the philosophy of the past.

Philosophy, therefore, repudiates not merely the attempt to prove that particular pleasant things are true, because they are pleasant, but it declines to inquire into any problems of the nature or conditions, the presence or absence in the universe, of satisfaction or satisfactoriness : that is, the character of objects which produce satisfaction in intelligent beings. Philosophy, in the work cited above, deals with nothing but general and a priori propositions, such as state properties in which all abstractly possible worlds agree. The typical problems in which the new philosophy already claims successes are such as number, infinity, continuity of space and time. Philosophy, I think it would be fair to say, is considered as dealing with the pure logical forms common to every

[1] I speak from memory.

possible universe. It is the theory of the universal factors in all possible theory.

In contrast with this conception of philosophy it is charged against the philosophy of the past that it has been biased by human interests and the desire for agreeable results. It has thus investigated matters which, as I understand, either are obviously facts to be determined, if at all, by special empirical sciences, such as whether or no there is a future life or, at all events, are *de facto* qualities of particular things in particular worlds, like the presence of good and evil, and therefore are, compared with true philosophical problems, also mere questions of fact.

Here, in my judgment, a fundamental issue is raised as to the object-matter and area of philosophy. But I by no means hold that the criticism just referred to is altogether groundless. I should answer as follows.

You cannot define what questions should be asked until you know a good deal of the form which the answer will take. You cannot rule out this or that investigation unless the course of the inquiry has already shown you that it is not going to lead to an answer relevant to the sense of the inquiry. Two things follow from this. First, it is natural and normal that, within the general province of the desire to know, particular problems should have to be discriminated by degrees. Thus there is a perpetual progression of questions being raised by philosophy which cannot in the end be answered by it. Its curiosity, the general desire to know, is omnivorous, and only points out the peculiar channel which it has ultimately to assume as the varied inquiries which it originates diverge from it and form particular routes of their own. And so, secondly, when we raise the question what problems and of what nature really belong to philosophy, it is again impossible to rule out subjects of inquiry otherwise than because of the line taken by the investigation itself. It is nothing to tell us that our interest is to be purely theoretical. There is a purely theoretical interest whenever anything of any kind can be found out. What we want to know, with a view to determining the limits of our subject, viz. philosophy, is what connected object-matter, other than that of inquiries which prove themselves to have the limitations of a special science, there is revealed by the actual pursuit of the general desire to know. If I am asked what I mean by the limitations of a special science, I answer unhesitatingly that the investigation itself must decide. The more an inquiry burrows into its own hole, neither depending on a general view of what we experience, nor contributing to one, the more nearly it is a special science, and the less it belongs to philosophy. And once more, positively, what inquiries belong to philosophy, only the investigation itself can show. It is not dependent on our antecedent ideas, and all prescription of methods is futile. It grows like a tree, or burrows, to use our former metaphor, like a mine. And what hangs together in its progress belongs together, and what is discriminated as we go forward is distinct.

But the view we are discussing suggests an antecedent limitation, and it seems to me that in the suggestion a very obvious confusion is operative. The confusion is this. It is implied that because the interest of philosophy is purely theoretical, therefore the matter about which it theorizes must itself be theory and its objects. Thus philosophy is confined to the theory of theory, including under the second reference to theory those forms of being—number and the rest—which are specially taken account of in physical and mathematical science. Philosophy becomes equivalent to Logic and that the Logic of the objects of science.

Now, is there any ground whatever for this restriction? There are great worlds of human interest, embodied in structures and experiences which prima facie have as good a claim as anything else to become the objects of disinterested consideration. Such worlds, for instance, are the world of æsthetic experience and the world of religion, morality, society. They themselves, indeed, are not, like the world of science, primarily structures of theory. They are, in a sense, not impartial as to human interests. They are themselves human interests—interests of finite minds—in a concrete form.

But the impartial and theoretical nature of philosophy furnishes no reason at all why these existing interests, themselves not theoretical, should not be included among its objects. They are, to describe them in general, worlds of satisfaction. And there is no reason that I can see a priori to exclude from philosophical investigation the nature of satisfaction and the objective character which it involves, and which may be called satisfactoriness. If the course of the investigation proves that no result can follow from pursuing this line of inquiry, then the question falls to the ground. I only say that prima facie the character of satisfaction and satisfactoriness is an object of general theory which is in no way ruled out by the fact that it is not necessarily itself of a theoretical nature. The only question is whether it is capable of being investigated by logical processes of thought, and that, surely, nothing but the attempt can show.

I am obliged so far to differ from an expression employed by Mr. Carr in his interesting work on *Change*. He seems to me, in agreement with a very considerable movement of philosophy since the return to Kant, to adopt the principle which I am disputing. I do not know that it really makes much difference to his fundamental contention. But he considers, if I follow him rightly, that philosophy is a peculiar study just in the fact that it is the theory of theory and not the theory of the world. I believe that the restriction of Philosophy to the theory of cognition, which follows from this assumption, is a false route, due largely to Kant's aspiration after the sure march of a science.

For the sake of illustration, as the point seems to me all-important, I will briefly refer to another writer who unwarily at one time fell into a similar view, and I will explain where it now seems to me that he was mistaken. When I wrote about Logic I am afraid that I really thought, though I did not loudly proclaim it, that Logic was the whole of philosophy. I argued thus to myself : Philosophy is the connected system of the form or ultimate universal essence of all objects, including, of course, all systems of objects. Now about all objects or systems of objects, the pure truth, so far as ascertainable, is to be sought for in the sciences and not elsewhere. Therefore, if it were possible to analyse out of the sciences and exhibit in their connection the universal essence of all objects and their systems, one would have in the result at once a logic and a philosophy.

But I now seem to myself to see that the common oversight of all such argumentation is just this : Philosophy no doubt is a theory and its interest is theoretical. But no presumption arises from this that its object-matter is in turn a theory, or objects or kinds of being as apprehended through theories. Its object, prima facie, is the universe, with all its activities and values, among which the theories of exact science with their objects form only a certain proportion.

And we are not to be told that this is to subordinate truth to our subjective desires. Such an objection, like the views which I have referred to above, would rest on a mere confusion. Satisfaction in the subject prima facie involves satisfactoriness (value) in the object, and to rule out the problem of satisfactoriness in general from philosophical inquiry is to anticipate the course of philosophical investigation and to violate the law of method, that the true form of a question can only be determined in so far as its answer is known.

Thus it appears to me that the very plausible position, which I once shared, must be fundamentally modified. Logic, as the theory of theory and of its objects, is not the whole of Philosophy. The object-matter of Philosophy is much more than the object-matter of Logic—unless, in a way which I shall suggest, and the idea of which to some extent influenced my former position, the area of Logic is very widely extended. For philosophy deals with the universe, in which the characters fundamental for science form only a single province, by the side of others no less illuminating. Besides the theory of what concerns the sciences, a philosophy which is to have any claim to deal with the universe is bound prima facie to undertake a theoretical consideration at least of beauty and of goodness. There is no less and no more reason, to start with, for the former than for the two latter. Whether each can maintain itself as a fruitful investigation depends on the course of the investigation itself, and cannot in any way be determined beforehand. All of them, as branches of philosophy, are alike theoretical, and the demand is rightly to be maintained that their interest shall be the pure interest of knowledge. But to suggest that a pure theoretical interest can only apply itself to the investigation of pure theory and its objects is at best, it seems to me, a mere verbal confusion.

But we have not yet completed our view of philosophy. For, applying to logic itself the conception which we began by eliciting in the case of other branches of philosophy, we see that it also is liable to be described as an inquiry into a form of satisfaction, with the necessary correlation of a certain form of satisfactoriness. This character of logic is prima facie obvious, and nothing but the detailed investigation can further confirm or can overthrow it. But supposing that investigation reveals a common and fundamental character in the objects studied by the several branches of philosophy whatever they may be, it is clearly possible that this common character will afford the object-matter for a more general mode of consideration, which will be the only one applicable to the whole of experience and of what is experienced as such. This most general mode of consideration will be metaphysic. It will differ from logic in two obvious ways. It will not restrict itself to the area of the forms concerned in the sciences, but will look directly at all the provinces of what is experienced. And, reflecting upon Logic itself, it will find in it and its objects and its criteria just one case among others of the main principle of reality ; the principle which investigation detects as satisfactoriness in all provinces of the universe, though not in all equally.

The result would be, as indeed recommends itself unconquerably to common sense, that Metaphysic, as the central philosophy, would be altogether a wider theory than that of logic, dealing primarily with all great modes of satisfactoriness which the whole body of experience presents to the theoretical spectator. Of such modes logic itself is one, and, dealing directly with the ultimate forms of connection and completeness, has a prominent place in helping to detect the characters which pervade all reality and constitute its cohesion or interconnection. I insert the latter term so as not to exclude *ex hypothesi* all forms of plurality.

For of plurality, as of other possible characters which might be selected to push forward against our suggested account of philosophy, one can say in a preface or general study only that their claims must be referred to the investigation itself. So, again, if it should be said—and in a preface or introductory essay anything may be said—" You give prominence to beauty and goodness because you like them and like to think they are prevalent ; why not take evil, disorder, natural appetite as your clues and names of provinces, and treat your universe as made up of such departments as these ? " The answer is simple. It makes no difference where you begin. The inquiry itself takes charge of the form of the question, and cannot but lead to the same recognition of structure, from whatever isolated phenomena we may make our start. The difference between good and bad, for instance, resolves itself into a fundamental difference in types of order, such that the bad necessarily presupposes the good and falls within it. So that any investigation which starts from the phenomena of the former is necessarily led to affirm it in its real correlation with its foundation in the latter.

Now we are prepared to estimate the criticism that our theoretical interest in systems of satisfactoriness is one with a bias in favour of the aims of private desire. The technical point is that on which we have just been insisting. The inquiry into reality as such may begin anywhere ; and it is very natural that in the process of defining itself it should pass through a phase of taking up and sifting the suggestions propounded by personal and private interests. These interests exist ; they must indicate some character of the universe ; and they are, therefore, to the problems of metaphysic as particular parts of daily observation are to the theories of science. When confronted with the problems of reality, they have undoubtedly some contribution to bring. In a theory which has to face the universe as a whole, nothing which is can be treated as if it were not. The attempt to do so at once convicts the theory which attempts it of arbitrary superficiality.

But what has to happen is this : Every personal bias and desire has to be scrutinized—it is the mere consequence of the large aim of the theory—with reference to what it indicates in the completeness or incompleteness of the universe. The natural thing, then, historically speaking, is for problems of this kind to split in two. The significance of such a problem being raised remains for philosophy. The problem as one of particular fact may or may not prove possible to be attacked by the methods of science. It is easy to observe the progress of this discrimination in such a question as that of the continued existence of the higher and lower animals after what we call death. *Sentimus experimurque nos æternos esse.* This is plainly an experience demanding philosophical consideration. You may rule it out as mystic after a metaphysical inquiry, but hardly before. On the other hand, there comes the question of fact as to the survival of living beings, which has nothing specially philosophic or of religious interest about it at all. We can see in the historical attitude of philosophy to the latter how the discrimination between the two attitudes is promoted by the actual investigation. But we seldom or never see the attitude of Plato, for example, correctly represented. It is in the main an inquiry what sort of perfection can be held possible for a finite soul, and how this perfection would be subserved by the various forms of continuance familiar to popular imagination, supposing any one of them to be real.

Now that we have cleared away, I hope, the prejudice that would deny to philosophy the right of direct inquiry into reality at first hand, we are ready to approach the relation of philosophy to science, and to compare the progress of the former with the sure march of the latter.

It is true, we shall find, and for good reason, that philosophy does not emulate the advance of the particular sciences by making discoveries after the manner which their problems prescribe to them. It is not true, we shall find, and for reasons equally good, that philosophy fails to make the kind of progress which her own problem dictates and demands, and which is necessarily and essentially different from making discoveries of the kind by which the several sciences advance.

In the gradual discrimination of the inquiries initiated confusedly by the omnivorous appetite for knowledge, two classes of truths come to be plainly distinguished—statements of particular fact, and statements of general connections. These constitute the branches of knowledge which fulfil less and more completely the ideal of science. What they give us are laws of the world of objects in shapes less or more separated from unessential matter—less so in statements of fact, more so in statements of law. Assuming these two classes of truths to be segregated, the appetite for knowledge has not yet received its fullest and characteristic satisfaction. There still remains before it, as an object of investigation, the whole body of what is experienced, taken together, including both what comes through truth, and also what comes directly in the various forms and structures of living. About this whole body, not of what is known only, but including what is given in feeling, in action, in valuation and the structures and systems which realize them, the appetite for theoretical understanding is compelled to make affirmations. As analysis has amply demonstrated, these affirmations, and these alone, are what directly and ultimately satisfy its demand. For they alone are what directly and ultimately affirm about the totality of things, which is its final and characteristic object. Truths of particular fact, which in a certain sense give reality, can give with it no rational connection. Truths of principle and connection, which in a certain sense give rationality, give nothing persistent or actual—nothing but the linkage of possibilities. The sort of reality which sequences of possibilities demand as their basis, and which actuality demands as its rationale, cannot be expressed either as a fact or as a law. It demands affirmations of what is at once actual as contrasted with the linkage of possibility, and necessary as contrasted with fact. These alone can satisfy the appetite for knowledge, which has discriminated and set aside the more elementary types of statement, as steps in its approach to these. They alone are true categorical judgments, and the system of them is philosophy.

So far I have avoided the traditional expression that philosophy is the investigation of reality as such, or of being *qua* being. Because in a sense everything is real or has being, and before we had made some progress in discrimination it would have been impossible to answer the question what was intended by the additional phrase " as such." But now we have at least a negative answer. When all particular facts, and all abstract connections, have been discriminated within what we are endeavouring to know, there still remains the demand, which so far nothing at all has been done to satisfy, that we should make some effort to apprehend the universe which surrounds and penetrates us, in its own character, by affirmations which characterize it and not merely factors within it. This attempt, to speak about the whole complex to which we belong in its own character, and without isolating part from part by selected conditions or reservations, gives the meaning of the expression " an inquiry into reality *as such*." The feasibility of the inquiry cannot be determined a priori. If we find out anything, we find it ; if not, not. It is an old and true remark that anyone who professes himself able to deny a priori the possibility of any type of knowledge, already pre-supposes his own possession of some part of the knowledge which he denies to us. To protest against mere thinking is meaningless. Nothing but thinking can give knowledge ; and all thinking without any exception is the endeavour of certain experiences to affirm themselves as a whole. From what depth and width of experience such a process can produce results of value, nothing but thinking itself can tell us. Obviously not ; for there is nothing else that can give to knowledge any results at all, and therefore you can overthrow the results of thinking only by those of other thinking, and any issue between the two is simply a theoretical conflict, like another, to be decided by theoretical considerations.

This characteristic of philosophy, that it speaks about the whole complex of being without any reservation, brings us to the point in which we are interested at this moment. The peculiarity is, we said, that its affirmations are fully categorical. As it makes no reservation, so it isolates no problem and admits no working hypothesis. This must be so of necessity with any endeavour of thought that tries to speak of reality in its own character. Plainly no affirmation about reality can be true which is inconsistent with any true affirmation about it. Fictions, and consequences drawn from mere possibilities, are altogether excluded. This seems to me, I may add, to be the moral of Husserl's curious view of the a priori, which stands alone, I believe, among doctrines of this subject, in admitting that a priori propositions may often contradict each other, and need reconciliation. That is to say, what passes for a priori is usually mere prima facie. Such an a priori has no place in philosophy.

Now this characteristic affects the problem of progress in philosophy. A famous teacher used to say, it is reported, with reference to people who wished philosophy to be scientific : " They want to make discoveries." The implication is that philosophy ought not to make discoveries in the sense in which the sciences make them, and prima facie admits the censure of unprogressiveness. What distinction between science and philosophy is here signalized ?

The answer follows plainly from what has been said. The essence of philosophy lies in the connected vision of the totality of things, maintaining in every point the subordination of every element and factor to every other element and factor as conditioned by the totality. It may be compared to the best theory of Impressionism. You may perfect your detail and finish as much as you please, but there is one inexorable condition. Lose subordination to the whole and all is lost. You must never violate the singleness of the impression.

And the impression whose singleness is the condition of philosophy is not, we saw, that of the mere encyclopædia of the sciences. It includes the direct contemplation—the valuation —of the whole spectacle of life. And nothing can be affirmed as true in philosophy which does not sustain itself in a thinking process to which the whole of this experience is contributory.

The result for our immediate argument is twofold. Philosophy can never be revolutionized by discovery; and it can never fail to be progressive so long as thinking is possible and human nature changes.

It can never be revolutionized by discovery, as, for all I know, a particular science may be, and as a particular branch of technique certainly often is. This, I take it, is the meaning of saying that in it you cannot make discoveries. Philosophy rests on the whole spectacle of the ordered universe, and on the judgments of value which are essentially and rationally implied in that vision. To revolutionize it would be more than to pass from one civilization to another, though that is perhaps the nearest realizable analogy. It would almost be to pass from one universe to another. In estimating such sayings as these, it must be remembered that philosophy does not make itself. It is in the main a reading of civilization.

And it cannot fail to be progressive. A limited technique, which is readily revolutionized by a discovery, can hardly be progressive. A whole way of doing is abandoned, and a new one takes its place. But the vision of reality, which embodies the changes of life and knowledge, while retaining the singleness of its first impressions, must necessarily progress so long as thought survives. It must progress, because it incorporates new matter with old. If it dropped the old in passing to the new, then indeed there would be change, but no certainty of progress.

What I have been saying may be more simply put by referring to what will commonly, I think, be admitted—that there are subjects, and those some of the greatest, on which the judgments of great men are of especially permanent value. I do not believe it to be true that the acquired content of philosophy, with its reactions on the world, is second in importance to that of any other intellectual activity. Any view of the history of culture which suggests this inference I take to be a caricature. It is not a matter, I should contend, of belief in specific dogmas. It is a matter of the recognition and appreciation of great structural worlds. The apparent differences of dogma which divide philosophers are as nothing compared with the differences of recognition which divide all philosophical students from those who have not seriously busied themselves with the matter. The relation between Kant and Hume is a good example of substantive agreement between thinkers who rank as polar antagonists.

Of course I know well how open to objection and even to mockery is such a picture of philosophy. I am just identifying it, I may be told, with the subjective impressions of individuals upon things in general guided by their likings. I am allowing it nothing at any point precise or verifiable or scientific.

Now I have been endeavouring to be positive rather than negative, and to explain as frankly as possible what sort of thing I took philosophy to be, in preference to guarding myself against obvious criticisms on special points. But I will indicate in a few sentences the line of my answer in principle to censure of that type.

There is, I am convinced, no demand for accuracy so severe as that which is inherent in the criterion applied by philosophy to the categorical judgments which compose it. For their essence is to be tenable only when corrected and sustained by the whole body of propositions which can be affirmed of the real as such. Isolation, which is as I understand the essence of working hypotheses and of the strictly scientific method, is here inadmissible. Only the hypothetical can be isolated ; the categorical challenges all reality, and is false if it anywhere in the universe of experience meets with an insuperably refractory element, and I think that many students will agree with me that, where the method of working hypothesis is introduced into philosophical reasoning, there does appear to result an extraordinary want of precision. To me this seems natural. It is only in philosophy that you may not suppose what you please, as long as for your immediate purpose it will help you to obtain a result. In philosophy you must take things as they are, that is to say, if you are going to make use of special points of view, you must show that these points of view are not in conflict with well-established facts. If you follow a method which does not conform to this requirement, then I think you fall greatly below the standard of precision and verification demanded by philosophy. The whole treatment of data, for example, in the work which I began by referring to, seems to many of us to rest so entirely on fictions *ad hoc* that it has no place in a philosophical argument at all. I appeal to any modern account of the objects of sense perception.

I can illustrate this contrast of total attitude, without going into metaphysical argument, by the impression which I gather from some remarks on Interrelatedness in the work in question. I take this example, as one which prima facie in a careless statement tells against my view, in order to show how much agreement may be pointed out between the supposed paradox of the philosopher and the deliverance of common experience, on condition that both are seriously examined with completeness and impartiality.

We are told that Mr. Bradley pronounces relations impossible. But there is more likely to be error, the author continues, in his very subtle argument, than in so patent a fact as the interrelatedness of things in the world. And then mention is made of experiment and the empirical outlook in contrast with a priori errors, quite after the manner of John Mill.

Now the author seems to me not in any way to imagine how totally foreign all this suggestion appears, rightly or wrongly, to the problem at issue as others among us see it. The very intimate affinity of the outlook of traditional philosophy for such a doctrine, for example, as naïve realism, and the very special and limited sense in which alone it can have to do with a priori thinking, seem not in any way to be present to him. The sort of difficulty it is dealing with, and the kind of way in which it is approaching it, do not seem to us to have come near to his mind at all.

Without going into the dialectic of relations, but treating the matter on the basis on which the author puts it, as a question of the estimation of facts, I begin by saying that all the absoluteness—the rigidity of statement—is on the critic's side. Mr. Bradley has, one might say, exhausted his very considerable resources of language in pointing out the two-sidedness of the problem, and how, if you cannot do with relations, no more can you do without them. It is the rigidity of the critic's dogma that philosophy and fact appear to join in impeaching.

Now my modest contribution is merely this: Whatever, I urge, may be the ultimate truth in metaphysic or in science, certainly a complete and sympathetic outlook over our world does not warrant the critic's attitude. In common experience throughout life the interrelatedness of things, if strictly construed, is no doubt at times a very valuable point of view, but is not a very prominent or patent fact.

The first point that strikes one is that, by the ordinary mind, in quite commonplace and unreflective apprehension, a great part of our surroundings are not considered as things at all. We do not analyse them so. Out of doors, in the country, the conception of things hardly ever occurs to us. Fields, hills, moors, roads, the sky—these are not thought of as *things*, as terms of relations, each at arm's length to others, a discriminated unit. "I see no lines in nature," said the French artist, and I think he might well have said, "I see no relations." Interrelatedness belongs surely to the sort of stage at which you begin to think in terms of maps or diagrams, and set down positions or reactions of isolated units with reference to one another. For relations in the strict sense you surely must have strictly bounded and distinguished terms; and in ordinary life we recognize nothing of the kind, except when we are handling portable objects, from which our notion of "things" is, in the main, derived. Continuity, in the popular sense, is the leading character of our world. I do not know exactly how one's kinsmen come to be called one's relations; but I think that this narrow reference of the word in everyday usage shows how unfamiliar is the general or logical idea of interrelatedness in common life.

An obvious objection will carry us further. You are talking, it may be replied, of spatial relation; and you are using as your *schema* to represent them a sort of line or thread, which presupposes terms removed from each other by spatial boundaries like islands on a map. But relations are of more and richer kinds than this ; they need not be spatial, and they may include any kind of combination or meeting point or reaction or common frontier.

Very well ; it is admitted then that this sort of inter-relatedness, which is shown e.g. on a map of a countryside, as opposed to the intimate knowledge of the countryside itself and loving habit of intercourse with it, is not a thing common or present or patent to the ordinary mind of the country-dweller. But it is urged that you can find much richer inter-relatedness than that symbolized by a map, and this, it is implied, *is* something patent and predominant in our daily experience. Let us see. Before going further, we may ask, in speaking of interrelatedness, though of course it need not be spatial, there is yet a limit to its unity, is there not ? We are not to say all or any unity is interrelatedness, are we ? If so, of course, *cadit quæstio* ; but with it falls all attempt to represent philosophy as objecting to interrelatedness.

I suppose when you speak of relations and terms you do necessarily isolate them from the rest of the world. You exclude, *pro tempore*, the bearing upon them of any thing or fact, not specified in the terms, or in those relations between them which have been named. I do not mean that you deny the existence of anything else ; but *ex hypothesi qua* thinking relationally, you disregard it *ad hoc*. It is this negative aspect of relations that makes them *suspect* to common sense. Let me give a non-spatial instance. Two persons are described as in the relation of master and servant. Now the relation thus stated—take it e.g. as a basis of jural obligations—does exclude, does it not ? all consideration of them except as master and servant. Now plain fact and common sense protest that no such relation is a real fact of the world. It is a good point of view to take into consideration ; but it is no solid fact ; and no solid fact can be of such a character.

And if you rejoin, " Of course that is understood, but relations are to be reasonably interpreted with regard to what they imply," then I say you are being carried away along a path on which there is no necessary halting-point. You are, and this is our complaint of all non-philosophical method, not insisting on your distinction to the bitter end. You are taking your hypothesis lightly and easily, and working it just as you please, without strict and severe attention to what it actually says and demands when confronted with the great body of experience. For what you have now before you, in the "relation" thus leniently interpreted, is no longer a relation, but some complete form of unity, some real totality such as the community, or the moral world, or humanity, within which, of course, there may be countless relations, but none of them strictly taken suffice to constitute a real fact or entity, and none is in ordinary life ever dreamed of as doing so.

Thus relations, strictly speaking, not only are never thought of by the unreflective mind, but they are, if strictly understood, unsatisfactory to the mind which contemplates things at all completely. *Summum jus, summa injuria.*

Let us think of a familiar human face. The pupils of the eyes may be three inches apart, and when the head is erect the line that joins them would be horizontal. Undoubtedly the eyes can be considered as thus interrelated. But would anyone, looking at a human face, still more at a friend's face, think of it in this way, except for some special purpose, such as fitting a pair of spectacles to it ?

I may be told that selection does not falsify. But I am not at this moment arguing that it does. I am not saying that such relations are false, but only that interrelatedness of this kind is not a patent fact, because, in reality, no one even thinks of it. But, it may be rejoined as before : That is your fault ; there are plenty more relations of the eyes to each other and to the rest of the face, relations of all kinds, not merely spatial. If you took in all these, you would be reproducing quite a fair idea of the face, and there would be nothing odd or unusual in your account of it.

Yes, but in as far as you approached something like a portrait, you would be getting away from the point of view of relations. It would then be straining language to say you had got a complex of relations between the features, instead of simply saying you had reproduced the face. When you had once recovered the singleness of the impression, however much you might seem to have built it up out of relations, the relations as such would have disappeared, and that which replaced them would be an experience of a different type, an individual unity.

In fact, relations are thought of in the main at certain stages of experience. The interrelatedness of things can only be a prominent fact when we are thinking about the world in terms of discriminated things or persons and when we are not thinking about it in terms of breadths or unities, the singleness of impression with regard to which has either never been destroyed or has been fully recovered. If we mean by its being a patent fact that it is a way of thinking which is often necessary and whose truth in a way cannot be denied, the interrelatedness is a patent fact and I do not think that any philosophy rejects it. But if we mean, as the antithesis to the view of traditional philosophy implies, that it is something generally obvious, and thoroughly endorsed by common sense and experience, and of wide value and influence in every-day thinking or in the fullest knowledge of things, then *negatur*. A categorical view of the world does not bear it out.

My contribution has arrived at nothing more than showing that interrelatedness occupies in the world of fact and common sense and sound judgment a position closely corresponding to that which it occupies in, for example, Mr. Bradley's philosophy. Philosophical consideration explains, and on the whole justifies, the verdict of a really serious and careful empirical outlook and the usage of common sense. And that I am convinced is the typical position of traditional philosophy. And, while its essence does not lie in discoveries that revolutionize it, if a doubt is raised whether it has something valuable and of its own to reveal to thought, I point to the simple facts. Its demand for precision is so intense, and its valuations are drawn from so universal and critical a survey, that its opponents can be shown, I think, in quite definite and assignable respects, not to see at all what sort of requirements they are up against. Not that by any means they fail to bring valuable material, which in time will find its due place and rank ; but they do not see the necessity of using in philosophy any such propositions as will stand a criticism motived by the whole character of the Real. Failing this, the attempt to philosophize becomes a game of play. I gather that in regard to Haeckel, on the one hand, and Mach on the other—I do not know Mach as I ought, I am thinking of Schiller's remarks—this would now be an accepted description, and I cannot help believing that it would extend further.

## II

## THE PHILOSOPHICAL IMPORTANCE OF A TRUE
## THEORY OF IDENTITY

I SHOULD like to explain very shortly why I have chosen this particular subject. Those of us who are especially accused of being interested in German philosophy are tempted either to give battle along the whole line, as by discussing the nature of reality, or to make everything seem all the same in all systems, as may easily be done by a sympathetic treatment of any special subject. I was desirous, if I could, to select a point which should be important in its bearings, but yet perfectly definite, so as to be explained, I hope, with some approach to precision. I believe myself that this is the *only* fundamental question which is or ever has been at issue between distinctively English thinkers and German idealist thinkers, as such ; but when I say the *only* question, of course I include in it its consequences, and it is the object of this paper to indicate very briefly how far-reaching these are. Other alleged differences, such as the distinction between a priori and experiential philosophy, or that between a belief in the absoluteness and in the relativity of knowledge, I take to be pure misunderstandings.

In order to state the question precisely, I will take it first in its logical form, although in this particular form English writers have sometimes seen and satirized the absurdity of the view which, in my opinion, they accept in all other provinces of philosophy.

The logical law of Identity, A is A, is susceptible of many interpretations ; but they all fall, I think, between two extremes. The one extreme is to take the principle as a demand that in every judgment there shall be some identity or positive connection between subject and predicate, which is merely symbolized by the repetition of an identical letter. This view we need not trouble ourselves with; it is nothing at all, unless further explained. But the other extreme is to take A is A as a statement of the *sort* of identity which the judgment aims at : i.e. as a type of the fullest, completest, most thorough identity, compared with which the identity in an ordinary intelligible judgment is incomplete and falls short of being genuinely identity at all. Hamilton's statement (*Logic*, i, 80) is of this kind. The law of Identity means "Everything is equal to itself." I should state the view, then, which I propose to apply and to controvert as being that perfect identity consists in the entire exclusion of difference.

The importance of this view consists in its atomic tendency. If we were to attach moral implications to theoretical views, this doctrine might be burdened, more fairly than materialism, with the chief associations which are supposed to be objectionable in materialistic conceptions. I say this by way of illustration of its importance, and not in the least believing that such associations ought to be introduced into philosophical reasoning. But the ground for connecting any such associations with this ideal of perfect Identity without difference lies in what Plato would have called its *eristic* character, that is, its tendency to exclude from judgment, and therefore from truth and knowledge, all ideal synthesis. Not, of course, that ideal synthesis ever has been or can be excluded from judgment; less deception would be possible if this were so ; but what may and does happen is that an arbitrary line is drawn across various contents of knowledge, and their identity is denied from the point at which some little effort or some little education begins to be needed in order to recognize it. In fact, all ideal syntheses which we can find out to be such are pronounced to be fictions.

If we take A is A in the sense to which I object, as meaning that the real type which undeilies the judgment is an identity without a difference, we simply destroy the judgment. There is no judgment if you assert nothing; and if there is no difference between predicate and subject, nothing is asserted. Of course in "A man's a man" we make some difference between the two terms : one means man in his isolation, the other man in his common nature, or something of that sort.

If I were asked how I should represent a true Identity, such as a judgment must express, in a schematic form with symbolic letters, I should say the problem was insoluble. Every A is B would be much better than Every A is A ; but as the letters are not parts in any whole of meaning, they are things " cut asunder with an axe," and such a formula could only correspond to a proposition like " London Bridge is one o'clock," i.e. to a spurious judgment, which would be mere nonsense.

One might try Every A is AB, which would be suitable in some respects ; but then, what is the use of repeating the A when you have it once already in the subject ? The whole difficulty would arise again in endeavouring to explain the connection between A and B in AB ; and besides, a qualification in the subject would be demanded to account for the qualification in the predicate, and we should have to recur to AB is AB. In point of fact, the letters, taken as mere letters, are atomic existences, and the judgment cannot be represented by their help. If they are used algebraically, i.e. for elements in a numerical whole, the question is different.

What, then, is Identity ? The judgment is the simplest and perhaps the ultimate expression of it. An identity is a universal, a meeting-point of differences, or synthesis of differences, and therefore always, in a sense, concrete. Or we may speak of it as the element of continuity that persists through differences. We may illustrate this idea by comparing it with Locke's notion of identity. " In this consists identity, when the ideas it is attributed to vary not at all from what they were that moment wherein we considered their former existence, and to which we compare the present " (*Essay*, Bk. ii, ch. 27). In spite of this demand for the exclusion of difference, Locke gives a very fair working account of personal identity, by limiting the points within the personality which do not vary, and ascribing identity in virtue of them. But he forgets that these points are not isolable from differences, and cannot be treated as identities simply on the ground of their not varying. If a thing is pronounced truly identical with itself only in as far as we exclude the differences of its states, attributes, and relations, identity falls into tautology, which is really incompatible with it.

Let us take such a judgment as " Cæsar crossed the Rubicon." In order to give this its full meaning we must not try to cut it down as Lotze in one place does (*Logic*, § 58), reducing Cæsar to mean merely a creature that crossed the Rubicon ; this would be A is A again. Precisely the point of the judgment is that the same man united in himself or persisted through the different relations, say, of being conqueror of Gaul and of marching into Italy. The Identity is the Individual, or the concrete universal, that persists through these relations. And if you ask what in particular this is, and try to whittle away the differences and leave the identity, you will find that when the differences are all gone the identity is all gone too. In the case of two outlines which partly coincide, you cannot speak of the coincident part as the same, except by an ideal synthesis which identifies it first with one of the two outlines and then with the other.

Identity, then, cannot exist without difference. In other words, it is always more or less conciete ; that is to say, it is the centre or unity or continuity in which different aspects, attributes, or relations hold together, or which pervades those aspects, or persists through them. It is quite accurately distinguishable from difference in known matter, but it is not isolable from difference. The element of identity between two outlines can be accurately pointed out and limited, but the moment they cease to be two, it ceases to be an identity.

This is the most vital point of recent Logic. The universal is no longer treated as an abstraction, but, so to speak, as a concretion, so that violent hands are laid even on the inverse ratio of intension to extension. We can no longer see why the universal, within which a certain element falls, should be more abstract than that element ; why, for example, the state should be a more abstract existence than the citizen.

A very good instance of this way of looking at universals is the treatment of proper names [1] as indicating universals, because they indicate persistent subjects. Most people have some sort of *schema* which helps them to handle their philosophical ideas. The traditional *schema* of the universal—even

[1] E.g. Sigwart, *Logik*, i, 83.

Mill's, I should say, though he helped to show the way out of it—was, I suppose, extent of area. The greater universal included the wider surface, and was more abstract. The *schema* I should now use would be more like a centre with radii, or simply a subject with attributes, the greater universal having the more or more varied radii or attributes, and being therefore the more concrete. Such a *schema* is particularly in harmony with taking an individual as designated by a proper name for the example of a universal.

The recognition that a universal is an identity, and vice versa, is to be seen dawning on Mill, who usually denies the operation of identity in inference, in a very interesting foot-note in the *Logic* (i, 201) directed against Mr. Spencer, who answers it in *Psychology* (i, 62, note). Mr. Spencer is more of an atomist, I believe, than any one else has ever been, for he says that the syllogism must have four terms ; i.e. the middle term is not identical in its two relations, but only similar.

The concrete view of the universal has a result antagonistic to the whole tendency which began with the class-theory of predication (closely connected with the law of Identity), and ended with Quantification of the Predicate and Equational Logic. Of course these researches have been both curious and important ; but in as far as they aim at reducing the judgment to an identity without difference, they are off the track of living thought. Jevons's idea of Identity is very difficult ; I can hardly suppose it to be thought out. But what he says (*Principles of Science*, pp. 16, 17) about the negative symbol which indicates difference, " or the absence of complete sameness," means, I think, that he considers difference an imperfection in identity. Jevons writes the judgment, " All Dicotyledons are Exogenous," as " Dicotyledons = Exogens," which he takes to mean, I suppose, that the two classes are composed of the same individuals ; i.e. their identity is in the mere sameness of the individuals. What this judgment really means is that in a particular kind of subject, a kind of tree, the different attributes of having two seed-leaves and of making fresh wood on the outside are conjoined, with a slight presumption of causality. The whole point and significance of the identity depends on the depth of the difference. So that though you can, under certain conditions, take the one term and deal with it as if it was the other, yet that is only a *consequence* of the real import of the judgment ; the real point and import is to look at the two together, as united in the same subject.

In Psychology the difference between the conception of concrete and abstract identity shows itself in the theory of Association, especially in the attitude taken up towards the law of Association by Similarity. If Identity is atomic or abstract, i.e. excludes difference, then you cannot speak of your present impression as being identical, or having identical elements, with a former impression which, *qua* former, is by the hypothesis different ; and, consequently, you must say that the first step in Association always is to go from your present impression back to another impression which is like it, before you can get to the adjuncts of that former impression, of which adjuncts the revival by association is to be explained. This first step is Association by Similarity, which, according to what was till recently, I believe, the received English theory, must always precede Association by Contiguity, that is, the transition to those adjuncts of the former impression, the recalling of which by something in present consciousness is the problem to be explained. The *theoretical* question at issue is mainly the degree in which the processes of consciousness are homogeneous at its different levels. Association of particulars might lead up to Inference from particulars to particulars, but could never lead up to the activity of judgment and inference considered as the interconnection of universals.

The question of *fact* which is involved in this question of theory is one of extreme interest. It is whether we do, in what is called transition by association, go from the presented element to the quite different context which it recalls, through a distinct particular reproduction of a former impression similar to that now presented. If this is so, we go to Contiguity always through Similarity, and in doing so we revive our former impression (I adopt the language of the theory, though, if there is no identity, we cannot *revive a former impression*, but only one like it) with complete exactness, just as if we were taking a print out of a portfolio. And the idea that we do this is attractive, because in some cases we appear to be aware of doing it in a striking way—of going right back into a former and similar state of consciousness, before we go on to the further adjuncts contiguous with that former state of consciousness.

But I do not think that this popular idea will really bear examination in the light of facts. It is plain that, as a rule, the element in present perception which sets up an association is not a particular complete in itself, and operative by calling up a former separate or self-complete particular resembling it. On the contrary, the element which sets up an association can be seen very easily (if we think of hourly, normal occurrences of the process, and not merely of striking examples in which a picturesque memory is at work), to be a characteristic *in* a present *complex* perception, not itself sensuously isolable, but identical with something *in* a former complex perception, and recalling directly, without intermediation of a similar particular, some adjunct of the former complex perception. And this adjunct, the idea whose reproduction is to be explained, is not itself a particular, but is a complex dominated by a type or rule of interconnection, which does not appear in the mind with its old particular content, but with a new one largely furnished and modified by the present content of consciousness.[1] The more closely we examine the matter, the less we shall think that contents brought up by association reappear in their old form, like prints out of a portfolio, or involve an intermediate reproduction of the old case similar to the new perception which starts the process. The illusion comes from seeking out very elaborate examples. The common cases in which association and inference can barely be distinguished are perfectly good instances, and show the continuity of the intellectual function. I hear a rumbling in the street and think that an omnibus is passing, or a double knock and know that the letters have come. I do not go back to the last particular rumble or postman's knock, or expect letters like the last which came.

The interest of those who believe in concrete Identity, in thus reducing the two " Laws of Association " to the one Law

[1] It will be obvious to all who are familiar with the subject, that I am borrowing largely from Mr. Bradley's chapter on " Association " in *Principles of Logic*.

of Contiguity, is to enforce the idea that the content of consciousness is never merely simple or particular, and that in association, as in judgment, the universal or meeting-point of differences furnishes the true guide to the intellectual process.

This reduction is beginning to be accepted (e.g. Mr. Sully mentions it, and Mr. Ward in some degree adopts it), not perhaps in the full sense here claimed for it, but merely as a preferable statement of the operation of ideas which are particulars. I doubt, for example, whether Mr. Sully has abandoned the Scotch or English ground of atomism in ideas. But to recognize identity as the universal makes the associative process far simpler, and homogeneous with the whole remaining evolution of consciousness.

In Ethical Philosophy the desire to exclude difference from identity produces analogous difficulties to those which we have noticed in Logic and Psychology. If, in short, difference is excluded from identity, how are you ever to get from one self-identical particular to another, whether in inference, or in association, or in moral purpose, or in political obligation? In the sciences that deal with human action the natural atom to start from is, simply putting atom into Latin, the individual human being. Of course an individual human being is a concrete universal, as we saw in speaking of what is meant by a proper name; but as his unity is pressed upon us by merely perceptive synthesis, we are apt to treat it as a datum, or to draw a sharp line between the unity of the individual human being, as a datum of reality, and the unity of human beings in identical sentiments, ideas, purposes or habits, as something not a datum, not real, the mere creation of our comparing intelligence. A striking example of such a point of view on Ethical ground is the passage in *Methods of Ethics*, p. 374, where Professor Sidgwick speaks of testing the feeling of common sense towards the sum of pleasure as an ethical end, by supposing that there was only a single sentient conscious being in the universe. Of course it is allowable to suppose, for the sake of argument, alteration in a state of things which we know to be actual; but nobody—least of all so cautious a writer as Professor Sidgwick—would remove in his supposition so enormous an element of the case as man's social life, unless he supposed it to belong less really to the individual's moral identity than his existence as a living body does. This is simply not the fact. Of course, if a plague carried off all men in the world but one, that one might *retain* his social consciousness and habit of mind. But apart from further religious assumptions, that consciousness would be an illusion, and the man's self would be a mutilated fragment for which no real life was possible. The fairer case to put, which we can observe in fact but too often, is to suppose that the body lives on, but that the real identity with society and humanity—the universal consciousness—is extinguished in that one body by disease. Then we see that it was not in the least a metaphor, but an absolutely literal truth, to say that the man's real self— what he was as a moral being and in part as a legal person— consisted in a system of universals, or identities including difference—viz. the consciousness of certain relations which, as identities in difference, united him with family, friends, and fellow-citizens. " Identities in difference," such e.g. as a man's relation to his son ; it is like the case of the two outlines which I mentioned. The two men are bound together by certain facts known to both of them, certain sentiments and purposes, all of which they both share, but in regard to which each of them has a different position from the other, apart from which difference the whole identity would shrink into nothing.

In Political Philosophy, again, we may notice Mr. Spencer's social atomism, curiously doubled with a comparison of the body politic to the living body, in which the state is taken, roughly speaking, as a unit, among units, instead of being taken as a real identity throughout the whole. It is a strange fate for Plato's famous simile of the organism to have its contention retorted in this way. A justification might be found for Mr. Spencer by pressing home the idea of a spiritual identity as against an external or legal one, and probably that is the sort of meaning which he has in mind, but he is barred from saying so by disbelieving in identity altogether ; and it would not be true, for a spiritual identity will always express itself as a legal one.

I should like to try and illustrate this point of real identity by one further example. We here, the members of the Aristotelian Society, have in our minds, *qua* members, a really identical purpose and endeavour, and consciousness of certain facts, just as actually and truly as we are actually and truly sitting round an identical table. It is not the fact that we are a number of separate individuals or atoms, each completely real in his sensuous identity, and merely cherishing, in addition, certain ideas which happen to resemble each other. In as far as this is fact, it is so in the sense that our moral being has enough in other relations to fill it up and make it real, apart from what we are and do as members of this Society. But in as far as our membership plays any part in our consciousness, so far this real identity actually and in sober earnest forms a part of our being as the individuals that we are, and our solidarity as a Society is only another aspect of a real identity which is recognized in a different form by each several member of the Society, according to his individual relations to it. It may be said : " But our ideas and purposes in respect of the Society are not all the same ; they are probably not all even in agreement." But our ideas of the table are not all the same ; our perceptions of it are certainly all different—the different angles at which we see it answer for that. No one can prove that we all see it of the same colour, and if we do not, our perceptions of it are even discrepant. Yet we say it is the same table, because, in our worlds which we severally construct and maintain, it fills a corresponding place, and so we do not say that there are as many tables as people ; but we call it one and the same table which we all perceive. And so, because this Society to which we belong is recognized by each of us in certain purposes which are relative to the corresponding purposes of others, and which assign different people the places necessary to common action, we call it the same Society, which really exists in the ideal and practical recognition of it by its members, and is something in them which is the same in all of them, and without which they would be so far devoid of a real solidarity which they now possess.

If we once begin trying to exclude difference from identity, we can never stop. The comparison of Locke's discussion with Hume's is interesting in this respect. Hume follows much the same lines as Locke, but bears more distinctly in mind that in explaining an identity which includes difference

—e.g. personal identity—he is not expounding a fact, but is, according to his own principle, accounting for a fallacy. The problem is, of course, as old as Heraclitus. If we want to free identity from differences, we must go to atomic sensation, and then we cannot. Any limit which we place upon real identity has only a relative value, depending upon the aspect in which the terms are compared. If we try to make such a limit absolute it at once becomes arbitrary.

And by accepting such a limit we may be driven into an opposite extreme, through lumping together all that lies beyond our limit. It seems to me that the Comtists do this in erecting Humanity as an object of worship ; they know that all ideas of solidarity or real identity among men are apt to be taken as fiction, and they think it as cheap to have a big fiction as a small one. So they take an object, I think, in which it is really very hard to show a centre of identity. You can do something with an ideal human nature embodied in an individual, or with a national consciousness and history ; but is there really anything at once definite and valuable that links together all humanity as such, including the past ?

It often occurs to one to ask oneself, whether all this question is not largely verbal. Supposing we take identity to exclude difference, and therefore practically banish identity from the world altogether, and instead of it use the term similarity or resemblance, and attach certain consequences to certain degrees and kinds of similarity, would philosophy suffer any loss ? When Hume explains continued identity as a current fiction, does he not explain it quite as well as any one could who called it a fact ? When Mill treats consciousness as an ultimate inexplicability, does he not in that very passage state the nature of consciousness as well as any one could who professed to be able to explain it ? There is something in this, in so far as we analyse contents, as Locke and Hume do in their discussions, and distinguish what consequences attach to what resemblances, or, as Hume would call them under protest, identities.

This can be done, by the process of defining and precisely limiting the points of resemblance in respect of which inferences are drawn, such as those inferences which we draw from what we call personal identity. An indiscernible resemblance between two different contents, in specified respects, will do whatever identity will do, because it is identity under another name. The self-contained identity of the separate contents is broken down when you admit that one of them can be indiscernibly like the other, and yet also remain different from it. In that case the contents form a coherent system or unity in multiplicity, which is the essence of identity.

The only objection to this is the confusion of terminology, and so of thought, which is involved in putting ordinary similarity, the essence of which is not to be precisely analysed and not to establish a middle term or centre, on the same level as " exact likeness," which establishes a middle term or centre of unity. We know that in ordinary similarity the things pronounced similar remain separate, and you cannot infer from one to the other. On the other hand, in indiscernible likeness or identity there is a systematic unity between the elements in question, which is as real as the elements themselves. Therefore, to dispense with concrete identity involves a confusion of the case in which the transition of unity is " objective "—i.e. as real as the content itself—with the case in which the content is self-contained and merely has a certain echo of another content, so that the similarity of the two may be called subjective ; that is to say, that it is not precisely referred to any element in the content itself. In the one case the unity of the contents is real, in the sense that it is definitely a part of themselves ; in the other case it is a fiction, in the sense of being somehow added on to them by a confused perception.

It is quite possible to examine into the bearings and nature of a fiction or artificial structure, and English philosophy, from Hobbes to Mill, has done much good work in this attitude. But putting aside the theoretical inconvenience, which I have tried to point out in detail, of assuming the wrong kind of unit, there is also an important practical effect on the theoretical interest. People will not pay the same attention to what they think secondary or artificial as to what they think a reality in its own right. Reality means to us something that resists efforts to destroy it, and refuses to be remodelled at our pleasure, and everything which is artificial or made up, though of course it exists, seems arbitrary and capable of being remade in another way, especially if we believe that the units when separated would retain a value which, in fact, they only have in synthesis. And for that reason anything artificial seems less fundamental, and less worth detailed investigation, than what is thought to have a nature that cannot be got rid of, and that includes all we need care about.

I should like, in conclusion, to illustrate this effect by more general considerations. The effect is, I repeat, the outcome or embodiment of an idea that difference is detrimental to identity (the logical formulation of the doctrine is not, of course, responsible for the whole effect or embodiment) ; and it consists in a sceptical attitude towards the real unity of every system or synthesis which can be seen to be a synthesis. And by " real " I mean having equal reality with the individuals which enter into the synthesis, so as to form an integral part of their nature, and not to rank as something which may be thus or otherwise without fundamentally affecting those individuals.

This feature is extremely remarkable in the otherwise brilliant history of British philosophy. I suppose that in the theory of material evolution England stands unrivalled. In the theory of spiritual evolution, apart from some excellent recent treatises on the simpler phases of anthropology, and apart from the recent Germanized movement itself, England has not a single work of the first class, and hardly a single work of the second class, to show. Of course Herbert Spencer fills a large place in the world's eye, and has no doubt made important general contributions to the theory of evolution. But I think it would almost be admitted that he is more of a theorist than of a historical inquirer, and at best his inquiries are very limited in range. On the evolution of fine art we have not merely no philosophy, but we have not the material for it ; we have no native *history* of fine art of any distinction, if we except the life-work of Mr. Ruskin. The history of religion, of morals, of law, of philosophy, and also history as such, have met with no complete philosophical treatment. I believe there is no tolerably good edition of Plato's *Republic*, or of

Aristotle's *Ethics* or *Politics* (till the last few days),[1] that has been made by an Englishman for the use of Englishmen. The same is true of the New Testament, though there I am told that other nations share our deficiency ; but they do not share the deficiencies of our general treatment of theological subjects, which till lately testified to the same curious apathy on the part of philosophical students.

Our logic, even, has only of late—I should say not till Mill's *Logic* appeared—really attempted to assume a vital and organic character as a genuine analysis of the intellectual world. Our analytic psychology and metaphysic, while it has from time to time shaken the world by the acuteness of its questions, has, as it always seems to me, almost wilfully declined to engage in the laborious task of answering them.

Such observations as these may be taken as an attack on British philosophy. I do not mean them to be so ; I do not doubt that the philosophy of Great Britain will creditably stand comparison with that of any nation in the world, excepting always, in my judgment, the ancient Greeks. But I do think that not enough attention is usually paid to what is, so far as I know, the wholly unparalleled fact, which a mere glance at a bookshelf containing the works of the great British philosophers will convince us of, that they have understood the limits of their subject quite differently from the philosophers of other countries. The qualities which have hitherto been displayed in British philosophy—I mean in the really effectual part of it —have been, as it seems to me, only a portion of the characteristics of the race which has produced it. Penetration and audacity, a power (so to speak) of leading the forlorn hope, have been the characters by which British philosophy has at times left a decisive mark on the thought of the world ; but it has hardly shown the power of comprehensive organization and continuous growth which in practical life, and I suppose in physical science, put the British people at the head of the nations. We do hear sometimes that even in practical organization, when it has grown so elaborate as to demand conscious and reflective development, we tend to come short ; e.g. in education and in the means of modern war.

[1] Mr. Newman's edition of the *Politics* was published shortly before this paper appeared in *Mind*.

This national peculiarity, which can hardly as a matter of fact be denied, is no doubt a defect of our good qualities ; and it is perhaps not fanciful to connect it with our insular position, which may cut us off more than we are aware from the impression of a real unity and continuity in a very various life. No one can read Goethe's recollections of his boyhood without feeling how, for example, the pageants of the empire which he witnessed at Frankfort helped to call out his pregnant sense of organic continuity. More especially I suppose that the secondary results of the Renaissance which led up to the splendid development of genius in Germany, about a hundred years ago, were choked in England largely by the political causes which led to the victory of Puritanism.

It seems to me, therefore, that the recent interest in German philosophy, which has shown itself in some meritorious and perhaps in some rather laughable forms, is not an accident, but is an aspect, however humble, in the great intellectual movement of the nineteenth century, and brings with it, however awkwardly, an element in which the abstract thought of this country has hitherto been deficient ; that is, a faith in those higher forms of human solidarity which are only created, maintained, and recognized by intelligent effort. We must remember that while Kant and Hegel are annoying our philosophers, Rousseau, Schiller, and Goethe, who have the same ideas in their practical shape, are at the other extreme of society, under the name of Froebel, reforming our infant and elementary schools, and that perhaps our very economical and commercial existence is at stake in the degree to which the national mind can be awakened to the real value of the world of truth and beauty. The actual history of the Germanizing movement in England would be well worth tracing. I suppose Coleridge and Carlyle represent two early aspects in it ; Carlyle's laborious historical work is quite as characteristic of it as Coleridge's rather ineffective philosophizing.

The logical aspect of such a movement as this is the transition from an idea of exclusive or abstract identity to one of pregnant or concrete identity. I should say the transition began in England between Hamilton and Mill. This idea has not been overwhelmed by the reaction which has set in in Germany against Hegelianism, but remains a permanent and vital gain to logic. A nation does not lose what a teacher like Goethe, not to speak of Hegel, has taught it ; and we should be much mistaken if we fancied that our common logic was already on a level with that of Prantl and Sigwart because it is innocent of Hegelianism, against which they are in re-action. The reaction is simply a way of thoroughly appropriating what has been done, and making sure that we understand it. The state of innocence is something very different and inferior.

# III

# ON THE PHILOSOPHICAL DISTINCTION BETWEEN "KNOWLEDGE" AND "OPINION" [1]

I AM privileged to speak this evening before a society of philosophical students in the city which has been called the modern Athens. It appeared to me, therefore, that I might not inappropriately lay before the Society some thoughts on that central question by the treatment of which in ancient Athens the first foundations were laid of a European philosophy.

The question, " Is there such a thing as knowledge, and, if there is, by what features may we recognize it ? " had, I take it, a far more radical bearing in Plato's time than in our own. For us, it is a matter of extreme scientific and also of ethical interest to define the grounds and principles on which, and subject to which, human thought can claim to apprehend the nature of things. The idea of the unity of the world is vital even to those who think that they deny it. But, except in some remote theoretical sense, no one does or can deny it to-day. The great inheritance of science and philosophy is to logic, as civilized law and religion to moral reflection, or as the fine art of the world to the perception of beauty. If anything bewilders us in the proceedings of nature, we set it down, as a mere matter of course, to our own ignorance. Nor does any one seriously dispute the main content of civilized morality, or the universal value of beauty. Our theories are tested by these things, and not these things by our theories. But in Plato's time these great objective supports were largely wanting to philosophy ; though doubtless the civilization which he knew seemed much larger to him than, by comparison, and owing to our ignorance, it now seems to us. In the way of

[1] An address given before the Edinburgh University Philosophical Society.

systematic knowledge, we think there was only a little mathematics ; in the way of moral consensus, only the institutions, and the not very stable convictions of his own small country, and to some extent of the Hellenic world ; in the way of realized beauty, the products of the short-lived maturity of one only, though that the most gifted, among nations. I cannot but think that the suggestion that these principles and activities belonged to no coherent unity, and possessed therefore no absolute and universal validity, was in his day a natural and probable suggestion to a degree which we cannot for a moment imagine. If now, for example, the mysterious debility were to strike Great Britain, which has struck other nations that in their time have led the world, we should look, I suppose, with confidence to Europe and to America for successors who could carry on the torch of science and of civilization. But if in Plato's time the educated and politically civilized society of Hellas, and more especially of Athens, was to be crushed, or, as he clearly foresaw, to deteriorate, where was the philosopher to look for the hope of humanity ?

Therefore, it seems to me, we should consider Plato's account of scientific knowledge, although drawn from the acutest analysis of experience, as in part a *prophecy*, which the later history of the world has wonderfully accomplished and defined. To complain that Plato did not say, and did not indeed know in precise detail, what he meant by his dialectic, is to complain of a philosopher for possessing the genius that could lay down the universal conditions of a science for which the actual materials did not in his time exist. He had to work with only a few fragments of organized experience, and in face of a world apparently relapsing into moral chaos ; but perhaps the difficulty thus occasioned is compensated not only by his genius, but by the burning reality which the questions of philosophy thus acquired for him.

Of these burning questions the chief and typical one was that which I mentioned : Is there such a thing as knowledge, and what are its distinctive features ?

We all know how the question is introduced in the fifth book of the *Republic*. Politics, Plato says in effect, are a science ; you will never get government properly organized till it is in the hands of people who have some grasp of

principles. And in support of this suggestion he goes on to
explain where the distinction lies between the mind as grasping
a unity of principle, and the mind as wandering through a
variety of particulars. I will not follow the discussion in
Plato's sense, but will merely mention what throws light on the
question before us. Plato draws many contrasts between the
world of opinion and the world of science ; but the central
contrast which is the focus of all the others is this, that opinion
may make a mistake, but science is infallible. And the fundamental question which I should like to discuss this evening is
what we mean by any such conception as that of the infallibility
or necessity of science, and what limitations we must observe
in applying it.

In the main, we shall not improve much upon Plato.
According to him Opinion was liable to err because, in fact,
it constantly contradicted itself. And it contradicted itself
because its content was *relative*, but *not defined*. And its
content was not defined, because it was merely an aggregate
of perceptive or traditional judgments, which no attempt had
been made to analyse or to reconcile. The " many " or
" manifold," which is constantly recurring in Plato, as the
characteristic content of popular opinion, obviously means not
merely separate *objects* or *sensations*, but isolated and therefore
conflicting *judgments*. Thus we hear of the many popular
formulæ, νομιμά, of " beauty and justice," and again of " the
many justices," that is, cases of justice regarded as rules of
justice ; and so of the " many beauties," i.e. conflicting standards of beauty. He is thinking of minds filled with unrationalized instances which appear as fluctuating standards
and conflicting judgments.

And because its content is unrationalized, therefore the
world of opinion tends to coincide with the world of sense,
and is, of course, spoken of as the world of the things that are
seen in contrast with the world of the things that are understood. The Greek expressions δόξα and δοκεῖ (" seeming,"
and " it seems to me ") lend themselves to this distinction. I
do not suppose that these words indicate sensuous appearance,
as do φαίνεσθαι and φαντασία, but they do indicate a contrast with active thought, a sort of personal acceptance as
opposed to a universal conviction. And Plato, in the *Republic*,

as we know, sweeps into the category of opinion or fallacious appearance even the representations of fine art, because
they can be considered as images or imagery, and therefore
as sensuous.

Science, or knowledge, on the contrary, was infallible, in the
sense that its content was single, and its inmost nature therefore excluded the possibility of contradiction or fluctuation.
Not that its content was other than relative, but that, being
relative, it was defined. Of course there is no confusion or
contradiction in relativity when you know to what your terms
are relative. Relativity in this sense is the root of scientific
necessity.

And thus, moreover, being defined, the content of science
was necessarily *intellectual*. It is impossible to have a connected system of conditions in the shape of unanalysed perceptive or traditional judgments. And so the object or content
of science was spoken of as the world of things understood, in
contrast to the world of things perceived by sense. We are
not here concerned with any materializing misconceptions, of
Plato's or of our own, respecting that intelligible world. There
is no question whatever that the unseen world which Plato
was labouring to describe was the world of science and of
morality—the connected view which gives meaning at once
to nature and to human life.

I suppose that the account which we should now accept of
this distinction between knowledge and opinion would be
essentially founded on that of Plato ; but the conditions of
modern thought have driven home one or two important points
on which his language is not and could not be absolutely
unambiguous.

In the first place, we must be very cautious in accepting the
opposition between the world of science and the world of
sense. We have not in exclusive use the convenient Greek
term, " it appears to me." We recognize no peculiar connection between opinion and sense. We speak without a blush
of " *scientific opinion*," and even of " *scientific authority*." Our
opinions are a sort of debris of antiquated science and political
or theological tradition, of general maxims and half-understood
principles. They have not, we are inclined to think, enough
immediate touch with the world of sense-perception. Their

fault is rather intellectual confusion than imperfect abstraction from sense.

Our science, on the other hand, seems closely bound up with sense-perception. Nor, again, should we ever dream of ranking Fine Art among unreal illusions, because it is, and must be, largely sensuous. The extremes of our mental world seem to have met, and even to have crossed. Our chaotic opinion is intellectualized, and our coherent science is materialized. If we try to distinguish the world of things seen from the world of things understood, where are we to bestow that act of seeing which a distinguished microscopist begins by describing as " an act of the pure understanding " ?

The fact is, that there are correlative misapprehensions attaching to this idea of a world of sense-perception, which we must take care to avoid. Sensation, we are too apt to say, is illusory or false. This is incorrect. What we ought to mean is that sensation is not true ; but for the same reason for which it is not true, it is also not false ; for it is not a judgment at all, and nothing but judgment can be true or false. On the other hand, if we mean to say that sense-perception, such as human seeing or hearing, is illusory, as Plato too often appears to imply—that may or may not be ; these activities are judgments, and may no doubt be false, but also may be true.

There is, indeed, a secondary difficulty affecting the truth of any perceptive judgment which is *bona fide* a singular judgment, because its subject is to some extent unanalysed, and therefore not accurately conditioned. But when you are once fairly started on the continuous evolution of judgment, you will find it very hard to draw any intelligible line between judgments affected by this secondary difficulty, and judgments which are not so affected, or are so in a less degree. And granting that judgments affected by it may intelligibly be called " nearer to sense," it still remains quite untrue that judgments dealing with the determinate concrete objects of our perceptive world are necessarily judgments thus near to sense. As Plato says, our primary remedies against sensuous illusions are number and measure ; and so-called sensuous objects, as they exist for civilized and for scientific minds, are penetratingly determined at least by measurement and enumeration.

Thus, we must clearly realize that knowledge and opinion both exist in the medium of judgment, that is, of thought. That marvellous dialectician, common language, forces *us* most commonly to say, " I think," when a Greek would have said, " It seems to me." And though one may be tempted in a moment of irritation to exclaim with Dr. Whewell, " Do you call that *thinking* ? " yet, philosophically speaking, if a judgment is made, it *is* thinking, and we must be quite clear that our distinction between science and opinion is a distinction within the world of thought, which is a single world, and to which the objects of human sense-perception emphatically do belong.

Then, in the second place, and as a consequence of this generic oneness of our world, we must guard ourselves against finding the differentia of knowledge in any isolated principle which may seem to commend itself to us as peculiarly intellectual in origin or by contrast. We shall do no good by comparing one isolated judgment with another in order to accept that which is more remote from experience or concrete reality. We need not hope, that is to say, to distinguish part of knowledge as the content from part as the form of thought, or to enumerate a list either of innate or of a priori principles of the mind. It has been said, and by an illustrious Idealist thinker, " Two pure perceptions, those of time and space, and twelve pure ideas of the understanding, were what Kant thought he had discovered to be the instruments with which the human spirit is furnished for the manipulation of experience. Whence these strange numbers ? " Directly you mention them, you feel that you cannot insist on them in that rigid form. And if, or in as far as Plato meant that science was in the long run to hit upon an abstract ultimate first principle, or principle external to its content, from which knowledge was to be suspended as a coat hangs from a peg, then, and so far, he wavered in his conception of the nature of truth. It might be questioned, for example, what he had in his mind when he said of the mathematical sciences, " How can the whole system amount to knowledge when its beginning, middle, and end are a tissue of unknown matters ? It is, in fact, no more than an elaborate convention." We should of course say, and should have expected him to say, that in any conceivable system of knowledge the beginning, middle, or end is only known by being in the system, and *ipso facto* becomes unknown, if regarded in abstraction from it. And I do not think this would be at variance with what he had in his mind. Probably his difficulty was that, as he constantly hints, the greater whole of knowledge was beyond his power to construct ; there was, therefore a *saltus* or discontinuity round the edge of the mathematical sciences relatively to the whole of knowledge. It was not that he expected to find some law of Causation, or law of Uniformity, or Principle of Identity to which they could all be attached. He evidently was convinced that " the truth is the whole."

Thus we must look for the infallibility or necessity which distinguishes knowledge from opinion, *not* in the distinction between intellect and sense, *nor* in the distinction between an empirical and a necessary judgment (unless explained in quite a peculiar way), *but* in the degree of that characteristic which makes it in the first place thought, and in the second place knowledge at all.

All thought is determination, or connection, or definition ; but popular thought is insufficient determination, and for that reason is self-contradictory. Every judgment determines a unity by a relation ; but as every unity is a centre of relations, it is plain that until the unity has been exhaustively analysed, all its different relations will seem to conflict, because each of them will claim to include the whole of it. And the only remedy for such conflicts is, accordingly, further determination, as Plato explains with unsurpassed clearness in the seventh book. As determination progresses, then, the unity of thought is maintained ; but its differences, which were at first merely found together, come to be systematically arranged, and to have their reciprocal bearings quite precisely defined. So then every part of the system becomes charged with the meaning of the whole, and the relativity of the different elements becomes a source of necessity, instead of a source of confusion. Two terms are relative in this scientific sense when you can tell what form the one will have, by looking at the form of the other. Plato is apt to allude to the apparent contradiction between the appearance of an object seen at a distance, and that of the same object seen close at hand. But of course to an educated eye there is no such contradiction ; the one appearance under one condition necessarily involves the other under another condition. The contradiction *would* arise if the angle subtended by the object were the same at two different distances. The estimate of real size, as formed by an educated eye, is a consequence or combination of the various appearances combined with other evidence, and does not vary with the distance at which the object happens to be seen. We do not judge a man to be very small when we see him a long way off, nor to grow bigger as he comes nearer. In fact, we more generally make too much allowance for distance, and think a man taller at a distance than he really turns out to be when we see him near. The various angles subtended at different distances do not contradict but confirm one another, because their conditions are made explicit ; if we confuse their conditions, they will contradict one another. A railway engine coming towards one at full speed does seem to *swell*, because one has no time to adjust the perception of distance to the angle subtended by the object, i.e. to distinguish the perception under one condition from the perception under another.

Thus it results that the possibility of contradiction is removed and turned into confirmation in as far as experience is organized as a single system of determinations. It is in this sense alone that science has a claim to be infallible or necessary.

But now, if this is so, how far does this kind of infallibility take us ? To what extent does it justify us in even asserting that we have knowledge at all ?

To begin with, we cannot show, strictly speaking, in this way or in any other, that it is impossible for a change of relations to occur without a change of conditions. We can only say that the suggestion is unmeaning to us, as it involves the saying and unsaying, or being and not-being of the same matter in the same relation. To do and undo is for us simply to leave nothing done ; we therefore disregard this contingency ; in other words, we assume the unity of reality, which assures us that what is once true is always true, and that what turns out to be not true never was true. *Our* problem is, how can we be assured that we are making no mistakes ? We are powerless if it is suggested that we may be making no mistake, and yet may be in error. That falls outside our discussion to-night.

But there are difficulties more relevant to our problem.

The necessity of science does not provide against our determinations being insufficient, as is plain from the progressive character of science.

There are at first sight two degrees of this insufficiency, though ultimately they may have the same root.

First, there is confusion of conditions. That is to say, you may lay down a connection between condition and consequent, in which by some error of identification you have simply placed one condition or consequent where you ought to have placed another. I will give two examples, one of a more or less debatable case, the other of an extreme case.

The old Wage-Fund theory said, as I understand it, that the wages of labour with a given population depended on the total amount of capital available, and destined in the minds of capitalists, to be paid in the shape of wages. In one sense, this is a truism, i.e. on a given pay-day the whole amount paid, divided by the number of persons to whom it is paid, gives the average wage. But in the more real sense, viz., that this fund is a pre-existent fixed quantity, the amount of which actively decides the rate of wages, the doctrine is now disputed, and generally held, I believe, to have been overthrown. Wages are paid out of the produce of labour, and not out of a pre-existing fund, and the capitalist very likely gets his hands on the produce actually before he parts with the wages, which therefore are not limited by the amount of a pre-existing fund. The old Wage-Fund theory perhaps rested on a confusion between the truism which I first mentioned, and the very real connection that exists in various ways between the amount of plant or stock in a country, which is Auxiliary capital, not Wage-Fund capital, and the productivity and general employment of its labour, which in their turn affect the rate of wages.

Now how, if at all, does the necessity of science maintain itself in the overthrow of this doctrine ? In some such way as this, that the postulates and conditions which made such a doctrine necessary to the scientific system, will continue after its overthrow to be fulfilled by some more or less cognate doctrine, liberated from the confusions which disfigured this one. We shall still speak, I suppose, of the importance of saving. We shall still be aware that an undertaking like the Forth Bridge could only be carried out by a country with an enormous command of accumulated wealth, and that, with a given population, the best chance of raising wages lies in increasing the amount of capital productively employed. Only we must not restrict capital to wage-fund capital, but must include in it, for example, machines and materials.

Now the necessity of the science consisted in the demand for a representation of all these relations and conditions, which, as their determinations advance in accuracy, mould and remould the doctrine that is to satisfy them, but *without sacrificing its identity of content or function*. The alteration of such a doctrine is like the transformation of gills into lungs, or the substitution of a Westinghouse continuous brake for a hand-brake on a train. You pass from one fulfilment of certain organic demands to another.

As an extreme case where the connection seems quite irrational, I will just mention what Swift wrote, that once when he was half-asleep, he fancied he could not go on writing unless he put out some water which he had taken into his mouth. He was confusing between writing and speaking, of course. There really is a necessity in the background even there.

In the second place, a science may be precise as far as it goes, but may omit some entire sphere or branch of fact, as Euclidean geometry is now said to omit certain kinds of space. Against this possibility there, prima facie, is no theoretical resource except in a postulate of exhaustiveness, viz., that our knowledge bears some appreciable proportion to the whole of Reality. I incline to think that we take this postulate on ethical grounds, i.e. we are convinced that Reality will not so far dwarf our knowledge as to annihilate our life or wholly frustrate our purposes. It ought to be mentioned, too, that probably a science which is not complete cannot be *truly* systematic.

Of course you may cut the knot of all these discussions by saying that sciences which make mistakes are not science. But this would not help us, because then we should say that our question is, how far the sciences are characterized by science.

In the third place, the systematic character of scientific necessity is in itself a limitation on the extent and application of that necessity. For if and in as far as the systematic character is lost, then and so far the necessity is lost too. It has been said of political economy, that if you do not know it all, you do not know it at all. This is true in strict theory of every science and of all science. So that the scientific judgment transferred by the help of language into a mind not equipped with the body of knowledge, is science no longer. It has become mere opinion, mere authority. This explains the curious contempt which practical men have, as a rule, for the evidence of scientific experts. Scientific authority is a contradiction in terms. Unhappily the scientific mind itself often forgets this, and offers, like Thrasymachus, to put its doctrine into men's souls by physical force. But this is impossible. Knowledge can only be communicated as knowledge. You cannot claim the necessity of science for a scientific conclusion torn from its organism and hurled into the sphere of opinion. Think of the popular interpretations of any such propositions as : " The soul is a substance," or, " Sensation is subjective."

But here we have arrived at the end of our negatives, and the balance begins to turn.

If, for the reason just stated, Knowledge cannot refute Opinion ; neither, for the same reason, can Opinion refute Knowledge. An individual judgment and a universal judgment cannot be contradictory in the strict sense. The judgment, " If A is B, then C is D," is not affected by the judgment, " C is not D." They are in different planes, and do not meet. Before you can bring the two into relation, you must ascertain how A and B are behaving in the case, when it is alleged C is not D. Then we shall find, in proportion as the hypothetical judgment belongs to a thoroughly organized body of science, that it is easy to incorporate the new determination in the old system. I will once more take an example from political economy. The economical doctrine says that prices determine rent, and rent does not determine prices. But of course it is a common opinion that a tradesman in a fashionable street is compelled to charge higher prices than a tradesman in a less fashionable street, in order to recoup himself for the higher rent which he has to pay. If we put out of sight the alternative of his obtaining a larger sale, I should suppose that this *might* be the fact, although one would imagine that he would have fixed his prices so as to obtain the greatest profit, even if his profit was not to go in rent. But waiving this argument again, and admitting the alleged fact, what does it amount to? What made his landlord ask for that high rent, and what made the tradesman contract to pay it? Why, that both of them thought that the prices necessary to pay this rent could be got out of the public in that locality. You cannot put up your prices just as you please; and if you cannot get the prices necessary to pay your rent, why, then you cannot pay your rent out of the proceeds of the business, and the rent must come down; and no doubt if you are under a lease *or competing for houseroom with other occupations that pay better*, you may say to the public, "Really I am *forced* to *try* to keep my prices up." But strictly the reason for this is not that the prices do not determine the rent, but that they obviously do, and the tradesman is crushed between two determinations of his rent, legal and economical; only, being unable to revise his bargain, he may try to hold the prices up with both hands, so to speak; and with a friendly circle of customers, or a circle who need him in their district, to some extent he may succeed. But in some such way as this the relation between the scientific doctrine and the popular opinion is not, I think, very hard to see, when you look at the matter all round. And of course it does modify the doctrine a little bit; but on the whole, *when you analyse* the alleged case, it joins on pretty easily to the science. The science, of course, primarily considers what a man will freely bargain to do; it never denies that a man may have a loss thrown upon him by a bad bargain which he cannot revise, and that *so far* his rent, which is naturally the consequent, will become for him the condition, because he cannot alter it.

If, then, we try to state the positive value of the so-called infallibility of science, it appears to reduce itself to this—that the organization of a province of experience is an affirmative or actual achievement, which may be subsequently modified or transformed, but cannot be lost or cancelled. We cannot guarantee the particular formulation of an isolated principle;

but then we know that identity does not depend on particular formulation, but on continuity of function. I should be very sorry to predict in what precise terms the Principle of Sufficient Reason may be stated by philosophers a hundred years hence. But that the determinate relativity of the parts of experience will be embodied in some principle or other, is as certain, I think, as that there will be science at all.

It may be objected that we are guaranteeing the whole of knowledge in general, but no element of it in particular, and that this is illusory. To those who cannot conceive a concrete continuous identity I think it *is* illusory, and ought to be. You cannot, as they would wish, fix and separate any portion of knowledge. Every element of it must take its chance in the systematic development of the whole. Therefore, when speaking of knowledge in general, you can only affirm its self-identity in general. But to any one who can see a meaning in saying, for example, that Christianity to-day is the same religion that it was 1,800 years ago, this idea of continuous pervading identity will present no difficulty. A substantive identity, we think, can persist through difference, and can, indeed, only be realized in differences.

While, on the other hand, if a certain difficulty attaches to this view, yet it throws an all-important light on the nature of knowledge. It shows us that the necessity of knowledge depends upon its vitality. Axioms and dogmas, traditions and abstract principles, equally with unanalysed perception, are not knowledge but opinion. The life of knowledge is in the self-consciousness which systematically understands, and you cannot have it cheaper. We know *not* " as much as is in our memory," *but* " as much as we understand." A science which accepts foreign matter, data to be learnt by heart, is so far not a science. But one who has *understood* anything has a possession of which he cannot be deprived.

Any one who speaks thus confidently is sure to be asked " What are his metaphysical presuppositions ? " It would be more to the point, in my judgment, to ask him if he has obtained any metaphysical *results*. His only presupposition is, I think, that there is something presented to him which it is worth while to analyse. The principles involved in this analysis such as the unity of Reality, are no doubt operative from the first, but are only established in a definite form by the analysis itself. And any view, more strictly metaphysical, as to the precise ultimate nature of the unity of Reality, would be a still further result, which may or may not be obtained. That mind, in its essence, is one, and that the unity of man with himself and with nature is a real unity, seem to be principles demanded by the facts of science and of society. It is also true that a reality which is not for consciousness is something too discrepant with our experience to be intelligible to us. But whether the human mind will ever form to itself a conception that will in any degree meet the problem of a total unity of Reality, is a question the answer to which must lie in the result of analysis, and not in its presuppositions.

Thus we abide by the position that the characteristic in which Knowledge differs from Opinion is the degree in which, as a living mind, it has understood and organized its experience. The criticism of Goethe's Mephistopheles on the traditional logic is perfectly just. It is well to take every mental process carefully to pieces ; but it is essential to bear in mind that the pieces are elements in a living tissue, in a single judgment, and that in their detachment as " one, two, and three," they are not knowledge. So far from being a mechanical science, logic is perhaps the most vital and scientific of all the sciences. It accepts nothing from perception or from authority, and gives nothing to learn by heart. It depends on no intuition of space, and on no list of elements. Its only task is to understand the process of understanding, the growth and transformations of thought.

This is the conception with which logic began in Plato, and which has never been entirely lost. In the old Dominican Church of Santa Maria Novella, at Florence, there is a series of frescoes illustrative of education, familiar to us through Mr. Ruskin's description under the name of the Strait Gate. One of these paintings has a peculiar attraction for the student of modern logic. Next but two after the Narrow Gate itself, which indicates the entrance to good life, there is placed over a head of Aristotle the allegorical figure of Logic. This beautiful figure is drawn, as Mr. Ruskin points out, with remarkable strength and grace ; it is most probably from the pencil of Simone Memmi, of Siena, early in the fourteenth century. In her left hand the figure holds the scorpion with its double nippers, emblem of the dilemma or more generally of the disjunctive or negative power of thought ; but in her right hand she holds the leafy branch, symbolizing the syllogism, conceived as the organic or synthetic unity of reason. This suggests an ideal worthy of the age of Dante, however little it may have been attained in the explicit logical theory of that time.

It is some such ideal of knowledge that has, as we may hope, been making itself more and more imperatively felt since the revival of letters in Europe ; and the view which it involves, of the true distinction between Knowledge and Opinion, is merely one branch of that principle of the unity of mind, which is fraught with consequences of inestimable importance for all aspects of life in the present day. We cannot—such is the lesson we have to learn—we cannot elevate the human mind by any fragmentary treatment, by any communication or assistance which does not stimulate its healthy growth as a single living thing. In fine art, in the province of social rights and duties, in morality, in politics, and especially in the interconnection of all these spheres, it is no less true than we have found it to be in science, that the mind must grow and advance either all together, or not at all.

# IV

## ON A DEFECT IN THE CUSTOMARY LOGICAL
## FORMULATION OF INDUCTIVE REASONING

1. THE point on which I desire to insist, though by no
means new, has been brought into prominence by the attitude
of M. Bergson, with the imitation and repetition theorists
whom he appears to follow, to the creative and constructive
activity of the intellect. I cite a typical passage (*Evolution
Créatrice*, p. 218) : " L'intelligence a pour fonction essential
de lier le même au même, et il n'y a entièrement adaptable
aux cadres de l'intelligence que les faits qui se répètent." [1]

Such a statement is in the sharpest possible conflict with
the view of intellectual activity which to many of us seems
natural and obvious. But when we refer to the most accredited
expositions of the logical theory of Induction, which attempts
to deal with the characteristic working of the scientific
intelligence in the advancement of natural knowledge, we find
them dominated by ideas which appear to justify M. Bergson's
position. What I wish to attempt is a brief reconsideration of
the exact meaning and function of these ideas in Inductive
Logic.

The basis of Induction is usually stated in some such
formula as " Same cause, same effect." It is unnecessary for
our present purpose to raise the questions connected with the
converse formula, " Same effect, same cause." It is enough to
understand the simplest truism of Identity, that a thing does
what it is its nature to do under given conditions,[2] and cannot
do otherwise except by some change in the conditions ; from
which it follows, that if, in an alleged causal nexus, the alleged
effect is sometimes absent while the alleged cause is present,

---

[1] Cf. Tarde, *Lois de l'imitation*, pp. 14–15.
[2] Cf. Mr. Joseph's *Introduction to Logic*, ch. xix.

*ceteris paribus*, it is impossible that the alleged cause should be the real cause of the effect in question. The principle is sound, beyond any doubt, as far as it goes. It is, in fact, nothing more than can be read off from the law of non-contradiction, as formulated, for example, by Plato. The same thing cannot behave differently to the same thing in the same relation. If it seems to do so (Plato's condition " at the same time " is superfluous), you can infer that there is a difference in the supposed agent. The same, so far as *it* is concerned (i.e. if no condition is altered), produces the same ; what produces something different, out of itself, is not the same. If this much is not to be assumed, we cannot treat anything as having an assignable nature. Truth ceases to have a meaning. Anything might behave anyhow.

Now it is from this law or truism that, according to accepted logical theory, the fundamental Inductive test of causal connection is derived. The Inductive process is thus regarded as one of elimination.[1] You have before you, it is assumed, one or more suggested connections of cause and effect, and you labour to eliminate from among them all alleged causes that are present in the absence of effects with which they claim to be connected. Such elimination leaves, it is presumed, a surviving statement which approaches more and more closely to a true, i.e. an invariable, causal connection. The principle is simply that which M. Bergson refers to : What is the same, does the same ; if the same product is not there, the same agent is not there. The same produces the same. And yet, if this were all, we should have a difficulty in denying M. Bergson's doctrine which I began by stating. It *would* then seem to be the case that the essential work of the intellect lies in binding the same to the same, and that the true type of the logical universal—the essence of cognition—would be, as M. Bergson says, the relation of an abstract statement to examples which repeat its tenor wholly without variation. That water boils at sea-level at 212° Fahr. would be such a generality ; and according to the number of instances

[1] The rules of elimination which depend on the further principle, " Same effect, same cause " (i.e. on the exclusion of plurality of causes), rest merely on a more precise consideration of the ideal of identity, which it is not necessary to take account of in order to understand the point at issue in this discussion. See Joseph, ch. xxii.

in which people boiling their kettles at or near sea-level [1] found the water to be about 212° would be its rank and power as a piece of knowledge.

2. But why *should* we deny M. Bergson's doctrine ? Perhaps it may be true. As a prima facie answer to this suggestion, we need only refer to such a criticism of tautology as we find, for example, in Mr. Bradley's *Principles of Logic*.[2]

M. Bergson's doctrine is logically bound to deny not only the advance from one truth or connection of fact to another, but the possibility of apprehending or of uttering any significant truth at all. It may appear that this criticism is exaggerated, because the doctrine explicitly treats (so far as I am aware) as outside the principle of the intelligence only the difference between the corresponding terms of one nexus and those of another nexus, and not the difference between the terms themselves—alleged cause and alleged effect—which are constituents of a single nexus. But there is no escape by this road. If tautology is the principle of the intelligence, the connection of any two distinct terms, say, as cause and effect, stands on the same ground as the connection between two different connections. With tautological identity as the principle of intelligence, all systematic coherence between term and term, equally as between judgment and judgment, inevitably vanishes.

But, in fact, there is (i) some misinterpretation involved in setting up the principle " Same produces same " as the dominant principle of scientific Induction and as governing the nature of the generalization which is the aim of that process ; although

(ii) I admit and maintain that the current logical statement of the theory of Induction lays itself open to this misinterpretation.

(i) When you postulate as the basis of Inductive Inference the principle " Same cause, same effect," you do not mean that the effect is the same as the cause.[3] They must be different,

---

[1] I am satisfied to take a case in which strictly accurate repetition is all but impossible, because it illustrates the real fact, which is that the interest of the generality lies in the differences which it binds together. A *strict* repetition could have no interest at all.

[2] E.g. p. 29.

[3] In a remote sense some such meaning might be assigned to the true Inductive principle which I desire to see established, and it may be that

if the relation of cause and effect is to be worth establishing
You do mean ($\alpha$) that assuming the truth of an alleged causal
nexus A—B, it only applies in cases which are absolute
repetitions of it, i.e. where you have exactly the same A as
before without any variation ; and ($\beta$) that in examining the
truth of an alleged causal nexus A—B, your rule must be that
if you find a case in which, *ceteris paribus*, B is different
(C or $B_1$) and A is unvaried, your alleged causal nexus A—B is
disproved. For if it were true, the same cause would be
producing, *ceteris paribus*, two different effects, which is impossible. (If A is plural and B singular, this is not literally
a case excluded by the formula, " Same cause, etc.," which is
strictly taken silent about it, and no negative inference follows,
unless we are making what usually counts as an additional
postulate, " Same effect, same cause.")

What you mean by " Same produces same," then, is an
assertion that the cause, in a nexus guaranteed by this
principle, is unvarying compared with itself, and the effect
unvarying compared with *itself*. You imply no comparison
between cause and effect.

And your principle makes no suggestion towards the
estimation of any possible cause and effect allied to or
developed out of those forming the nexus whose truth we
assume to be accepted. According to a proper interpretation
of the word " same," some such expansion would be permis-
sible, passing from $a$—$b$ to $\alpha$—$\beta$ and from $\alpha$—$\beta$ to A—B. But
what makes it impossible is the demand for a methodic rule.
Plainly there cannot be a general rule that will tell how much
variation in your cause and effect, each from each, will be
justified under the principle, " Same cause, same effect." And
therefore, if you want a rule, you must take one which
justifies no variation at all, and makes your " generalization "
cover nothing but sheer repetitions, and degrades your procedure in connecting the same with the same into one which
admits of no novelty or true inference.

But the two types of connection thus disregarded (that of
cause and effect, and that of any generalization and its more

some hint of this possibility prevents the formula under discussion from
seeming as naked as it really is. Its strict meaning can only be that stated
in the text.

advanced but kindred form) really contain the very life and mainspring of Inductive thought. How the suggestion of the effect B issues from the fact of the cause A ; or how the more complex and advanced *a* (*def*)—*b* (*xyz*) came to be substituted for the cruder A—B, this is where the real work of the scientific intelligence lies. This is the work of invention or discovery, of which the imitation and repetition theorists, whom M. Bergson appears to me to follow, have never succeeded in giving any serious account.[1] It is the process by which isolated observations are built up into a science, through an assignment of conditions which is always becoming more systematically complete on the one hand, and more relevantly precise on the other. Examples of such an inventive pursuit of a universal relation would be the rise of the science of acoustics out of the old observation that the pitch of musical notes has a ratio comparable with that of the lengths of the stretched strings which produce them ; or the development and limitation of the conception of equi-potentiality as applied to organic growth in recent embryology. Here we have the plain fact, that it is the essential character of intelligence to bind different to different in binding same to same ; and that it is for the former character that the latter is valuable, and, indeed, it is through the former only that the latter can exist. But the sameness here in question is not the sameness of M. Bergson's doctrine or of the formal Inductive test. We can see this from the nature of its aim. The universality or generality, which is the goal of such a process, is not the relation of the terms of an abstract judgment, term for term, each to each, to the terms of repeated cases which fall under it. It is the relation of the different terms of a judgment to each other, or of an organized system of conditions, representing a certain range of experience (e.g. our experience of musical sound or of embryonic growth), to the several connected factors or conditions, whether constant or varying, which it embodies and explains. Its universality is not measured by millions of repeated instances, but by depth and complexity of insight into a sub-system of the world.

(ii) The logical theory of Induction gives but scanty attention to this work of the universal in suggesting and

[1] Cf. especially Bergson, *Évolution*, p. 177.

pursuing new connections, because, for good logical reasons, it cannot be reduced, like the eliminative test, to something like a formal rule. Nevertheless, this work is the true spirit and mainspring of the inductive advance of knowledge ; and to disregard it, while insisting on an eliminative test, is an error analogous to demanding a general criterion of truth. But truth has no criterion except the fuller truth. And the real interest of logical theory in the advance of knowledge is to note how, by the analysis and purification of its conditions, a perception passes into an organized system of understanding.

The existing connections or universals with which the mind is stored act as clues among the new experiences which confront us, selecting those that are kindred or complementary, and inventing new systematic ideas after the manner of what have been called proportional systems, and by means of relative suggestion.[1] That is to say, that an existing connection of thought, when confronted with new matter, is able to reproduce itself in a new form which is at once appropriate to the new matter, and continuous with the connection as previously thought. This is not a question of reproducing objects of thought which have previously been connected in the mind. It is a question of continuing some elements of such a connection into new forms of nexus, because the connection between the new objects has a real kinship with the connection between the old, although differentiated by the nature of the objects themselves, and made, as a connection, something new, and not a repetition of what it was before, like the continuation of a varying curve from the datum of a given fragment of it.[2] Such a continuation is plainly not a repetition, and I think that in view of the current theory of Inductive generalization, the notion of repetition as a condition of knowledge is not meant to apply to such an inventive construction as that of which I am speaking.

Let us look at an example. In recent embryological

---

[1] Cf. Stout, *Anal. Psych.*, ii, p. 80. I note that Professor Stout here observes that relative suggestion " would not of itself enable (the discoverer) to fix in exact detail the special variations." In the case he is dealing with, calculation was necessary. In our instance from embryology, observation is necessary. But it seems to me that the question what calculation ? what observation ? is answered by the governing idea in both cases, and the relevant conclusions are selected by it, and it is it that they develop.

[2] Cf. Bradley's *Principles of Logic*, p. 281 ff.

discussions,[1] covering the old ground of preformation and epigenesis, we read of experiments which prima facie suggest two precisely opposite causal connections.

Half an ovum, we are told, in certain cases will produce only half an embryo ; but in other cases the half ovum may develop into a perfect embryo. The former fact suggests a complete preformation of the organism, each part of it in a fixed part of the ovum ; the latter suggests that the ovum has a structure of which " every part may become anything." It is of great logical interest to look at the course which these two alleged types of connection have imposed upon Inductive research. Sheer prelocalized preformation is an idea, it would seem, that the experiments undertaken to confirm it immediately destroy. And if a universal nexus had no power of developing into novelty, this check would have been checkmate, and the idea would have been dead. But a universal can take on new shapes as demanded by new matter ; and though, as it seems, the " mosaic theory " (of the independent preformation of parts) must be abandoned in its rigid shape, yet the most various experiments on the tissues of organisms in later stages have shown that some of these are necessary to the development of some organs, and that therefore something essential to special development (perhaps " organ-forming substances ") is preformed, though not necessarily prelocalized. The logical interest is, that the idea of preformation, disputed in its primary and rigid shape, has been able to act as a clue to new experiments in a different region, such as to confirm it when restated in a more subtle and flexible form.

So with the idea that every part of the ovum has the capacity of becoming a whole. It is easily seen that this capacity is limited, and is sooner or later lost ; but the idea of the kind of causation at work modifies itself according to the limitations which are discovered, and seems to suggest new lines of research which promise to account both for the capacity and for its limitation and arrest. And the logical interest is, that by means of this suggestion, that of " organ-forming substances " and their distribution, it appears as if the two universals in question, " preformation " and " epigenesis,"

[1] My example is drawn from Driesch's Gifford Lectures and Jenkinson's *Experimental Embryology*.

might coalesce in an idea different from either, but satisfying the requirements of both.

Of course, I am offering no opinion upon the value of these investigations. I only adduce them as striking examples of the ordinary course of a universal in its Inductive development. What works throughout is a continuity through differences ; and its value is in the differences it connects. This is throughout the essence of creation and invention, which permeates the whole of life, and so everyday a process as the use of language is a striking example of it. No one ever used the same word twice in precisely the same sense ; in " finding the right word " there is always a creative effort.

Now the general rules of Inductive elimination, based on " Same produces same," are simply the minimum negative criterion of truth, and can do by themselves no Inductive work at all. To rely on them alone is to reduce Induction to trial and error.[1]

3. Thus, I do not think it is true to say that " Same cause, same effect," is the basal principle of Induction ; and if this is so, there ceases to be any ground for maintaining that it is the essential function of the intelligence to connect the same with the same. The true principle I should rather state in some such form as that every universal nexus tends to continue itself inventively in new matter. It is true that to guide this process we can have no general criterion, because, as we have said already, the only criterion of truth is the fuller truth—the science at a more developed stage. And, therefore, there can be no rules for it, and it tends to drop out of logical theory. But none the less, it is this process to which the whole positive construction or invention of our inductive knowledge is due ; while the principle " Same produces same " can only eliminate what, having been suggested, is found on further trial not to produce the minimum characteristic of a real nexus. We have seen, indeed,[2] how a good experiment may sometimes reveal a

---

[1] It is a subtlety that in fact the underlying positive nature of negation often asserts itself, and the " just-not $a$ gives just-not $b$ " affords a positive extension of the nature of $a$ and $b$ respectively, which may be theoretically valuable (see my *Logic*, ii, p. 136). Thus in Driesch's Tubularia experiment, it is now alleged, the capacities of different cells are just not equal, as they just belong to different elements of the body. And this suggests that differentiation is present in a certain degree—a positive correction and extension of Driesch's conclusion (Jenkinson, 292 $n$.).

[2] Pp. 66–67 above, and the preceding note.

correlation of serial variations, which is in itself a positive expansion of the suggested nexus.    But this is only incidental to the strict process of Inductive Elimination.

The neglect of the positive continuity between differences as the inventive factor in Induction appears to me to show itself in the doctrine that Inductive progress consists strictly in mere elimination of the unfit,[1] in reducing the number of nexuses that can claim the position of the true invariable law.    This doctrine seems to me to subordinate the more important process and element of proof, because it can have no abstract criterion, to the less important, which is nothing but an abstract criterion.    But if the aim of logic is not to give rules of practice, but to understand the nature of knowledge, this ground of subordination is invalid, and it remains true that the mainspring of inductive advance in natural knowledge, as of knowledge in general, is the power of ideas to make experience coherent, and that therefore the demand of continuity between term and term or between nexus and nexus—of a positive explanatory character attaching to the nexus—is a fundamental requirement of inductive science, which is, in fact, merely an elementary stage of knowledge, and shares all its positive characters.[2]

4. The modification outlined above in the idea of Inductive universality or generalization follows from this conception. The value of an Inductive conclusion, as of any piece of knowledge, lies in the amount of reality which it enables us to grasp, and this is very slightly tested by the number of cases in which the nexus is repeated in fact.    And if the idea of identical repetition could be realized (which it cannot, for every so-called repetition is differenced by a new context) the frequency of recurrence would have no connection with universality at all.

What is here advocated as the true view of Inductive advance has been suggested by Green's treatment of logical theory,[3] and has in some degree been embodied by the writer,[4]

---

[1] See Bradley's criticism of one form of disjunctive reasoning, *Principles of Logic*, p. 515.

[2] See, however, Mr. Joseph's example from the discontinuity between physical cause and psychical effect, p. 453.    I think it could be discounted.

[3] *Works*, ii, pp. 288–90.

[4] *Logic*, ii, pp. 169–70, 174.

at the point where he deals with true Inductive generalization as consisting in the range of differing data and conditions welded into a system by any investigation, as contrasted with the number of recurrent cases which may fall under a single abstract statement, and there is a definite logical necessity for making the former type of universal the goal to which the latter is a half-way house or less. For, as Plato [1] pointed out and as Mr. Bradley [2] has recently emphasized, statements of fact (implicit statements of nexus), but slightly hedged with conditions, must always be at the mercy of unexpressed factors for their truth or falsehood. They tumble backwards and forwards between " is " and " is not " ; Plato's famous expression, which Mr. Bradley's argument in the passage just referred to strictly and precisely justifies. The remedy, as Mr. Bradley says, is to get the conditions into the subject ; and this means either an explicit or an implicit reference to a complete system [3]

The normal and natural working of intelligence, then, is creative and constructive, tending towards the concrete and to continuity within differences. The universality which is its mainspring is in itself a nisus to the concrete. This operative continuity is not represented by the linkage of the same to the same. Its law—the law of intelligence—is not the law of Identity, unless the law of Identity is construed in a way that takes it deep into the postulates of organic systematization. [4] And phenomena which should merely repeat themselves would present an absolute barrier to the central nisus of the intellect. Mere repetition, in fact, if it were possible, would be incompatible with understanding.

I am, therefore, still confident that the restriction of Inductive proof to the disqualification of competing hypotheses is a fundamental error of principle. [5] What really works in the proof is the same as what works in the discovery, the power, that is, of an idea to harmonize experience. No doubt the

[1] *Republic*, p. 479, c.
[2] *Mind*, No. 72, 499.
[3] See my *Logic*, i, p. 260, for judgments which imply, though they do not expressly include, a relevant scientific system.
[4] See my *Logic*, ii, pp. 207-8.
[5] I am afraid that here I find myself in opposition to Mr. Joseph, whose *Logic* I greatly admire. There is perhaps a difference in what we call " Induction." But I could not admit a distinction of principle. For my ultimate answer to the disjunctive theory of Induction, see my *Logic*, ii, p. 166.

hypothesis which best satisfies this condition would also be the least likely to fall a victim to the rule of elimination. But yet, theoretically speaking, if accepted for this latter reason, it is accepted, so it seems to me, for the wrong reason, and its value as knowledge is not genuinely apprehended. But this point is only incidental to my discussion, and I will not pursue it here.

# V

## CONTRADICTION AND REALITY

THE purpose of this paper is to insist on the familiar view which treats Negativity as a fundamental characteristic of the Real ; to exhibit this view in connection with one or two points in logical theory, and to insist that its value depends on the principle being pressed home in its full force.

1. I start, then, from what I take to be the nature of pure formal or logical Contradiction. The crucial point seems to be that no predicates are intrinsically contrary to one another. They only become so by the conditions under which they are drawn together. Contradiction consists in " differents " being ascribed to the same term, while no distinction is alleged within that term such as to make it capable of receiving them.

This is Plato's law of Contradiction—what does or suffers " opposites " (it is enough to say " differents ") in the same relation must in itself be two and not one—and it is the root of his distinction between Opinion or Appearance and Knowledge or Reality. It is a formal contradiction if you say, " This colour is both beautiful and ugly, i.e., not-beautiful." It ceases to be a contradiction if you say, " This colour by daylight is beautiful and by candlelight is ugly." Are not, it may be asked, those terms intrinsically contrary which can in no case be affirmed of one another, such as the circle and the square ? Why, no. They do not impede one another or the process of thought unless we bring them together in a special form, to which their content is inadequate. They may quite well be conjoint predicates of the same complex term, and when thus affirmed, and protected by adequate distinction, have nothing in them contrary to one another. It was a friend, I think, of Mr. Verdant Green who described a college cap as an abortive attempt to square the circle, and better examples of the conjunction would not be hard to find. There are places for all predicates ; and when all predicates are in their place, none of them is contrary to any other. It is the bringing them together on an inadequate basis of distinction which is the essence of contradiction and contrariety ; and this may happen with any diverse terms whatever. I may venture to note that even Dr. McTaggart, by implying in his description of contradiction [1] that the predicates are antecedently " contrary," suggests to my mind that he has not completely analysed its nature. It is a trivial point in itself ; but perhaps it indicates that he would not agree with me in taking Contradiction as a mere consequence and symbol of something much more fundamental.

Logical Contradiction, then, is an intellectual deadlock caused by the attempt to bring together two or more different terms without adequate adjustment of content for their reception. Contradiction in this sense is rightly pronounced unthinkable, and cannot therefore be a characteristic of Truth or of Ultimate Reality. For these, if they are anything, are experiences in which Thought is triumphant, and harmonious with itself at least, even if with more besides.

It will be a first step in our argument if we can decide at this point how far even such bare formal Contradiction is in some sense an actual existent and a characteristic of Reality. We see that it cannot be a characteristic of Ultimate Reality, and we are disposed at the first look to agree with eminent thinkers that it is simply a blunder of our own making, something subjective, and incapable of belonging to the actual world. But in saying this, we seem to have unduly idealized the world of fact, and taken it as equivalent to Ultimate Reality. For the unrest of action and cognition seems to arise from the perpetual presence of implicit Contradiction in the nature of actual fact, a presence which becomes explicit on the slightest reflection and forces us to go further in the hope of faring better. It must, I infer, be admitted that fact, as given in ordinary experience, is both actual and self-contradictory. To deny this is either to pronounce all objects of cognition subjective or illusory so long as cognition is

[1] *Studies in Hegelian Dialectic*, p. 9.

progressive—for its progress is a proof that it still meets with contradiction—or to stake out, within experience, some fixed world of realism, which would, after all, not coincide with actual fact in the given variation and development of the latter. Logical Contradiction, then, is a characteristic of Reality so far as presented in the actual world of fact. In the form of pain, dissatisfaction, and unrest it may almost be called itself an actual existent. It consists in an attempted synthesis, which fails owing to the inadequate adjustment of the contents employed ; and it is actual over the whole region of progressive action and cognition, which is equivalent to the region of finite experience. The view of its range is established by the fact of progress.

2. Our next step is to ascertain what form or spirit of difference survives when a logical contradiction is resolved. The point I would draw attention to is that we are here dealing with a survival of what was present in Logical Contradiction. Nothing is changed, except that what was attempted has been achieved. The contents are diverse, as they were ; they rush towards each other through the same rational impulse, whether in its practical or in its intellectual form ; the difference is merely that now they have been re-adjusted, and can carry out their union. How are we to describe the form or spirit of their difference ?

I may illustrate—it is merely an illustration, for I do not wish to raise purely historical questions—by Hegel's view of contradiction. It is familiar ground that Hegel has been accused of denying or disregarding the logical law which pronounces Logical Contradiction to be unthinkable, and that his best interpreters (Dr. McTaggart and Mr. Bradley) have cleared his reputation of this impiety. The dialectic, so far from disregarding the Law of Contradiction, rests, as they have pointed out, entirely upon it. It is because Contradiction is unthinkable and intolerable that a conjunction of judgments which makes their predicates irreconcilable demands a readjustment of contents and the formation of a new totality.

Now, while I admit that this is contained in Hegel's view of Contradiction, I cannot but think that there is something more behind. Hegel obviously feels himself fundamentally in antagonism to the current formal view of Contradiction as merely unthinkable. No words are too strong for him to express his scorn of such an attitude. " What moves the world is Contradiction ; it is ridiculous to say that Contradiction is unthinkable. What is true in this assertion only comes to this, that Contradiction cannot be final, and that by its own action it cancels while it maintains itself (aufhebt). The cancelled and maintained contradiction, however, is not abstract identity, for this is only one side of the antithesis." [1] Here, I admit, we are in the region of Essence, where oppositions are sharp and pointed. But this does not account for the whole of Hegel's feeling, which is fundamental with him. " Whereas people say Contradiction is not thinkable, the truth is that in pain which a living being feels it is actually a real existence." [2] He says the same of motion in space : " Formal Thinking prescribes to itself the rule that Contradiction is not thinkable ; but, in fact, the thinking of Contradiction is the essential moment of the Notion." [3] These latter passages are from the discussion of Life and of the Absolute Idea. All this is nothing new ; but it is relevant to my purpose to call to our minds how uncompromising Hegel's position really is about what he calls Contradiction, and how little he enters into the current isolation of that feature in experience, while admitting and maintaining that it is essentially provocative of change.

A suggestion can now be made in answer to the question, " What survives when a Contradiction is resolved ? " The reply might be, " A successful expression of negativity." Not that we are taking Hegel's views as authoritative ; but this is a consideration that occurs to us as accounting for the fact that he, on the one hand, with all logicians, sees in Contradiction something that cannot be tolerated ; and on the other hand, evidently with his deepest insight and conviction, holds that there underlies it something which is the pulse of life and the movement of the world, not through the fact of unthinkableness, but through the structure of Reality. This something he often calls Negativity, and it would seem to express the whole aspect or tendency of anything real, which

---

[1] *Encyclop.*, 119, Zusatz 2.     [2] *Wiss. d. Logik*, Theil ii., s. 249.
[3] *Ibid.*, 332.

finds imperfect manifestation in what has been described above as Formal or Logical Contradiction. Negativity, then, it is submitted, is fundamental in all that is real. It is the same characteristic which Dr. McTaggart describes as the tendency of all finite categories to complete themselves (notice the limitation to finite categories), and the same which Green expresses as the nature of a Self which is Self-conscious or at once its Self and its other. And in defining an answer to the question immediately before us, What form or spirit of difference survives when a logical Contradiction is resolved ?, we may take our bearings from Dr. McTaggart's description of this attribute of Reality. For him it is a tendency not to negation, but to self-completion. Negation, he holds, is incidental, and in the progress towards perfection tends to disappear. Even self-completion is only in the finite categories. In perfection, therefore, as I con-strue the implication of his conception, both would disappear altogether. Not that Dr. McTaggart is careless of the con-sideration that Reality must include and do justice to every-thing. But some things, as I read him, may be absorbed without leaving a trace, and negation is one of them. This is not unconnected with his view of the importance of pleasure. The view here submitted may give its bearings, as I said, by referring to Dr. McTaggart's account of the matter. Logical Contradiction, I admit, is a vanishing element, belongs to the sphere of the finite, and minimizes itself in the higher types of experience as the character of finiteness approaches a minimum. With negativity, or with negation, the case seems to be different. This belongs to the fundamental structure of everything that is real. It is not a disappearing quantity in the progress of experience, and for this reason: that it does not, like Logical Contradic-tion, depend on inadequacy. So long as there is no science, and the world baffles and contradicts the mind of the savage at every turn, there can be no such sense of a reality not-ourselves beyond and over against the mind as there is in the days of Newton or of Darwin. The negation is cor-relative to the affirmation. The important question about negation always is, not how much meaning can be conjured out of mere denial, but why, in the most highly developed experience, negation bears an equal part. And the answer, as I read it, is fundamental to the nature of Reality. Affirmation and negation may even become co-equal and interchangeable in content, but a real whole must always *bona fide* hold them both together.

This, therefore, it is submitted, is the spirit of differences which survives even in a resolved contradiction, and where we possess what is most real and thinkable. Everything contributes to the whole, and the failure which made the contradiction no doubt depended upon the distinctness of the two sides, which survives in and tends to perfect the completed union. But it appears to me that we are running away from the problem if we treat the mere fact of failure as something which, surviving as such, qualifies the successful union. The qualification, whatever it is, can surely count and work only as it survives within the completed whole, and it is in the character of this whole itself that we have to find the experience of negativity, which is not, according to the view here insisted on, a note of imperfection, but is a characteristic that deepens and does not fade as the other characteristics of Reality grow more complete. Negativity is not all Reality, but the completer the Reality the deeper the Negativity.

How, then, is Negativity experienced ? And if it only means the distinctness necessary to identification, is not a term connected with the idea of negation too violent and exaggerated to use for it ? Now no doubt Solutions of contradiction, Completeness, Satisfaction, are possible at many levels of life, and compatible with very easy and effortless experiences. But it is here suggested that in a true typical satisfaction there is always a certain exaltation which depends essentially on the fact that in satisfaction the self goes out into the other, and, though or because it becomes enriched, is beyond its normal barriers, and in a word, to put the whole paradox brutally, is undergoing an experience technically, and in its fundamental nature, homogeneous with self-sacrifice. How can this be construed of anything but a finite being ? Obviously not by help of such words as have just been used, presupposing limits and a temporal modification in the self. But there is a point of some interest which may at least serve to bring out the distinction of principle between taking Negation as, like Contradiction, an incident of Finiteness, and taking it as fundamental in Reality.

3. It has already been implied that the current view of experience, influential even among philosophers, confuses Contradiction and Negativity. The principle that an element of Reality can be completed only through what is not itself is confused with the imperfection of adjustment in finite beings or contents which so far hinders such completion from taking place. And thus it comes to be held that Negation, like Contradiction, is a vanishing quantity, and that in a complete experience it would disappear. The point of interest which was just now referred to as emphasizing the distinction of principle is the extreme difficulty of avoiding this confusion. When we endeavour to insist upon the nature of self-consciousness, as self and other in one, by instances and analyses drawn from actual experience, we constantly find ourselves appealing to characteristics which depend upon ignorance and imperfection. The ideal which we have in mind is the self *in* the other, but in actual experience we have little more than the self *and* the other. Nettleship observes upon this in the biography of Green. Now the crux in the distinction of principle arises at this point because of the apparent fact that it is the discrepancy of self *and* other that *for us* gives interest to the realization of self *in* other. We may take as a characteristic case that apparent responsiveness of external Nature to human moods, the perception of which is at least a great part of the apprehension of the beautiful. The freshness and strength of the feeling which such perceptions bring with them is surely in a great measure dependent on the fact that they come to us as undesigned coincidences. It is for this reason that they seem to bring to us a confirmation of our own sentiments which is rooted somewhere beyond the foundations of our own self. If we were convinced that Nature was somehow just another offshoot of the same principle as ourselves, and not merely convinced of it, but able to see it pretty completely in detail, then we are inclined to think the return upon ourselves would lose in vigour what it gained in perfection, and the fascinating sense of something beyond would

be transformed into a dull feeling that it is all one. Now the case thus stated emphasizes the opposite side of the question from that which was insisted on above. The sense of the beyond and of something over against the mind must be immensely greater, it was urged, for Newton or for Darwin than for a savage to whom Nature is chiefly an incalculable interference. Both points of view seem prima facie justified, and their contrast just illustrates the parting of the ways. In a word, it seems *natural* to take the characteristic which distinguishes the other from the self as lying in discrepancy and unfamiliarity, which may be symbolized by Logical Contradiction as described at first. But it is also plain that such a characteristic excludes *pro tanto* the correspondence of the two sides in their full detail and complexity, and must be a vanishing characteristic as experience approaches completeness. We must then elect, it would appear, to conclude, that to interpret the beyond or the other which confronts us in experience, as due to our ignorance and defect, and as a vanishing quantity in the progress of the mind, is to confuse the incident with the essence ; and that as in the example of natural knowledge, the otherness becomes more definite as the object becomes more adequate to the subject. It is partly perhaps with the view of construing these appearances that many thinkers have embarked on the adventure of treating all the content of life as a translation of the interaction of conscious beings. Then no doubt we have the conception of an " other " which is able to maintain its independence—its otherness—along with almost any degree of transparency or familiarity. And I mention the speculation chiefly for this reason : to make clear, if it does not seem clear, what the particular crux is which I have had in mind. We may try to conceive an intelligent being who has learned all that a sunset or even a toothache can teach him, and in that case we feel a difficulty in comprehending how they can any longer seem experiences from which, as his other, his self has anything to gain. But a person, however well you know him, is still an independent source of response, and it may be argued that here, and here only, you find the true other of a self.

I feel a difficulty about this speculation which may rest on misapprehension, but which I will indicate in a few words, because it stands in the way of our first conclusion. What we must have for any theory of Reality, and especially for Negativity, to work in is the content of life, pains, conflicts, sacrifice, satisfaction. Now there is a difficulty, is there not ? in getting these contents out of a universe of persons, except by presupposing, in the outside or other of every person, what might as well have been presupposed as the outside or other of the persons commonly recognized as such. It is things, is it not ? which set the problems of life for persons ; and if you turn all things into persons, the differences which make life interesting are gone, except in as far as for practical purposes you turn the persons back again into things, i.e. your food, or your own body, or the place in which you were born. In making the outside adequate to the highest claims, you have turned it into an inside, and so, while professing to meet the problem of the outside in the highest degree, you have, it almost appears to me, really abandoned it altogether. If the instruments and attributes of my life are turned into other persons, I, surely, am reduced to emptiness and deprived even of my character, for my character is not, without external activity. This criticism may be mistaken, but it may pass as affirming that we must perceive as actual the distinctions which give life its content.

4. It is time to indicate the conclusion—an old conclusion —to which I have nothing to add, except by pleading that its point is lost if it is not conceived in its whole depth of paradox.

I will try to express it through antitheses to current opinions, which will bring out the reasons for which it seems to me worth caring about ; and these are also the characteristics which define its peculiarity.

a. It is a mistake to treat the finite world, or pain, or evil as an illusion. In answer to the question whether they are real or are not real, I see nothing for it but to repeat what Hegel says of Space and Time, " Everything is real, so long as you do not take it for more than it is." Finiteness, pain, and evil are, on the view here accepted, essential features of Reality, and belong to an aspect of it which does not disappear even in perfection. The view that they are illusions says that if we knew everything we should see that there was no pain or evil at all. In a certain sense the two views may be brought near together, but my plea is that all depends on being in earnest with the idea of negativity, and that from that point of view the idea of *illusion* is rejected, though that of *appearance*, as something *actual* but *contradictory*, is accepted. Hegel mentions the name of illusion in the matter; but, as I understand, the illusion which he speaks of is not the belief that finiteness is actual, but the inference that this being so, there is nothing more to be said, or in other words, that the actual is necessarily ultimate. At all events, as against the idea that finiteness, pain, and evil are an illusion, the view here indicated would maintain that conscious beings actually suffer and do wrong because it is their nature to complete themselves; and the general form of this completion involves as one factor in it the loss of self, and in the finite world this is emphasized by various degrees of what we have called Logical Contradiction—that is to say, inadequacy of the elements in which completion is sought. It would follow (and this seems to agree with the best ethical theory) that the ultimate logical structure, if I may so speak, of suffering and of evil is the same as that of satisfaction and of good. This is noticeable, of course, in Green's theory of morality. The difference between them is one of the adequacy of contents to self-completion, and their kinship is seldom altogether latent even in finite experience. I may refer to Mr. Haldane's observation on the death of animals in the second series of Gifford Lectures, and to the nature of the fullest æsthetic exaltation.

β. The same mode of thought would be hostile to any conception of the divine nature, which should involve stability and perfection in such a sense as to exclude activity and the general form of self-sacrifice. It is not intended to adhere to the view of those who conceive the divine being as finite and possibly as one of a number. The intention is rather the reverse, namely, to maintain that finiteness *ipso facto* arises if negativity is not given its full significance in the conception of the supreme nature. The Master of Balliol's criticism of Aristotle's Theoretic life,[1] as literally interpreted,

[1] [See Edward Caird's *Evolution of Philosophy in the Greek Philosophers*, vol. i, Lecture xii.—ED.]

puts this point very clearly. It is not an imperfection in the Supreme Being, but an essential of His completeness, that His nature, summing up that of all Reality, should go out into its other to seek the completion which in this case alone is absolutely found. The other in question can only be finite experience, and it is in and because of this, and qualified by it, that the divine nature maintains its infinity. And therefore it may be said that the general form of self-sacrifice—the fundamental logical structure of Reality—is to be found here also, as it is everywhere. Not, of course, that the infinite Being can lose and regain its perfection, but that the burden of the finite is inherently a part, or rather an instrument, of the self-completion of the infinite. The view is familiar. I only plead that it loses all point if it is not taken in bitter earnest. I have had much in mind Nettleship's fragment on the Atonement.[1]

I have used remorselessly phrases which imply time—" activity," " going out of oneself," " seeking and finding." The objection to predicating time of the supreme experience lies in the nature of self-completeness, and if on the one hand succession seems incompatible with this, on the other hand the idea of instantaneousness, which is a temporal idea, must not here be introduced to embarrass our thoughts. I must not dwell upon the matter at this last moment, but I think we must distinguish the conception of changing or progressing as a whole, from the conception of uniting, in a self-complete being, characteristics which for us demand succession. I may refer again to one of Nettleship's fragments, that on Immortality.[1] If we were to be barred from ascribing content to the Supreme Being, because for us all content is developed in time, the end must be that for us the Supreme Being will be nothing.

γ. Finally, the point of view is hostile to the form in which questions of optimism and pessimism are usually raised, as to the surplus of pleasure over pain in the universe. Even Mr. Bradley has discussed this question with reference to the Absolute, but I cannot help thinking that it is improperly stated. What we as factors of Reality demand is not, if I am right, essentially pleasure, but satisfaction ; that is, the

---

[1] [*Lectures and Philosophical Remains*, vol. i.—Ed.]

sense that by help of the negative we have attained our-selves. This no doubt implies some pleasure ; but the point is, if I am not altogether wrong, that in satisfaction the pain or difficulty as a moment—i.e. a phase which remains an element—contributes actively to the positive attainment, while in comparing pleasure and pain as experienced facts of feeling I suppose they must retain their first positions as *plus* and *minus* quantities. This is one point, and another follows from it. The comparison of pleasure and pain in respect of quantity—even if we disregard the difficulties pointed out in anti-Hedonist controversy—betrays an in-organic point of view. The question cannot surely be how many moments of pain you have experienced, and whether you have had enough moments of pleasure to outweigh them, but whether the experience has done its work and returned you to yourself a complete or at least a completer being. So, it would seem, the problem should be stated about the universe. Not, if we could reckon up moments of equal pleasure and pain, which of them would be found to out-number the others ? but rather, is there reason for think-ing that pain and finiteness are elements playing a definite part in the whole, such that its completeness depends upon containing them ? Broadly speaking, I suppose, experience suggests to us that a soul which has never known pain, like a nation that has never known war, has no depth of being and is not a personality at all. Of course this way of looking at the matter does not by itself dispose of the suggestion that the cost even of perfecting a soul may be too high ; but the conviction that there is and essentially must be a certain cost, corresponds to our best insight in the sphere of every-day experience.

And so, in the end, *if* such a question as that of pleasure or pain in the Absolute has reality for us at all, it seems important where we look for the suggestions from which we are to start. We ought not surely to start from common-place experiences, but only from those in which self-expres-sion is at its fullest, rare moments such as those to which Aristotle alludes in the discussion of the Theoretic life. It may be noteworthy that Aristotle consents while Plato refuses to ascribe the feeling of pleasure to the Divine nature ; and this may be connected with Aristotle's apparent omission of negativity from his conception of ideal experience. In his distinction, however, between the enjoyment of self-realization and the enjoyment of recreation he throws out a hint which we might do well to follow. And for him as for us, apparently, the activities primarily devoted to sheer enjoyment and delight are wrested by the very structure of man's soul to severer forms of self-expression ; so that the completest of all the creations in which as yet man has freely and spontaneously sought what he most enjoys, is, I presume, for us, as for Aristotle, that of poetical tragedy. This does seem to be a paradox worth noting, and it might be driven home by all sorts of considerations. I am only using it to set the question of optimism in a certain light ; that is to say, to state it not by looking for pain to be as it were quantitatively submerged or neutralized by pleasure, but by looking for a completeness in which souls have found themselves, or realized their inherent structure ; which completeness, considered as a whole, cannot be quantitatively compared with the factors or elements, such as negativity, subordinated within it. If we had to depend on Contradiction as such, then I suppose completeness could only be in its abolition ; but the distinction between Contradiction and Negativity seemed to be suggestive on this point.

# VI

# LIFE AND FINITE INDIVIDUALITY

## DO FINITE INDIVIDUALS POSSESS A SUBSTANTIVE OR AN ADJECTIVAL MODE OF BEING? [1]

1. IN considering some recent literature of this question,[2] I am strongly impressed with the result that there are two lines of argument to be regarded.[3]

i. The one set of arguments appeals to the fact of existence. It rests upon the proposition that finite individuals are individual existents. Using, then, the unrestricted premiss that all individual existents are ultimate subjects, it applies this conclusion to spiritual finite individuals, together with all existent " things," including things that are parts of things. I shall suggest that a proof depending on so wide a premiss is precluded from supporting, in a serious sense, the thesis that spiritual finite individuals possess substantive or substantival being.

ii. The other set of arguments appeals to the intentional character of spiritual finite beings as such—to their pretensions and their implications—a question of unity as an object or ideal rather than as a subject. It deals with such matters as

---

[1] [The opening paper of a Symposium. The terms of the question were suggested by the book named in note [2] below. For the papers which followed see *Life and Finite Individuality* (1918), a volume edited for the Aristotelian Society by Dr. Wildon Carr.—ED.]

[2] I note that Professor Pringle-Pattison, *The Idea of God*, uses indifferently the terms " substantive " and " substantival." " Substantive " (p. 272) I take to mean of the nature of a substance, and " substantival " (p. 282) of the nature of a noun substantive. This is not unimportant, as the meaning of " substance " is lowered by his argument, in agreement with others, almost to that of " noun substantive." It should be noted in advance that if the latter meaning were all that is in question, there could be no doubt that any object of thought could be subject (in the sense of having " substantival " being) and any could be predicate. Though not decisive, this fact is significant, and was, of course, fully recognized by Aristotle.

[3] A conceivable interpretation of one of these would remove the difference. I will refer again to this point (see p. 112).

the self in morality and religion, with its pretension to assert a unity which it does not find existent, to be free and responsible, to remain itself even in the social bond or in oneness with God. A conclusion from such considerations would be strictly applicable to the finite spiritual individual. But I shall urge that from such considerations the conclusion must be that which I advocate, and not that which is advanced against me. The spiritual individual has a solid claim to substantive being only indirectly, and through an admission and recognition that his immediate self is of a nature which, to speak in terms of the antithesis before us, cannot be called substantive, and must by preference be set down as adjectival.

2. I will begin by stating what I take to be the essence of the first set of arguments. They turn, not upon anything peculiar to a finite spirit, but upon the fact of thinghood. Aristotle's doctrine of substance seems to be typical of them, and is adopted by Professor Pringle-Pattison,[1] who at this point only, I think, strikes into this first line of argument. Indifferently, as I gather, the individual man and, for example, the stone in his signet-ring, are taken to be substances, as subjects that cannot be predicates.[2] So, according to Professor Stout, following, as he rightly says, the popular opinion, is any existent thing or existent part of a thing, an orange,[3] or a dog's tail—it does not matter how subordinate to other individuals, or how far from such self-existence as belongs to the universe. It need merely have the independence of a substantive in relation with its adjectives.[4] It must be a concrete—that is, though its relatedness to other things may determine its special nature (no unrelated [5] nucleus, so far as I gather, is reserved in contrast with such relatedness), its particular existence must not be derivative from this. But, I suppose, it is only in its fully determined relatedness that we could think of it as substance or subject. In its existence behind or abstracted from this it would be empty, a *Ding an sich*.

The limits of the class of substances which are ultimate subjects are, as I said, taken to be those of thinghood.[6] Any

[1] *The Idea of God*, p. 272.    [2] Cf. Joseph, *Introd. to Logic*, p. 50, cf. 167.
[3] *Proc. Arist. Soc.*, 1902–3, pp. 2, 22.
[4] Stout, loc. cit., cf. note [2], p. 89, above.
[5] Such as, e.g., Professor Parker assumes, *Self and Nature*, p. 247.
[6] This, as I understand, is Professor Laird's view, *Problems of the Self*, pp. 348 and 354, and also Professor Parker's, op. cit., p. 267.

" thing " is an ultimate subject, a substantive, and, I presume, a substance (Professor Stout does not use the latter term) and, *pro tanto*, self-existent. An abstract quality may be existent, but cannot be self-existent.[1]

In Professor Laird's most solid and instructive discussion we get the best that can be done on this method.[2] The soul is a substance because it is an existent unity of existent experiences—cognition, conation, and feeling—each of which is such as to imply a unity of itself and the others. These experiences are substances, though not self-subsistent substances. They are parts of the soul-substance, and not merely qualities of it. They are ," parts of its existence " in Professor Stout's sense. The soul-substance *is* its acts in their continuity and unity, and not including their objects. But we can identify the acts and estimate their continuity—so I read the theory—only through their objects. The soul-substance's continued identity, from beginning to end of its experienced life-course, is but little, fluctuating, and full of gaps, and I add, for my part, full of positive incoherence, self-rejection, and self-contradiction. And we are, according to Professor Laird, not entitled to affirm its pre-existence nor its post-existence to the life we experience, though neither are we entitled to deny them. We are told, indeed, of a claim to freedom, independence, responsibility.[3] I cite a characteristic sentence. " We know what our souls are, we know the meaning of their identity, we know the sense in which they are distinct and independent in the world. Because we know these things we should hold fast to them," etc.

It is a great thing to find a clear issue. These words, taken in their context and supported as they are supported, precisely express what I am anxious to deny. They define, as I gather, the conclusions of that first line of argument to which I am referring, and the position they lay down exactly embodies the popular misconception which to me appears most at variance with fact.[4] For here, as I understand the issue, we can assert

[1] Parker, loc. cit.
[2] See especially the conclusion, p. 360 ff., and cf. p. 195.
[3] Op. cit., pp. 356, 366.
[4] Cf. Professor W. E. Hocking on " The Holt-Freudian Ethics," *Papers in Honour of Josiah Royce*, p. 270. " It is not by the possession of any soul-substance that I am defined a self, but it is ' by this meaning of my life-plan, by this possession of an ideal ' " (cf. p. 278).

nothing without passing into argument of the second type.   The proof of distinct existence is no basis for predicates such as those connected with freedom.   That proof applies to all things and parts of things, and to all minds of brutes.   And for these it clearly carries no such implications.   Therefore, by itself, it cannot do so for other beings.

So far as the first line of argument has carried us, the distinction between substantive or substantival on the one hand, and predicative or adjectival on the other, amounts to nothing more than the distinction between a complex of predicates, presupposed as connected in a single focus of apprehension, and a predicate or predicates separately referred either to such a nexus, or to the one ultimate subject whatever that may be.   There is no such thing as a predicate or adjective which is not referred to any subject at all.   Now, we know that thinghood or existence gives no guarantee whatever for the relevance, either to each other, or to the propositions made about the existent, of the predicates presupposed to be connected in it.   Locke's wonderful section [1] tells us that nothing can be guaranteed to exhibit within itself the conditions of the attributes we ascribe to it.   In other words, the conception of any thing, as a unitary subject, though we assume that it has some degree of intrinsic connection, can have no definite limits assigned it.   There is no proposition about it which can be known as strictly and adequately true. The familiar impossibility of determining what is and what is not so much as to be called a " thing," reinforces this argument.[2]   There is no ultimate reason for taking one complex, at least below conscious individuals, as a single thing more than another.   They include one another in innumerable subordinations, from the Sahara, for example, or any patch of it, down to any grain of sand in it.   A thing, therefore, as an existence, can have no claim to be an ultimate subject.   It is, as such, a provisional subject, and has, of course, a being and reality, and is necessary to the universe.   But it is selected for convenience of special knowledge or practice, and justifies its selection in indefinitely varied degrees.   This, we have seen, the argument before us admits.

[1] Essay, IV, vi, 11.
[2] Laird, p. 353 ; my *Logic*, i, p. 129.

It should be noted at this point that the phrase " ultimate subject " suggests a type of subjects to which subjects of all types are reducible. If we apply the words in this sense to finite individuals, then either the proposition which applies them is obviously false, or finite individuals must include, for example, such subjects as civilization,[1] society, nature, propositions about which are certainly irreducible to propositions about persons or things. This result would destroy the pre-eminence claimed for singular beings in the pluralistic sense. It would force us to recognize a series of subjects progressively nearer to being ultimate, up to the universe.

But can a thing, even considered as a provisional subject, ever be regarded as adjectival or as a predicate ? Mr. Joseph [2] says very reasonably, in explaining the general view which I, for one, have adopted : " There is no desire to deny to individuals a relative independence, or to pretend that the relation of attributes or universals to the concrete individual is the same relation as that of an individual to the system of reality which includes him." And of course this is so, while we are in the attitude presupposed by the first line of argument. The whole point of this is that it forgets the abstraction under which it apprehends the structure of experience.

What follows, however, from the above explanation is this. The complex taken as one with some existent, and commonly accepted as a thing or solid starting-point, substance or subject, *de novo*, is in truth, as we saw, a set of determinations which, with or without some pretence to system, are wholly inadequate and self-contradictory as a subject to the proposition in which they stand. Their real function and position, therefore, is like that of other adjectives or predicates which are identified with an existent as conditions explaining some of its characters, or as predicates explained by some. You cannot ascribe predicates truly to the existent as you apprehend it. You ascribe them to reality on conditions roughly indicated by the marks of that existent. " Reality as indicated by the characters of gold is heavy." " Reality as including certain aspects of the geological history of our globe is the Atlantic Ocean." In short, " Reality is such that at or in S it is P."

[1] Joseph, *Introd. to Logic*, p. 168 ; Laird, p. 339.
[2] *Logic*, loc. cit. I do not mean that he adopts this view.

This is the formal account of the existential affirmation. Its essential truth seems to me obvious. Locke's section is enough to justify us in setting down most existents as subordinate to the universe in such a way as must surely be called adjectival. Adjectival does not mean abstract or in the air. The adjective "agrees with" its substantive. Its name implies at once attachment and detachment. Any point in the nature of a substantive can be taken apart and made an adjective of it. We do not, indeed, think of the features currently presupposed in the solid subject, the starting-point of judgment, as adjectives. Yet the adjective, when distinguished, remains attached, and presupposes in its own nature the nature of its substantive.

When this is considered, we are driven to treat highly subordinate existences as adjectival to their superordinate existences. They are emphasized in detachment from them, but they qualify them, and lose either significance or, in some cases, the conditions of existence if viewed as detached from them. It is mere formalism, dependent upon a substantiation, of provisional subjects, that hinders us from saying so. And we have seen that the formula which says otherwise—the current formula S is P—is false. R in S is P, or R as S is P, applicable to part as qualifying whole, is the formula which we want, and which we shall find expressing the spiritual truth in the second line of argument with precise fidelity. It leads us somewhat to extend the usage of the term "adjective," in proportion as we note the superficial and provisional nature of ordinary substantives. To take Professor Stout's homely instance, it is plain that the dog's tail qualifies the dog. It is among the first things you note as decisive of his kind or his beauty. When we are told it is a part of the dog's existence, and not of his nature, this is a plain overstatement. It is meant that it *also* attracts attention for its own sake, and is a "this thing" with a nature of its own presupposed in it. And you can try to look at it so ; but you cannot really adhere to such a point of view. Neither existence nor nature belongs to it by itself. The possessive genitive, which marks it as a part and as having its value in being a part, marks it no less as being of a predicative nature. You cannot think or speak of it without such a genitive. If you try to do so, you think or speak falsely, making an abstraction which you forget. If you remember the abstraction you are making, the term becomes predicative at once. The same applies to all parts of things. When we come to parts of spiritual wholes, the argument is at a different level, and yet more decisive. But there is still a word to be said to emphasize the predicative nature of parts in highly unified wholes, even on an existential basis.

You can predicate any part of a structure, of the whole as subject taken in a certain aspect. It is what, so considered, the whole becomes. It is no bar to such subordination that it may possess a particular structure which repeats that of other particulars, and so is distinct from them and side by side with them. Its particular structure, e.g. as a unity of acts which imply each other,[1] is no bar to its taking on a special shape and character expressive of its subordination to and within an inclusive structural system. At this level, in the comparison with common thinghood, it is a fair parallel to point out that the unit divisions within the whorls which are irrecoverably merged into the single orchid blossom have, each within itself, overlaid by the inclusive structure, the whole leaf-nature with its appropriate equipment of spiral vessels. Our minds, if they could be visualized, although they repeat in each an analogous structure, would not look like self-contained shapes, each repeating the other side by side like our bodies set in a row. They would look like bits of machines or organs of organisms fragmentary and incomprehensible till the whole were supplied to which they respectively belonged, each with its driving-bands or nerves or wireless aerials hanging loose around it, all senseless and self-contradictory apart from the inclusive structural system. This would be the case even if their internal structure were ultimate. It would be merged and overwhelmed as instrumental to a wider identity. It is so continually in the daily life of fully developed intelligences. But, further, the alleged internal structure is secondary.[2] We can have experience below any such structure, and we might have it above.

I note the common refuge of semi-pluralist reasonings in admitting that finite individuals are interrelated, but only *in*

[1] Professor Laird's soul-substance.
[2] See Bradley, *Appearance*, p. 477.

*some degree* determined by interrelatedness.[1]  To me this seems
an evasion.  It is meant to suggest a crowd of co-ordinate
individual reals, like Herbart's, entering into relations which
are secondary to their private being.[2]  But these co-ordinate
reals are pure assumption.  There is nothing in experience to
suggest drawing a line between interrelatedness and non-re
latedness :  and the plain fact is that of super- and subordinate
reals.  You cannot possibly draw an absolute boundary line
round any reals but spirits ;  and they, as we shall see, have
power explicitly to negative the boundary which, in a sense
they suggest.  When I say that certain apparent subjects are
adjectival I do not merely deny non-relatedness ; [3] what I aim a
denying is co-ordinate relatedness.  We are speaking of the
typical relation of an individual to the universe.   I am surprised
that this should have been compared to the relation between a
shoe and a foot, or a son and a father.[4]

We shall see further reasons below for admitting that pro
visional subjects taken in their whole reality [5] are best con
sidered as characters predicable of the universe.  And the
analysis of the judgment which I have suggested agrees funda
mentally and especially with the nature which full experience
demands for the finite individual spirit.

It is urged that individuals are none the less apprehended
as they really are, if apprehended as distinct individuals in
spite of belonging to a superior whole.  Abstraction or analysis
does not involve falsehood.[6]  On this the comment indicated
above seems to me simple and decisive.  The question is
whether, in considering the subordinate individual, the abstrac
tion involved in attending to it *par excellence* is forgotten or is
remembered.  In the popular attitude—the attitude to which
pluralist or semi-pluralist reasonings appeal—it is forgotten
And the individual taken as real on that basis is, therefore
partly unreal, and its appearance is in some degree illusory

[1] Stout, loc. cit., p. 21 ;  Pringle-Pattison, p. 274 ;  Parker, p. 246 ff.
[2] It is most remarkable how Professor Parker favours such an assumption
by instances naïvely taken from superficial wholes.  The terms " pre-exist,"
"native," and " acquired," applied to the individual, betray this fallacy
pp. 246, 254, 271.
[3] Pringle-Pattison, loc. cit.
[4] *Id. ib.*
[5] The soul-substance, as we shall see, is not the whole reality of the finit
individual.
[6] Stout, loc. cit.. p. 23 ;  Parker, pp. 257, 265.

In the attitude to which we shall finally appeal, which regards the substantiality ascribed to the self as intentional, the abstraction involved in apprehending the subordinate individual is unforgotten. This means, in other words, that it is annulled, that the claim often made in argument [1] is really justified, and that the provisional individual is apprehended in its true place, and in unity with the superior whole. So far as it can be thus apprehended it is or would be real. Its appearance is so far not a " mere appearance," and involves no element of illusion. So apprehended, as in the second line of argument which I shall consider, and not otherwise, it may fairly be called substantival. But this is not in its own right, for it is then revealed as an adjective at once attached to and detached from its substantive.

3. I now approach the second line of argument, and must address myself to Professor Pringle-Pattison's position. In the main he and I are arguing on common ground, a ground much narrower than that on which my discussion has so far moved, though at one point, as it seemed to me, he retreats to that less relevant basis. For the most part, however, we are both reasoning about spiritual finite beings and on the basis of their claims and implications.

Our common ground, as stated by Professor Pringle-Pattison himself,[2] includes a negation and an assertion. We both *reject* " the old doctrine of the soul-substance as a kind of metaphysical atom." We both believe that the mere individual nowhere exists ; " he is the creature of a theory." " Both his existence and his nature (his ' that ' and his ' what ') are derived. It is absurd to talk of him as self-subsistent or existing in his own right." I need not multiply citations. Again, we both *assert* that if we could possess ourselves entirely " we should be . . . either the Absolute *in propria persona*, or Browning's ' finite clod untroubled by a spark.' " " All this, then, is common ground."

The main difference between us is indicated in the sentence which forms the theme of this discussion. So far as the term substance is implied by Professor Pringle-Pattison, its meaning is lowered [3] to something like noun substantive, and expressly

[1] Stout, loc. cit. ; Parker, loc. cit.    [2] *The Idea of God*, pp. 257–60.
[3] See notes, p. 89, supra.

guarded against implying Spinozistic substance, or self-sub-sistence. It is expressly identified with Aristotelian substance, or the character of any and every subject which cannot be a predicate. The argument here drops down, as I said above, to the level of resting upon distinguishable existence or concrete thinghood, taking no account of what is special to a finite spiritual being. He would even admit that an individual might be adjectival, if that only meant interrelated with other reals. To me, as I said, the term would imply subordination in place of co-ordination—the character of being something which has its main being and value as a qualification of a whole which includes it. So far, our disagreement is marked. I should have held, indeed, that our previously noted agreement covered this point and re-quired him to admit the finite being's intrinsic subordinate-ness. But he does not understand it so. All this, however, as we saw, amounts to little more than an argument from distinct existence.

Appealing, also, to a further line of argument, he has more important characteristics to insist upon. These may be fairly summarized under two heads. There is the topic of membership of the Absolute, and in connection with this, what I may coin a phrase to express as the teleological status of finite spirits in the universe. And there is the kindred problem of freedom and self-distinction in the great experi-ences of which love, social morality, and religion are typical examples.

I am criticized for rejecting the notion of the membership of finite spirits as such in the Absolute. I partly explained my position on this point in the *Mind* notice of Professor Pringle-Pattison's book, and I need not be lengthy here. I rejected the term membership, because I thought it would commit me to what we both repudiate—eternal substances, differentia-tions of the Absolute, identified with finite selves. Here I follow Dr. McTaggart's logic,[1] though not his opinion. In view of our imperfections there must be, he argues, a chasm either between the Absolute and the finite self as we experi-ence it, or between the finite self as we experience it and its own reality. He accepts the latter alternative, I find

[1] *Studies in Hegelian Cosmology*, sect. 39.

myself driven to the former.[1] So far as this choice goes, I may claim my critic's assent. He rejects with me the pluralist's eternal substances. And I would call attention to the expression, which he cites with approval from Professor Laurie, that the predicates of the Absolute are the worlds.[2] Something of this kind was also in my thoughts, both in conceiving finite individuals as predicative in character, and in holding at the same time that some more inclusive differentiations than finite selves would be more fittingly considered predicates of the whole.

It was a motive to this opinion that I could not bring myself to hold finite selves to be necessarily eternal or everlasting units. I cannot be sure whether this is intended to be a subject of complaint against me. My critic nowhere rejects my view, but he seems to find fault with my theory for implying it. And I do not say that transience is incompatible with membership in a non-transient whole. But obviously, taken along with the other imperfections of existent selves, it affects the kind of membership which can be ascribed to the transient. The analogy with the lower animal mind presses upon us here. Do I understand it to be urged that M. Arnold's Dachshund [3] *was* or *is* an individual member of the Absolute? If he was, I should hardly object to calling all finite spirits also members of it in at least a parallel sense. For he was individual, surely, rather for others than for himself; and this is very noticeably the line of the critic's argument at this point. If we rely on such superior insight into individuality, we abandon the position that the self has membership in the shape in which it experiences itself. If he was not an individual member, and I should have thought this the more appropriate language, I should urge that the high and unique value which my critic claims for that "little self" shows that what we really need for our estimate of finite beings can be satisfied without our taking upon us the hazard of asserting membership for every finite spirit as it stands and experiences itself, with all its imperfections on its head, and all its gamut of degrees.

---

[1] Unless in a further sense the Absolute were taken as the reality of all finite selves.

[2] *The Idea of God*, p. 174.          [3] Op. cit., p. 268

Therefore, I think that my critic's teleological status of finite spirits,[1] though in the general line of my own convictions, is too rigid and exacting a view. He holds that the development into finite spirits—our spirits as we know them—must be the chief end and aim of the Absolute. I cannot escape Dr. McTaggart's argument. I cannot believe that the supreme end of the Absolute is to give rise to beings such as I experience myself to be. And I recur to my critic's own words. If I possessed myself entirely, I should be the Absolute, and, I continue, I should not be what I experience existentially as myself. Suppose the " worlds " to be realized were not you and I and the Dachshund, but beauty, truth, and love in different renderings through different " created " systems. We, perhaps, might be instrumental as trivial elements to one such world.

Membership in a sense, of course, there must be in the Absolute for all its elements. It is the form of membership, whether as we exist in experience or otherwise, that sets the problem. If reality is temporal, a transient existence as such can have but a very passing tenure of membership ; and, surely, must possess some other form of reality than individual being as a member. If reality is timeless, the transient existence must symbolize some participation which is not confined to its passage in time. I will try to fill out these hints below.

I could have modelled my statement into an almost complete agreement with Professor Pringle-Pattison, for the explicit difference between us is one of proportion and degree. But as there underlies this a real contrast of tendency, which he has rightly felt, and as it depends on a point of view which I am exceedingly desirous to emphasize, I will express my position as uncompromisingly as possible. I was not asked to open this discussion in order to gloss over a radical discrepancy of feeling, but, I suppose, in order to make it explicit. And, therefore, I will state the rest of my argument in terms of the distinction between the two attitudes to life, which, as I suggested at first, are respectively embodied in the two sets of arguments we are concerned with, and between which I am desirous to express my preference.

The remaining issues which I have to discuss with my

[1] The phrase is not his.

critic amount to the problem of free self-determination on the part of the spiritual finite individual, and the conceivability of confluence between such individuals, or their transmutation and absorption in the Absolute. I believe that I can best sum up my own whole argument, and explain my position as to the points just mentioned, by trying to set out the two fundamental attitudes to which I have just referred. The distinction between them is founded on the idea that the truth of our apprehension of individuals within a whole— that is, the reality of the individuals so apprehended—is relative to the degree in which we have forgotten or have not forgotten—are unawake or awake to—the abstraction involved in apprehending them.

i. The popular attitude in considering finite individuals, whether things or persons, is frankly pluralist. Alike in contemplating the natural and the human world, it models itself on the apparent self-identity of the movable and self-coherent body. It is reinforced by the current conception, an alternative expression of itself, which confines identity to linear or successional continuity, the so-called existential or numerical identity of individual things. In one of the most recent and capable discussions of the self we have this assumption quite naïvely expressed. Identity is only within one thing. Between two things there can only be similarity.[1]

This attitude is further confirmed in the case of human beings by theories of the first look,[2] which deal with them as members of a crowd. The apparent self-completeness of our bodies, and their external repetition of a single type, side by side, as free figures devoid of material co-adaptation or connection, occupy our vision, blinding us to the moral and spiritual structure which lies behind the visible scene.

And, once more, all this is emphasized as the very basis even of our spiritual lives by our religious individualism, which re-echoes the metaphysical doctrine of substance in a popular shape. We are brought up to identify our self and our destiny with the history of a substantial soul, by implication pre-existent to our experienced life, and certainly post-existent

---

[1] Parker, p. 42 ff. The assumption is most remarkable in view of the extended use of identity in difference which Professor Parker makes *within* the " numerical " individual.

[2] Cf. *Philosophical Theory of the State*, p. 80 ff.

to it ; continuous, therefore, throughout our passage in time, and concentrating our hopes and fears upon its particular development through life and beyond as the sum and climax of our value.

This attitude of mind, the outcome of a natural bias and prolonged tradition, is very far from giving way when the orthodox dogmatism which reinforced it has decayed. Our being and our destiny are still thought of in terms of a linear progression ; and the inherent demand for self-completion is construed as a desire to " go on " and continue our achievement *in propria persona*. The reality of life's issues is made to depend upon their prolongation for each of us beyond the existence which we experience between birth and death. If we do not " go on " in person, so it is implied, our values lose their reality. The connection is expressed in the familiar rhyme :

> Life is real, life is earnest,
>   And the grave is not its goal ;
> " Dust thou art, to dust returnest,"
>   Was not spoken to the soul.

We see here how naturally the reality of values seems to connect itself with the persistence of particular souls. For a younger generation, the vehicle of such an ideal is probably different, but the moral atmosphere, if I read our literature right, remains for the most part the same. Hope, anxiety, and expectation fix themselves at every moment on the linear future, and if this basis is shaken, the substitute is not a wider outlook, but despair.

I do not see how it is possible to maintain that any attitude even remotely resembling that which I have indicated does not involve forgetting the abstraction by which we attend to finite individuals within the whole of experience. The doctrine that identity is exclusively numerical, or of existence, is enough by itself to determine this point of view, of which it is indeed a concise rendering. And the contention that a substantive character, or that of an ultimate subject, is coincident with thinghood exhibits at once the obviousness of the position and its untenability.

ii. I pass to the further attitude which comes to us partly

through the experience of life, as in morality and religion,[1] partly through science and philosophy. Here we find that in various degrees we are becoming conscious of the abstraction, subject to which in everyday and practical life we conceive both the " thing " and the spiritual finite individual. In fact, we had already transcended it in the recognitions which morality and religion imply. But our power of abstaining from explicit reflection on what we have practically recognized is, as we all know, extraordinary. Thus, it is only in science and philosophy that the abstraction under which we currently conceive the thing and the person is at all completely undone " for us," as contrasted with " in us."

The case of the " thing " is simple ; but, as the essence of the first attitude was to treat individuality on the basis of thinghood, it is well to recall, what was mentioned above, that there is really no standard of thinghood.[2] Distinct individuality, at any rate below the level of mind, is a question of degree ; and there is none such whose boundaries cannot be indefinitely extended into the natural world, whether in scientific or in æsthetic[3] experience.

Turning to the spiritual finite individual, we feel ourselves here at last attempting to deal with him in his proper character. We have no doubt of his unity, his freedom, his real and substantive being, which in principle and on the whole, though still subject to limitations springing from our impotence, yet reveals the individual in the general or typical light in which he must be taken as truly experienced within the universe.

I will recur to the two features[4] which I proposed to treat from the present point of view. I will try to explain, that is, how in this attitude we should approach the individual's claim to unity and to freedom.

We are confident of our individual unity. It is in our experience as existents continually interfered with and broken down, but all this failure we resent and repudiate. In existence, however, as we feel every day and every hour, it is not realized. The continuity of our whole succession of experiences

[1] Which themselves exhibit different degrees of it. Morality is very far more " forgetful " than religion.
[2] See reff., p. 92, supra.
[3] As when a painter is said to paint on the whole of his canvas at once.
[4] Cf. pp. 89–90, supra.

amounts to little, and much which existentially attaches to it we reject and deny to be truly our belonging.[1] None the less, it is our nature to be a single self. We claim it as a right, and accept it as a duty. Our very repudiation of elements within our existential complex means the rejection of what we cannot unify. We carry with us a pretension to be ourself, which includes less and more than we find in our existence. Our unity is a puzzle and an unrealized aspiration. It is demanded by thought and action, but we cannot find it in existence. This, and not our experience of our acts, is the secret of our confidence that we are one. We are so, because to be a thinking being is to demand a unity, and every act of such a being is an attempt to realize it. But philosophy tells us, as we agreed, that if we possessed our unity, we should no longer be what we experience our existence as being. Here, then, is our substantive reality, in which we are not mere features, predicates, characters, but are seen, apart in principle from abstraction, as substantival solidly founded entities, possessed of an indefeasible unity.

Yet, what is the nature and structure of this reality? Is it the self as we experience it in detail? Surely not; or it is that self, but in an illumination more intense than the customary, and revealing a further structure. It *is* a substance and an ultimate subject, but not in its own right. Its existence, as an existence, bears the unmistakable stamp of the fragmentary and the provisional. Can there be any one who does not feel it so in every act and every thought? But through all this, and operative in it, there shines the intentional unity. It is not my monad nor my star. It is the life which lives in me, but it is more of that life than I succeed in living. I *am* substantive and subject, then, but only so far as I recognize myself to be adjective and predicate. If, forgetting the abstraction, I set up to be in myself a self-centred real, I become *ipso facto* in the main a false appearance and all but worthless. This is when I come nearest to being a substantive in my own right, in error and in sin. How can I be a false appearance if I actually appear? Is not the answer very simple? I can mistake the

---

[1] If by a miracle a man of sixty could have himself, as a boy of ten, introduced to him and open to his insight, is there anything, apart from external history, or bodily marks, by which he could identify the boy with himself?

character in which I appear. I seem to myself, perhaps, to be the King, and I am the fool. There is, then, just this much truth in me, that I am here upon the stage, thus much, and no more.

Then, let us think of freedom—man's character in morality and religion. The paradox of its nature is familiar, and needs only a few words to exhibit its connection with the present argument. The attitude from which we started sees freedom wherever the objects of volition are selected by any response of the self. Thus, at every point, the linear self—that which lies in a serial continuity of acts—is accepted by this attitude as substantive and independent. And it is true, as I have argued throughout, that this self has existence, and a status which represents itself as independent on the basis and analogy of thinghood.

But on reflectively weighing the experience of religion and morality we necessarily supersede this attitude by that other of which we are speaking. We become aware of lateral, so to speak, as well as of linear, identity, and are forced to undo the abstraction under which we were judging. We find that we were like a horse in blinkers, blind to all that is not straight ahead. We begin to apprehend the individual as within the super-ordinate wholes to which he belongs, and so to estimate in their reality both him and them. For the individual, as we are accustomed to accept him, there could be, we begin to understand, no self, no will, no knowledge, no morality, no religion. Apart from the content of his centre there could be no feeling self ; apart from their objects his acts are an empty form ; and in all his objects there is no object that is not universal and derivative. His identity with the community, we observe, is not reducible to similarity between him and other individuals. It lies in the participation of moral substance, and in the reciprocal adaptation of structure, on the part of all apparent units, to identical and indivisible function.[1]

A man is free [2]—we now restrict the expression—in so far as he wills the universal object. The reason is obvious. It is only what is universal that is free from self-contradiction. It

[1] See above, p. 95.
[2] It is a mistake of fact to say that freedom is most strongly felt in mere choice, Parker, p. 296 ; contrast Laird, p. 124.

is only what is free from self-contradiction that can be willed without obstruction. Every contradiction in my world of experience obstructs my action and embarrasses my will ; and every pain or defeat or confusion of which I am aware, in any subject or object apprehended by me, is a contradiction in my world. I am only free in such objects of volition as confront with adequate solutions the situations which I apprehend.

Thus, in accordance with a familiar paradox, it is only in a will above my own that I can find my own will and my freedom and independence. Here, again, it is only by acknowledging myself adjectival and under necessity that I can become substantive and free. Observation of life at its highest effectiveness fully harmonizes with the analysis of the judgment suggested above. In all serious moral action, in all social volition or religious self-determination, the form of experience is " Reality in S is P." The moral universe in me expresses itself thus. There is always an incoming wave of identical object-consciousness. Nothing can come of nothing ; and by itself myself, consisting of its acts, is nothing.

I will speak of two special points that might cause a difficulty—the question of initiative and the question of confluence.

If every community consists of individuals, and if the wills of all individuals are derivative, where is the source of derivation ? Everything seems derivative from what is itself derivative, that is, from other individuals. The answer lies in the recognition of lateral as well as linear identity. The communal will, for example, though revealed in a number of individuals, is a single thing as much as external nature, which is revealed in the same way. Participation in its structure makes every particular unit an individual, that is a particular, in which the universal or the identity assumes a special modification. His will is made out of the common substance, and, even when he rejects and reverses the form in which it is seen elsewhere, his volition is still dependent on it. The relation is familiar to us in every structure of elements. If all the elements are gone, the structure is gone ; but yet the functional character of the structure is not co-ordinate with all or any of the component elements as such. It is really in the universal function that they have even their structure.[1] It is this property of being a centre, in which the universal spirit applies itself to the concrete situation, which gives the spiritual individual just that note of independence which is claimed for him. If nothing beyond, so to speak, the local centre were in operation, there could not be the growing sense of necessity which is the mark of all serious will, and indicates the shaping of the common life to the special environment. Some compare the volition to the judgment. The comparison is illuminating for volition. The judgment is not the response of a punctual centre, but the self-shaping of a full world.

Then, again, is the confluence of selves conceivable, and is there any analogy or example in its favour ? I might argue that the knot is cut by the admission that if we possessed our self we should be the absolute ; for certainly we should then include or be blended with innumerable other selves. To explain further. What seems to me important is to set free the idea of the self ; to recognize that the self is constituted just by what it is and what operates in it ; and that its limits and distinctness flow from this, and not this from any given thing or being. Two theoretical points are here concerned. There is what I have called lateral identity—identity of co-existent being as contrasted with that of a thread continuous in succession. It seems to me all-important for a free and full understanding of the self to make at least as much of co-existent as of continuous identity. Otherwise, we unnaturally narrow down the basis of our self. And there is the emptiness of the ego, which it appears to me that Professor Pringle-Pattison and Mr. Balfour misconceive with really amazing perverseness. The point, as I take it,[2] is that if the ego has a prior content, apart from what it unifies, unification becomes impossible. If the self is to be free and self-modelling, the ego must be a mere spirit of unity working in and throughout experiences. Otherwise, it must bring with it some character or nature which would be an antecedent condition biasing and restricting the development of the soul or self.

I am accused of not at all appreciating the idea of the self.

---

[1] J. S. Haldane, *Organism and Environment*, Lect. IV.
[2] See *Principle of Individuality and Value*, p. 325 ; *The Idea of God*, pp. 128–9.

I will try to summarize and distinguish precisely what seems to me right in the common view, what I should like to see recognized in addition, and what associations of the common doctrine I wish to repudiate.

1. I agree that the self has existence as a function which is a system of functions.[1] It is not a mere adjective in the sense in which P is so taken in the formula S is P.

2. But I think it should be recognized that—

i. Belonging to the self is a matter of degree, and all its belongings, including its not-self, are contributory to the being of a finite individual.

ii. The self and its not-self are concretely real only as identified by modifications of universal content [2] and by appercipient systems.

iii. The existence of the self is not adequate to its implied unity, which is a pretension inherent in a thinking being.

3. Such an attitude to the soul as is expressed in Swinburne's very splendid lines, " Because man's soul is man's god still " (Prologue to *Songs before Sunrise*), ought, as it seems to me, to be rejected.

In face of current commonplace assertions about the independence and initiative of the finite individual, or of the self, there are some undeniable, though hardly less commonplace observations, which should not be forgotten, and which I will summarize by way of recapitulation.

a. The self as defined in (1) above has no content and can originate nothing. The finite individual thing in nature has, so far as we know, no separately distinguishable nucleus. The spiritual individual is the utterance of his place and time— a sub-variant of the content of his age, and a derivative of his family stock like a bud on a plant.[3] And, if we abstract from these conditions, he is nothing.

β. Judgment is said to be my act, and is even compared with volition (not by me). But is it controllable by my self, whatever that can mean ? It is, surely, the conclusion of my self-moulding whole of knowledge ; and, if it is genuine, I, as my punctual self, cannot affect it at all. The world judges in me, though from my point of view. The analogy with volition would extend the application of this remark.

[1] My *Logic*, i, p. 2.     [2] See Laird, pp. 199, 246.     [3] *Ibid.*, p. 358.

My love and hate are not controllable by others. True, but the remark is too narrow. For they are not controllable by me. No one, I think, has said that you can love and hate as you wish. How easy life would be, if you could ! It is urged that in the " great experiences," say, love, social morality, and religion, you must yet remain distinct from other personalities ; you must have " otherness." [1] But the remark appears to me to miss the point. Your regeneration in these experiences does not spring from anything which the other personalities previously contained. It is an introduction to a higher individuality, of which the plural persons are instruments like the carbons of an arc light. They are contacts which draw on the forces of the universe, not on themselves.

γ. The individual's expressive powers belong to his free communication with nature and the thought around him. They may be impeded any day by obstructions to memory or apprehension, and he can do nothing to help it, but so far ceases to be.

δ. A simple analogy from knowledge supports the conception that the perfection of the finite individual would imply a change in his identity, and possibly an absorption into another's. If my philosophy were made complete and self-consistent, I am sure my critics would admit, it could no longer be identified with that which I profess as mine ; but would probably amalgamate with that of someone else, and in the end with that of all. I do not know why the same should not be the case with my self.

We must remember that the claim to have synthesized distinct personalities has actually been made,[2] and the stability alleged to have been gained by the process is in harmony with all probability. The difficulty of separate bodies was absent in the case alleged, but it seems as if this might be no more than a practical difficulty. Common language admits one self in different bodies, and the " general will " seems to be an indisputable fact.

All this is matter of degree, of which the extreme psychological curiosities are not the only or the more important cases. The illuminating comparison is between the extremes within our recognized, our normal self, and those " selves," whether

<hr>

[1] Pringle-Pattison, p. 289.     [2] In the Beauchamp case.

vicious, morbid, or exceptionally great, which we feel unable to reckon as fully belonging to the former.    Even the identity of selves which are prima facie external and side by side is none the less real for being mediated, and can become, as we know to be true of the reciprocal recognition of intelligent beings, all but immediate.    Fully to " enjoy " the self, we want much more freedom in repudiating the self sequential upon us, and accepting that beside us.    Our continued self-identity is apt to be a fetish which becomes a slavery.    I may add as an illustration that while no one feels the facts of moral responsibility more strongly than I do, it always strikes me as a grave injustice that a man should be severely punished for an offence of very old date ; though, of course, it would not be practically permissible that intentional evasion should involve escape.

There is one more word to say.    Our theme is not the soul or self, but the finite individual.    And the reality of the finite individual is not confined to his temporal existence as a soul or self.[1]    Where his action and influence extend, he is so far real, beyond his existence.    Our failure to grasp the connection where it is remote seems simply to mean a want of apprehensive power on our part.    It seems impossible to hold that men who have lived in the past are not real so far as their thoughts and characters are present and operative [2] to-day.    They are not here in full personality, but their reality would be diminished if its activity of to-day were subtracted from it.    It is often maintained that what is a fact once is a fact for ever.    But this must not be taken to mean that the whole reality of the fact is compressed within its existence and eternally petrified.    The reality of the battle of Waterloo is still liable to change and increase.

It seems to follow from this point of view that spiritual individuals must qualify the universe not merely as subordinate existents, which declare themselves adjectival in claiming attachment to their substance, but, more finally and completely, as predicates *pur sang*.    The point becomes plainer and more urgent when we hold their existence as selves to be very transient.    If the series of events is the reality, then a

[1] See pp. 96, 102, above.
[2] See Nettleship, cited *Value and Destiny*, p. 264.

quality of individuals, outside their existence, is the chief way in which they are present in the reality.  If reality is non-temporal, it is timelessly characterized through them by such a quality, reinforced by whatever character corresponds to a brief passage in time.  In any case, we have seen, this problem presents itself, on the current view, about the minds of brutes, on the unique value of each of which nevertheless so much has been said.  The whole question is analogous to that which is now being raised about the localization of objects in space. They are, it is suggested, wherever their very various appearances are operative or are perceived.[1]

Thus, individuals not merely exist for a brief space in the world, but characterize it as permanent qualifications.  This is what the poets have said, and it seems to be true.  I need not quote the *Adonaïs*, but I will cite some humbler verses of a recent writer :

> Walking through trees to cool my heat and pain,
> I know that David's here with me again.
> All that is simple, happy, strong he is.
> Caressingly I stroke
> Rough bark of the friendly oak.
> A brook goes babbling by ;  the voice is his.
> Turf burns with pleasant smoke.
> I laugh at chaffinch, and at primroses.
> All that is simple, happy, strong he is.
> Over the whole wood in a little while
> Breaks his slow smile.[2]

We all, so far as we know, exist in the world for a very short time ;  of course, we make a difference in it, and are necessary to it.  But this is only to say that we have existence, and there is no thing, nor part of a thing, of which so much cannot be said.  It does not, therefore, seem to follow, from our existence only, that we are worlds into which the universe is primarily organized ;  and our transitoriness and imperfection are such that to draw a sharp line between ourselves and inferior existents on the ground of our given unity does not seem feasible ;  while, if we appeal to our intentional pretension to unity, the moral of this, as we saw, points in another direction.

[1] Parker, p. 69 ;  Dr. Haldane, loc. cit.
[2] *Fairies and Fusiliers*, Robert Graves,

It is more natural to suppose that our brief existence is the temporal appearance of some character of the whole, such as, in any case, constitutes a very great part of the finite individual's reality as experienced in the world. For what appears as a passage in time, the Absolute has need to express itself through us as very subordinate units. And there are indications which point in this direction, and suggest in what kind of worlds, or higher complexes, we might find our completion. While we serve as units, to speak the language of appearance, the Absolute lives in us a little, and for a little time ; when its life demands our existence no longer, we yet blend with it as the pervading features or characters,[1] which we were needed for a passing moment to emphasize, and in which our reality enriches the universe.

I reserved a conceivable interpretation for the primary attitude which I described, reinforced as it was by traditions from the metaphysic of substance. Suppose that this metaphysic or theology [2] dealt with substances eternal indeed but created ; and that such creation ought to be understood, as Kant apparently must have understood it, though the fact is seldom noticed, to imply an underlying oneness with the creator.[3] Then, what the doctrine really signified for religious thought was a communicated and derived substantiality, founded on a sense of unity, whose ultimate meaning was unity with the creator—a unity not conditioned by time. Then, the conception of substance, whose withered husk has become the support of pluralism, and has been lowered to the level of thinghood and existence, would have meant essentially an attempt to insist on the eternity of all spirits in God. I presume that this was not so for Aristotle. But Aristotle did not speak the last word on the subject.

[1] I may refer to the paper, " Unvisited Tombs," in my *Some Suggestions in Ethics*, 1918.
[2] I admit that my idea of it comes chiefly from Dante. For the point in question, see *Purg.*, 17, 109.
[3] Abbott's *Kant's Theory of Ethics*, pp. 188, 196.

# VII

## TIME AND THE ABSOLUTE

THE Problem of Time has of late attracted attention. I have not any startling theory to propound. My purpose is to insist upon certain simple cases and elementary principles, in order, if possible, to clear the ground for a just apprehension of the data *ab initio*. The discussion falls naturally into two parts :

1. The actual position of Time in our experience.
2. The necessary admission that Time is in the Absolute, in relation to any attempted inference that the Absolute is in Time.

1. I am not attempting to argue from genesis to reality or unreality, but am only taking the facts of genesis as illustrating by concomitant variations the conditions essential to the reality of that which is generated. And this, I think, is fair.

a. It is an old remark, which merely needs recalling, that psychical succession pure and simple is not enough to constitute a temporal consciousness. Not to speak of the animal intelligence, it is clear that the growth of a sense of time in human beings depends on developed attention to the relatively permanent. Adaptation of action to circumstances, as in choosing noon or night for repose, implies no estimate of the duration of intervals at which these circumstances recur. Something that lasts through a period, and so raises the question, " Will the period be long enough, or too long ? " seems needed to account for an estimate of Time ; and this something is a relatively permanent interest, say, for example, a journey which must be completed before nightfall. Such an interest confers on the succession of perceptions the indispensable continuity which causes it to be bound up into a whole of duration by comparison of passing perceptions with some perceived unity which runs through and outlasts them. Time arises with this relation—with the sense that a set of perceptions is carrying us forward towards a change the point of incidence of which upon a relatively permanent background (really another set of changes) has interest for us. This is measurement, a case of the principle of enumeration. There must be a general interest which constitutes the motive for the construction of a certain whole by equation with an assumed standard.

The temporal consciousness, then, is not constituted by mere psychical succession or discretion, but involves continuity, as indeed is generally admitted. Our present point is that this continuity means a relatively permanent interest embodied in an element running through the perceptions, and this involves the recognition of a world in which permanent elements have a place. From the first, then, the temporal consciousness is two-sided, and although we may say that the two sides are equally essential to it, yet beyond doubt they tend to change their relation. The mind which is most immersed in succession must have least temporal consciousness.

$\beta$. In the developed intelligence of the civilized world, as shown in history and in some forms of science, the temporal consciousness reaches its maximum of importance. The constant ratio which material movements bear to each other, so long as their physical conditions are unchanged, is hypostasized into a real, uniform, and standard duration, although the comparison of successive parts of Time is *ex hypothesi* impossible. The vast system of historical chronology, and the still more far-reaching constructions of astronomical or geological theory, are treated as if they were presentations of actual reality, and the temporal order comes to be regarded as an infinitely extended line or procession, which marches away and away so as to separate the extremity of the past by an ever-lengthening interval from the moment of the present.

Now, this single chart or picture—the stream of Time—is a gigantic constructive extension of anything given to us in experience, and though true in the sense that it is useful for certain purposes, it does not represent our whole apprehension of the facts. First, it reduces our private experience of duration to an abstract standard. For the purpose of a common measure, especially with a view to practice, this is plainly necessary. I may live a lifetime of anxiety while the train brings me from Oxford to London, but the hour and a quarter measured against the earth's rotation will be an hour and a quarter still. Great care is needed in criticizing abstractions of this kind. It is a dangerous attitude to set up the merely given in any kind of experience as possessing a clue to reality which is lacking to its methodical unification. I do not feel sure that Mr. Bradley has wholly avoided this danger in his observations on Time in dreams. Nevertheless, sometimes, as in defending the secondary qualities against the ascription of exclusive reality to the primary, we have to resist the mutilation of experience which is carried on under the name of reduction to an objective standard. And thus what may roughly be called the reduction of subjective to objective Time is in some degree analogous to the case just referred to, or—taking a particular instance—to the representation of all kinds of light in terms of ethereal vibrations. For certain purposes the actual perceptions can be standardized in these ways, but this fact does not dispose of their own richer characteristics. It should at least be noted, then, that what may be called personal Time is relative to standards which are variable judged by those equable motions which we assume as objective Time-measures. Taken apart from the mechanical world our private Time-feeling may be much more deeply interwoven than that world is with the whole content of actual life. If we want to judge of ultimate reality, rather than of immediate practical necessities, it is possible that this consideration may assume importance, just as the reality of secondary qualities assumes importance when we come to consider the objectivity of the æsthetic judgment.

Secondly, this infinitely extended past, as presented by history and science, is, to a great extent, a vanishing form. It belongs very noticeably to the middle stage of our knowledge. Intelligence, it might be said, begins by creating Time and Space, and goes on to destroy them. Nay more, from the beginning of its work in creating them, it is *pari passu* destroying them. If we think of the rise of historical chronology, we observe that it represents a period of immature reflection on the unity of history, and a desire to think the historical process as one. Just so with astronomical and geological science. The more that history and science bring before us a unified past, the more closely do we weld it to the content on which we base our construction of the future, and the less do we actually live in a world of temporal succession.

I have pointed out elsewhere that the relation of reality and unreality, by which we characterize the present and the future in the moment of succession, has truth for present practice only, and is transferred to the ordered past solely by an association at the mercy of criticism. The imperfect theory of temporal causation—imperfect, for no complete theory can be stated in terms of sequence—has no genuine bearing on occurrences which are no longer partly unreal, and it is impossible in a system which has become in every part equally real and unreal, to separate effect from cause, as something derivative and, so to speak, unnecessary. It is all-important, of course, in evolutionary science, to avoid the prejudice that what comes earlier in time can limit the interpretation to be put upon what comes after it. This prejudice arises from transferring relations of reality and unreality directly from sequence into the ordered whole of experience. But if so, the essential attribute of sequence in time has disappeared. It cannot be said that in the past there is an earlier which is real and a later which is unreal. The true simile to describe our actual experience of Time, in the civilized mind, would be, I have often thought, that of a sort of dropping, which, as it drops, distributes itself over some great crystalline structure, such as to grow and organize itself, not at any one point only, out of the material thus accruing. To resolve the whole structure into an infinite sequence of the dropping process, is a wholly artificial idea, and does not represent the course of our actual experience.

The question of direction may also be raised. Science and history run back as easily as forward. Their actual constructive movement is indeed backwards rather than forwards, and our Time view acquires its character much more from our attention running to and fro along the chronological chart than from our own experience of succession, which all this chronology and construction really tends to dwarf. But this running to and fro in our attention is not a true experience of succession. We have no experience of succession outside the immediate now ; and as we stretch out the arm of our constructive chronology as a first endeavour to bind together for our imagination the increasing bulk of our world, we are building up a background against which our experienced succession becomes increasingly insignificant. We may even be said in a very real sense to be enlarging our possible present ; for if we have once admitted duration into the present (and how can we keep it out ?) it seems hopeless to deny that any period of succession which can be conceived at all, may from some point of view be looked at as a present, that is, as a totality within which the element of succession can be neglected in consideration of its causal or qualitative unity. It cannot be too strongly insisted on, as a mere fact of experience, that a great constructive work, such, for example, as Grote's *History of Greece*, operates mainly to destroy and not to enhance the importance of temporal succession in our knowledge. The history so presented is in course of transmutation from the form of successive occurrences to the form of a systematic unity, causally connected together, and logically and ethically in the closest possible proximity to ourselves ; in it we are beginning to shake ourselves free from the form of bare chronology which marks the most meagre and hungry stage of the imagination, when it first feels the yearning for a comprehensive historical unity.

It is hardly necessary to labour this point further, or it would be possible to illustrate in many ways the connection between what might be called the middle intellectual level and the ascription of great importance to temporal succession. The doctrine of causation alone, with its temporal relation to practice and its non-temporal relation to systematic theory, amply suffices to explain the difference of attitude with which we are concerned. Succession may be for us the dominant type in which our lives are cast, or merely the inlet by which new formative material is added to our permanent world.

And the difference, though only of degree, cannot be wholly insignificant in philosophy.

When we come to deal with the higher achievements of the mind, with Art, Philosophy, and Religion, we find that the Time-spirit has practically lost his power, or rather, has become the spirit which conquers Time. He presents us with the quintessence of the ages, but the process of distillation is lost, and only the spirit remains. We absolutely refuse in these kingdoms of experience to find the criteria of comparative reality in the bygone order of succession. If we remember the facts of sequence at all, it is only to note that the earlier did not contain the later, but, on the contrary, borrows its whole character and value from what in fact was yet unreal in Time when it—the earlier—was already real. Any analysis of the part played by Time in the logical judgment, of which the above-mentioned stages of causation are indeed merely a case, is sufficient to illustrate the evanescence of Time in all the higher intellectual processes.

But it may be asked what we can expect to show by considerations of this kind. Assume, for the sake of argument, that we could show ourselves to be approaching a state of experience in which succession would have ceased, or would be wholly, as it is now partially, reversible at pleasure. This would not remove the fundamental fact that by the hypothesis we should be no more than approaching the condition in question, and the affirmation of some kind of future condition does not seem a possible road to cancelling the reality of Time. It might be urged, indeed, in reply, that—again by the hypothesis—the attainment of such a standpoint would of itself show the past, which as a past would then have become inconceivable, to have been an illusion, or more than that, would wipe it out of existence even as an illusion. In the latter case, of course, the problem would disappear with the experience which caused it : but the application of so violent an hypothesis would tend to present our world as emptied of all its content, along with all its problems. If no partial standpoints are to survive within the whole of experience, then there certainly could be no difficulty, but it would be questionable whether there could be anything.

The former hypothetical case, though incapable of being

realized in experience, seems to share the essence of our actual position, and to set the problem which our theory would have to deal with if it professed to be able to do so. On this hypothesis the illusion, although explained, would not be explained away. It would then be, to use the phraseology of Mr. Bradley, whose argument to a great extent I am merely expanding, an appearance. It would be there, and meet us in experience, like the sun's apparent diurnal motion, although we should see behind it. And we should not be able to say that temporal experience did not exist, or had never existed; but only that it was a mere appearance, and that we could see the reason of it, and how and why it was false, and how it was transcended.

No problem, then, would be solved by saying that a timeless experience might come into being in Time, not having been before. That, by itself, would be to accept the reality of the Time-process and to limit the Absolute by it. To look to the cessation of the Time experience in the future as in itself a reconciliation of the difficulties presented by Time is a fundamental contradiction. It is placing eternity outside and *after* Time, as the popular imagination has often attempted to do. The only clue to a solution which would be afforded by such an experience would be in the light thrown by the supposed new insight on the nature of the Absolute and of its relation to the Time-succession. It would not be that the Absolute had come into being after Time, but that in the temporal succession it had more or less completely manifested itself, and something as to a deeper reality might be inferred from this manifestation. But for this we require, not the annihilation of temporal experience, but the power of seeing through it.

And even to our way of knowledge and feeling, separated by a wide gulf from the hypothetical case in which Time would be transcended, some such analysis seems to be provoked by the peculiar nature of the phenomena. Time comes into being along with its opposite, viz. the unity of what appears discrete in Time. Up to a certain point the two seem to grow together, but at that point—the point where genuine causal or evolutional unity is explicitly insisted on—we become aware that the half-scientific Time-consciousness has immensely departed from anything warranted by our experience of succession, has extended itself chiefly into the past, which it has projected in a form quite inadequate to causal unity and systematic reality, and is, so far as the main portion of our experience goes, reversible at pleasure. The standard of hypostasized equable duration suffices as a first arrangement of occurrences, and no more. What we cannot be rid of is the personal momentary transition from present to present as new sense-perceptions arrive. This is incident to our way of existing, and we cannot transcend it. But we cannot shut our eyes to the concomitant variations of its importance relatively to the perfection of our experience.

2. As regards the second part of my subject, I propose nothing more than to claim attention for the antithesis involved. There have been recent indications of a tendency which in my judgment rests on a confusion of its sides. In bringing the question of Time, as involving change and imperfection, to its climax in the question of evil, it has been asked, as I understand, whether a perfect whole can have imperfect parts. I am not sure whether the self-consciousness of the parts as finite souls is held to make a difference of principle. I cannot see that it makes any. The question then is, whether the imperfection of parts as parts, is incompatible with the perfection of the whole. Perhaps, if we press it hard, the phrase " parts as parts " will prove equivocal. Part implies whole, and a part fully grasped as a part, it may be urged, must be seen under the species of the whole ; that is, no longer as a mere part, but as having a perfection inseparable from the perfection of the whole. On the other hand, a part given as a part, in a whole which as such is incompletely known, is compatible with, or even implies, obscurity and confusion in its relation to the whole. And it is this, the part as given, with which we are dealing. Perhaps the above equivocation has affected the discussion of the question. It is a truism to say that if a part remains imperfect when seen under the species of the whole, then the whole is itself imperfect, or in other words fails to be truly a whole. But in dealing with a part as given in a whole which is not given, the presumption is the other way. The part would not be of the nature of a part in a truly concrete whole—it would not possess the substance

and individuality which belong to the member of any such complex—unless, taken in relative isolation, it presented, so to speak, a harsh and jagged contour and an appearance of unresolvable ultimateness in this contour. This is what we are startled by, in minor instances, every day of our lives ; and I must insist that daily experience, often as it is cited, is as a rule most crudely and coarsely analysed when applied in philosophical problems. The hardness and ultimate given-ness of fragmentary appearances, and the miraculous alchemy with which the touch of thought and progressive experience is perpetually dissolving them, are fundamental facts of practical and theoretical life, which none but the very greatest philosophers seem to have adequately appreciated. I may instance, in work which in my judgment is in general of very great value, Mr. Ellis McTaggart's constant use of the term delusion, to represent the imperfection of an appearance within experience, and his insistence on the difficulty presented by a sense of imperfection—pain, evil, thwarting—on the part of the individual mind. Neither of these facts appears to me to carry the importance or the character which he finds in them. An appearance is not a delusion, it is the form of reality, and the beaten track of experience. Our life is made up of appearances, in process of resolution ; they become delusions only when persisted in against experience which to a normal mind suffices to resolve them. The individual's sense of imperfection is no harder a datum than many which we transfigure into a higher unity from year to year and from decade to decade ; it has no fixedness or finality, and we can often see quite clearly that the sense of shortcoming within a given mind, fact though it is, is also an appearance of a kind which can at least relatively be transcended. Knowing that it may accompany the most complete achievement, of which it is often merely a reaction on certain feelings, and that this reaction itself can be absorbed into the sense of achievement as a characteristic element of it, we see that we can never tell how far this really happens for the individual, much less how far the self-containedness of the individual, involving the separation of his subjective suffering from his objective self-realizedness, is a mere appearance.

I apply these ideas, then, admitting that the application is very modest and limited—an endeavour to remove needless prejudices rather than to solve ultimate problems—to the antithesis between Time in the Absolute and the Absolute in Time. The real question seems to me to be whether we are in earnest with the relation of part and whole. If we are going to say that the part as given qualifies without reservation the whole which is not given, then the knot is cut, and by admitting Time to be given, we admit that the Absolute is in Time. But if we make any attempt to face the daily facts of experience, such a conclusion seems to become merely fantastic and unrelated to the real world. Within our experience there is no limit to the transformation which a given part may undergo by being seen in connection with a whole which was not given along with it. And unless this is the case the conception of part and whole is destroyed. A whole which made no difference to the part would no more be a whole, than a part which made no difference to the whole would be a part. The general tendency of our experience, then, together with indications particularly concerning the reality of temporal succession, suggest that but little more inference lies from the given-ness of Time in the Absolute to the Absolute being in Time, than from the given-ness of colour in the Absolute to the Absolute having a colour.

# VIII

# THE PERMANENT MEANING OF THE ARGUMENT FROM DESIGN

THE point of view from which I desire to start in approaching this question may be thus stated : that while it appears to me that nothing is gained for the interpretation of the world by the assumption of a divine intelligence underlying it, it also appears that beyond the abandonment of an otiose hypothesis nothing is determined in the interpretation of the world by surrendering this assumption. The problem, if I am right, remains, then, exactly where it was before. We desire to know something of the fundamental nature of the system in which we find ourselves. I speak of it as a system without hesitation, because in these days no one denies it unity in the bonds of mechanical causation. From this point we start.

Before proceeding further, I would lay down another principle, which I think is usually disregarded. Granted that we are not to assume merely what we desire, I further maintain that we are to defend in theory what we *are* forced to assume in practice. Interpretation and analysis are here in place to any extent ; what we *are* forced to assume is one of those troublesome problems in which opinion as to facts actually modifies the facts within very considerable limits. I only maintain that, when all is said that can be said, we must not allow the basis of life to be incompatible with the basis of thought, and that to do so is a co-ordinate form of cowardice with that which assumes in theory the reality of whatever we desire in practice.

It seems to me quite plain that as soon as the conception of the Supreme Being passes from that of a person outside the forces of nature to that of an intelligence which is one with the forces of nature, the element of intelligence becomes otiose, being merely the accompaniment of a system of causation which it can in no way control. But this does not bring us a step nearer to answering the question, of what kind is that system of forces itself ?

In the form which especially interests us this question refers to the position of man, as a being with purposes, in the machinery of nature ; and in this shape it has attracted the attention of the most untheologically minded of philosophers—notably, of Kant and Herbart.[1]

What reason have we to suppose that the causal system in which we live will permit the realization of any of the more important and remote purposes which make up our moral life ?

Of course we have a certain amount of knowledge about the mechanical properties and tendencies of the earth, and at least of the solar system, and, it may be said, we must form our judgment about the probable future of climate, and of the earth's surface generally, on scientific grounds, and we must frame our plans and ideas accordingly. Now this is clearly the least that we must do, and this the interest of curiosity, not to speak of higher motives, makes it quite certain that we always shall do. But I do not in the least believe that our *de facto* habits of action can now be explained, whatever may be the case in the extreme future, by our particular knowledge.

I do not believe that it bears any such proportion to the bulk of the universe as would make it of serious importance in judging our course for the future. I do not separate it from the convictions on which we act ; I regard it, so far as it goes, as the accurate embodiment of these convictions ; but I do not believe there is enough of it to do much in justifying them. I think we have to go further afield, and in so far as we reflect at all, to justify our practical faith, without which action is wholly impossible and inconceivable,[2] by reflection on the tendencies of the world. I see no theoretical objection whatever to doing this, in spite of the abandonment of the idea of an intelligent designer. We are not bound to know, we never shall know, what brought the universe about ; but we know that a system of forces may be of the most various characters, and that we think quite differently of different

---

[1] See Herbart, *Werke*, 8, 401.        [2] *Ibid.*

systems, according to the results which we have partially observed in them.

I will now go briefly into the question, beginning with formal characteristics, and proceeding to more positive ones.

We start with a causal system, which is assumed to be a unity in the sense that its parts are assumed to act upon one another. Technically, I think I am justified in saying that every inductive inference, however exact and however trivial, involves a judgment as to the nature of this unity. We cannot go in any inference, straight from one particular to another particular. We always do go, and always must go, by the circuitous route through the nature of the process, or continuum, or system, to which they both belong. It is well to remind ourselves sometimes of the old platitude that experience, as sensuous experience, does not and cannot contain the future. If we want to get the future, or unknown of any kind, out of particular experience, we must go behind the particulars, and make out what sort of continuum it is that they enter into, and read off what we want to know from the proportion of this continuum. Thus all the judgments which make up the *Nautical Almanac* depend on convictions which we have formed as to the continuous nature of certain motions and attractions in the bodies of the solar system.

As calculations in exact science, we may say that they are all hypothetical ; but in the sense of conditions of action we take them as real predictions, and if they were seriously falsified our civilization would be thrown out of gear. In comparison with what we call design or plan, the unity involved in the continuance and interdependence of these motions is a formal unity, that is to say, the detail which we infer from it is all composed of parts added together, such as we are acquainted with already ; therefore we are within the limits of simple inference according to causality. We are expecting the underlying unity to do what formally it has never done before, but nothing which in type and substance it has not done before. It is simply continuing on its way, though in doing so it does meet and conform to a necessity of human life as we know it.

Now we know that the parts of Nature can " destroy " one another, as we say, that is, affect one another's form of existence by turning it into something wholly different from what it was. Man is a part of nature. Is the causal system which produced him of such a kind that his fundamental purposes can find realization in it, or that it will not destroy him, as man, at any casual moment ? Of course I am quite prepared for the counter-argument that the system of things does not conform to man, but he has conformed to it, and must, further, in making his designs, conform to it. But all this, taking things as they are, has very narrow limits. A simple change in atmosphere or temperature, the disruption of the globe, or very considerable convulsions on its surface, and he is gone with all his morals, and his purposes, and his theories.

Is there any reason, outside the imperfect evidence of exact science up to date, itself ultimately resting on the conviction of a continuity in nature, to suppose that such changes or convulsions are not to be looked for ? Can we infer anything from what has been called the appearance of design in nature ?

When the question is thus stated, I do not think that the mode of origin of species touches it. If the whole system is a single chain of causation, I do not think that the order of determination in it makes any difference to its character. Within a causal whole there is no distinction of priority. Granted that the hierarchy of services between the different orders of creation does not mean that the subservient creature is made with reference to its superior, but only that the survival of the higher creature was determined by the existence of the subservient one. This does not alter the character of the great machine ; the tendency to co-operation and to consciousness remains a fact ; and it appears impossible that it should not be reflected in our conception of the unity of the world.

Two arguments, directed against the interpretation of this unity on the analogy of a plan, demand examination.

The first of these depends on the question of alleged waste and failure in creation, which, on the accepted doctrine of the origin of species, is in a sense not incidental, but essential to the causal process. Here, again, I feel compelled to retort the emphasis, having however first conceded that pain and death are factors in animal life which a human being naturally deprecates.

But as they are general factors of the very life with which our purposes are identified, they do not by themselves interfere with the only relation which we are now seeking to establish, viz. that of a conformity between the continuous nature of the world and human life at its best.   We can see that, as life really is, pain and death are essential to its nobleness and its possibility.   Having said this much, I must insist that to introduce the purely moral terms, failure and waste, into our judgment of the lower orders of creation, is a far worse piece of anthropomorphic fallacy than to see a plan where there is a causal system of a particular nature.   The conception of failure as applied to the individuals of a variety which is defeated by a better adapted variety seems to me quite unreal.   Every individual has to die ; I do not know that, if these individuals die soon, they are conscious that their life is shorter than that of others, nor do I know that their deaths are more painful than those of any other individual creatures. As for waste, this is again a moral idea ; and I cannot see its application to the regions below human purpose.   Most species of the orchid, with its cunning contrivances for fertilization and its enormous number of seeds, remain comparatively rare plants, at least in England ; but I suppose the matter thus employed may as well be doing that as anything else, and if we take in human ideas, for otherwise I do not see how to suggest a purpose at all, its clumsiness and wastefulness make it a very curious and interesting plant.

The strongest objection under this head is that drawn from the less fortunate ranks of mankind.   And here I cannot help illustrating the alleged coldbloodedness of science by saying again that for the limited purpose which we have in view we must not apply our ideal standards to intelligences whose happiness is not relative to them.

It may have been a deprivation to a palæolithic man that he was not a Christian and a Londoner in the nineteenth century, but he could not feel it to be any misfortune, and it is a tremendous anthropomorphism to read back our ideal into him and say that he was a failure and a wasted life.   In the same way we must judge throughout, accepting as a standard of success the mixed life which enters even into our ideal, and in the case of those who cannot possibly be tormented by an ideal, only requiring the success or absence of failure which depends on the conformity between their life and their instincts Looked at in this way, though the world is a rough place, it has not the fiendish horror which comes of applying our ideal morality and happiness as the sole test to every human being The idea of waste and failure is a survival of the theological idea of universal condemnation. The sense of failure is probably greatest just at the moment of favourable change such as we have among the wage-earning class to-day. I protest, then, against applying the conception of waste and failure in the non-moral world, and to a great extent against applying it in the less fortunate ranks of mankind. You can only apply to each life the test of success which it in itself suggests.

The second argument against conformity to purpose in Nature is that of the separateness of man. Here the new teachers, say Professor Clifford, seem to me to ride on two horses. If man is to gain anything by being supernatural they say man is natural; if nature is to gain anything by man's being natural they say that man is supernatural—or at least extra-natural. They must choose between these two principles which are incompatible. I do not think the question is verbal When we read Professor Clifford we really might think that we were reading some very superstitious theologian who thinks that nature is as savage as can be, but man is inspired by a good spirit, and has for his task to put things straight. Now of course an evolution may change its direction; but not, one would think, so that its latter part is purely incoherent with its beginning. If we are to call man a natural product, which is certainly my inclination, we cannot omit all reference to intelligence when we come to define the unity of nature through which alone, as I said, the very commonest and simplest inference can be made. There is one feature in respect of this argument which seems entirely to upset the alleged difference between man's sphere of purpose and the supposed purposeless sphere of nature. This feature is to be found in the greater achievements of man's intelligent volition These achievements, which affect us with the strongest sense of intelligent design, are essentially organic and not volitional Let us think of such examples as the development of philosoph or of art, the British Constitution, the Roman Empire, the Church of England, even a great cathedral building. Now a purpose, in the very strict sense in which we distinguish man's conscious purposes from natural results, can only exist in the individual mind ; but none of these things, as they ultimately came to completeness, was ever a purpose in any individual mind. Of course the same thing extends into the purposes of numbers of minds, but only as the same coral reef enters into the instinctive purposes of countless coral insects. The conscious adjustment of purpose is enormously greater in the work of man than in the coral reef, but the real factor in both lies somewhere below, in that which causes the insect and the man to find himself at the right moment in the right relation to the other workers. And this something, the cause of the relation between instincts and between purposes, does not fall within the several instinctive aims or conscious purposes themselves. It constitutes their nature but it is not their aim nor their doing. The individual man consciously aims at what he knows, and provides for the conditions which he understands ; but when his work is done it bears a relation to the rest which no one fully foresaw, and which is owing not to the wisdom of the individual, but to the wisdom of nature— of course a metaphor or a problem. If you force me to choose between the notion that rationality only exists within the purpose of the individual man, and the notion of an overruling Providence, I must choose the latter, i.e. simply as a view of the *de facto* course of the world.

I only insist on this so far as to infer that you cannot dissociate human purposive action from the causality of nature. Its greatest results are natural, although on a higher plane than the products of unconscious nature.

Therefore, though it is fallacious to gloss over the difference between intelligence and the unconscious, I do think that the truth lies in the direction of assuming the greatest possible kinship between them which is compatible with their actual difference. And I believe that if we lay aside the shallow optimistic standard which is at the root of pessimism, and only ask for the possibility of such a life as forms our proximate ideal, we shall find reasons to think that the causal power which has created man is probably of such a nature as to give room for his development up to some marked grade of completeness, and for some sort of new tendency and appropriate change of ideal if and when the race is to come to an end.

I have not laid protracted stress on the necessary relation between faith and action, because it seemed to me too plain ; but I will quote a straight forward passage from Herbart,[1] whose principal thesis is on the opposite side, i.e. against any dogmatic creed about the future. It would be no more than true to say that all action implies a belief in the possibility of the end proposed.

" ' But there is inherent in our minds a sort of augury of future ages ; and in the greatest intellects and the noblest spirits it exists most strongly and is shown most readily. And if it were withdrawn, who is mad enough to live continually in labours and perils ? ' [2] After all repudiation of groundless world-plans there assuredly remains not only the need but the right to extend our gaze into the unbounded future. Everything incites to it which man can think of as the possible result of his noblest endeavours, everything great and beautiful that has been achieved by others, by the State, by humanity, demands it. The point is only, as in every other contemplation, to have firm ground under one, and avoid caprice and misinterpretation. Man should not appear small in his own eyes ; his action or abstinence should not seem insignificant to him ; great efforts ensue only from great anticipations ; but also it is only well-founded expectations that can sustain courage through long periods and in changing circumstances and renew it after every necessary repose.

" What has been said of politics and education would lose all meaning if the future were so closed to our eyes that man could consider himself all the wiser, the more his thoughts and cares were limited to the immediate present."

Then can we deduce conclusions of particular fact from moral necessity and natural tendency ? No, I think not. This shows the extreme profoundness of Kant's discussion on these subjects. We must conceive of our principle as a general faith in the *de facto* reasonableness of the machine in which we are a part, which faith is gradually taking shape in

[1] Herbart, *Werke*, 8, 400. *Tel. R. d. Moral*, Sect. 212.
[2] Cicero quoted by Herbart.

science, and cannot take a *definite* shape in any other way, but nevertheless, as a general postulate, is the basis even of science itself, which consists from beginning to end of conclusions about the unity of nature, and all vanishes at once if we do not believe that nature is fairly stable and fairly accessible to reason. I feel the danger of these considerations and of everything that seems like casuistical optimism, but for the mere interest of the matter I may end by calling attention to Kant's treatment of the fact that progress is by conflict,[1] and that nature undoubtedly uses man as a means and not merely an end, when he suggests that for moral development this is a necessary method, though for sheer hedonistic development it might not be so.

[1] *Kritik d. Teleol. Urtheilskraft. Werke,* 4, 327 ff.

B.—ETHICAL, SOCIAL, AND POLITICAL

# IX

# THE PRACTICAL VALUE OF MORAL PHILOSOPHY

In proposing to discuss the practical value of Moral Philosophy, I had a double object in view. I desired to criticize, on the one hand, some current conceptions of what is meant by practice ; but no less I was anxious to maintain, without the slightest indulgence to dogmatism or to doctrinairism, that there is a way in which moral philosophy can usefully affect the guidance of practical life, in the commonest sense of the words. Both parts of this problem seem to merit consideration at the moment. In the present clamour for a " practical " education, it is probable that the full and true meaning of " practice " is in some degree forgotten, partly through the prevalence of a false philosophical theory. While, on the other hand, " where there is smoke there is fire " and it is very possible that the clamour has some justification, not only, if it be so, in the case of the chemist or the engineer, but in that of the publicist, the philanthropist, the minister of religion, the employer and the representative of labour— of all, in a word, on whom it is directly incumbent to influence social conduct. It is conceivable that for all of these there is something to be gained from a study of human nature in its leading principles, which would prove of value for practice in the simplest meaning of the word. Can we, indeed, bring ourselves to suppose that there was nothing at all of truth in Plato's conception that the supremely important thing is the manner of mind of those who are to influence society ? It is noteworthy that many of our universities are setting themselves the definite task of training the captains and the officers of commerce and industry for their part in the working world. No doubt this training is to deal in a great measure with matters of specialized knowledge and the machinery and routine of business.  But I am confident that there are those among the leaders of the movement who well understand what is involved in an education which is to treat of commerce and industry as subjects worthy to absorb the entire attention of the most capable men.  In one way or another, in a special curriculum or out of it, there will, I think, be brought before such ᵗtudents the meaning of those forces of the human spirit which play so enormous a part in " efficiency."  And I do not care in the least whether you call it Moral Philosophy, or by what professors or instructors it is taught, so long as we are agreed that a large and careful consideration shall be devoted to the real forces of human nature and the deep conditions of its power and of its impotence.

1. First, then, I wish to call attention to the truer and larger meaning of the term Practice.  Genuine cognition, I suggest, is strictly within the true meaning of Practice, and, moreover, ἰs in certain respects its most central and typical case ; and its nature affords the highest test of value for every practical achievement.

There are current, as it seems to me, certain popular errors which obscure the true state of the matter.

(i) To begin with, I think there is a confusion resting on the very truth which I desire to enforce.  Theory, it is felt, does indeed in some sense belong to practice ; but practice, it is supposed, must always operate through producing changes in the arrangements of the bodily world ; and as operation of this kind plainly is beyond the power of theory by itself, it is inferred that the relation of knowledge to practice must be that of instrument to end—that of " Bradshaw's Railway Guide " to catching a train.  Theory or Cognition, that is to say, is supposed merely to exist for the sake of practice, which is taken to mean that knowledge exists for the sake of pointing out the means to exterior action.  This is what I understand by the view now advocated as " Pragmatism."  I do not say that those who are of this opinion consider reason to be the slave of the Passions ; or neglect the fact that the ends of practice are stated and conceived through the intelligence.  But yet an end of action, for them, has always an external side ; it is at first a dealing with material objects, even if

plainly understood to have other then material consequences.
Theory, the labour and aspiration of the intelligence, is thus
held to be essentially a means, always having an end of a
different nature from itself.

This conclusion I steadfastly deny. Theory does indeed
belong to practice. It is a form of conation. But Practice or
Conation is not restricted to operation in the so-called outside
world ; and such operation, we might almost urge in return,
is strictly, in itself, never anything but a means. Practice
is the direction of our powers by an end and to an end ; and
of Practice in this sense the effort after truth is among the
purest and clearest examples. For the general description of
our ends is the production of harmony in our experience ; and
the simple type of the activities which go directly and un-
conditionally to the realization of such an end is the conation
which aims at relieving us from contradiction within our
intellectual world. A man who builds a house or sets up a
business could hardly tell you how much in his purpose is
means, and how much is of the nature of an end ; but it is
certain that very many incidents of what he proposes to
undertake are alien to what his heart is really set upon, and
alien also to the true and fundamental aims of a human life.
This is due to the mixed and conflicting nature of our so-
called practical activities, and is therefore unavoidable in
what is commonly understood to be the workaday world.

The direct effort after harmony of experience, complicated by no merely incidental conditions, we are acquainted
with only in certain forms of spiritual endeavour, of which
the struggle after truth is perhaps the most easily verifiable.
For I will not yield to the temptation of a facile retort, by
affirming that Cognition simply is the end, and that Practice
simply is the means. In the first place, as we shall see more
fully below, Cognition, at least in the modern sense, is not
equivalent to the full conception of " Theoria " or the theoretic
side of life, to which other forms of the endeavour after unity
must also contribute. And secondly, the effort which is con-
cealed within what the world calls practice, is no doubt a part,
and in finite life a perfectly necessary part, of the whole
endeavour after unity which expresses the nature of the mind.
Thus I am not to be censured, as if I were propounding the

Nirvana for a moral end ; though apart from the material and the purpose of life as a whole, the cognitive aspiration could mean little more than Nirvana. I am only contending that in Cognition and the kindred elements of the theoretic life we possess in their purer form—and therefore more nearly as an end—the endeavours which latently and without consciousness of their purpose permeate the whole of the life we know. I have not at all suggested that any portion of our life is conceivable or desirable in severance from the rest. At the same time, if, for controversial purposes, a relative preference has to be assigned, then I hold it truer to say, as Aristotle, I suppose, has said, that the end and criterion of Practice lies in Theory (which then should no doubt be understood as Theoria or the entire unimpeded life of the soul), and not that theory has its end in Practice, as I imagine Pragmatism to maintain. In everyday fact, it may be added, the former relation is at least as obvious as the latter. Strike out of practical life, in the most commonplace sense of the phrase, all that genuinely done for the sake of Art, Truth, and Religion, and you will find that more has vanished than you would care to lose.

(ii) There is also an unhappy popular contrast, in respect of reality, between Cognition and Volition, which we inherit, I presume, from the limitations of Kant's period, in a great degree perpetuated by him. The new name, Pragmatism, designates, as I understand, the doctrine that Practice in the narrower sense is the end of life, to which Cognition has value only as a means. That term appears intended to remind us of a passage in the Foundations of the Metaphysics of Morals ; where, however, it should be remembered, Kant is occupied in explaining that the Pragmatic Imperative " Do it if you want to be happy " is in nature not one with, but profoundly opposed to, the Practical Imperative " Do it because only so are you yourself." The connection of this true Practical Imperative with the true and ancient conception of the theoretic life is obvious at once. It consists in the innate aspiration of intelligence to affirm itself in the law and order which is its nature. Practice, for Kant, whatever it may mean, is not compatible with Pragmatism. It is the fact, however, on the other hand, that he conceives Cognition as distinct from and inferior to the Practical Reason. Cognition from his standpoint deals with Phenomena, while Volition expresses Reality. The distinction is extraordinarily characteristic of that debasement of the conception of knowledge which followed, I presume, from the separation between world and individual, characteristic of the modern mind. Kant, of course, retained it only to destroy it. But here, as so often, there are followers who follow, in the great thinker, only the vices of his age. Every one who has to compare notions of Cognition, familiar in ancient and in much of modern thought, must have been struck by the fact that they have hardly anything in common. The completest and intensest conceivable experience on the one hand, and the faded image of an impression of sense on the other hand—these are the poles between which the meaning of knowledge has varied. In the facts, I imagine, there is justification for both ; but it makes a world-wide difference which you have in mind.

The same variation has been traversed by the meaning of the term " Theory." Theory, a mere theory, is to us something akin to a fiction ; it is a logical contrivance by which the interconnection of facts is rendered possible. Theoria, which indicates the enjoyment of vision or contemplation, was to an ancient philosopher that form of activity in which we both apprehend the world most intensely, and put forth our own nature most completely.

The reason for which certain modern thinkers, believing themselves to be following Kant, have transferred this attribute to ordinary practice, to Volition which seems to affirm itself against material hindrance, may readily be gathered from what has been said. Cognition, we have learned to think, is secondary ; practice, in the narrow sense, primary. Things are outside us, and Cognition copies them inside us ; but we too are things, and our will reveals ourself to us from the inside. Cognition, in a word, is of Phenomena, Will is the essence of a thing in itself. Or, as Hume has said, " Will always places us in the world of realities." We may be reminded of the famous lines—

But here is the finger of God, a flash of the will that can,
  Existent behind all laws, that made them, and, lo they are.

We shall see, however, that here the poet's thought is really on our side.

Now, in this whole conception, that Cognition is something secondary, it seems to me that we have a mingling of obsolete logic and meaningless spatial metaphor. The entire fabric is annihilated when we realize a single point. Knowledge is not a reproduction of an outside world, but an endeavour to realize our nature by the construction of a harmonious experience. The truth of Cognition is not its correspondence to something else, but its degree of individuality in itself. The faint reproduction of impressions, the veil of formulæ, imperfectly apprehended, which enwraps and disguises the effective being of things—these are not Cognition, but its failure. To philosophize, we have heard, is to " vivify," to get rid of the husk, the dross and slack, which the tired or baffled mind will fail to penetrate, nay, indeed, actually creates by its effort to penetrate. In a word, Cognition is one great aspect of the life of the soul, in so far as it is lived apart from the struggle against matter. I have not repeated the ancient doctrine that it forms by itself the essence of morality and religion ; but genuinely to understand how this doctrine fails to be true, is a problem which modern popular philosophy has never approached at all. Certainly it is true that in Cognition our nature affirms itself after a completer type than in the Volition of everyday life.

It is, further, an almost universal opinion that Cognition has the attitude of acceptance, and Volition of self-assertion. Yet it seems to be founded on a false analogy, influenced probably by the error which has just been explained. No doubt the soul has aspirations towards a truth in which it can repose, and in that sense acquiescence may be spoken of as the ideal of cognition. But as there are two different terms, cognitive process and truth, so there are two different terms, volitional process and satisfaction ; and of these terms process corresponds to process, and attainment to attainment. It is by fallaciously comparing the attainment of truth with the process of volition, and not with the attainment of satisfaction, that we seem to establish the difference which stamps Cognition as secondary and imitative, while Volition is primary and original. The popular phrase " to be satisfied " might teach us better. When a man says he is satisfied of a truth, he means that he has removed a contradiction which threatened his intellectual peace, and has attained a relative self-consistency. Cognition, like practice, desires indeed to accept Reality, but is the very negation of the acceptance of appearances. When I say, " I want to know," I mean that the facts before me are unsatisfactory, and I feel compelled to adjust them by an inquiry which transforms them. It is this inquiry, and not the " being satisfied " of truth, which corresponds to the effort of volition in altering the appearance which withstands it. For, again, if a man has achieved a practical purpose, he also acquiesces and is " satisfied," for the same reason as in truth, and in a similar degree. He has brought out a result which lay in the mass of appearance, like the statue in the marble, and that the only result by which the given appearances could, for him, be made harmonious and complete. In both cases—in the Cognition as in the Volition—something unreal, which could not stand, has given way to the self-assertion of the reason, and passed into something relatively more solid and self-consistent. In neither case can there be ultimate acquiescence or satisfaction short of the full attainment of perfection or reality. The difference between the two ways of self-assertion is merely that in one the mind exercises its own nature more directly and distinctly than in the other.

(iii) Cognition is further disparaged as a form of Intellectualism. It is in Feeling, we hear, that you find the interesting and the real; it is in unsharable Feeling that the individual possesses the sanctuary of his Individuality. The intelligence is dry, cold, formal, and general; Philosophy is a mere apotheosis of Knowledge, and has nothing to do with Religion.

First : There is a question to be asked about the unity of the mind. No doubt it will endure a good deal of conflict and division within itself; but if, when it is at its fullest in one great self-assertion it is necessarily at its emptiest in another, there is a poor outlook for its perfection.

Secondly : It has been well pointed out, that to the greater minds which have lived on a level of experience which we share with effort, and only now and then, the opposition of knowledge and feeling has not commended itself. Plato, for instance, or Spinoza, hardly seem as if they would be able to understand it. And I cannot but think that if we frankly made the best of our best moments, instead of being afraid to claim the greatest things as our own, we should discover indications to the same effect even in ourselves. After all we too know what it is to enjoy a great idea. For the moment, at any rate, the mind expands. It seems to enter upon a new freedom, and things that before were alien now are known to it as friends and kindred. Love does not seem separable from the development of Self-Consciousness.

Thirdly : This becomes clear if we appeal, as we are justified in appealing, to Theoria in the full conception, and not merely to cognition in the narrowest sense. It is impossible to make a fundamental separation between Cognition and Philosophy, or between Philosophy and Art or Religion. I do not mean that they are the same ; but they are very closely allied. They all belong to " Theoria," the expansion of the mind in harmony with its own nature, and they are all co-ordinate forms of the relatively unimpeded life of the soul.

And lastly, When we are told that feeling is unsharable, or that it tends to be inversely as Intellectualism, we are transported to a world where the familiar doctrines of Kant's third Critique, of Goethe, and of Schiller—the very roots of modern Idealism—are as if they had never been. Feeling, they taught us, as it became more powerful, more characteristic, more individual, became also universal, necessary, communicable, and social. The individual comes to himself as his nature is completed in the social order, and it is only in the greater creations of intelligence that the higher powers of emotion can be embodied. In a word, the lessons which are most readily learned from Æsthetic Philosophy are at the core of modern Idealism, and a wide range of data will have to be reinterpreted before they can be treated as obsolete. After all, and most remarkably, it was not everyday practice, but the art of music, itself a form of Theoria, in which the poet found the expression of the ultimate will; for, let us complete our quotation :

But here is the finger of God, a flash of the will that can,
    Existent behind all laws, that made them, and, lo they are—
And I know not if save in this, such gift be allowed to man,
    That out of the three sounds he frame not a fourth sound but a star.

The idea of the poem is almost pure Schopenhauer. Schopenhauer's " Will," which for him is the thing in itself, finds its fullest expression not in practice but in Theoria.

Thus, if the comparison—of which we may not approve—is pressed upon us controversially, we must say, I think, and are perfectly safe in saying, that Theoria, as contrasted with everyday practice, has more of the nature of an ultimate end, approaches nearer to the completeness of mind considered as a whole, and in particular involves and demands a higher individuality and a stronger feeling. The controversial comparison is dangerous, because it suggests a false exclusiveness. Life has to be dealt with as a whole, and none of its elements can be omitted. Lack of energy and robustness in everyday habits of action must infallibly reappear as a defect in theoretic life. It is only a question of the spirit, the tendency, the proportion, in which life is to be organized. And here, I contend, it is well to remember, and as against Pragmatism—the exalting of everyday practice—even well to insist in the spirit of Aristotle, that Theoria, of which Cognition is a typical case and an integral part, is itself the essence and the highest form of practical activity. It does make a difference whether we aim on the whole at the things which are essentially common ground and which bind men together, or at the things which cannot be entirely common, and which present at least an aspect of rivalry and division. Nor, I may observe in passing, will such a spirit be found hostile to that success in the businesses of life which is alone worth winning. A wholesome and friendly attitude to our fellow-men, the direction of expenditure, whether public or private, to what has real value, freedom from self-indulgence, the habit of serious attention to what is important for mankind, these are characteristics by no means disadvantageous to the prosperity of nations and of individuals. To stand well above the necessary activities of life is no bad qualification for directing them to the best effect. In spite of all satire and of all calumny, there appears to be a moral secret worth looking into behind the successfulness in business of the Jew, the Puritan, the Scotsman, and the Quaker.

I have so far been controverting the view that Cognition in general is simply ancillary to Practice in the narrower sense.

2. Now I turn to the opposite contention, dealing with Moral Philosophy in particular, to the effect that Ethics, as based on Metaphysics, has no guidance at all to offer on ordinary matters of conduct. And I will say at once that in this position I find a notable element of truth ; and what I wish to do is to explain carefully the precise nature of the distinction which here seems to me important.

(i) It is clear to me that Ethical theory cannot either lay down the rules for conduct or pronounce judgment on particular actions.

But it is worth while to note exactly what are, and what are not the reasons for this disability.

(a) It is not because Metaphysic, on which moral theory depends, deals with conditions too remote to be in any sense applicable to human life. Metaphysic falls short of its office if it does not deal with all degrees of reality, and with all the leading experiences of our world.

(b) It is not because morality fails of being ultimate, and is superseded by Religion, in which morality is absorbed. In Philosophy, the higher involves the lower, and Religion annuls in Morality nothing but its failure.

(c) Nor, again, is it true on the whole to deny that Morality is rational, and implies a single end to which, as a matter of principle, all good action *qua* good can be held contributory. It is true that we are in a world of limitation and choice, and that in every course of action something must be forfeited if anything is to be achieved. But this aspect of hazard and of sacrifice, which attends upon all finite action whatever, is not to be magnified into a conflict of principle between incompatible obligations, as for example the obligation to seek one's own welfare and that to seek the welfare of others. The end is single and clear : it is to make the most of human nature. The means are but means, and may seem conflicting ; they can only reveal themselves through the working logic by which life is organized, and this will often seem equally favourable to opposite courses, as science will seem equally favourable to opposite theories. But this imperfection no more impairs the unity of morality than the same imperfection impairs the unity of science. Whatever is rightly chosen in either case is chosen as contributing to the end, to perfection or to truth, though whether it really is so contributory only a larger experience could show.

(ii) The true reason why Moral Philosophy can neither lay down general rules for conduct nor pass sentence on particular actions lies in the nature of any attribute which involves completeness of Individuality. Such, certainly, are Perfection the end of Morality, and Truth the end of Science. Plainly there can be but one criterion of such characteristics as these. And this must be the individual system concerned in its own further advance, or, what amounts to the same thing, another system such as to include it. Of course you may describe the action of a criterion in general terms, but such a description is not itself a criterion, because it cannot be applied. We may say, for example, that the criterion of scientific truth is agreement with the facts. But when we approach a theory and begin to apply our criterion, we find that either we understand the facts as the author of the theory understands them, or we understand them differently. In the former case we no doubt approve his theory, but that is because we understand the facts as he does. On the other hand, if we understand them differently from him, we can go no further in applying our criterion until we have shown that we know more about the facts than he does, and are better able to interpret them. This being so, our criterion has really broken down, and the principle we are relying on reduces itself to this, that if you know more about a thing than another man does, you then are able to judge whether his theory is true or false. The criterion of a science, that is to say, is simply the science itself in its further advance. The same applies to morality. We may have a general knowledge of the end and be able to illustrate it by many hypothetical applications. But to know whether a subordinate rule or a particular action is, or points to, the best course under all the circumstances of the given case, we should have to include as part of our experience the entire context which makes up the individuality of the moral agent in that action. And in morality there is the peculiar difficulty that the most important part of this context lies within the agent's own mind, and cannot possibly be known to any one else, and is indeed but imperfectly known to himself. It is, therefore, a degree more impossible for Moral

Philosophy to prescribe or pass judgment on particular actions or courses of action than it is for Logic to contrive or pass judgment on the special theories of the particular sciences. The person who can judge and help, if any one can, is the person who shares both the special experiences and the confidence of the moral agent. And he is only too likely to be the victim of the moral agent's self-deception.

3. It seems to follow, then, that the general nature of the moral end can be established, that its roots in human nature can be displayed, by the help of metaphysic, and that conduct contains a real and positive relation to this end, as science does to the end of Truth. Only, for both general and special reasons, it is not the task of Moral Philosophy to prescribe rules of conduct or to judge particular courses of action in given cases. To judge hypothetically and by way of illustration is a different thing, and is permissible, because then, as Lord Westbury is reported to have said of actual legal decisions, " You should be accurate about the law, but the facts are always at your disposal."

Now, when we have stated the matter in this way, it is perfectly plain that, if we are right, Moral Philosophy is important and influential for conduct, though not by entering upon casuistry. So long as ideals affect human action the criticism of ideas must affect it too.

Let us recall for a moment at random some few of what may be described as the great moral ideas of the world. " Goodness is knowledge and Vice is ignorance," " Character is destiny," " Life is the practice of dying," " Man is social by nature," " Men are born free and equal," " Man has natural rights," " Society is based on contract," " The end is the greatest happiness of the greatest number," " One is to count for one and for no more than one," " From all according to their abilities, to all according to their needs," " Society is an organism," " Society is a mind," " There is nothing good, in the world or out of it, but a good will."

All such ideas as these, though ultimately drawn from experience of life, were brought plainly into men's minds, and prepared to serve as mottoes of conduct, or perhaps as watchwords of fanaticism, by the speculations of Moral Philosophers.

They have played in the building up of reflective morality something like the part which has been played in the construction of science by such conceptions as Causation, Evolution, the Conservation of Energy, Natural Selection. And if we were to strike them out of human thought, the moral consciousness of the civilized world would have lost its framework.

Now the service which can be rendered by Moral Theory to Conduct consists, according to the view we are suggesting, by no means in dogmatic deductions from thoughts like these, or in the attempts to draw rules of conduct out of them. But it consists in ascertaining the true connection of such principles with one another, and with the realities of human nature, in discovering the aspects and amounts of experience, so to speak, which every one of them may be said to cover. Thus it is its function to render the mind justly appreciative of the various principles of conduct which have summed up the behaviour of intelligent beings under the stimulus of various demands, and have been embodied in institutions, in theories, in ideals. Some of the narrower of these may well be the more obvious : some of the deeper and truer may be more subtle and less in evidence. Yet the blindness which misreads them, and substitutes a more mechanical for a more spiritual conception, is not only a stupid, but a dangerous thing. To take an extreme example. A man who does not believe in honesty except as the best policy is not only a fool, but a very mischievous knave. And so, more excusably, a man may never have turned his attention to the implications of such an idea as freedom, or to the real nature of the desire which he describes as that of pleasing himself as much as possible, or to the real conditions, which from his common sense he more or less observes, of doing good to other people. It is true that the education and the membership of a Christian society, together with common sense, will take you a very long way, and I have most distinctly disclaimed the idea that you can make a man out of ethical theories. Nevertheless, a false or fanatical theory *is* a hindrance to conduct which is not wholly negligible, especially in appreciating the influences which affect the lives of others. We do see every day that bad theories produce bad observations and bad observations

produce dangerous action.   I will venture so far, for example, as
to say that if the logical relation of individual and universal had
been more familiar than it is to Herbert Spencer and his antagonists, we might have escaped, to the general advantage, something near a generation of irritating social controversy.   Or if
more serious ideas were current of the intricate and delicate
factors involved in all problems of character and circumstance,
we might be spared the incomplete and superficial observations
which occupy the public mind as " Statistics of Poverty."
In technical language, special criticism is necessary to enable
us to appreciate the forms of unity which are higher than the
common-sense categories, or the conceptions of physical science ;
and, apart from special criticism, we are liable to see a blank
when the greatest things of life are before us.

In a word, then, we say with Plato that " neither we nor
our pupils can rank as morally educated until," in his language,
we have learned to read in the moral world ; until, that is,
we have learned to discern something of the true powers and
excellences of human nature, and to have a fair judgment of
them both in real life and in the literature and art which form
so great a portion of our moral environment.   At any rate, it
would be a sure and definite gain if each of us who studies
moral philosophy in this place could lay the foundation of a
lifelong friendship with some one or two of the great ethical
books of the world.   They would not, indeed, instruct us
how to act in cases of conscience.   But probably we should
become both more appreciative and more secure in our point
of view ;   we should respond more readily to the excellences
of others, and yet the simplest fallacies would no longer find
us quite so easy a prey.   It is a chance which comes to us at
the University, and to most of us comes never again.

And such a friendship with a thinker of the past—for it
is almost a personal relation with a great man, when he gives
you the very best that he was able to give the world—is in
itself a great thing.   Here, in conclusion, I return to the point
which occupied us earlier in the lecture.   We have just now
been saying that a deeper study of man's mind and his world
must surely make us wiser on the whole in judgment and in
everyday conduct.   But we will conclude as we began, by
insisting that the introduction of greatness and consistency

into our intellectual experience is of the nature of an end in itself ; and that to conceive the true aim of life, not as restricted to cognition, but yet as kindred with it, and in the light of a mind at one with itself rather than of objects in which we are the prey of rivalry and competition—that to conceive the aim of life to some such purpose as this is to conceive it justly, and in a way for which the world would be the better.

# X

## RECENT CRITICISM OF GREEN'S ETHICS

1. THIS paper will deal with some special points in Mr. Taylor's work *The Problem of Conduct*. Professor McGilvary's article in *Mind* (October, 1902) did not come to me soon enough to be included in my treatment, although I believe that the first part of the paper will meet the criticisms which he makes.

I hope that it will not be thought that I am reviewing Mr. Taylor's book. If that had been my object, I should have been bound to treat fully of the author's positive ideas as a contribution to ethical science. This I have made no effort to do, further than was implied in trying to estimate his criticism of Green. The book contains suggestions with many of which I strongly sympathize, falling in, I almost hope, with ideas which I have myself attempted to express.

But there were two special reasons which made me wish to say something about it. One was, that Mr. Taylor's impression of Green's main argument was very different from my own, and I was glad to go back to the *Prolegomena to Ethics*, and try to come to some clearness as to what it really meant to say. It may seem an odd observation to make, but I doubt if the *Prolegomena* ever received the strictly philosophical attention which it merited. It was, one might almost say, superseded in the general attention seven years before it appeared by Mr. Bradley's brilliant first essay, *Ethical Studies* (1876). His *Principles of Logic* appeared in the same year with it (1883). And though Book III of the *Prolegomena* has generally been studied and admired, I question if Book I, which largely refers to a controversy bygone for the moment, though permanent in principle, has been very thoroughly understood. I shall show reason, I hope in no carping spirit, to doubt whether Mr. Taylor has studied it profoundly, or, at any rate, recently. My grounds will be drawn from a tendency to harp upon particular phrases and doctrines, as if literally extracted from Green's book, whose presence there may be substantially demonstrable but is not a matter of literal fact. His idea of Green seems like the general notion which any one may retain who looks back upon a great but naïve thinker from a more developed standpoint. I do not think this is an unfair thing to say. I was so ready myself to believe that my old impression was wrong, and Mr. Taylor's was right, until I re-read the *Prolegomena* carefully *ad hoc*, that his attitude seems to me quite natural, and I suspect that it is widely shared. It is, moreover, I shall admit, in some degree justified. This, at any rate, is one reason why I desired to speak of Mr. Taylor's book, that it gives us a chance to refresh our recollection and readjust our estimate of the *Prolegomena*.

And my second reason lay in the nature of the advanced position which Mr. Taylor shares with other recent thinkers. Within a narrower province of thought I might almost claim to have predicted [1] that this position must emerge as soon as the distinction between ultimate and empirical truth should reappear after the sensationalist deluge. It was natural and necessary that the revival of metaphysic should accent the distinction between the truth *ad hoc* of common sense or the natural sciences, and that which should refer to a perfect experience, as arrived at by metaphysic. But this tendency is now pushed so far that metaphysic is tending to become a necessary and abstract science of the possible, as opposed to the empirical sciences of the actual, with the result of practically returning to the position for which the possible is wider than the real, and necessity is divorced from actuality. This position, due, as I should urge, to establishing as a principle the abstractness which is an imperfection of metaphysic, threatens the unity of the philosophical sciences, and tends to break the connection between life and the completest thought. Now we may be very ready to grant that, in the past, too few gradations may have been admitted between morality and perfection. But it is one thing to interpose gradations and another to fail in maintaining natural groupings. It must be demanded, I suggest, of the philosophy of the

[1] *Logic*, ii, p. 228.

future, that it shall be able to utilize our best ideas in throwing light upon life, while noting the distance between actual human experience and the highest that it implies. Mathematics has done much, I suppose, to make the actual appear as a mere case of the possible. I have no right to say a word in criticism of mathematical speculation as such. But I should like to ask whether it would not be equally free and valuable if it were regarded as an exercise of intelligence in pursuing the consequences of imaginary conditions, rather than a study of real possibilities. I do not see how any injustice could thus be done to the ideas in question. For at the first hint of an actual superiority as explanation of the given, they would spring up *ipso facto* into candidates for reality ; while, in the absence of any such contention, it seems more correct, logically, to let them stand as a pure intellectual experiment.

At any rate, the difference of principle between Green and Mr. Taylor turns upon this question of the unity of the philosophical sciences, and that was my second reason for writing this paper.

2. A word is necessary, by way of precaution, about the ideal of science as the " complete description of phenomena reduced to their simplest terms," [1] which Mr. Taylor borrows, as he tells us, from Avenarius. I regret that I am not acquainted with Avenarius's theory at first hand. As Mr. Taylor states it, it appears to me to raise one very important question, which is this : When the term " description " is qualified as " complete," and referred to " phenomena reduced to their simplest terms," is anything left of the connotation of " description " ? The word has a suspicious history in the theory of explanation.[2] And when Mr. Taylor charges Green with supposing that the full reality of the sensuous world could never be the object of " direct perception," [3] we ask ourselves, Does Mr. Taylor imply that the full reality of anything could ever be an object for *sense*-perception ? The

[1] *Problem*, p. 19.
[2] It is enough to refer to Mr. Bradley's *Principles of Logic*, p. 490, for a mistake made by G. H. Lewes in the way of a descriptive theory of explanation and a criticism of it. I imagine that something of the same mistake must be imputed to Mr. Stout, *Analytic Psychology*, Introduction.
[3] *Problem*, p. 450.

difficulty may be stated thus : If " description " has a distinctive meaning, it means the statement of particular detail.
It is essentially of the particular, and of sense-perception.
Now, sense-perception never is nor can be " complete " nor
" of phenomena reduced to their simplest terms " ; that is, as
I understand, experienced as free from contradiction. It is
necessarily a mere heap of irrelevancy and inconsistency.
Directly you select and state a universal connection, you have
got beyond description in the only distinctive sense of the
word. But if so, apart from further definition of the theory,
the characteristic which gave it plausibility is gone, and nothing
is left but the demand for a coherent experience, of whatever
nature that may be. That it is to be an actual experience tells
us nothing. The question is whether the term " description "
gives us any help as to the nature of the required experience, or
merely pretends to do so. Description seemed to be a familiar
idea, and to indicate that the whole thing would be there
immediately, and nothing omitted—a perfectly full experience.
But in the sense in which we commonly use it, it is incapable
of coherence, and therefore it does not help us as an account of
the required experience, which is above all things to be coherent.
It looks like defining an ideal by putting together two conditions
destructive of each other.

If this is meant and admitted, in the sense that we do
demand an experience at once perfectly full and perfectly
coherent, though we do not know how it could be realized,
that is a fair procedure. But then there ceases to be a
ground for backing " description " in the ordinary sense against
explanation, i.e. statement in terms of universal relations.
Both are in that case admittedly required ; but the crux is
that as we know them they are incompatible. With regard
to the defects assumed to be necessary in conceptual knowledge, I would call attention to Nettleship's remarks on the
two meanings of the concept.[1] We are apt to forget that
thinking ought really to mean a far fuller and completer
experience than sense-perception. The neglect of this
consideration has much to do with the acquiescence,
which I have spoken of, in the abstractness of Metaphysic.

[1] *Remains*, vol. i, pp. 166–7.

3. I pass to the question of what Mr. Taylor calls the "Eternal Self." I will first state shortly the impression which I have formed of Green's doctrine of eternity in connection with the human self, and will then attempt to remove what I take to be misunderstandings of it ; and after that, to show how, if at all, it differs from the view to which Mr. Taylor inclines, as a follower, if I read him right, of Spinoza. My statement in chief, if I am right, may be very short and simple. In my judgment, Green's very elaborate exposition and reiteration were due to the necessity which he accepted of maintaining the general Idealist position against a popular Naturalism of the crudest kind.

The gist of his doctrine, I believe, is no more than this, that the human mind is capable of apprehending a " whole," and does, in fact, apprehend a world as a whole, though imperfectly ; and further, that the world is thus apprehended in its real character, in so far that it really is a whole and has the only kind of unity which analysis of experience suggests to us as possible, namely, that of " some unifying principle analogous to that of our understanding." [1]   The caution of Green's statements, and his openness to the alternatives consistent with a fundamental principle very widely conceived, are what impress one most in a study of his work, in contrast with what I might almost call the legend of his views which appears to have become current.

The rest of his essential view follows from drawing out the character of a true whole, or whole of consciousness. It must be a system, or something closer than a system, all-inclusive, and thoroughly one. This he seems also to express by saying that it is " eternal " ; that is to say, present to itself in all its parts, if the term " parts " is even applicable to it, with an intimacy which we cannot imagine, but can more or less remotely illustrate from our highest experience, say, of knowledge and of love.[2] This conception has, in fact, arisen altogether from insisting further on characteristics partially present in the experience of particular human minds. It is at once implied, therefore, that the human mind partakes of the nature which is thus supposed to make the total world-experience what it is. Thus, it is urged, the human mind is

---

[1] *Prolegomena*, sect. 29.      [2] *Memoir*, cxxxviii, xciii.

rightly inferred to be continuous and partly identical, as a mind and not merely as a natural fact, with the consciousness which is the whole. And this partial identity, evinced in human minds by their partial apprehension of the world as a whole, through knowledge and feeling, constitutes a perceptible contradiction with the limitations of such minds, resulting in the endeavour towards various types of totality which may be traced in all their actual experiences.

The world-consciousness, then, as continuous in character with the human mind, but perfect where it is imperfect, has been called the higher or the real self of man. That is to say, it is conceived as the only thing which could be for him the completion of what he is in ordinary fact. It " communicates to him " " his own nature." It is therefore at once " eternal " in its own right, and also the true or ultimate self of man. Therefore the human mind or self might come to be spoken of as eternal, in virtue of its relation to the world-consciousness, and in so far as that relation is realized through apprehension of the world as a whole. Thus, for example, in proportion as man attains to his ideal of knowledge, he considers together, as intimate parts of a single system and equally and reciprocally bearing on one another, facts and events separated in apparent succession by the whole range of historical time. The consciousness in a particular human self of the identity of its own experiences is merely, as I understand the argument, a case of the apprehension of a whole. It is determined in detail, I suppose, like the apprehension of any subordinate whole of experience, by the continuity discoverable in the set of experiences in question. And it is very noticeable that the true or real identity of the self is not, for Green, present prima facie in the intermittent consciousness of man.[1] Like other matters of our experience, it comes to us darkly and imperfectly, and could only be grasped in completeness by apprehending the fuller experience which the world-consciousness includes. Of course, *de facto*, the experiences which our life is spent in trying to unify are happenings in our own soul, and therefore we may say, with Green and Mr. Taylor,[2] that all our knowledge consists, logically speaking, in the unification of our private experiences. But the principle which is implied in

[1] *Works*, i, p. 115.  [2] *Prolegomena*, sect. 101 ; *Problem*, p. 13.

the whole process is the same ; " the experience of a thousand years ago and the experience of to-day, the experience which I have here and that which I might have in any other region of space—forms a single system." [1] My apprehension of my own identity in my own experiences taken as a whole is, as I read Green's argument, a part of this system, dependent on the same capacity, and, like it, subject in particular experience to differences of degree and to imperfection. Green's inference always rests on the unity and unalterableness ascribed to reality, or, as in the place just cited, on the inclusion of events supposed previous to any consciousness on our earth in our system of experience. Granting that reality only is through unity in some form of consciousness, how can our extension of a homogeneous experience beyond possible human perception fail to imply the continuity of our mind with the consciousness which is the whole ? Eternity, as I said, is the name given to that characteristic of a true whole by which its parts (if we may use such a term) are in absolute intimacy of unity with one another. In as far as a particular mind is able to identify itself with a whole of this character, it may be said, in a derivative and imperfect sense, to possess eternity, or to have laid hold on eternal life. And the human mind, as such, appears to be distinguished by the capacity for apprehending a whole of this nature, and therefore so far, and in this partial sense, it may be considered as eternal; not merely in the same sense as any fact within reality, say a blade of grass, but in a sense really, though no doubt remotely, analogous to that in which the whole itself has eternity.

This is my impression of Green's central view, after carefully re-reading the *Prolegomena* and portions of the *Works*, and studying Nettleship's *Memoir*, which merits more attention than, as I suspect, it receives.

And this brings me to the first of what I take to be mis-understandings in Mr. Taylor's work. There is no meaning, Mr. Taylor urges, in speaking about the Eternal Self, which he considers to be a defiance of empirical psychology, unless " not only consciousness in general, but finite selves, are ultimate underived realities." [2] And he proceeds to argue that Green held this opinion. Now, in order to make clear my

---

[1] *Prolegomena*, sect. 32.  [2] *Problem*, p. 70.

xact position and a great part of my object in writing this
paper, I will say frankly that when I read Mr. Taylor's book
I thought to myself : " Well, I did not remember that Green
used language implying the finite self to be ultimate. I
thought he meant something quite different, and I believe that,
judging from the *Memoir*, Nettleship thought as I do.  But it
sounds very serious, and if the terms used really imply what
they appear to imply as cited, I should not be able to defend
them even in a modified sense."  I will return below to the
phrase " Eternal Self."  At this point I will merely note that
in re-reading the *Prolegomena* I could find no justification for
the suggestion made in the passage I have quoted.  I do not
think that there is anything in Green to suggest that he
referred to an " Eternal Self " which empirical psychology
could not admit.  The whole context of his views would indicate that to call the finite self an ultimate underived reality
would have appeared to him rash, if not blasphemous.[1]  He
does seem to argue at times,[2] very modestly and tentatively,
for something like a continuance of personality after death ;
but the nature of this argument itself, and the width of its
conclusion, prove absolutely that it was not derived from any
preconception of an eternal finite self.  The expression, indeed,
in his essays would be self-contradictory.  Therefore there is
no misunderstanding when Mr. Taylor ascribes this view to
Green ; but there is, as I hold, another grave and fundamental
misunderstanding in suggesting that its absence would be
inconsistent with his notion of eternity in connection with
the self.

Mr. Taylor holds that Green's rejection of a Natural or
" Physical " Science of Ethics places him in antagonism to
psychology and evolutionary science as such.  But it must be
remembered that *Physical Ethics*[3] was a current idea of the
days when Green was in the height of his activity.  His
criticisms of Spencer and Lewes (published 1877, and later)
show plainly that he felt himself in presence of a strong body
of opinion tending to derive consciousness from a universe in
which no such thing existed, and, partly in consequence of this

[1] *Works*, i, pp. 124-5.
[2] *Prolegomena*, sects. 182, 185.
[3] *Physical Ethics*, by Alfred Barratt, 1869 ;  Barratt was one of the most
distinguished Balliol men of his time.  Cp. *Works*, iii, p. 96.

derivation, to confuse the nature of psychical and physical units. It was a concession on his part, as on that of Mr. John Grote,[1] to allow that occurrences in the way of feeling, considered as temporal events in a purely sentient life, might be dealt with by a naturalist as physical facts [2]; that is, I suppose, as very simple reactions, of which as they occur in the animal world the naturalist certainly appears to know the chief external conditions. The admission, perhaps, was rash ; but to have withheld it would, of course, have strengthened his case. If it is denied to-day, by the purest psychology,[3] that in human experience at any rate a sensation, as a simple reaction to a single stimulus, has any existence, Green's analysis of experience was the anticipation, if not the actual source, of such a view. He conceded a " mere sensation " or " feeling " to his antagonists as a possible *terminus ad quem* but he denied that the experience which we know contained anything analogous to it. If he was wrong in speaking of such a *terminus* at all, of any feeling or sensation which could be looked at as a physical fact, this actual inaccuracy is a substantial confirmation of his view.

So, too, with the terms " nature " and " natural." He explained with his usual care the sense in which he used these terms—the sense of his materialist opponents—when maintaining that a spiritual principle must be non-natural and could not be accounted for by any natural science. " Nature " in this sense, he points out, is nature considered as the object of knowledge.[4] In other words, it is nature as one side of an antithesis, as a manifold of bodies and occurrences, from which the consideration of their unity, except in a very subordinate sense, has been omitted. And when nature is taken in this sense, the spiritual principle of its unity cannot, *ex hypothesi*, be found in it, or derived from it by any evolution which involves an identity between its beginning and its end. I take it that neither Psychology nor Biology as they stand to-day has any real quarrel with Green on behalf of the method thus rejected. But he has pointed out most fully [5] that there is no reason for

---

[1] *Exploratio*, ii, p. 17.
[2] Cp. *Prolegomena*, sect. 5.
[3] See James *passim*, or article " Brain " in *Baldwin's Dictionary*.
[4] *Prolegomena*, sect. 8.   Cp. sects. 52, 18.
[5] *Ibid.*, sect. 54.

estricting ourselves to such a meaning of nature, if we prefer
o employ the term in a more inclusive sense. That would be
he usage, I should add, of the great Greeks, of Goethe, and of
Vordsworth. In that sense it includes the " spiritual principle
—necessary to the possibility of a world of phenomena." [1] And
his is the sense, no doubt, in which it is meant to be spoken of
a much of our evolutionary science and popular philosophy as
 an independent agent," and as " more or less complete or self-
ontained." [2] The fact is, as Green points out, that the two
neanings are played fast and loose with. Nature is apt to be
reated as the whole, and yet conceived under restrictions which
elong solely to the part. He only demands that those who
mploy the term should make clear the sense in which they
mploy it, and be consistent. Thus there would be no objection
rom Green's standpoint to treating the mind of man as natural
r as having a natural history, if this did not lead us to falsify
ither the beginning or the end of its development. His very
areful statement [3] on the subject of the animal mind shows
learly that it was a problem on which he did not feel bound to
ronounce categorically. All that he contended for was that
ve should be clear in what sense we supposed the development
o have occurred. *"If it "* (such an intelligence as forms the
asis of our knowledge) *" is absent "* [4] (from the animal mind),
hen such a mind as ours cannot in the strict sense have
eveloped from such a mind as theirs. " But [5] this hypo-
hetical negation is quite compatible with the admission that
here may have been a progressive development, through hered-
:ary transmission, of the animal system, which has become
rganic to the distinctive intelligence of man," and so on. In a
vord, our intelligence either can be traced back in essence to
he animal mind, or, if it cannot, must have supervened upon
nodifications of sensibility in non-human beings such as to
repare the way for it. The only important matter is not to do
iolence to the facts of either extreme in the development ; and
: is the human mind from which we really start, as knowing it
t first hand. In the light of these distinctions, Green's obser-
ation that the preceptive part of Ethics is endangered by a

---

[1] *Prolegomena*, loc. cit.  [2] Loc. cit.
[3] *Prolegomena*, sect. 84. Cp. 83.  [4] Green's italics, loc. cit.
[5] *Ibid.*

natural theory seems, as he says, obvious.[1]    A natural theory
in the sense explained by Green, as a theory in terms of nature
as an object, is bound to disregard the factor on which the
humanity of the human mind depends, and must fetter the
inquiry a priori.

The term " empirical," again, appears in inverted commas
as the name of something which Mr. Taylor holds that he is
defending against Green, and as if Green used it as an epithet
of the " natural science " which he rejects.    The word is so
ambiguous that if Green did use it the fact would mean very
little, apart from further explanation, but I regard it as
characteristic of him that in the *Prolegomena*, so far as I
can see, he does not.    When therefore Mr. Taylor bases,
as I understand him, on the suggestion that the term has
importance for Green, the further suggestion that Ethics for
him (as I suppose) " contains some non-empirical element of
immediate intuition or a priori axiom of unquestionable
authority," [3] or that the precepts of Ethics are for him
" absolute and final," I think we have got into a region of
legend growing out of legend.

We seem to have lost hold of the central principle and its
careful and patient elaboration, exhibiting the mode in which
the universal good takes individual forms according to the
nature and history of individual minds.    I may add that
it surely is not sound to treat the " ought " recognized by
ethical science as on all fours with the " ought " which
expresses the expectation based on a general principle applied
to any object of natural science.    " Ought " implies the contrast
of rule and case for consciousness ;  in any science, therefore
you can have it, but in ethical science, if we are to speak in
this language, you have it twice over.    You have it both in
the expectation of the student, as in any other science, but
also in the consciousness of the objects studied by the science.
The " ought " surely remains peculiar, if not to Ethics at any
rate to the philosophical sciences.

In the same way, to the best of my belief, the actual
expression " Eternal Self," on which Mr. Taylor continually
harps, does not occur in the *Prolegomena to Ethics*.    I hope

[1] *Prolegomena*, sect. 7 ;  *Problem*, p. 60.      [2] *Problem*, pp. 65-6, 52.
[3] *Ibid.*, p. 52.

I am not captious about this. Of course, very similar expressions occur ; and the actual words are to be found in a criticism of Locke,[1] and very possibly elsewhere in the *Works*. But then it seems to me that where this or any equivalent phrase does occur, it does not bear the meaning which causes Mr. Taylor to reiterate it in inverted commas, and which he thus drives home in the reader's mind. In the place just referred to, for example, it very plainly means the world-consciousness or divine mind, sharply contrasted with the " thinking thing " in you or me ; which has, I suppose, its identity outside its given self, as is the case more or less with all finite existences. In face of this fact, and of my general statement of Green's view, it seems to me that the criticisms of Mr. Taylor's Chapter II are wholly beside the mark. They are directed against an Eternal Self which is a supernatural and changeless nucleus within each finite centre of consciousness. Its timeless character is parodied as indicating, not man's living grasp, the constructive spirit by which he enters upon consciousness of a whole or unity, but a changeless element, persistent through the experiences of the concrete self, and, as changeless, unaffected by them.[2]

Thus it appears to me quite idle to argue, as against Green, that only continuity, and not changeless persistence, is needed as the basis of individual identity. The question is, as I understand it, how successive and diverse experiences can be conceived as a whole at all. Assuming that this can be done, it is useful to analyse the conditions of continued identity, which apply to every case of individuality whether in minds or in things. Such an analysis shows us what things consciousness will recognize as identical, but does not enable us to deduce the nature of a consciousness for which there is identity.

The *punctum stans* argument,[3] to which Green frequently recurs, is that most liable to misunderstanding. I will not deny that if it stood alone it might cause a difficulty as to Green's general position ; nor that some of Green's expressions in connection with it might have been the occasion of Mr. Bradley's criticisms in a well-known passage.[4] The first thing

---

[1] *Works*, i, p. 115.
[2] Cp. section 100 of *Prolegomena*, directed against this misinterpretation.
[3] E.g., *Prolegomena*, sect. 81.
[4] *A. and R.*, 49 ff.

L

to remember seems to me to be that it does not at all stand
alone, but that the main foundation of Green's argument is
clearly and continually expressed in other terms,[1] referring to
the nature of a true whole, and the progressive realization of
such a whole in the human mind. The difficulty of the *punctum
stans* argument is, I suppose, that it appears to suggest an
apprehension of succession by an act that has no duration ; and
the relation of this act to the duration of the ordinary consciousness is unexplained. The metaphor of the *punctum
stans*, we may note, is borrowed from an allusion in Locke,[2] and
I think is applied by Green with a modification of its apparent
meaning. (I do not know the original meaning to which
Locke refers.) " The presence of consciousness to itself," he
says, " is the true *punctum stans*." [3] Expressions like this, in
harmony with his analysis of what is implied in actual succession,[4] indicate, I believe, his true meaning. I think it is this,
that consciousness, at any moment, in cross-section so to speak,
is a complex of reciprocal determinations, thus bearing witness
to its proper nature as a self-contained totality. It is quite
true that the parts of its content are more or less in succession,
and consequently that its phases occupy duration. But still,
the tendency to build up a self-contained whole is never entirely
absent, and even if we are specially apprehending a succession,
the conditions of doing so bear witness to the logical ideal of
knowledge, through our inability to admit that any event in
the succession exists in its own right or as undetermined by
the rest, whether before or after it. The self-contained whole,
which as such, internally, is not in time, always sets the
standard which our apprehension aims at attaining. It seems
a strong thing to say that in the perception of something
moving from point to point, the consciousness of it as at the
second point is not an event sequent upon the consciousness of
it as at the first,[5] but still, if we strictly distinguish, as he does,
between the perception of the movement as a whole, and the
process of arriving at the perception, we can see the nature of
his reference to the complexity of a whole in consciousness.
Of course he does not mean that the whole process has no

---

[1] E.g., *Prolegomena*, sects. 36 and 83.    [2] See reference in *Works*.
[3] *Memoir*, lxxix ; *Works*, i, p. 121.    [4] E.g., *Works*, ii, p. 73.
[5] *Ibid.*, i, p. 478.

duration. He means that the consciousness at the end approaches the nature of a self-contained complex. His expression may be rash, but it is quite plain, I think, that he does not really depart from the lines of his general argument, resting not on the processes of discursive thought, but on the implications of knowledge and morality.

I cannot therefore think that there is any meaning in ascribing to Green " a metaphysical theory which, like that of the ' Eternal Self,' attempts to attribute to the inmost core of selfhood an *absolutely* unchanging character," or a timeless centre of identity in our own inner life.[1]  I hardly understand how anyone could read sections 47 and 67 of the *Prolegomena*, for example, and retain any such conception.  It seems very plain that, for Green, our eternity is not something which we start with, except as a capacity of a special kind, but is something to be won in making the most of our individuality.

Therefore I think that Mr. Taylor's reduction of the Eternal Self to the subject-object consciousness, and his insistence on the acquired and intermittent character of that consciousness, are also irrelevant.  The Eternal Self is the highest and fullest concreteness.  It is inevitable that in the aspiration to be one with it we should sometimes fall below and at other times rise above the separation involved in the mere opposition of subject to object, which marks, on the whole, our everyday relation to the world.  It is one which self-consciousness in the full sense, of a unity realized in difference, has already transcended.

" Well, then," Mr. Taylor may very fairly reply, " supposing that I were to admit your interpretation, you would have shown that I was mistaken in thinking that Green's metaphysics differed seriously from my own.  I am interested to hear that you think he on the whole would have agreed with me, but that does not, of course, impeach, but rather confirms, my own philosophical position.  Only, why then do we differ so utterly as to the relation of metaphysic to ethics ? "

I will go on directly to the relation of metaphysic and ethics.  But it is a prior question, whether, discounting all that I take to be misunderstanding, Mr. Taylor is in substantial agreement with Green's metaphysics of the self.  The question turns on the connection between the human mind (including in this phrase any limited intelligence) and the consciousness which is reality. I am not quite sure of Mr. Taylor's position on this point.[1] Judging from one controversial passage I should have imagined him to hold that there could be no meaning in treating the human self as having any sort of eternity, unless we held that it, as we know it, had no beginning in time such as evolutionary science could trace. Such a view seemed to me wholly alien to Green. But on the same page Mr. Taylor points out other senses in which the term " eternal " may be used. Passing over the sense in which everything—a blade of grass, as I said above—may be treated as having eternity in the whole, we find the only meaning in which Mr. Taylor recognizes the term as differentially applicable to the human mind to be one derived from Spinoza. To this Mr. Taylor recurs elsewhere, and it appears to represent his own conception : [2] " The ' eternity ' of the human mind, instead of being identified with its power of understanding its own history and destiny, etc." The same view is referred to elsewhere,[3] in a footnote, which shows, I almost fancy, that Mr. Taylor found himself nearer than he liked to the " Hegelian fetish of the Eternal Self," even in the form which, as I believe, a mere legend has conferred upon it. Here we found it stated as Spinoza's doctrine that it is only as you know yourself identical with the Deity that you become identical with Him. Again, the author speaks of Spinoza's view [4] as admitting degrees of eternity, a conception which is essential to Green's doctrine.

The only difference of principle that I can see is this, that Mr. Taylor (I am not competent to speak of Spinoza) does not admit any participation in the world-consciousness to be implied in the ordinary human intelligence—the mind of the natural man. *His* eternity is only that of a blade of grass. The mind has no identity with the eternal, *qua* mind, but only in so far as it explicitly apprehends such a relation with reference to its own history and destiny. This idea no doubt gives some sort of rationale for the distance which the author maintains between metaphysical and ethical science, as well as between religion and morality. But it is hard to see how it

---

[1] *Problem*, pp. 70, 73, 83, 429.  [2] *Ibid.*, p. 83.
[3] *Ibid.*, p. 429.  [4] *Ibid.*, p. 73. Cp. *Prolegomena*, p. 75.

can stand before an analysis of the whole facts of the rational
consciousness in their continuity which should accept the idea
of degree. I have urged that it is on such an analysis that
Green's conception of the two-sided self is founded.[1] And it
seems to result in a much larger and simpler estimate of
man's relation to the real than any which makes it rest on
a special preoccupation with his private history and destiny,
or on specifically religious faith. *Laborare est orare* implies
an identical faith—and as Mr. Taylor well reminds us, *Denken
ist auch Gottesdienst.*

There is indeed a defect in much of Green's language,
as judged from a standpoint like that of Mr. Bradley's
Metaphysic, which there are signs that he himself would have
admitted. At any rate an incautious reader of the *Prolegomena*
would be apt to believe our relational and discursive thinking much more nearly akin to the world-consciousness than
probably any student would admit to-day. It almost seems
as if Green thought at times that reality might fairly be
described as a self-consciousness (which we naturally think
of after the pattern of our own) considered as the unifying
principle of an unalterable system of relations.[2] In the same
way, it would appear as if he thought that the supreme moral
good could be conceived as realized in the divine consciousness
without transcending its specifically moral nature. In general,
therefore, it might be said that he allowed too small an
interval between experience specifically moral and specifically
religious, and again between human experience and perfection.

Suggestions in such a direction he would, to all appearance,
have been very ready to admit. I may cite a striking passage [3]
written in 1880 : " If thought and reality are to be identified,
if the statement that God is thought is to be other than a
presumptuous paradox, thought must be other than the discursive activity exhibited in our inferences and analyses, other
than a particular mode of consciousness which excludes from
itself feeling and will. As little can it be the process of philosophizing, though Hegel himself, by what seems to us the one
essential aberration of his doctrine, treats this process as a
sort of movement of the absolute thought." His argument,

[1] *Prolegomena*, p. 88.        [2] *Ibid.*, p. 17.
[3] *Works*, iii, p. 142 ; *Prolegomena*, sect. 47.   Cp. *Memoir*, lxxxi and lxxxv.

as I insisted above, and as he emphatically affirms in this paper, is always from the implications of reality, and never, essentially, from the processes of thinking. So too in the *Prolegomena* we can see that he did not really suppose the machinery of terms and relations, by which our thought proceeds, to represent the mode of consciousness in which reality can consist, or that of a perfect intelligence.[1] So far as we can judge from his writings, he would have welcomed a theory by which the " something analogous to our own understanding," which was all he ventured to postulate, should receive a closer and a larger definition.

Undoubtedly these considerations are in some ways akin to Mr. Taylor's criticisms. They tend to diminish the metaphysical importance of mere morality, and to decrease the supposed homogeneousness of the human mind and a perfect experience. But we must remember that if reality cannot be relational or purely moral, that does not mean that it is less, but rather that it is that and more. How much substantial difference they make to Green's position could only be explained by a theory of degrees of reality. But it seems safe to say, for the reason just assigned, that they will not overthrow the conviction which indeed Mr. Taylor expresses,[2] and to which Green, as I believe, had given a simpler and truer form.

4. So far then we may say that the general doctrine of man's identity with an eternal whole is pretty much common ground, although it is held by the author in a different form [3] from that which Green maintained. For every conscious attitude towards life it must have at least the sort of bearing which Mr. Bradley has explained in defending his own doctrine from the imputation of Agnosticism.[4] "According to the doctrine of this work that which is highest to us is also in and to the Universe most real, and there can be no question of its reality being somehow upset."

But it might be held that such a conviction, though important for the estimate and confirmation of the general ethical attitude, could give no special help to the problems

[1] *Prolegomena*, sect. 43.
[2] *Problem*, p. 429.
[3] *Ibid.*, p. 429.
[4] *A. and R.*, ed. 2, p. 560.

of ethical science.   This is Mr. Taylor's view when he urges
that metaphysic cannot be the foundation of Ethics and
points his assertion by affirming that the true foundation is
in Psychology.[1]

In examining this criticism of Green I will begin as before
by stating briefly the impression which I have formed for
myself as to the essential nature of Green's argument ; because
it appears to me that in face of such a simple statement many
misunderstandings might fall away of themselves.   I will then
attempt to deal with Mr. Taylor's doctrine of the radical
contradiction in Ethics, as affecting its relation to metaphysics
and as a criticism of the self-realization theory.   I should have
wished to show further that the judgment of approbation
in Ethics is as superficial a datum as (it is Mr. Taylor's own
comparison) the judgment of taste in æsthetics.[2]   Then it
would follow that a failure to start from the self as a logical
whole was what precluded him from making full use of his
own excellent suggestions.   His work is very full of matter
and would repay a much more protracted treatment.   But
space and time force me to be content with a narrow choice
of topics.

As I trace for myself, then, the course of Green's Method of
Ethics, it was his great object to be unfettered.   Hedonism on
the one hand, and the Physical Naturalism of his day on the
other, seemed to him, as he says of the former, to stop you
*in limine*.[3]   That is the essence of his objection to them.
What we want is to look at man's life as a whole, and not to
rule out parts of it at starting.   And Common Sense, too, like
Hedonism and Naturalism, tends to stop you *in limine*.
Experience criticizes itself, carries itself on from point to
point, modifying the notions with which everyday routine
has furnished it at starting.   It brings you to factors which
imply the identity of self and other, the unreality of mere
particulars, the nature of a genuine whole.   In ethical experience these elements meet you at every turn.   But common

---

[1] *Problem*, p. 88.

[2] I do not know whether Mr. Taylor, in the passage referred to, is criticizing
my views on æsthetic theory or not.   Anyhow, I agree with him that the
cases are parallel, and I have elsewhere given my reasons for thinking, in
Æsthetics, the reverse of his method to be the right one.   But, of course, a
complete theory must, first or last, deal with all data.

[3] *Prolegomena*, sect. 170.

sense, or, in technical language, the categories of the natural sciences, are unable to apprehend these elements, and when confronted with them, simply report a blank.  So that, unless you have recourse to some of the more concrete ideas or standpoints furnished by philosophy, you have not the eyes to see the objects of your study.

The necessity which the ethical student thus finds himself under of having recourse to philosophical ideas has nothing to do with preconceived or a priori principles, or the dictation of one science to another, or the deduction of one from another. The ideas may indeed be called preliminary,[1] if they are necessary to clear the ground from theories which would otherwise be obstructive, or, according to Green's careful statement, "the foundation but not the whole" of your science, if they prove to be the central conceptions on which it hinges.  If they are stated in the beginning of a book and not at the end, that is a matter of the order of exposition, and does not at all necessarily follow the order of investigation. The essential point is simply, as Green has said,[2] that when you try to put the whole thing together (as is necessarily implied, after your experience has confronted you with the inherent difficulties of the data) you find that without the conceptions in question the facts simply will not come together, and unless you are going to employ unexamined conceptions, you must have recourse to metaphysic or philosophy.

I think it is just, and philosophically important, to claim that the serious survey of human conduct in the concrete has always, from Plato downwards, been the special tendency of Idealist philosophy.  As Mr. Taylor points out, it is the unquestionably admirable part of Green's own work, and I am surprised that Mr. Taylor should ever have fixed on a metaphysical ethic as the marked feature of Hegel. Perhaps metaphysics are nowhere in Hegel very far off; but the remarkable point in his ethics, the point in which they are really peculiar and characteristic, is that they come in as a part of his science of society.  This relation to the concrete is no accident in Idealism, it is because by drawing to its assistance the notions of a true whole, identity in difference, the unity of self and others, and so forth, it is enabled to

[1] *Memoir*, cxxv.          [2] *Prolegomena*, sect. 174.

observe and analyse experiences which without these ideas
cannot be noticed or recorded. Common sense has no organs
for dealing with a true totality. It is Bacon's fallacy—the
most fatal of all fallacies affecting research—to suppose that
facts can be collected first and theorizing put off till afterwards.
Of course it may always be urged that an individual philosopher
is prejudiced by his own theories ; but a reproach so absolutely
general to human nature cannot expect any particular application. It was clearly, I think, Green's sincere conviction, after
long familiarity with common-sense ethical theories, and upon
an acquaintance with men and affairs unusual for a student,
that no unfettered survey of ethical experience was possible
unless common-sense ideas were transcended. Can you, we
might ask, and I believe the question would express his spirit—
can you seriously attempt to expound the nature of a human
being's satisfaction, without using, in one terminology or other,
some idea equivalent to the " good " of Plato or Aristotle, or
to an infinite whole as stated in Bradley's *Ethical Studies*, or
to Self-consciousness as used by Green and similar writers ?
And can you possibly state any of these in terms of natural
science or of a phenomenalist Psychology ? I hope that this
impression of Green's attitude may shake some misconceptions, and I will now say something on the difficulties which
Mr. Taylor raises.

Mr. Taylor's view is, in a word, that you cannot apply
metaphysical principles to Ethics, because Metaphysics can
only deal with the nature of a pure experience, and that in
the abstract ; while Ethics is shown, by its radical self-
contradictions, to be an imperfect experience, such as can
only be apprehended by the help of working hypotheses. If
Ethics were a metaphysical science, he urges, it would be
certain in every detail and free from contradiction. He does,
indeed, admit a critical employment of Metaphysic upon
Ethical Science " after " the completion of Ethics ; but the
work of Metaphysic in this employment can never, he contends,
be constructive. I am not sure that, if pressed home, this
admission might not lead to all that I require ; but as the
author does not intend it to weaken his disapproval of Green's
method, I must construe it as prima facie excluding what
I mean to maintain.

It is, further, Mr. Taylor's positive view that the present need in Ethics is a very complete collection of ethical phenomena, and that the root phenomenon of Ethics is not the act of will, but the judgment of approbation. On this, with its developments as known to psychology, sociology, and anthropology, a complete ethical system could, he thinks, be founded.

Now I hope it is clear, from my admissions at the close of section 3, that I recognize that more stages must be interposed between morality and perfection than Green's usual language seems to admit. Still, there is no doubt in my mind that in Ethics, as in all the sciences which have for this reason been called philosophical, we have on our hands certain categories or conceptions with which no natural science, and therefore no phenomenalist psychology, can properly deal. It is, in part, a verbal question by what science they are to be dealt with. If it is to be a matter for the philosophy of spirit, I should not have much fault to find ; but then it would be necessary that the philosophy of spirit should ultimately depend upon logic or metaphysic. In saying this I assume, as against all ideas of dictation or mere deduction as possible relations between sciences, that ultimately experience is a whole, and none of its spheres are without a bearing on its central character.

It seems to me, however, that metaphysic itself has no sufficient content unless, in attempting to exhibit the nature of a pure experience, it uses as starting-points the leading conceptions of experience as given. For, after all, it is only by criticism and readjustment of these that it can get to anything beyond them ; and in motiving its advance it must surely use what we have. If it does not understand what we have,[1] I do not see how we can rely upon it for what we have not. I am suggesting, in fact, that Mr. Taylor has neglected the doctrine of degrees of reality on its positive side. The content of a complete metaphysic would be, I take it, just this—the degrees of reality. Especially the philosophical sciences—those which involve the notion of a spiritual whole—must, as I have urged above, give some philosophical account

---

[1] I am speaking of general conceptions, and am not disputing Mr. Mc-Taggart's view on this point (*Studies in Hegelian Dialectic*, p. 248).

of their central conceptions. This group-formation seems to me quite a well-established relation between sciences, though it is not, I think, one of those which Mr. Taylor has touched in his reference to the subject. It is the case in which a central conception binds together a complex of connected sciences, to all of which it is essential, but some of which deal with it more and others less directly. Such is the relation of the biological sciences to the idea of life, carrying along with them other disciplines in which also that idea is central, such as medicine, hygiene, horticulture, and agriculture. Something of this kind, *mutatis mutandis*, is the group of philosophical sciences, though metaphysic may have a special place which there is no single science of biology to fill.

Now, if we compare the ideas either of different thinkers or of different ages of the world, can we seriously doubt that the philosophical sciences form such a group, having a common centre, of which logical or metaphysical theory is the most direct formula ? To some extent, indeed, this view is double-edged, and I readily make the concession which it implies. Ethical science (to speak of it alone) is bound up with the general notions of an age for the same reason for which I have urged that it is bound up with philosophy as the formula of those notions. And therefore it can be pursued in a way and for a time on the basis of these ruling ideas, and without direct reference to their technical form. Especially this is so, when after a period of philosophical excitement a certain store of advanced ideas has become public property. I do not doubt that in the present day a great deal of good work in ethics may practically be done on the basis of working ideas with which all cultivated men are now familiar, but which are very different from those of a former day. The very fact that this is so— that the possibility of an advance in popular ethics depends on a change in the level of common-sense, illustrates the connection which I am affirming. But a science carried on upon the basis of notions which happen to have been popularized is in a very precarious state, and the thinness of its ideas will always be tending to show itself. I may venture to observe, however, that as long as the votaries of common-sense Ethics are to be found among our most highly-trained metaphysical students, it is to be expected that they will not, in deference to a methodological distinction, allow their ethical science to perish for want of ideas.

The aloofness of pure Metaphysic, then, does not discourage me from demanding a metaphysical or, at any rate, a philosophical foundation for Ethics. I propose to exhibit what seems to me a crucial example of failure in the attempt to dispense with it by briefly examining Mr. Taylor's view of the fundamental ethical contradiction. But it follows from what I have admitted that I am not going to deny the existence of this contradiction. It is true, I have no doubt, that ethical experience is very far from a perfect experience, that it contains some kind of contradiction, and in some degree implies an infinite progression. What I am going to deny is the division of the moral life, by the alleged contradiction, into two heterogeneous halves, in such a way that morality can fairly be termed an unprincipled compromise, and the possibility of theorizing moral situations denied. For this, as I understand, the denial of a single end which can be consistently stated and applied as a principle in action, is the essence of Mr. Taylor's position. If I am wrong in this estimate of his view, my argument loses its bearing.

Readers of Mr. Taylor's work will remember that in drawing out the contradiction between self-realization and self-sacrifice he has returned to the common view, abandoning Mr. Bradley's subtler distinction. The terms of the contradiction therefore are for him, as distinguished in principle, self-realization or satisfaction of self, and social service or the service of others. I say " the service of others " in order to maintain the opposition in principle, because it is, as I understand Mr. Taylor's fundamental view, that the two terms are opposed, and opposed as " self " to " others " ; otherwise Mr. Taylor's favourite statement of the second term as " social justice " or action for the good of the community, in which, as he points out, my own good, so far as compatible with that of others, is included, would have compelled us to suppose that a common ground had been discovered on which my good could be compared and combined with the good of the rest of society. This is only one of the difficulties in which the author is involved by deserting Mr. Bradley's form of the distinction. For no one, I think, has pointed out more successfully than the author [1] the bankruptcy of sheer altruism. Nevertheless, he accepts it as an ethical principle when it is a question of establishing a fundamental contradiction between moral ends equally approved. " Neither egoism nor altruism can be made the basis of moral theory without mutilation of the facts, nor can any higher category be discovered by the aid of which their rival claims may be finally adjusted." [2]

Against the view thus stated and the consequences which the author draws from it I shall try to show :

1. What is the philosophical conception really in question and the defect incurred by neglecting it.
2. That the alleged contradiction does not split morality into two irreducible principles, but rather constitutes a risk and imperfection in it equally throughout.
3. The pessimism which the author deduces from this contradiction is false, and reveals an ethical experience blinded by defective philosophy.

1. The conception which the author rejects as untrue and useless for Ethics is, discounting misapprehensions, that of a Self-consciousness whose inmost nature is to be itself and another in one ; which again is an alternative expression for rationality and for an infinite totality (in the sense of *Ethical Studies*). The completeness of such a nature can obviously be found only in the whole of reality, as the only true self-contained whole. It follows from this that the real self of a particular self-conscious animal lies largely outside his given self, and his satisfaction consists in removing the contradictions of his given self by acquiring his real self. Thus obviously distinguishable elements are involved in his satisfaction, on the one side attainment and on the other side negation. You cannot become something you were not except by ceasing to be what you were, but in ceasing to be what you were you may become all that you were and more. (I apologize for this repetition of familiar ideas, but it seems essential to following out the connection.) I cannot see why the author's interesting views of the impersonality of the primary desire for pleasure, and of the analogy between the relation of myself to others and of my present to my future self, should not have developed

---

[1] *Problem*, pp. 194-5.    [2] *Ibid.*, p. 184.

on the lines of a real or universal self rather than on the lines of a progressive opposition between egoism and altruism.

2. My opposition to Mr. Taylor's view of the total hetero-geneity of these two parts of morality starts from his abandon-ment of Mr. Bradley's position. The radical moral antithesis for Mr. Bradley, many readers will remember, is not Egoism and Altruism, or self-development and the service of others, but rather what we might call, in terms for which he is not responsible, self-systematization and self-dissipation. In both cases, as I understand him, you are in principle realizing the self, but in the former case, we might say, you do it more directly, in the latter more indirectly. In the former case the whole which you aim at subserving is in a great measure to be completed within your direct experience, and so perceived within your private self. The implied ideal might be called self-cultivation, if we understand that it does not imply restriction to any one side of the self, such as culture in the current sense presupposes. In the latter case the whole which you propose to subserve falls, as a whole, mostly outside your private experience, and you treat yourself as instrumental to it, abandoning the hope of rounding off your private life into any kind of completeness. You " let yourself go " in obedience to some impulse which will not find its completion within your private existence. The point then is, it appears to me (Mr. Bradley is in no way or degree responsible for my inter-pretation), that what is commonly called social service, or the service of others, may quite well fall on either side of this antithesis ; and the same is true of self-culture as currently opposed to social service, that is, as covering all devotion to ends which are not personal. A man may, and often does, make a man of himself and feel his feet and his strength, first through social service, while he may, and often does, feel that half his powers are rusting when he devotes himself to what is currently called self-culture.

It is the excellence of this view, as I read it, that it alleges no ultimate disparateness between the two great aspects of morality. There is indeed a divergence in application, owing to the finiteness, which makes it always uncertain which element of our double nature will be predominant in any single act. In all our mind, then, and throughout all our actions, there will be variable elements of self-affirmation and of self-negation, according to the situations and their possibilities. When the situation involves so much contradiction that the best attempt to harmonize it still denies a great part of our existing self, we may call the act self-sacrifice ; when it admits of completeness and self-organization, the act will be called proper self-affirmation or self-assertion. But in both cases alike we are, in acting for the best, impelled by the logic of the self, that is to say, by the nature of the totality which has roots in our actual being. It can take, in our finite lives, innumerable shapes, corresponding to the variety of situations in a finite world. But all of them are attempts to realize our nature as a whole, in terms of our working theory of the situation as it stands. The logic of the self is the nature of the whole working through our given mental formation and our circumstances. The factors with which it has to deal, though exceedingly complex, are not theoretically disparate. Ethical science is so far in a position analogous to that of any natural science on the assumption of the uniformity of nature. No science, as a science—and this Mr. Taylor seems to me to forget—can deal with individual situations as such. All individual data must come from trained perception. It is futile therefore to make a mock of Ethical Science for not being able to answer questions about hypothetical situations for which no complete data are given. Engineering science would be in precisely the same plight, I take it, if asked to give directions for building a bridge without a survey of the ground or details of the service required. Only, in morality, the necessary data are in possession of one person alone. The judgment of others must be scientifically worthless. It may be objected that the fundamental conceptions of every natural science are in contradiction and that this is just what is alleged about Ethics. But I am speaking of the possibility of theorizing an ethical situation ; and in this respect the parallel with the natural sciences is good for my purpose, namely, that the metaphysical defects of their concepts do not prevent them from forming coherent theories of their data for practical purposes. And this is what the extreme view before us denies to be possible for ethics.

The Logic of the self endeavours to raise life into a whole.

If there were divergent ideals such as Egoism and Altruism, then, because of the logical bankruptcy of Altruism, there could be no meaning in affirming a simple end for morality. There could not even be a working principle possessing any clue to unity. But if negation and affirmation are inherent aspects of the whole, divergent only in finite application, and as inseparable as they are distinguishable, then making the most of human nature according to the logic of the self is a sound principle throughout life, though its realization may fall beyond morality.

The result of these considerations, if I am right, is that, in principle, self-affirmation and self-renunciation extend alike over the whole of morality. The hazard of apparent total loss accompanies moral action throughout, and that not unconsciously, but known and faced. " Why, that's certain ! 'Tis dangerous to take a cold, to sleep, to drink ; " much more to devote a life to study or to art. Suppose we have mistaken our powers, and the whole life comes to nothing. And again, there is no moral action which does not spring from a positive ideal, evoking contradictions in the self which only the effort after a fuller reality can appease. A false theory, however, may stimulate a devotion which is all but purely negative—which all but realizes the contradiction of pure altruism ; and such beliefs have been the curse of Christendom.

3. Thinking in this way, I should view very differently some matters in which Mr. Taylor seems fairly to merit the name of pessimist.

Self-realization or self-satisfaction is for Mr. Taylor a subtle form of Hedonism. This view, I think Mr. Taylor would admit, means pessimism at once. It makes us look for compensation as essential in a case of right self-sacrifice where, of course, it cannot be shown. Then right self-sacrifice, though admitted, seems sheer negation, and this is pessimism. I cannot in the least see why Mr. Taylor should take the view that self-realization is Hedonism, unless because of his acceptance of altruism, which, having, as I understand, proved it purely empty, he retains as a moral ideal. Then, to make a difference between self-realization and altruism, you must say that the former looks to get something and the latter does not ; and contrary, I should have thought, to Mr. Taylor's own excellent analysis, he assumes that if you look to get something you must be a Hedonist.

α. Thus, I cannot help thinking, he fails to explain either the actual experience of self-sacrifice, or the account which Green gives of it, following Aristotle. Green insists on the absence of compensation as the great merit of Aristotle's view, as, I suppose, it is. Mr. Taylor on the contrary enlarges on the absence of compensation, as if he thought the " self-realizers " ought to find some difficulty in it. But the matter seems almost simple, both in experience and in theory. The act is, Aristotle says, τοῦ καλοῦ ἕνεκα. That is to say, it is the recognition by you of your place in the whole which you belong to. This is what τὸ καλόν means ; the quality of unity depending on the self-assertion of the whole in the part. You have a scheme, or, taking the less intellectual mind, you have an organized habit of life, which identifies you in part with a certain ideal whole, engraved in your mind and feelings. When a supreme hazard arrives, as an incident of this total life, you cannot break off that bit of your being from the rest, and treat it on a different basis. It comes to you, as we say, all in the day's work. And such a scheme or habit is not blind or irrational (by which I mean, failing to be teleological). It embodies a theory of the situation, and discriminates circumstances in which retreat is allowable, and others in which it is not, according to the nature of the whole to be maintained and of the entire case.

One might *illustrate* the position, the relation of the life to the incident of self-sacrifice, by introducing the idea of compensation, in this way. You might say, that the whole life, right through, the consideration which the man enjoys in his own mind, and in that of others, his very feeling that he is himself and can rely on himself at all, *are* the compensation. It is a vulgar way of presenting the relation of a universal to a detail, but may serve to emphasize it. Every soldier, every workman in a dangerous trade, has, I suppose, for himself and for others, a certain position and consideration, owing to the severity of the chances which he may be any day, or is every day, called upon to take. It could make no difference to an honest man that he had had his compensation beforehand. But this, as I say, is only an illustration.

The essence of the matter is, as it seems to me, that utter self-sacrifice is only an intensification, to which finite beings are liable in the chances of life, of an element which in principle attends all moral action.[1]   It would be interesting to apply and defend this principle in some typical extreme cases ; but space forbids, and I really think experience is quite decisive on the point.

β. The unity of the moral end is curiously illustrated by Mr. Taylor's treatment of the scholar's life.   He puts the contradiction together for us in his own words ; [2] " it seems hardly possible to deny that the scholar's life, which we thought at first a typical example of satisfaction found in the consistent following of a principle of self-development, is full of internal anarchy and dissension."   The ideal case of self-culture turns out to be nearly the ideal case of self-sacrifice, which on our theory seems natural enough.   And we may cap this for ourselves by the case of social service ; for there can be little doubt that this, which we were given as the ideal case of self-sacrifice, indeed, as constituting the altruistic side of the antithesis, is pretty constantly the ideal case both of self-culture (in the best sense—the cultivation of strength, breadth, and character) and of self-satisfaction.   Now it would not be fair, I submit, to charge me with unveracious optimism, and with the assertion that self-sacrifice always pays, and therefore does not exist.   What I am saying is that it is not one dissociated half of the moral life, but extends throughout it as an essential principle.   And as a proof of this I show that, on a scrutiny, the cases which were offered as the extremes of the opposing types show a decided tendency to change places. If I said that they really do change places, that would be an exaggeration, and would put me back into the very contradiction which I am criticizing.   What I say is that there are no such places, exclusive of one another, to change.   There is not one place of self-sacrifice and another of self-culture. There is a whole to realize, which has, for us, many kindred forms, and all of them involve some self-negation, and, owing to our finiteness, may come to us as hard and hazardous.

In all the different kinds of lives which are apt to be taken as types of conflicting moral ideals, self-affirmation and self-

[1] *Problem*, p. 423.          [2] *Ibid*, p. 259.

renunciation play in principle precisely the same part. In every case there is an immediate self to educate and to subdue ; and it is impossible to say, as a matter of principle, that more of this self is negated in one case than in another. It is enough, for general theory, that part is always negated.

Therefore, if I am right, the heterogeneousness of the ideals in principle falls to the ground, and with it the irrationality of ethics, and the impossibility of theorizing ethical situations. Institutions, which provisionally guide us, are in the position of theories framed by long experience, partly by foresight. partly by trial and error, and dealing with immense masses of varied fact, which they embody and harmonize. And if it is said that to accept institutions because we are born into them is an abdication of reason and a mere compromise, I would ask how the scientific furniture of our minds is acquired. To be born into the mind of our day, and readjust it a little, is all that we can do alike in pure thinking and in moral action.

As a minor case,[1] but a very important one, of false conflict between egoism and altruism, I may refer to " philanthropic expenditure." This presents itself to the author, as to most people, in the light of a minus quantity in income, decreasing the resources of self-culture to some extent, the only question being, how far ? And this question, according to the view before us, there is no rational way of determining, so we fly to social custom. There could hardly be a more instructive instance. It is the problem in a nutshell. Such expenditure, *ex hypothesi*, is not on an object which grows out of the general spirit of a man's life, and takes equal rank as a part of what his heart is set upon. If it were so, the expenditure would settle itself according to the relation between its object, as linked with the man's whole aim in life, and the other interests of which his life is made up. I do not say the problem is easy, nor that it cannot involve self-sacrifice. I only say that the interest to be satisfied is a positive interest, *in pari materia* with the other interests of life, and instrumental to a good which belongs to the same web with them. And if it is not so felt and understood, the philanthropic expenditure is a loss to recipient and to donor alike, and a poison to the community through the separation of resources

[1] *Problem*, p. 200.

from ideas. If otherwise, it is not a minus quantity; the object, not being disparate with the general object of life, can be treated theoretically as a case of that object, and assigned its place in the whole. The forwarding of human nature is the same work in kind whatever may be the particular aspect of the universal in favour of which we have to deny our immediate selves. And the question what in particular is to be done turns, as a rule, frankly on the problem what, given ourselves and the situation, can be done. I see no reason for being afraid of questions about our personal gifts and likings, so far as they mean our special capacities. They seem to me almost the main element in practical ethics; and this seems to solve the question of differential treatment of others, which the author finds more difficult than I can see ground for. When we look into it, we see that we help the nearest first, because that is what we can do best. If any one thinks he can go out into the wide world and do good to the first comer, let him try it and see.

The unity of the real self seems to help us with the truly pessimistic circle of the irrationality ineradicable from the life of social service.[1] Satisfactions do not make you happy, and yet the best you can do is to try and get the same—generally rather less of them—for others. Surely this is atomism in theory, and error in practice. If you consider the life of a community as a number of individual lives, each possessing the satisfactions of its immediate self, you have cut the roots of life. This I take to be the point of the beginning of *Republic*, iv, which the author thinks inconclusive. It follows from the view—in essence, I believe, that of Green—which I have been urging, that—

α. Everyone has a nature, whether he knows it or not, in which real happiness would lie for him, except in unusual chances, if it could be awakened.

β. This nature being common to all, everyone who is in contradiction with it contradicts it in everyone else as well as in himself.

γ. Thus every unit *really* made better off not only comes nearer to a satisfactory life himself, but removes contradictions in the lives of all others, including the social reformer.

[1] *Problem*, p. 266.

Thus it is not a question of merely adding a number of persons with certain comforts, more or less discontented, to an existing number of such persons, the good done being measured by the doubtful advantage conferred on the number of units added to the quasi-comfortable total ; it is a question of removing obstructions to a satisfactory life, the problem being of such a nature that an obstruction removed, or a life awakened, in any unit, affects in principle the life of all other units for the better, bringing all nearer to the life which they are bound to lead. It may also happen that not the essential improvement, but some incident of the improvement of one life may tell hardly on another. This is a possibility which Mr. Taylor insists on at length. The first thing to remember is that granting the fact, it is another effect over and above the tendency to better the whole which lies in the bettering of one, which so far always exists. Then, further, even in economic problems, the main rule is the other way. Pessimism here tends to fall into the fallacy of the work-fund. Even displacement by machinery, the author's one really formidable point, loses its terrors if frankly faced, as we face and provide against other risks of life.

It is necessary to break off. I will only observe, in conclusion, that metaphysical theory seems to demand a general convergence of the aspects of the ethical end as well as a divergence in occasional application. It is no objection to this that the point of complete fusion may fall beyond the sphere of ethics. If we consider the account of morality on the side of its true infinity which was given us in *Ethical Studies* we shall not be at a loss to look for the beginnings, within the moral sphere, of the process which is completed beyond it.[1]

[1] *A. and R.*, ed. 2, p. 426.

## XI

## HEDONISM AMONG IDEALISTS

It is interesting to observe that Hedonism appears to be making way among Idealists. There are reasons for this in the modifications which criticism has brought to the views of both the extreme parties to the anti-Hedonist controversy. Psychological Hedonism, more especially, seems to be dead, and its disappearance has brought the disputants nearer together. A certain air of *odium theologicum* has faded from the argument. It is probable that the influence of Sidgwick's views, co-operating with the deeper analysis of recent psychology, has had much to do with bringing about the present position.

Even those who, like myself, are still definitely anti-Hedonistic, must welcome this state of things. It affords some hope that we may attain, as R. L. Nettleship desired,[1] to a genuine appreciation and comparison of the experiences to which we give the name of pleasure, and may learn exactly where the difficulty lies which causes their nature and value to be so divergently estimated.

I have been greatly interested both by Mr. Taylor's and by Mr. Rashdall's treatment of the subject. But on the present occasion I wish to consider Mr. McTaggart's chapter " On the Supreme Good and the Moral Criterion " in his brilliant book, *Studies in Hegelian Cosmology* (Cambridge, 1901). This, however its main thesis may stand the criticism of years to come, is for the present a leading document of modern Idealism. Now in such a work, a quarter of a century ago, we should as soon have expected to find a defence of materialism as an advocacy of Hedonism. Mr. McTaggart's view has therefore, for those who learnt, say, from Green, the interest of a paradox,

[1] *Remains*, 1, 7.

while, as I have indicated, it unquestionably belongs to a tendency of the Idealism of to-day.

I should feel very uneasy in differing from the argument of the chapter in question if I believed that by doing so I finally severed myself from the author's position as a whole. But this does not seem to be a necessary consequence. The author's idea of the Hedonic criterion does not depend so much on his doctrine of the nature of reality and the supreme good, as on his view of the means by which approximations to either can be ascertained. And a difference of opinion here would not, I think, be fatal to agreement there.

My object in this paper is twofold : (1) To argue that the use of pleasure as a criterion, advocated by the author, necessarily passes into another criterion of a different kind ; and (2) to explain and defend this other criterion in a way which I believe would harmonize with Green's ideas, but which I do not profess to find definitely stated in his works.

(1) I need not explain to the reader of *Mind* Mr. McTaggart's theory of Reality. It is enough to say that in this reality, not because it is real, but because it includes the perfection of the nature of individual selves, Mr. McTaggart is prepared to find the Supreme Good. For him, therefore, the Supreme Good contains pleasure, for it contains the satisfaction of conscious beings ; but it is not purely and merely Hedonistic.

But, the author contends, the Supreme Good may be one thing, and the criterion of morality may be another. And the criterion, he urges, must be Hedonic so far as a criterion can be operative at all. His chapter aims at establishing this point.

That there must be a criterion of morality, as the following section (100) argues, may be admitted. Moral judgments claim to be objective, and therefore imply a standard by which, at least in theory, their claims are capable of being tested.

But in the conception of the criterion as indicated in the sections 100–102, preliminary to the main argument, we must note certain points.

i. The criterion, it is said, may be other than the Supreme Good itself. The Supreme Good, indeed, we shall find it argued, is so abstract in our knowledge, and in its abstract completeness so remote from our world of matter and of choice, that it cannot form a practical criterion to be applied by comparison with our actions. But (*a*) an extraneous criterion is of very doubtful value, and in fact may almost be said to constitute a danger, in all complex affairs of conduct and science. It is all very well where an arbitrary sign is annexed by convention to ready-made alternatives; but a criterion other than the essence is just a concomitant circumstance; and to attend to concomitant circumstances instead of the essence, where the alternatives have to be constructed out of a continuous mass of experience, is a pretty sure road to fallacy. Ideas become fruitful, say in law or politics or science, just in proportion to the precision with which essentials as opposed to concomitants are retained before the mind.[1] Moral action is a very strong case of this principle. It is a very serious matter, indeed, for the mind to be preoccupied throughout its practical deliberations with ideas which are not of the essence of what it really aims to achieve. It seems likely that such considerations must obtain a weight in the moral disposition to which their nature gives them no real claim.

(*b*) We should note the admission that to some extent we can see what conduct embodies the Supreme Good least imperfectly (sect. 102.) It the later argument (sect. 105) this is, I think, hardly admitted to the same extent. And it might be asked in general how we can judge the fitness of our criterion if the lower degrees of perfection which it is to indicate are in themselves unknowable. But I suppose the answer would be that we presume its appropriateness on abstract grounds (sect. 125.)

ii. It is important to bear in mind that any criterion must be individual in application, though the ultimate principle which it involves may be capable of being stated in the abstract. Thus when it is said, " Every moral judgment claims to be objective and demands assent from all men "—" if A asserts that to be right which B asserts to be wrong, one of them must be in error," these are merely the ideal logical postulates which apply to all science or rational

[1] Green, *Prolegomena*, sect. 308.

judgment as such. They do not mean, and must not be taken to imply, either that right and wrong, in any one's conduct, can, in fact, be readily judged by outsiders, or that right and wrong can be in detail the same for A and B, as long as A is a different person from B or in a different position. The application of a criterion to actual moral conduct must always be of the same nature as the application of scientific principles to the solution of a highly individualized problem. Such a solution is " universal," because it brings to bear the spirit and conduct of a highly organized system upon a single point ; but it is not " general " in the current sense of the word. The criterion, therefore, as applied, must be a concrete system, according to which solutions are framed to satisfy complex individual groups of conditions.[1] This the author presupposes in explaining his Hedonic criterion : but appears to me to forget, in discussing the criterion of perfection.

iii. That which can be measured by the criterion can only, it is urged, be likeness to the supreme good and not tendency to hasten or to hinder its advent. The view of section 135, that nothing we can do can hinder (or, I suppose, hasten) the advance of the supreme good, seems to me to supersede this argument, and to be truer. But the interest of the present contention centres on the view advanced in support of it (sect. 102), that a morally good action need not give rise to good, nor an evil one to evil. This is opposed to a well-known passage in Green ;[2] and I believe Green to be right. If, in the temporal succession of events, every characteristic of an action has its necessary sequel—and this surely is inevitable—then the character of good, that in virtue of which it is able, *pro tanto*, to satisfy desire, cannot fail to have a relevant consequence, in whatever shape. It is quite true that such a " good " may provoke evil, or from a higher point of view may itself *be* evil. But this consequence or character will not annihilate the goodness or satisfactoriness contained in the action, to which the nature of the evil which it is or provokes must always be relative. The conduct of a high-minded reformer and of a selfish demagogue may each of them lead to public disorder, which may call for repression and end in reaction. But the

[1] Green, *Prolegomena*, sect. 377-9.　　[2] *Ibid.*, sect. 295.

elements at work in the sequence will, so far as the reformer at all achieves his purpose (and if not, his relative good will not be attained), be different in the two cases ; in the one the evil produced will be of a higher type, farther on—so to speak—in the dialectic succession, and the relative solution arrived at will comprehend larger elements. In short, the necessity of evil is only tenable because evil has a common root and nature with good—is, as it were, good in the wrong place, as dirt is matter in the wrong place. It is possible, therefore, that good can enter into evil, just as evil can enter into good ; and the principle that evil must come, and must come of good, is no obstacle to the view that the good of a good action is always preserved.

I am not saying that we can help or hinder the advent of the supreme good, because I do not know that we can act otherwise than we do. But I think it clear that in as far as any one acts well, there are fewer stages to be traversed before the advent of the supreme good, than if he acted ill.

I have so far argued against the author (a) that in morality it is a grave defect for the criterion to be extraneous ; (b) that it can only be applied through a systematic individualized construction ; (c) that achieved good remains, even if it passes through the form of evil, and therefore if we see our way to what has the character of good, we need not be sceptical as to further tendencies, except on positive grounds which we must estimate in judging it good.

We may now approach the discussion on the two proposed criteria, Perfection and Pleasure, so far departing from the author's treatment as to take Pleasure first (points 2 and 3 of sect. 102), because I hope that the criticism developed in discussing these will be of use to us later on, in dealing with point 1, the alleged uselessness of perfection as a criterion.

I. Point 2, then, is thus stated (sect. 102), " that the Hedonic computation of pleasures and pains does give us a definite criterion, right or wrong." We should note that Psychological Hedonism being dropped, the Pleasure of All, of course, is the proposed criterion. The discussion of it begins with section 111.

(a) We shall readily admit to the author in general that "we know what a pleasure is, and what a pain is, and we can distinguish a greater pleasure or pain from a lesser one."

There are, however, states of consciousness, as he points out, about which we can hardly be sure whether they are pleasures or pains, and many cases in which it is hard to decide which of two pleasures or pains is greater. But, he argues, a difference of which we cannot be sure must be less than any appreciable difference, and a possibility of mistake thus limited can only concern a very small amount of pleasure. The uncertainty thus arising, it is implied, does not show that the criterion by calculation of pleasures fails to give a fairly precise decision. This contention, I think, must be admitted ; as here we are not raising the question whether the criterion is right or wrong, but only whether it gives an answer at all. In speaking of its correctness we shall have to recur to this point.

(b) Next comes the objection based on pleasure being an abstraction. It is urged, the author says, that for this reason "pleasure" is an impossible criterion, being something, in fact, which nobody experiences. The objection, thus stated, is prima facie readily disposed of, by help of the analogy of the exchange values of heterogeneous commodities. As regards the present question, whether pleasure gives a criterion that can be used, this is decisive so far as the mere fact of abstraction goes. But it does not show that a quantitative unit can, in fact, be applied to abstract pleasure—a point which will occupy us directly.

I am accustomed to regard this objection from the abstractness of pleasure as holding more especially against its correctness as a criterion. With a view to that issue I will here merely note that the author's defence inevitably implies that all equal amounts of abstract pleasure, including equal algebraical sums of pleasure and pain, are ethically interchangeable. This is subject of course to his final reservation on the limits of applicability of the criterion.

(c) I will follow Mr. McTaggart in discussing at this point (sect. 114) the objection that pleasures vanish in the act of enjoyment so that a sum of them cannot really be possessed, though this, as he points out, is an objection against pleasures forming the supreme good rather than against the Hedonic criterion.

The author's reply is in effect that while we live in time any good whatever can only manifest itself in a series of states of consciousness. If we say that the states in which perfection or the good will are manifested have the common element of their characteristics running through them and uniting them, he answers that pleasure states have the common element of pleasure. If we urge again that pleasure is an abstraction and so knits the successive states but slightly together, it is replied that every pure identity running through a differentiated whole is to some extent an abstraction, by abstracting from the differentiation. Perfection or the good will, therefore, if conceived as timeless elements of a consciousness existing in time, are just as much abstract as pleasure under the same conditions; while if a timeless consciousness could come into being, a feeling such as pleasure would be as fit, or fitter, to enter into it, than a state of cognition or volition.

Here I am strongly convinced that the anti-Hedonist does not get substantial justice from Mr. McTaggart. His analysis seems to let slip the peculiar nature of the experience in question. To begin with, I am for once not satisfied that the logical point is rightly stated. An identity which is sustained by the co-operation of differentiated parts is surely on a different logical footing from an identity which lies in a general quality, common to two contents, or persisting in a single content. The former is such as the power of a machine to do certain work, the latter is such as the colour it is painted. It is true that each can be stated in a single phrase, and thought of, up to a certain point, in isolation from the machine as a whole. But the former cannot be truly thought of in this way, that is, if so thought of, it cannot be understood; while the latter loses little if anything by being thought of in isolation. Identities of the former type I should naturally call concrete, and only those of the latter type abstract. It may be only my King Charles's head, but I almost suspect that a tacit confusion between identity and similarity is here playing us a trick. A true concrete identity is based on differentiation, and is curtailed by abstraction, *qua* identity, in the same ratio in which the differentiation itself is so curtailed.

Now a consciousness, even a consciousness in time in so far as it realizes a degree of perfection or of the good will, is an identity of the former type. A consciousness of which we only know that it realizes successive states of pleasure, need only contain an identity of the latter type. The former is held together by a unity touched only at its margin by succession. Its edges are washed by time, but its own elements are not in succession to one another. The latter, for all we know, may be a succession having in common almost no assignable element of unity at all. We really can say hardly anything as to the minimum conditions involved in a succession of pleasant states. But we can say, I think, that taken at any two points of the succession it need exhibit no tendency whatever to grow towards totality. The old criticism remains therefore unassailable, that the hundredth pleasant state need find us in possession of no more pleasure than the first. With perfection or the good will this is not so. The accidents of life may frustrate their development ; but in so far as they display their nature— and this is surely the case we ought in fairness to consider —they involve a certain structure of the mind and character of a logical type which necessitates an appreciable achievement of harmonious structure, and a progress in the same direction.

It may be urged that succession in time is a false appearance, and that in the reality the vanished states of pleasure cannot be lost, but must be gathered up as parts of the timeless whole.

But granting this reply to be just, it comes equally to the aid of the good will in respect of the successiveness which attaches to its realization in time. Only, whereas in the case of pleasant states the character of totality may hardly have begun to show itself, in the case of a realized perfection it already to some extent is achieved. In the former there is a new character to be created, in the latter only a defect to be removed. I feel sure that to call perfection and good will " just as much abstract " as pleasure, is an overstatement. I judge that in the general line of this argument I should have Mr. Taylor's assent.

No doubt the difference between Mr. McTaggart and myself as to the reality of the sum of pleasures is accented by our disagreement as to the Hedonic criterion. Pleasure indicates satisfaction much less closely and less correctly for me than for him.

(*d*) The next question to be raised is whether Pleasures and Pains can not only be compared in magnitude, singly each to each, but can be compared in sums themselves obtained by addition or subtraction. So far as the discussion hinges on the theory of intensive quantities I will defer it to the point at which the author deals directly with this subject (sect. 122).

Before coming to this, however, we have to meet an argument based on introspection (sects. 116–17), which urges that in everyday non-moral action, and also even in non-Hedonist morality, we do as a fact continually decide questions which involve the comparison of pleasure-totals formed by addition and subtraction. The appeal to introspection is particularly interesting, as I implied at starting, in the present situation of the Hedonist controversy. If it is conducted with care and frankness it ought to lead us far towards ascertaining the reason of our differences. I find the verdict of introspection on cases of the kind adduced to be not quite simple, and I believe there is risk of misinterpretation. The examples offered by the author are such as a choice between two dinners of equal cost and wholesomeness—must we not and do we not here add together the expected pleasures within each alternative, and come to a decision by comparison of the sum-totals? Or in choosing between means, themselves morally indifferent, to a given moral end, or in trying to give pleasures as such to others—a duty, the author urges, on any moral theory—or in weighing the importance of an intense feeling against that of a number of weaker feelings in the same person or in others; in all these cases, it is urged, we do actually come to a decision; and either we must arrive at it by addition of pains and pleasures, or we must admit that we are working in the dark.

The verdict of introspection in these cases seems to me, as I said, not quite simple. On looking into the author's account, we note that he appeals to introspection mainly for

 he fact that such cases exist, and that we feel ourselves able
ɔ decide them, and that we should not admit our decision to
e merely capricious. That, in deciding them, we compare
ɔtals of pleasure and pain, is not so much accepted from
ɪtrospection as argued from the impossibility of any other
lternative in face of the admissions of introspection.

Perhaps we might try to carry the matter a little further
ɪ the province of introspection, and see what result we can
et. There are well-known cases in which we seem to come
s near as we ever can to the attempt to balance totals of
greeables and disagreeables against each other on their own
ɪerits. I am thinking especially of the deliberations in which
ve make plans for a holiday tour, when we have to choose a
ɔute of travel with longer or shorter sea passage, to decide
·hether to take tickets for train *de luxe* or first or second
lass, whether and when to break the journey, and so on.

Now obviously we do go over in our minds the *pros* and
ɔns of plans consisting of such combinations as these, and
·e try, in some way or other, to balance the several plans
gainst each other with regard to their respective agreeables
r disagreeables. Probably experiences will differ as to how
ɪr we can make up anything like a sum-total of pleasantness
ɪ favour of each plan. I should be inclined to say that we
ɔ not succeed in getting anything like a single resultant of
leasantness or unpleasantness for each alternative plan, but
ɔntinue to think over the attractive and unattractive ele-
ɪents of each as so many distinct features of it. No doubt
·e arrive at being aware that one plan has more disagreeables
ttaching to it than another, and we form an impression
·hether another plan has any grave inconveniences which
utweigh this number of nuisances. But, so far as my
xperience goes, I do not believe that one arrives at a con-
ideration of each plan, including all its attractions and the
everse, as a homogeneous amount, in which the items are
ɪerged.[1] We keep recurring, rather, to the actual content
f each plan, and consider how far it corresponds to what
·e want ; that is to say, how far its details do or do not

[1] This is surely the true test whether or no we have got a quantitative
·tal. In a true " sum " the peculiarities of the ɪtems are lost. 200 lb. is
ɔo lb. whether you are weighing children or coal. If the nature of the items
ffects your choice, your choice is not based on quantity.

satisfy the conditions failing which we should pronounce ou
holiday " spoilt." This comparison then is hardly a tru
quantitative comparison. It passes from enumeration witl
very rough feelings of magnitude into something more lik
estimating the degree in which, say, a number of architects
designs meet the requirements in view of which they hav
been framed. " The degree," it may be replied ; " then you
comparison is quantitative after all." This example I thin!
extremely significant. Suppose there is a competition o
designs, and you give marks for the degrees in which re
quirements are fulfilled ; or, indeed, we may take the cas
of any examination in which marks are given. This is a
rough way of symbolizing the relation of performances t
requirements ; but it is not the result of a calculation, o
true handling of quantities, except in so far as requirement
are subdivided, separate marks assigned for conformity t
each, and subsequently added together. But we know tha
the more this is done, the less reliable the result becomes
and a highly skilled assessor or examiner, if compelled to us
marks instead of reporting in detail, is inclined, I suspect, t
make sure of his totals first, and subdivide them afterwards
i.e. to " cook " his marks for details. And the reason is tha
in each case you are translating the fulfilment of concret
conditions into the bare form of quantity, and the more th
arithmetical element enters in the more is the bareness o
this form perceptible. If I prefer this design very greatly t
that, I may simply give the one 200 marks and the other 100
but it would have made no serious difference if I had saic
instead, 180 and 100 respectively. I convey, roughly, th
fact that I think the one a good  deal better than the othe
But if I take 200 as full marks and try to divide the require
ments to be satisfied into ten heads with twenty marks eack
and assign marks on this hypothesis, and sum them int
totals, I shall probably find my total fail to express, eve:
roughly, my true preferences, unless I have as above sug
gested adjusted the subtotals to the total required. And th
reason is that the process is not a result based throughout o
the handling of quantities  The relation of each characte
in the design to a requirement, and of each requiremen
to the whole, is concrete and individual, and needs to b

represented in the intelligent language of a detailed report ; these relations are not quantities ; and the reduction or rough translation of the mere fact of preference into quantity, as a *memoria technica* for comparison *ad hoc*, has an accidental element. In a single preference this matters little, because re-translation is easy ; but in the arithmetical handling of a number of preferences it tends to monstrous errors. Or a simpler case may put the point clearly enough. Let the question be which of two pocket-knives, or guns, or microscopes, will suit me best. Of course in preferring one to the other I make a comparison which, *qua* comparison, has a quantitative side. But to try to reduce it to the bare form of quantity by, say, giving marks to the competing objects for their different qualities, would be darkening counsel. I have the requirements and the performances directly before me, and can estimate in the concrete how far the one is adequate to the other. To substitute an arithmetical process for this comparison would be a loss by abstraction, even if it were possible. The true typical case, under which all these choices should be ranged, is, I suggest, the comparison of theories with reference to their truth, that is, with reference to their comparative adequacy in view of a given scientific situation.

With reference, then, to complex totals of pleasantness, I am not maintaining that introspection wholly denies the possibility of comparing them. I am rather arguing that it gives the limit of the process, in the consciousness of a number of elements, which we do enumerate and more or less attempt to weigh against each other, And I urge that in the attempt to push this process further it inevitably passes into another, of which the ultimate type is found in weighing theories with reference to their adequacy.

And Introspection seems to convince me of a further point, which may be due to my prejudices, but prima facie is a datum deserving to be considered.

I am pretty sure that the ordinary mind does not like these attempts at complex comparison of sheer agreeables and disagreeables. We enter upon them only when considerations of interest and efficiency fail us. We find them most troublesome and unsatisfactory, opinions, even within one's own mind, varying about them in a remarkable way.

N

It may seem to contradict this statement when I agree that such a choice as that between the two dinners (though I cannot remember—and here others agree with me—ever to have made a choice that fulfils the supposed conditions) might be readily made. I believe the reason of this to be, however, that one would be guided by the first liking, or more probably, disliking, that came to hand. We should be uneasy to find ourselves reflecting in cold blood on such a subject, and we have, rightly as I think, been trained to make choice in matters of that kind without displaying deliberation. I think therefore that even this experience really supports the opinion that the whole business of calculation, as applied to pleasantness, seems to us a *pis aller*, an undesirable preoccupation of the mind, which we only submit to when we can think of nothing better.

When we come to anything so serious and demanding so much precision as weighing something important to oneself against something affecting a number of others, but probably much less important to each of them, I feel sure that we do not proceed by balancing a single intense feeling against a sum or indeed a product of weaker feelings. To multiply a weaker feeling by twenty or thirty, not to say a thousand or a million, and set the product against a single intense feeling, is, I am sure, something which we cannot even attempt, though the questions in which the use of a Hedonic criterion would require it to be done are of everyday occurrence. Our decisions in cases of this kind must rest, I think on the acceptance of some hierarchy among the activities of life, and an opinion as to which of them will be most hindered by our conduct under the circumstances.

It is to be borne in mind that taking perfection as our criterion we are not barred from recognizing pleasure as an evidence, when no better can be obtained, of certain elements in it, because we are working with a comprehensive idea of satisfaction ; while adopting a Hedonic criterion, on the very ground that it can be applied with precision while degrees of perfection are unknowable, we are barred from supplementing it by any other tests of satisfaction.

Indeed, one cannot help feeling that in some respects the Hedonic criterion brings us back to the standpoint of

Psychological Hedonism. It is much, no doubt, to have broken
the circle of Egoism. But still, though the abandonment
of Psychological Hedonism involves the position that our
main desires are for objects which satisfy, and not for
pleasures, the Hedonic criterion debars us from using directly
the character of satisfactory objects as such for a test of
what is likely to satisfy. I shall return to this point in
dealing with the correctness of the Hedonic criterion.

One word on the argument (sect. 117) that morality itself
requires us to choose, *ceteris paribus*, pleasure rather than
pain and to aim at giving pleasure to others—a requirement
which cannot be fulfilled without calculation of pleasures
and pains. I reply in substance by pointing to the results
which we drew above from the comparison of pleasure, as
a measurable aspect of action, to the exchange value of commodities. In strictness it followed that all equal amounts of
pleasure, however compounded, were ethically interchangeable.

I do not believe that the moral consciousness endorses the
alleged moral requirement, as it would have to be construed
in face of this strict interpretation of amount of pleasure.
We never, I believe, feel ourselves bound to compare abstract
amounts of pleasure either in our own behalf or in that of
others. We never, that is to say, try to compare them
impartially, going out of our way to look for the greatest
possible quantity. We do feel bound to promote the life
and satisfaction of ourselves and others ; but such promotion
always involves a reference, even if tacit, to definite lines of
living and enjoyment, presupposed in our general standard
of life. It may be objected that this is bringing in the
reference to welfare or perfection, which was *ex hypothesi*
to be excluded. It amounts, we may be told, to denying
that the *cetera* ever can be *paria*—that morality can be indifferent as between two ways of enjoying ourselves. What
I desire to urge on the other hand amounts to this, that life
after all is a unity ; and the very fact that two modes of
enjoyment seem to me ethically indistinguishable, and also
that I want one of them more than the other, is a fact, not
strictly indeed of my morality, but of the determinate structure of my being.

Now I deny that I feel bound to consider, as in strictness I should according to the theory before us, which of these, or whether any other course, will bring the greatest pleasure as such. I do what I want most, or what attracts me most, and, morality not forbidding, help others to do the same for themselves. Of course, Psychological Hedonism being dropped, it cannot be assumed that this *means* acting with a view to the greatest pleasure of myself or others. The question before us is, which way of looking at the matter is usually acquiesced in; as an argument to show which the moral consciousness demands. What I urge is, that we accept our wants as being along certain lines, grounded in the positive unity of our nature, even when outside morality. There is no impartial scrutiny of experience, to find where the greatest pleasures can be had, except *de minimis*, when we feel that we are out of touch with the true test, which is, simply, what we *really* want.

(e) In sections 122–3 we come to the direct argument against an objection to the effect that pleasures, being intensive quantities, cannot be added and subtracted. The way in which this is met seems to me unsatisfactory.

The form of the objection is taken as an admission that pleasures being intensive quantities are quantities. From this the characteristics of quantity in the fullest sense are inferred of them, e.g. that they can be brought into numerical relation with other quantities of the same kind; and that you can affirm the pleasure in A to = the pleasures in B and C together. Thus it seems to follow that the difficulty which is practically found in equating them is merely analogous to the liability to error attaching to all quantitative judgment whatever. And so there comes out the result that pleasure is as good a quantity as feet and inches, only rather harder to judge of in practice.

But this seems to me to presuppose the point at issue. It is clear that pleasure, so far as quantitative, is intensive, but the question is how far it is quantitative. Intensity, it may be agreed, involves the idea of a more or less of the same; but there are plenty of perceptions of more or less for which no measurement by a constant unit, and therefore no true quantity, has been or apparently can be established.[1] It is a matter of words whether we call such perceptions quantitative. But it seems clear that if they are quantitative it is in a sense which does not involve numerical relations. To judge that $A = B + C$, is beyond the mere perception of more and less, which involves neither a judgment of equality, nor an analysis of one term into two definite quantities. But it is short of numerical comparison, which surely must be taken to demand a total of units on one side of the equation at least.

Thus I do not find the difficulty where the author finds it. I do not see that "intensive" is a ground of objection, if "quantity" could be proved applicable. But to refute an objection based on "intensive" is, to my mind, in no way to establish the proof of "quantity." That must be independently sustained. The possibility of establishing anything like a true unit for amounts of pleasures and pains, even supposing the two could form part of the same quantitative series, is a psychological problem which I do not feel competent to discuss. It would seem necessary first to show not merely that all pleasure and pain is homogeneous *qua* pleasure and pain, i.e. distinct from other elements of feeling and content (which was admitted provisionally on sect. 112), but that it is capable in itself of being represented by degrees of a single series, i.e. has only one dimension,[2] so to speak. And then it would be necessary to show that the degrees of this series were true units, such that a number of them might be taken as a true multiple of one. Considering, e.g., the peculiarities of the sensation differences dealt with in Weber's law, it would seem as if great difficulty might be met with here. Though pleasure may be homogeneous, its stimuli are heterogeneous; and any attempt at measurement would here lack the support which the precise variation of the stimulus affords to experiment with the specific sensations. The economic analogue of Weber's law seems subject to extensive reservations.

(*f*) There is a further point, affecting the workableness

---

[1] I should say that the intensive and extensive aspects are both of them necessary to quantity in the strict sense. But without raising this difficulty, it seems plain that numerical comparison cannot be had without the establishment of a constant unit.

[2] Mr. Taylor has pressed this point upon me in conversation.

of pleasure-pain reckoning, to which my previous remarks on the tendency to convert it into another method may have served as a preface. I may call it the relativity of pleasure.

If Hedonic calculation is to be true calculation it must start from definite magnitudes, which must be traceable, through purely quantitative processes, down to the results obtained. If, in the deliberation which is to be represented as calculation, an object becomes more attractive, it must have been shown to carry with it a new pleasure which has had to be added to its original pleasurableness. If it becomes less attractive, it must have been proved to carry with it a pain which has had to be subtracted from its original pleasurableness. Its original pleasurableness, in short, is a magnitude which can only be modified by addition or subtraction. Even if outweighed by greater pleasure incompatible with it, the original pleasurableness should still remain as a weight in the lighter scale. The magnitudes should be constant for the whole stretch of life to which a single deliberation applies ; or at the very least throughout a single deliberation.

But in fact, as it seems to me, the magnitudes of pleasures and pains are reacted upon by the combinations conceived in deliberation, or met with in life, in a way wholly incompatible with that just described. A pleasure which seems strong at first, simply fades away in the light thrown upon it by a certain combination of objects of action. It need not be cancelled by associated pains, nor overbalanced in the scales by greater incompatible pleasures. For that ought to mean that it continues *per se* to be as pleasant as before, but is shown, owing to circumstances, to bring with it a pain not before observed to attach to it, or to be outweighed by incompatible pleasures not previously noticed to be possible at all, or to be incompatible with it. Its original magnitude should subsist, like that of a pound weight in the scales, whatever you add to its side or the other. Or even if you say that you subtract from it by cancelling part or the whole of its magnitude, by reason of combination with a negative quantity, as you may withdraw a pint of water from a quart, still its original magnitude should subsist ideally, and be traceable by arithmetical laws in the result of the deliberation.

But what happens in every deliberation upon serious matters is not in the least like this. The prima facie magnitudes of pleasures and pains change their amount or their sign with the combinations in which they are considered, because of the way in which those combinations alter the direction of our interests and our wants. Interest, satisfaction, expected pleasure, are not constant magnitudes attaching to particular acts or objects, but are determined by the whole fabric of purposes and satisfactions which life presents before us from moment to moment. Now it is the essence of deliberation to change this presentation by readjusting the emphasis of its outlines, completing some and obscuring others. In this process some things which fell prima facie in a main line of interest are shown not really to be so. Other things, not attended to at first, take the place of the former and promise a satisfaction which they cease to offer. A man is reading an ordinary novel with enjoyment. A newspaper comes in with exciting intelligence ; perhaps with the continuation of a controversy in which he is profoundly interested. He does not subtract the enjoyment of going on with his novel from the great enjoyment of reading and discussing his newspaper, and turn to the second in virtue of the surplus of pleasure to be gained by doing so. The momentary adjustment of his interests is modified. The novel, for the time, has ceased to please. Our interest, as we say, is called away. This is not an effect of relations of magnitude. It is an effect of the peculiar bearings of the various objects of life upon one another, according to the shape which our plan of satisfaction is able to adopt at the moment. Relations of magnitude, as we said before with reference to the assignment of marks, are the effect, but not the cause. It is as if one thing were not merely outweighed by another, but lost its weight in a certain comparison, or as a colour which is pleasant in one combination becomes painful in another. The new fact is not, or at least need not be, pain of discord less pleasure of colour, leaving overplus of pain of discord. The colour is now differently seen, and now seen as painful throughout. And deliberation just means readjusting the combinations in which things are seen. The object itself is altered. There is not a persistent Hedonic effect which is overbalanced.

It might be objected that these consequences cannot be lawless or irrational, and that if we knew the actual nature of the interests concerned we could, theoretically, deduce or derive their bearing on each other's Hedonic effects from their nature, and this would be the required Hedonic calculation. But my point is, that the laws of the combination, though certainly not irrational, are yet not arithmetical. They are the laws of the logic of desire, by which its objects include, modify, reinforce or supplant each other ; and they deal in every case with the growth of an individual concrete whole, perpetually modifying itself. Deliberation which consists in a phase of the life of such a whole differs in principle from the type of calculation.

In answer to these remarks Mr. McTaggart would perhaps refer me to that part of his argument (sect. 132) in which he maintains that Hedonic calculation is not always a correct guide to the fuller development of our ideals, but only to their fuller satisfaction by the environment. It is indeed probable that my difference from him consists in suggesting that the object of desire likely to give satisfaction under the conditions of present action is ascertained by a process much the same as that which he confines to the change or modification of our ideals in lapse of time. " Our desires," he says (loc. cit.), " have a dialectic of their own." The phrase seems just what is wanted to express the real determination of conduct with a view to satisfaction of which, as I believe, Hedonic calculation is a travesty. I will try to explain further below.

II. So far we have been dealing on the whole with the question (point 2 of sect. 102), whether the calculation of pleasures and pains gives a definite moral criterion, right or wrong ; though it has not proved possible to keep this wholly apart from the general discussion of Hedonism. Now we turn to point 3 of section 102 and ask (sect. 104), " Even if pleasure gives us a criterion which is applicable, does it give us one which is correct ? "

The author's answer involves the distinction which has just been mentioned. The Hedonic criterion would be a trustworthy guide to that element of the Supreme Good which consists in satisfaction of actual ideals. To development or perfection of the ideals themselves it does not bear a uniform relation. Subject to this distinction, the positive argument advanced occupies only six lines. Happiness is proportioned to harmony with surroundings ; if we aim at Happiness we aim at harmony between individuals and their surroundings, and this is to aim at one element in the supreme good. It should be noted that this argument if successful would destroy the relevancy of the objection taken above to an extraneous criterion. I believe, however, that this argument is itself irrelevant.

We are surprised to find a long chapter of a familiar controversy omitted at this point by the immediate identification of Happiness with the greatest quantity of Pleasure. I imagine that in the author's judgment his arguments to show that the summation of pleasures has a meaning, have removed the objections commonly made to this identification.

I am obliged to impeach this identification not merely from doubting the possibility of summation of pleasures, but for more direct reasons. I must therefore resuscitate the controversy in question, which, though it has the defect of belonging to an acute phase of the anti-Hedonist dispute, has the merit of turning our eyes directly on the experience under discussion.

I have tried to show that Hedonic calculation becomes unworkable just about at the point where if workable it would be applicable to the serious direction of life. And I now contend (point 3 of sect. 102) that if, by restricting ourselves to the more calculable levels we made it appear to be workable, the results would be unreliable or worse, even with respect to happiness or harmony with our surroundings.

I take the word Happiness to be primarily the name of a problem. It indicates, as I understand, that which would satisfy us, whatever it may prove to be. Whether it is or is not coincident with the greatest quantity of pleasure, is for me an independent question. Happiness, complete satisfaction, it may be conceded, must be what we mean by the good—that which we really want. But this does not establish the correctness of the Hedonic criterion until we know that this criterion points the way to happiness or satisfaction. This is the essence of the question before us. We have seen, in discussing the workableness of the Hedonic criterion, that it is extraordinarily impartial, i.e. that for it sums of pleasure and pain, compounded absolutely anyhow in complete abstraction from their contents, are equally choiceworthy if equal for Hedonic appreciation. We also saw that quantitative Hedonic calculation tends to pass into something else when we arrive at the more complex relations of life considered as a design.

Following up these suggestions, I am going to recur to the old topic of the pleasures of the natural man as the crux of ethical and æsthetic science. The whole *raison d'être* of these sciences, when one first approaches them, certainly seems to be in the paradox that what is pleasant to the natural man is not right nor beautiful. If, one is inclined to say, it were true that pleasure is the guide to the good and beautiful, then in face of so simple a clue these elaborate sciences could never have grown up. The contradictions which arise in applying that proposition have been the real ferment through which ethic and æsthetic have developed. Now it is quite conceivable that in the body of the sciences these contradictions may be overcome, and the above proposition victoriously reinstated. But plainly we are going wrong if we do not give some weight to the facts which make the conflict so serious—make it occupy, in fact, the whole working area of moral and æsthetic life. It may be said that the radical mistake of the natural man is to pursue his private pleasure and not the pleasure of all; and that when this is set right, the great contradiction between pleasure and good is in principle overcome. And the idealist Hedonist of to-day of course takes general and not private pleasure as his criterion. But I would point out that in æsthetic there is strictly no such distinction as that between private and general pleasure; and yet the contradictions which arise in taking pleasure as the clue to excellence are more marked perhaps than they are in ethics. I mean simply that, except with rare and gifted minds, the natural man, in as far as he follows what pleases him, is certain to be wrong. In æsthetic and in ethic alike, let him ever so much set his heart on general and not on private pleasure, the bottom fact is that his only chance of obtaining the fuller satisfaction is to make an effort which is in the direction of the greater difficulty. This effort corresponds to the apparent contradiction which the principle of pleasure has to explain away before it can even appear to cover the facts. If quantity of pleasure is the guide, why all this effort and explanation? A natural answer comes : " In the application of our pleasure arithmetic." I have tried to show that this does not really work. But now I want to make a more positive suggestion on the lines indicated above.

I will recapitulate the data as I see them, data presented equally by ethic and æsthetic. Up to a certain point of complexity pleasures and pains seem comparable by a direct quantitative process. Yet the natural man, man in as far as he adopts the direct process, is always tending to be wrong in his choice, to be wrong, because he misses satisfaction, both by his own admission and by the test of critical experience. And, in our choice, we are all constantly tempted to be the natural man, and so to be wrong. And in this way we daily and hourly miss satisfaction. It is further granted that right choices would and do bring a relatively full satisfaction, something which we ultimately prefer, and up to a certain point can acquiesce in.

Now, how does the natural man, in the sense of man *qua* following the greatest apparent pleasure, miss his satisfaction ? What would the effort, which admittedly he fails to make, achieve for him ? What is the source of the elaboration of ethical and æsthetic science ?

You may say, " He does his Hedonic sums too carelessly. If he made a more serious effort he would do them better. Ethical and Æsthetic science consist of the theory of Hedonic arithmetic."

But it is very hard to see, if calculation were all, how difficulty and resistance should creep in, as they do. I suggest therefore another answer. He goes wrong precisely by attending to the more obvious characters of facile satisfaction. These are just the characters which can, apparently, be quantitatively estimated. The difficulty of the right choice comes from the need of attending to other characters. And these other characters are what ethical and æsthetic science develop. I will try to explain. There are pleasures which it needs no effort to enjoy. There are others which need effort to enjoy and which need effort also to guard and sustain their enjoyment. The fuller satisfaction, by the unanimous voice of critical experience, belongs to a life in which the latter bear at all events a very considerable part. The fullest satisfaction to be had in human life is for normal natures only to be won and maintained with constant exertion. There can be no doubt that fairly full satisfaction is to be had, and there can be none, I think, that it is only to be bought with serious effort.

The " easy " pleasures, as I may call them in a word—those which are practically of universal attractiveness to healthy human beings—are the most readily treated as magnitudes by Hedonic arithmetic. They are on the whole I suppose what would popularly be called bodily pleasures. I do not mean to say that a hard and fast line can be drawn between them and the more arduous kind of satisfaction. But yet there is a pretty obvious distinction which runs through the whole of ethics and æsthetics. The " easy " pleasures, though they may vary from repose to the most strenuous bodily exertion, appear to " come natural " to the healthy body, and their excesses, though incompatible with true health, also " come natural." It is urged, as by Plato, that they lead to or are mixed with uneasiness ; but, at the moment of impulse, they have no uneasiness to overcome.

The " arduous " pleasures, or better, satisfactions, have a complex character which embodies the whole ethical and æsthetic difficulty of which we have been speaking. No one doubts that the satisfaction which they give is fuller and more harmonious than that of the bodily pleasures or those which relatively approach the nature of the latter.[1] But every one, except perhaps remarkably gifted natures, experiences a certain resistance in the enjoyment of them. They involve an exertion comparable to that of serious intellectual work, a resolution of discrepancies, and a maintenance of unusual and exhausting moods of feeling. Nearly

[1] Cf. in Mackail's *Life of Morris* " the physical craving for reading was unknown to him." I quote from memory.

every one, I take it, has some little shrinking from reading or seeing on the stage the *Oedipus Tyrannus* or *King Lear*. The spirit is willing, but the flesh is weak. The contradictions in a great tragedy are no doubt resolved, but their presence and the tension which they imply are just what gives the depth to æsthetic satisfaction. And so in ethics. To conduct a great enterprise bringing into unity jarring passions and interests is perhaps the fullest satisfaction in the world ; but the man who is doing it would often possess greater pleasure if he were cultivating his garden.

The distinction we are speaking of is the same that James refers to when he points out that we do not speak of a victory over our ideals, but we do speak of a victory over our self-indulgence. And it is the foundation I suppose of Spinoza's contrast between the strength of passion and the weakness of " active " emotions,[1] or between *titillatio*, local or partial pleasure, and *hilaritas*,[2] the pleasure attending upon a fully organized intelligence. It is the old prima facie distinction between yielding to temptation and doing right. The rejection of egoism does not destroy the difficulty in principle. We can yield to temptation for others as much as for ourselves.

Now it is a very heroic measure, as it seems to me, to assert in the teeth of this fundamental difficulty that quantity of pleasure is the clue to greatest satisfaction. Of course we are not to argue that the object which *de facto* we prefer must be preferred *qua* the greater pleasure ; if we said that, we should be back in psychological Hedonism. Yet no doubt we must maintain, what all experience and science agree to, the greater happiness or satisfaction of the more harmonious living. But to maintain this on the quantitative basis is, I suggest, to maintain a true conviction on the wrong grounds.

I believe that common instinct is right and that, so far as true quantitative estimates can be carried, the peculiar experiences which I have called the " easy " pleasures will always have an advantage in choice from the facility and obvious intensity which so easily turn them into temptations. I do not believe that the main difficulty of ethics and

---

[1] Joachim's *Spinoza*, p. 258.  [2] *Ibid.*, 263 *n*.

æsthetics can be disposed of in this way by simply ignoring it. We must admit, I am inclined to hold, at least a possibility that greater quantity of pleasure, so far as the phrase has a meaning, might often go with the less complete satisfaction. All satisfaction must be pleasurable ; but it is a misinterpretation of the appearances to say that the fuller satisfaction is the more pleasurable.[1] It is conceivable that pleasure should be a concomitant of satisfaction—which, I take to be synonymous with happiness—without being proportional to it. A relation of this kind seems not impossible. It would involve the presence, in quantitative pleasure *par excellence*, of some element which in the higher satisfactions was present in a less degree, either absolutely or relatively. Violence of sensation, perhaps, is an example of such an element in the case of æsthetic enjoyment.

What can be meant by a fuller satisfaction which is not necessarily a greater pleasure ? What I have in mind is such a difference as that between great art and literature, on the one hand, and " popular " art and literature on the other, or in ethics, between a serious and responsible undertaking and any kind of sport or amusement. The general theory of the contrast must be, I presume, that the former evokes our nature more nearly as a whole, and the latter more partially. But these phrases, " as a whole " and " partially," are deceptive when applied to an organized system, because in such a system the whole is not necessarily *more* in every dimension than the part. It is possible for the more total satisfaction to be preferred though possessing less violence or facility of feeling, because the logic of the desires works towards removing contradictions between their objects as much as possible. But intensity and facility of enjoyment may remain on the side of the partial excitement. And if intensity of absorption seems in a sense to be rather on the side of the great tragedy or grave enterprise, still this intensity, stirring up all the paradoxes of our being from its foundations, need not be

[1] The tendency to assert any superiority in the form of a quantity of the nearest measurable element is so enormously strong that we cannot be surprised at the difficulty which the very greatest thinkers have in resisting it. Plato's famous argument, *Rep.* ix., is brought to a numerical result, though, as I hold, by this very fact he shows that he makes light of the quantitative shape.

prima facie an intensity of pleasure. There is also the point that any one who does not know pain has plainly omitted a great range of experience. It must surely be in some sense included in a complete satisfaction.

No doubt there is a tendency for elements which appear to be sacrificed in the intermediate grades of perfection to be restored as perfection is approached. What is a loss, and how far perfection can involve what to us would seem a "loss," is a most difficult problem, both in metaphysic and in such sciences as æsthetic. But it seems clear, as indeed the author's theory most emphatically demands, that we cannot exclude all transformation of common experience in the higher grades of perfection on the ground that it would involve a loss. And if so—if for example the world of sensation must be sacrificed in ultimate reality—there can be no general reason why intensity or quantity of pleasure should persist in such a way as to merit the names we give them.

It seems to follow that in some form or degree, after all has been said that can be said for the unity of body and mind, it will be necessary to rehabilitate the distinction between bodily or relatively partial, and spiritual or relatively total, satisfactions. A pleasure in which the bodily system as such is harmoniously excited, as in a game or sport at its best, must be fundamentally different from a far-reaching emotion in which the body is but secondarily aroused, as in reflection on the triumph of a great moral or political cause. If it were possible that pleasure, in the direct and simple sense, could be proved proportional to the participation of the body in any activity, and not to the range of objective harmony signified to the intelligence through its activity (e.g. through a certain group of judgments or perceptions), we should have a theory which would come near to fitting the facts of introspection and of ethical and æsthetic analysis. Pleasure would then be a concomitant of satisfaction, but not simply proportional to it. The equivalent of pleasure in ultimate reality would not be annihilated by such a doctrine, for the body and all its feelings plainly must be represented there

## II

III. I return to point (1) of section 102, the author's contention that " the idea. of Perfection cannot give us any criterion of moral action."

What has been said above, first as to the true nature of a good criterion as (a) essential and not extraneous and (b) concrete and not abstract, and secondly as to the true process of judgment which is parodied by Hedonic calculation, belongs in substance to the present argument. It only needs to be applied to the author's contention in three respects, (a) as to his ruling out the work of a criterion in hindering self-deception ; (b) as to the assumption that the idea of perfection can only be applied by comparison in the abstract ; and (c) by showing that the process on which we rely is not confined to development of ideals as contrasted with their satisfaction.

(a) The argument of section 104—I am not sure whether it is directed against Green—amounts to ruling out the moral danger of self-deception. Yet I should have expected Mr. McTaggart to accept the principle " *Quicquid petitur, petitur sub specie boni* " ; and if so, there is no immoral choice which does not depend at bottom on self-deception. Even apart from this principle, the field of possible self-deception in morals is certainly enormous and extends over almost all, if not quite all, strictly ethical choices. Thus, I submit, it is a serious error of theory to separate the moral and intellectual elements of the choice. But this is, as it seems to me, the essence of Mr. McTaggart's argument. The supposed moral agent—he urges—*ex hypothesi* intends to do right, before he knows what the criterion says. Otherwise, he asks, of what use could a moral criterion be to him ? If he is not going to be deterred from a choice by its being shown to be wrong, he can have no use for a criterion that tells him which choice is right and which is wrong. This argument is directed against an alleged fault in the reasoning of those who advocate the criterion of Perfection. They take their examples, the author affirms, not from a choice between two courses alike prima facie moral, but from a choice between courses one of which is stated as good or in the name of good, and the other as either defiant or neglectful of morality. In such a case he agrees, the idea or, one might suggest, the mere name of perfection is enough to distinguish between them. But he contends, for the reason above mentioned, this is no test of the value of the criterion to a moral agent desirous to do right. His perplexity can only be between courses both of which appeal to him in the name of right. A criterion which only warns him against a choice which by its statement is immoral—a criterion which = " Do what you believe to be right and not wrong " —can be of no service to him.

I do not know whether Green is here aimed at, but his argument will serve to point out what I take to be the defect in Mr. McTaggart's. Green selects,[1] no doubt, as one example of the operation of his criterion, a choice which, *for the critical onlooker*, appears to be a choice between a moral effort and a self-indulgence. But the supposed chooser is to choose I presume by the light of one or other of the criteria in question, and is not to be imagined as in the possession of a moral touchstone prior to their operation. The question then is which of the two criteria will most readily help the supposed chooser to the choice assumed by the critical onlooker to be right. Green alleges that the Hedonic criterion will or may co-operate with the tendencies that make for self-deception, whereas the criterion of perfection, from the fact that it appeals to a standard heterogeneous from personal enjoyment, is more likely to effect a discrimination such as no confusing desires can blur.

It is implied that the choice is one in which a man could hardly go wrong except by serious self-deception. But this, from Green's point of view, makes the case stronger against the Hedonic criterion, which by operating *in pari materia* with the source of confusion, seems to him likely to permit such a confusion to take place even in a case where it should be easily avoided. It does not indeed make the positive case very strong for the criterion of perfection, because the choice selected is a fairly simple one, purposely with a view to its negative bearing against the Hedonic criterion. Nevertheless it suggests, what is Green's principle throughout,[2]

[1] E.g. *Prolegomena*, sect. 374.    [2] E.g. sect. 308.

that to be habitually preoccupied with an idea of perfection in application to life is the most practical and important safeguard against self-deception in moral choices. The separation of the moral resolve and the intellectual judgment on which Mr. McTaggart founds his objection, rules out this use of a moral criterion, because it supposes that the determination to do right being first and independently made, the chooser is henceforward an unbiased reasoner in the application of a criterion. But this seems to ignore the whole nature of the moral choice, which is essentially the maintenance of effective insight against blinding influences. In short then, *even if*, what has yet to be discussed, the criterion of perfection could give little or no guidance in absolutely bona fide perplexities between courses of conduct with a moral bearing, the fact that it is a safeguard in cases where the perplexity pretends to be but is not absolutely bona fide is enough to make it cover by far the most important part of the range in which Ethics can be asked for guidance. In all intricate matters of conduct, e.g. in law or politics, where varying and important emergencies press upon us, to keep the right principle and not the wrong one before the attention is of the very first practical importance. It makes constantly the whole difference between good and bad work. It may be admitted that if the proposed criterion only contained, as the author contends, such a rule as Do what you really think right, it could not be fertile of detail ; though preoccupation even with such a rule is of much more decisive importance in life than might be supposed, because distraction of attention is one of the great instruments of self-deception. But the question, what it contains, is now to be discussed.

(*b*) In bona fide moral difficulties, the author argues, preoccupation with the idea of perfection can give no guidance. For the supreme good, as we learn its nature from Metaphysic, cannot be realized perfectly by any action in a world of matter, time, and space. Nor can we determine by comparison which of alternative ends, or which division of resources between competing purposes, will realize it least imperfectly. For, in the supreme good, choice is precluded. No element of perfection is wanting and each is there to the

# HEDONISM AMONG IDEALISTS 211

full. But choice is the essence of our position.[1] In all ends, which we can conceive as moral ends, there is some good, complete good in none. Our question is which good to select and which to sacrifice, and how to compromise between them. And this a comparison with perfection, where all good is present in fullness but in shapes wholly different from those we know, can never tell us. The attempt to demonstrate it leads to sophistry. We insist that the element which happens to interest us most forms a link between a certain action and perfection. And we neglect the fact that other elements, absent in this action, are present in others which we happen to dislike.

1. If the means of guidance is to be such an abstract comparison as Mr. McTaggart suggests, I think his conclusion follows. It is impossible, as Plato points out, to go without intermediate steps from the most abstract universal to the most concrete particular. The attempt to do so involves Eristic, i.e. either the refusal to ascribe predicates, or the assertion that one predicate is as true as another. This is what Mr. McTaggart imputes to the Perfectionist views. But as constantly happens in philosophical discussions, Perfectionists would retort the accusation, and say that the intermediate steps are needlessly cut away and Eristic introduced by the operation of his theory.

The whole issue turns on the refusal to recognize our imperfect experience as a stage in which the idea of perfection is active, relatively to the capacities of that stage. By recognizing this idea only in the abstract shape which presents itself as the result of metaphysic, and failing to insist that this abstract shape is imperfect until charged with the life and power of all reality, the idea of Perfection is made a particular instead of a universal. It becomes a hard atom, which takes up an attitude of exclusion to the world whose core it should be. Thus the attempt to obtain moral guidance from it takes the shape of a comparison with it, and becomes parallel to an attempt to obtain scientific knowledge from inspecting the principle of the Uniformity of Nature. In each case we have taken the principle apart

[1] Mr. Taylor has put the same point very effectively in *The Problem of Conduct,* but I have not the reference.

from the stages in which its nature is revealed, and have thus incapacitated ourselves for seeing it embodied, though imperfectly, at every stage of our experience.

Our answer then to the argument drawn from the abstractness of our idea of perfection, by which it fails to show how it includes our reality, would be that in looking for moral guidance we begin at the other end. It may be true—I at least am not disputing it—that the central workings of our thought, which experience cannot undo, compel us to a result which may be stated in the abstract as Mr. McTaggart's view of Hegel's Absolute is stated. But the inevitable abstractness of this result, where experience fails to fill up the outline of thought, is a positive loss if it debars us from recognizing the working of the idea within the tissue of experience. We know that its work will be imperfect, because our experience is imperfect. But that is no reason against its being definite and right as far as it goes. The shape it takes would not do for ultimate reality; but the shape it takes for ultimate reality will not do for the given stage of experience. Thus in science Biology or Chemistry may be likened to growing forms, whose general life principle, when taken out in the abstract, becomes the Uniformity of Nature.[1] But so taken out in the abstract, though interesting for Logic and Philosophy, it is useless to the sciences. They *are* it, in shapes dictated by experience at every moment, but when it is separated from these they cannot use it. So with the moral life. Its shape at any moment is the idea of perfection working in experience down to that moment, as a striving after the completest harmony possible under all the conditions, in other words after what we really want. Taken out and pushed home in the abstract, it becomes useless, for this particular work. The forms which it had generated in the matter of experience have then been cancelled as inadequate to the whole, and therefore all links are cut between Perfection and human life. But they were not inadequate to the part; on the contrary, the effort which generated them is the same as, and an essential part of, that which as an *anticipatio naturæ*, regarding only the central lines

[1] Ultimately, of course, the Absolute. But I take it at a stage when the distinction of Knowledge and Practice still persists.

of experience, leads to the abstract conception of ultimate reality. The " tacking " of Dialectic makes no difference to this adequacy. Mistakes may be necessary ; but they are necessary only as efforts after harmony, and, as the strivings of reason, are relatively good. Indeed, everything but ultimate reality as such may be treated as a mistake. But there are mistakes and mistakes. Our object is to make only that mistake which our whole experience cannot help us to avoid.

The point may be put more simply by saying that we test courses of action not by the abstract metaphysical idea of the supreme good, but by the tests by which that idea itself is obtained—and which therefore form the rule of the entire process of practical experience—the dialectic of desire. The essence of the test at every point is the resolution of contradictions. Our action is precisely parallel to that by which scientific theories are remodelled and adapted ; and, like scientific theories, our morality is no doubt in the main a working habit or tradition, in course of constant readjustment.

I am convinced that the reiteration of such phrases as " choice " and " preference " is fatal to understanding the nature of the moral criterion. All voluntary action is " choice " in the sense that it is willed ; but the phrase suggests the selection of one ready-made course of conduct out of a number, as if there were hundreds before us on the counter of a shop. Thus the question why you choose " it," or which course you " like best," acquires a predominance unknown in real life. For, in fact, action is construction, rationality, invention of individual solutions for individual problems by modification of existing systems. This is what, I think, Green really meant [1] when he insisted that while nothing could follow from a bare definition of virtue, yet morality grows by habitual preoccupation with moral ideas in application to circumstances as they arise. The true analogy is the absorption of a scientific intelligence in detecting the true bearings of a principle such as natural selection. Such an absorption is fruitful, in morality and in science alike ; and fruitful in proportion as the principle is clearly and justly apprehended.

[1] *Prolegomena*, sect. 308.

Then, it may be asked, do we admit morality or Ethics, which we here compare with Biology and Chemistry, to be a natural science ; and do we not abandon the contention that a metaphysical idea is necessary for the guidance of conduct ?

This is very much a matter of degree. I admitted that the Uniformity of Nature as such is of no use to Biology or Chemistry, because it is notorious that these sciences can exist and flourish without casting a glance on Logic. But the total absence of a working faith in Uniformity would be and has been, I suppose, fatal even to the most purely natural science. So one might say that in a sense a logical faith is necessary and useful to the merest natural knowledge. And this logical faith itself has degrees ; and notions of system, method, and explanation may, though I am slow to assert it, be found really helpful in determining scientific problems.

Morality deals with higher categories, and its working faith involves a unity of a type not known to pure natural science. Such a unity is really a metaphysical idea, though to say in what forms and disguises it actually operates in the everyday mind would be a very difficult matter. But it seems clear that the clue which the mind follows, however ignorantly, is in substance that idea of perfection which pursued in its main lines beyond the details of experience becomes the Idea of the Absolute. No doubt it is the unity just in advance of where we stand, rather than an idea of the ultimate metaphysical Absolute, which at any moment, as Green insists, aids and guides the ordinary man. Morality depends on metaphysic, I am suggesting, not in the sense that it works with the explicit determinations of the Absolute, but that it operates through conceptions of unity which, if criticized or doubted, only metaphysical investigation can elucidate or justify. The idea of the Supreme Good is the ultimate elucidation of this conception, but cannot be the shape in which it actually operates within the everyday mind. This is Plato's doctrine, and Green's ; [1] and it meets, I think, in principle, the difficulty of an abstract comparison between a course of conduct and the Supreme Good.

[1] *Prolegomena*, sect. 309, cf. *Republic*, 505 E. " The good, which every soul pursues, as the end of all its actions, divining its existence, but perplexed and unable to apprehend satisfactorily its nature "—i.e. it is our guide throughout, but changes as we pursue it.

2. It remains to explain more in detail how, in the adjustment of moral conduct, we obtain guidance from the idea of perfection as thus understood. The essential point is that the situations which constitute the problems of conduct are highly individualized, and demand no less individualized solutions. Existing morality, and current knowledge of man and of the world, are the organs by which the impulse towards unity is brought into relation with specific character and circumstance. These play the part in practice which is played in the development of theory by acquired science and experience.

And it is very important not to demand too much. The idea of a magical possibility of absolute rightness in morality seems to be at the root of ethical pessimism. The best rightness we can hope for is to be right for us under all our conditions and limitations.[1] It is because these conditions and limitations are so complex that moral problems are not hopelessly insoluble. We have not got to say what is right for others, or what would be right for ourselves if we were other than we are. Our judgment in morality is about as good and as bad as our judgment in other complex matters. We attempt—whether by habit or by reflection makes no difference, for trained habit can make all adjustments of which reflection is capable—we attempt to harmonize the situation presented to us, including our own selves, following the logic of the objects of desire towards real satisfaction. We are not brilliantly successful; but we are about as successful in conduct as in the other matters which we approach in the same way; for example in science, or in practical organization.

We aim, then, at satisfaction, or the removal of contradictions in experience where our action can effect it, in short, at determining and attaining what we really want. It is a mistake of principle, I hold, to attempt to lay down beforehand in what our satisfaction is to consist, whether in pleasure or in any other predetermined form of consciousness. That is like binding a physicist before he begins his science to the

[1] This is the very type and essence of science. Mr. Taylor seems wholly off the right track at this point, in suggesting that individualization makes morality subjective (*Problem*, p. 361).

terms in which he is to explain phenomena. Every problem or situation is thoroughly concrete, though universal and the meeting-point of universal forces and principles. Our business is to invent the course which shall most remove contradictions; to theorize the individual situation, including our own resources.

This is why, though as a rule I have the utmost respect for Mr. McTaggart's arguments and examples, I cannot think his instances here to be of a relevant type. They rank, it seems to me, with questions which are carelessly propounded as puzzles to students of practical sciences, containing no possible data for an answer. It is like saying to a gardener, " Am I to prune an apple-tree in my orchard ? " or saying to a doctor, " My child has spots on him ; what do you think can be the matter ? " The answer comes at once : " Show me the tree " or " the child, and I will tell you what I think." Just so it is asked, Is marriage the best arrangement ? The moralist, if I am right, and as Green maintains,[1] has no immediate insight based on a comparison with the idea of perfection in the abstract. He will demand that the question shall be closely stated, with regard to the stage of social advance, the race and civilization about which it is asked, and will then treat the issue as a serious inquiry largely sociological but having an ethical aspect through its bearing on character. He can determine the general nature of the claims and capacities of selves in a definite type of society ; and may then be able to offer a judgment on the question what arrangement of institutions provides a conciliation of these with the least degree of injury. The point of view which makes him a moralist lies in his being alive to more and deeper aspects of unity than would appeal to the biologist or to the jurist as such. His eye is differently trained. This is exemplified by Green's investigation.[2] It flows directly from his conception of a spiritual unity gradually taking form through the working of an idea of good in the experience of certain types of men. For other types of moral being the conclusion might, conceivably, be different. In such a real investigation of an ethical question the Hedonic criterion, I believe, could never occur to the student's mind.

[1] *Prolegomena*, sect. 379.　　[2] *Principles of Political Obligation*, sect. 233.

So in the conflict of different ends, or in the distribution of resources, such as money and time, between different objects. The problem is altogether transformed when we state it as the endeavour to construct a solution for a highly complex situation, from what it is when we take it as a question asked in the abstract, out of all context. It is put to us again, Does a public school do a boy more harm or good? In general, I should say, no answer can be given. In view of a particular boy, whose character and surroundings we know, and of a particular school, there is no great difficulty as a rule in forming a fair judgment on the question. As regards the distribution of time or money, there is a difficulty which I have admitted, in bringing the higher forms of unity into relation with quantitative terms. But as in æsthetic or medicine, so in ethics, the result is obtained by a frank recognition that every solution of a problem is subject to mechanical conditions. A single question, how much a man should eat, or how loud a note must be struck, or how much colour must be put on the eye of a portrait, is meaningless; and so is the question how much money I should give to charity, or what time I should devote to metaphysic and to bicycling. In plain words, the distribution of money and time must be systematically theorized in connection with the possibilities offered by the situation. That we are born into our theories or conventions, and most of us never know that they do the work of theories, is no objection at all, for precisely the same is true of our mental furniture of every kind. Thus a particular decision is approached on the basis of a rationalized habit, dictated by the main aim and design of life. I have formed, or have picked up, or inherited, a notion or instinct of what I can achieve and how I mean to achieve it. On this all details are consequential, though, of course, in most lives, with a very loose logic. But logic is no looser in morality than in opinion, which admittedly is meant to be logical. From the main aims and method of life certain necessities follow as to adjustments of time and money; charity is or should be relative not only to the money I can spare but to the attention I can devote to its utilization, and that again follows from my line of life and special capacities. Recreation and work are adjusted by a concrete theory of the way in which the claims on my limited powers may best be met. I do not say for a moment that we are usually right, or even self-conscious, in our decision; but I do say that our life is probably a more rational whole than our opinions, and that the latter are admittedly a thing which ought to be logically coherent. There is no theoretical difficulty, therefore, in saying the same of our conduct.

If it is urged, as I think Mr. McTaggart means to urge in his demand for principles of distribution, that we must lay down beforehand at least what kind of things are more important, and what kind of things are to give way, I answer, as above, that in a sense this is obvious, but in a sense I believe it to be a dangerous fallacy. Our principle, the logic of our objects, will tell us in its working what are deep-lying contradictions, what are superficial, what apparent harmonies are pregnant with latent discords, or what apparent discords are introductions to fuller harmonies. It will tell us all this, so far as our knowledge and inference extend; and that limits the situation with which in morality we have to deal. We cannot escape its operation, so long as we act bona fide. The sense that " it is all very well, but there is something wrong," which attends a victorious self-deception by which we enter on a doubtful course of conduct, must be given its place, if we are true to ourselves, and must be tracked out to its significance. We are quite safe to miss our own satisfaction, unless we take sincere account of all we know and feel, and let each element have logical fair play.

But if it is meant that we are to prescribe the species of our feelings of satisfaction beforehand, that is, I think, a pitfall. Some solutions may bring pleasure, others intellectual repose; others " the approval of conscience "; others the tranquillity of endurance of completed tragedy. All we need to know is that we seek complete satisfaction; the clashing and harmonizing of objects will indicate our defectiveness or our success in ways which could not be adequate, if it were possible to lay them down beforehand.

It is, I am convinced, a profound theoretical error to think of current moral and social ideas and traditions as something arbitrary, which might just as well have been different. Just like the sciences, they are a tissue of adaptations, generated by the struggle of logic, with different degrees of insight, to harmonize situations from moment to moment. I am not saying that life is wisely or rightly determined by these adaptations, but I am saying that it is thoroughly determined, and that to suppose our own choices to be in principle capricious or irrational is to misunderstand our position and the essence of the moral problem. Not only is it scientifically wrong to treat the bulk of social tradition as irrational in its genesis, but it shows a lack of insight to treat conduct and modes of life as in essence irrationally determined. The logic of life is imperious, and conduct is guided by the dialectic of its objects in the minutest details. To urge that it is full of error and incoherence is irrelevant ; the point is that the machinery of determination is operative throughout, and is of an assignable nature. The imperfection of its results is itself necessary, and relative to the gaps of our experience.[1]

I may further illustrate my point by referring to Mr. McTaggart's evacuating interpretation of " my station and its duties." (I in no way attribute my views to Mr. Bradley.) The idea of his station and its duties, he maintains, does not teach a schoolmaster how to deal rightly with a particular boy on a particular occasion. This is something which I am tempted to say that I cannot understand. It must mean, no doubt, that the author reduces the idea of one's station to a general conception of one's place in society as distinct from other places. But surely this is a very poor idea of one's station. Who says " schoolmaster " says " a walking theory and practice of education." This is " what it is to be " a schoolmaster. His conception of his position as distinct, say, from that of the clergyman and the parent, is just the outline of an idea which theory and experience have filled in and adapted in detail, till his position involves for him a distinct conception of his individual duty to each individual boy who is entrusted to his charge, and this again carries with it the reaction of his trained nature upon every occasion and situation which arises. That his action is not in form determined by reflection or deduction makes, as I urge throughout, no theoretical difference at all. It is

[1] Cf. p. 212, above.

governed in the end by ideas and must be condemned or judged in their light. He is bound to have considered what, under all the conditions, can best be made of each boy so far as the schoolmaster is concerned ; and this is just his concrete idea of his station. It is a clear case of such a theory as I contend for.

Therefore, about the general method of the determination of conduct, there is, if I am right, no doubt or difficulty whatever. It is simply the logic of the objects of desire, by which we pursue the idea of perfection as our complete satisfaction. It is subject to blindness, due partly to lack of experience and inferential power, partly to self-deception by which partial objects, stimulating desire, are preferred to the whole. At every stage our idea of perfection represents our best construction of the whole ; and in proportion as criticism touches it Metaphysic is needed to sustain and develop it. Its working through habit and knowledge to resolve the contradictions of our individual situation is not to be taken as a pronouncement of abstract Metaphysic ; but acting through categories which nothing but Metaphysic can justify, it plays quite a different part in the science from that played by Uniformity of Nature in Chemistry and Biology. And even for these sciences the entire abandonment of the logical idea which works in them would mean annihilation.

A consequence of great importance seems to me to follow from the nature of this mode of determination, as compared with the summation of pleasures. As objects of action become more complex the translation of them into quantity tends to bracket them as equal in value. Every one knows how heterogeneous complexes, say, the marks of wholly dissimilar examinees, insist on summing themselves up to the same total. The linear numerical series has no way of representing the different composition of identical sums. Now between alternative complexes of objects which give the same sum of pleasure, though as wide asunder in their nature as the poles, a Hedonic criterion cannot distinguish. Whereas, as situations become more complex, the adequate solution of each in concrete science tends to become more clearly differentiated ; so that situations of modern life, on careful consideration, constantly seem to dictate their own solution beyond any doubt.

(c) From the point of view here taken, the two standards of immediate harmony with environment, and of development of ideals, become commensurable. Happiness, in the sense of harmony or satisfaction of the whole of which we are members, becomes the only test. Deliberation is incipient development, and development is for the sake of removing contradiction, or realizing satisfaction. How completely we are able to conceive the whole to which we belong must be a question of our individual experience and capacity. On this depends the soundness of our judgment in incurring immediate contradictions, that is, in making sacrifices (whether merely in our own persons or in the persons of those whom we are able to affect) with a view to possibilities of development either future in the lives in question, or wholly beyond them, or remaining partial and painful within them. This judgment is just of the same order as that which we are testing daily and hourly in accepting prima facie sacrifices or contradictions for the sake of the whole. It seems to me precisely analogous to our behaviour in the realm of theory, which mainly consists in deciding what contradictions are *ad hoc* to be disregarded, and what, as more fundamental, we must apply our scientific resources to reconcile. Ultimately, no doubt, the idea of the Supreme Good must include what for us are the separate aspects of theoretical and practical perfection. But speaking in more relative terms we may say that the idea of perfection is for conduct what the idea of system is for science.

## CONCLUSION

The most serious objection to these views which I should expect to be advanced, would be that according to them we make no use of the definite content of the abstract idea of supreme good, as metaphysically established (I suppose) for all possible worlds, in determining our conduct. We use it in a confessedly imperfect form, in which, I think Mr. McTaggart might probably contend, the empirical and metaphysical elements are undistinguishably mixed, and therefore it cannot be truly said that morality thus determined rests on a metaphysical basis, as Green for instance seems to assert. This point was referred to some pages back, but it may be well to recur to it in conclusion. The answer would, I think, begin by accepting the imperfection of morality as a whole, and of our morality. As Mr. McTaggart insists, perfection could not be realized in an experience like ours. In attained perfection we should have, or there would be, a complete experience forming one harmonious web with the idea of perfection ; and as all would be true and satisfying no question would arise how much was false. In our imperfection, we are haunted by this question, and we must admit that the whole tissue of our morality is tinged with falsehood. Nevertheless we are able, from a metaphysical standpoint, to verify *an* idea of perfection as working throughout the tissue of life. We cannot apply it to particulars of conduct by metaphysical considerations, but we can justify by metaphysical considerations the logical effort which is always constructing particulars in obedience to the idea. Though our morality is tinged with falsehood throughout, yet we know that it is truth, relevant and relative to our life, in as far as it pursues the line of effort which the nature of reason involves. And we know that somewhere in the central tendencies of this effort, the tendencies whose negation would be to us the most fundamental contradiction, there lie characters continuous with and implying those of ultimate perfection. After all, the Absolute needs us and our conduct just as we need it. We are in it, now if ever, and we can hold to it, if at all, with the full breadth of reason and need not allow our grasp to be attenuated to a thread of hope. Our experience, we must remember, is in one sense a fuller revelation than an abstract idea of ultimate reality, if in another it is less perfect. Its backwardness is due to the magnitude of the enterprise which it implies ; for it demands and begins the harmonization of a total world, and not merely the anticipation of its general nature.

# XII

# THE PREDICTION OF HUMAN CONDUCT: A STUDY IN BERGSON [1]

1. THE root of Bergson's views lies in his idea of "duration" as contrasted with that of mathematical time or time spatially symbolized, or taken as the measure of change in inorganic nature.

The mathematician's time, as I understand the contrast which Bergson draws, is symbolized by the uniform movement of a point, and his time-units are the imaginary successive positions of such a point, which he speaks of as $T_1$ $T_2$ $T_3$. Their meaning, as the mathematician employs them, is that a certain configuration of physical points coincides with each of these supposed positions of the uniformly moving point. Their meaning, therefore, has no reference at all to the intervals traversed by the imaginary point. They mark a number of simultaneities, or correspondences, between positions of different points and the position of the uniformly moving point.

As a proof of this it is pointed out (what the present writer has drawn attention to in combating the idea of absolute time) that if we suppose all physical movements to halve or to double their actual velocity, the change would not affect any mathematical formula, so long as the ratios of all the units to each other were preserved. The series of positions would run past faster or slower, but it would be no less complete and there would be nothing to indicate the change of absolute velocity.

Time, thus conceived, is not cumulative. It carries along with it nothing of the past. If a configuration recurs,

---

[1] This was an attempt to make clear Bergson's position on certain questions to a general audience.

it is as if it were a new thing. The fact that it is a recurrence in no way affects the points composing it. Hence, a previous position can be identically repeated ; for repetition awakens nothing of the past, and thus makes no difference. In a word, such a conception of time excludes the notion of history. Nothing is gained or carried forward. In the intervals between the positions, the system might as well not be.

Duration proper, on the other hand, is one with life, or rather, with living. Its successive parts are essentially not homogeneous nor uniform ; it is the experience of a being radically progressive and creative, whose states or acts are not outside one another, but carry their past with them. This is why the experience is essentially creative, productive of novelty. It is always gaining, by the addition of the new to an old which is retained. For such an experience, as opposed to mathematical time as above described, the *intervals* are the reality. It is what it is, by living through them ; growing and changing, gaining in every moment. Hence in this case no true repetition is possible. But there is a history, and the movement is irreversible. No prior state can be truly repeated. The fact of its being "repeated" would be enough to make it different, because its prior occurrence, and what has come between, have *ex hypothesi* left their mark.

Now Bergson makes his general complaint against both philosophy and common sense, that we confuse true and false duration ; we confuse life with the uniform movement of a point ; in a word, we confuse time with space.

For all our common wants and common sense are profoundly falsified by space perception and the analogy of space. Language, practical social needs, current natural science, are all of them deformed by spatial distinctions, e.g by the distinction of things, objects in space, which is rooted in practice and governs language. Concepts of things and events are all practical and spatial (it is almost the same at root. They provide us with a scheme of *what is where* and *what happens when*. This is all we want to know when or where we must act to be dealing with the due situation or configuration. The coincidence of an act with the relevan state of facts is what matters to us. The interval is as unimportant to our common sense as to the mathematician. Our intelligence is at home in geometry and mechanism, in repetitions of occurrences according to law. Its motto is " Same produces same," " Same cause produces same effect." In face of genuine life, genuine duration, it is bewildered. True, we can make to ourselves a picture, as we imagine, of history and continuous occurrence. But (it is a constant and characteristic simile in Bergson) our picture of duration is only a cinematograph picture. We snapshot in our minds a number of successive positions of occurrences and by running them rapidly past our mental vision, we produce or reproduce what seems to be an experience of duration, of continuous living, of uninterrupted time. But the thing is an illusion, like the bioscopic picture itself. We have not, in gathering these images, recorded the experience of the lapse of living. Our images mark the ends of short intervals ; and they give us no record, represent no intimate apprehension, of the intervals themselves.

So it is our tendency in all our current reflection to confound duration with so-called uniform time. But this time is really space, i.e. succession symbolized by the uniform movement of a point. We think of ourselves as being in time, just as we think of a thing's being in time, i.e. as passing through a succession of events. Our very self is disguised by superficial connections as in hypnotic suggestion, or association of an idea with an act. And thus we actually fail to enter into our own true duration. We are called in the morning and get up ; we have made it a routine connection, almost of the type of " pull the trigger and the gun goes off." The perception releases the action.

2. Hence Bergson's criticism of determinism and indeterminism alike. Both, he urges, are rooted in the spatial symbolism of time. We state, as the crucial question, " Could I have done otherwise than I did ? " In stating the question thus, we substitute for the experience of duration the picture of a hypothetical point traversing a uniform line, and, *ex hypothesi*, to an end which we already know. Then in order to express the fact of choice, we are driven to imagine the moving point confronted by a bifurcation of the line :

one way leading to X, the other to Y, and the moving point as oscillating between them, before it takes one of the two alternative routes.

All this means that we have split up the living self, which has all sorts of tendencies within it, by which it grows and develops its action ; we have split this up into an indifferent point and two tracks lying outside it, such as can be retraversed in our quasi-mathematical thought. This is really a gratuitous imagery. The developing consciousness, holding together within itself varying inclinations, and developing by their means into something new at every moment, is altogether a different thing. So, however common sense states the question of freedom, it naturally represents it in sharp verbal or spatial distinctions. Could I have done otherwise than I did ? Could the point, which has gone to X, have gone to Y instead ?

This statement of the question, Bergson urges, however you answer it, in the end gives up the game to the determinist. You have split up the conscious life into lines and points in space ; and if you take account of the knowledge which *ex hypothesi* you possess, you are driven to admit that the point was moving, all along, to X or to Y, and therefore was not an indifferent point. The indeterminist may assert, " You could have done otherwise ; at the place of bifurcation, it was still open to the moving point to travel to Y, instead of travelling, as it did, to X." But that is wilfully using only a part of his knowledge, which tells him what you really did, i.e. that you did the action X, and therefore, according to this mode of representation, were all along going to do the action X.

The fault which makes this result inevitable is representing time as space. Real time, or duration, is the growth of a being which contains the two lines—the conflicting tendencies —and much more besides, within itself ; and it will develop at a certain stage into a certain action. But there is no indifferent point, no homogeneous line, and no ready-made alternative routes, lying there like roads on a map, or objects waiting for choice on a counter. You cannot think back in spatial terms and say, I, being what I was before and after, was there, as I might be again, between these two alternatives laid down for me. This all comes from mapping your course after the action, like a route laid down and existent in space. It in no way corresponds to the nature of an action. An action is not free because some other action " could have been done," or unfree because the other " could not have been done." It is free, if it is free at all, because of a certain character in itself, which is not present in all actions, and where present, is present in various degrees.

3. What is a free action ? A free action is one which expresses the whole " me." That, of course, is not a new thing to say. If Bergson has a new point to make in saying it, this point lies in his hostility to our current self. For him, this is a sort of crust over our true or fundamental self, formed by language, common-place education, traditional ideas, social practice and social relations. In all this, he sees the enemy, the influence of spatial distinction and the spatial symbol of time, as expressed in the external world of things and the connections of simultaneous events, and the connection of events with the conduct which follows on them by a mechanical routine or habit of reaction. All this he thinks of, to repeat the phrase, as a crust [1] formed over the true self which lies in immediate experiences, in feelings, in the depths of personality. " To act without a reason is often the best reason." What does guide us when we are free is differently phrased as " the total of our sentiments," " our personal idea of happiness and honour." But, as a rule, Bergson is hostile to the term idea. He is inclined to identify it with all that he opposes to the true personality, with a superficial idea, a hypnotic or quasi-hypnotic suggestion,[2] which makes up a great part of what we mistake for ourselves. " Many people," Bergson says, " never do a free action at all," i.e. they act from routine in which by association the occurrence

---

[1] If I remember right, he does not refer to Wordsworth :

And custom lie upon thee with a weight
Heavy as frost, and deep almost as life.

[2] It will be remembered that for M. Tarde our consciousness of the social self as our own is of the nature of a hypnotic illusion. *Les lois de l'imitation*, p. 83 : " L'état social, comme l'état hypnotique, n'est qu'une forme du rêve de commande et un rêve en action. N'avoir que des idées suggerées et les croire spontanées ; telle est l'illusion propre au somnambule, et aussi bien à l'homme social." The conception betrays a total failure to apprehend the nature of identity.

releases the deed ; they act out of purely formal and traditional conceptions of social duty. They never enter into themselves and ask themselves what they, as complete personalities, really want. " They never once possess their souls," as Matthew Arnold has it. They are dominated by associationist images, and their mind is fixed not on their spiritual growth, the life and development of their whole being, but so to speak on what is to be done when the hour strikes, and the half-hour, and the hour after that. They live not in the lapse of duration, but in the conjunctures of occurrence. This is, as I understand it, the connection between his disparagement of the superficial self and his theory of the defective symbolization of duration by space.

4. Now we are prepared to consider Bergson's view of prediction in case of human conduct. From the above conception of duration flows a clear distinction between (1) prediction concerning purely natural events, e.g. in astronomy, and (2) prediction in matters of human conduct.

In the former case you have only to deal with time units as described above, which are in effect merely numbers, imaginary points in a uniform movement, and do not depend upon the intervals they divide. Prediction in this case only means, as it were, making them pass you very fast ; reducing the intervals between them to almost nothing ; doing the work of millenniums in a few minutes. This, as we saw above, makes no essential difference in the work to be done. All the occurrences occur without change ; the time units are rattled off ; only the intervals between them are shorter than those which occur in fact. In this case you can *do the thing before it occurs*, without affecting its nature. And this is everywhere the true essential of prediction. You can predict, where and in as far as you can do a thing before it happens or is done, and not elsewhere or otherwise.

In the life of conscious being the case is different. Here duration is a cause ; the intervals are experienced in transitions of feeling ; and to shorten one of them is to change the quality and outcome of its content. Shorten your day by one half, and you have cut out half the actual felt experience of it.

True, as appeared above, it is possible to run over past experiences very quickly in the memory ; and hence it may seem that they undergo no alteration by a change of the duration which they occupy. But the fact is not really so. To run them over in this way, it is essential to have named them ; and by naming them they are essentially altered. They are made into concepts, extracts or essences, comparable to the things and events of common sense. Language is one of the great falsifiers ; one of the great agents in the conspiracy to turn time duration into the spatial symbol of time. This distrust of language is remarkable, and from a philosophical point of view, ominous. However, it is the present point. Our experiences, thus recalled and reviewed, are no longer what they were in immediate experience, and would no longer suggest to us the results which in actual experience they would produce. Therefore, prediction being essentially to do a thing before it is done, you are in the case of human conduct shut up to two alternatives.

(Note at this point that Bergson makes a sharp distinction between probable prediction, based upon a man's past conduct, and absolute prediction, claiming to rest upon calculation. We shall see that this distinction coincides with one drawn long ago by Mr. Bradley in *Ethical Studies* (1876). Bergson appears to make too little of the type of prediction which he admits, when he denies that it is a true link between past and future.)

The case is, you, A, are to predict the course of action of B absolutely and by strict calculation or deduction from detailed data, not by mere analogy to conduct in previous circumstances. Then there are two sub-cases. You, A, may have the factors of B's duration (sentiments, motives, impulses) present in your mind symbolically, i.e. through language and in the medium of knowledge. Then, as we have seen to be Bergson's view, the factors are not in A's mind what they are, or will be, or have been, in B's mind. You cannot indicate their several intensities and their consequent result and bearing within the personal life, unless you know the total course of life within which they are to behave as factors. And this would be to know precisely what you are challenged to predict. You can have these factors in your mind, that of A, beforehand by way of knowledge and communication through language ; but then you do not possess them in their aspect of forces and portions of a life. They are stripped of the power to grow and combine and produce the result which, in their true duration, they would produce. A cannot, in this way, do B's action before it is done. Granting that he can intellectually possess the data, they will not, for him, live the life which belongs to them.[1]

Or again, you, A, may possess the factors, actually, as they are, experiencing their value and intensity and power, and not merely possessing these data in an intellectual shape. But then it would inevitably follow that your, A's, " duration " would be one and the same with that of the person B whose future action is to be predicted. And that means that you are one and the same with him ; for any deviation, a different body, a different date or life-history, would destroy some of the living experience necessary to the result. Therefore you fail in one of the conditions of prediction. You, A, would be doing B's act, but you would not be doing it beforehand. You would have turned into B, and be doing the act when and as B actually does it.

5. So, to sum up Bergson's view. By calculation, after the manner of astronomy, you can never predict a course of consciousness. For a course of consciousness can never be possessed apart from its own duration. You can predict, of course, probably, from knowledge of individual character and its expression in analogous situations. But that is not the kind of prediction in question. You cannot predict demonstratively from previous knowledge of psychical factors, because they have not their full nature except in being experienced. And you cannot take refuge in applying the idea of causation to the psychical nexus. Causation has no meaning in conscious duration, because repetition is there impossible, for the reason pointed out above ; and *the principle of causation " Same produces same " only applies where true or precise repetition can take place*, i.e. only in mathematical time, but not in duration. *For in duration there can never be any recurrence of the same.*

---

[1] Mr. Bradley, in stating the alternative of prediction by calculation, requires it to be from data such as can exist before the birth of B. Bergson apparently admits rather more, in suggesting that the actual factors of B's mind should be present as data to A.

Freedom, then, is the relation of the concrete " me " to its action. This relation is indefinable ; because, if fixed in a conception, and analysed, it drops out the nature of creative novelty which belongs to true duration, and you find yourself handling the spatial chart of time, and not the living experience. Thus every definition of freedom must establish determinism ; and yet determinism is false.

6. The above view, as I observed, coincides in certain points with that of Mr. Bradley's *Ethical Studies*. Calculation of a man's conduct from pre-natal data, it is there observed, if possible, would be objectionable in the highest degree to the plain man. Whereas prediction based on experience of an individually formed character, as displayed in his habitual action, is an everyday fact, and is not objectionable, but on the whole acceptable, to the plain man. And, in general agreement with Bergson, it is there pointed out that the instinctive objection of a reasonable man is not against foreknowledge, but against what I may summarize as " reduction." What a man minds, is being treated as something different from what he feels himself to be ; as something that can be mastered from the outside and put together out of alien data or factors ; out of circumstances and conditions disparate with himself. He does not dislike being known and understood as he really is, or at least as the sort of being he takes himself to be. What he dislikes is a process of understanding which seems to imply that he is not in the least the sort of being he takes himself to be. So far Bergson's views have a great deal in common with the best idealism.

But his opposition seems to be limited, so far as English philosophy is concerned, to such writers as Bain and Mill. And he therefore appears not to meet the contentions of idealism in their developed form. Idealism would, I imagine, accompany him in his campaign against associationism, but would make other demands as against his own antiintellectualism.

Here are some points by which such a criticism might be illustrated.

(1) The principle of intelligence is not bare identity, as Bergson throughout maintains. Causation, as the principle of science, is not dependent on mere repetition of conditions.

Therefore this alleged distinction [1] between life and inorganic nature, that causation is a principle which can apply to the latter and not to the former, ceases to be tenable. Everywhere, intelligence lies in the tracking of the universal, which is continuity through difference, essentially creative, and not dependent on unchanged recurrence. On the contrary, such recurrence is essentially destructive of intelligent comprehension, by leaving nothing for it to comprehend. Bergson, as it seems to me, is not really disposed to accept the extreme mathematical theory of homogeneous units of matter, but employs it as a *reductio ad absurdum*, by making it typical of the operations of intelligence and the principle of causation. But, as described by him and by other critics, it is not identical with either ; and you cannot at once apply it as a *reductio ad absurdum*, and assign it as the true principle of investigation in the inorganic world. In short, the distinction between true duration and the spatial symbolism of time—which may be a working abstraction—is one thing. But the suggestion that the latter gives the true characteristic of actual inorganic nature, and that it is adequate to the operation of intelligence and the nexus of causation, is altogether another thing.

(2) We find the same bias in the disparagement of thought, language, ideals, social relations. The general conception is that articulateness involves falsity. " Reality is richer than thought." Life, feeling, personality, become unknowable things in themselves. We are watching the rise of a new agnosticism, which necessarily develops into a new pessimism. It is always pessimism which tells you that ideas, language, social relations, take you away from the depths of reality and from the springs of life and feeling.

(3) To this point of view belongs the neglect of the conception that psychical sequence and the genesis of actions may be knowable as logically determined, though not, or not merely, a case of causation. We know that logic is latent in the most casual association, and this fact might give us a clue by which logical determination might be regarded as the true mode of initiative where free causes [2] are at work. Thus

[1] It is a distinction which Hegel maintains up to a certain point, but not absolutely.

[2] It is noticeable that the term " free cause " is common to Bergson and to Green.

much might be known and understood about the action of human beings without, or in addition to, prediction by calculation. Reduction might be avoided, but so also might the agnosticism of personality, into which the modern movement is falling as the opposite extreme.

If the three points just referred to were rectified, what is valuable in Bergson's attitude might be retained, while the agnosticism would go. Freedom of action might be held a logical mode of initiative, though not in the common sense a causal one. This would give a much better prospect of reconciliation with a causal system of nature, and with the whole of individuality, which is mutilated by the agnosticism we have described.

For example : Bergson rightly complains of the bad habit of taking very trivial choices as the tests of freedom ; mere cases of routine where the whole personality does not " vibrate." He likes to think of the typical choice as what happens when an appeal is made to your whole passionate nature, and it rises up and defies tradition and you do something worth calling new. Now I am disposed to turn the same objection in another way. It has always seemed to me that the really typical choices, those which show human freedom and the true nature of initiative at their fullest, are the great logical choices which occupy years in the making, as when a man chooses his religion, or his profession, or his political party, working by long processes of suggestion and elimination, till he has found, or nearly found, a self-expression which includes the whole of him, and in which therefore he can rest. Well, but it may be said, this is to make the typical choice nothing less than the whole process of experience which constitutes a man's life. So it is, no doubt, and so, I hold, it ought to be. If the free act is the act which expresses the whole self, it is here if anywhere that you get it. I certainly agree that you do not get it in the trivial choice, am I or am I not free to blow out this candle ? but neither, I think, do you get it at all completely in moments of rebellion against tradition and of upheaval of the whole passionate nature. You get it most fully, and see the working of it most plainly, when the self has time and opportunity to search for and to find the expression that is really appropriate to it.

And it is in as far as referred to such a process, and as stages in it, that momentary choices have their freedom.

When we take such a point of view, and return to the conception that ideas have hands and feet, and get rid of the agnosticism of personality, we are able to draw a deeper result from the discussion of foreknowledge, while adhering to Bergson's and Mr. Bradley's main results. Let us recall Bergson's own main principles in dealing with prediction. Prediction means doing a thing before it is done.[1] And you can do this for conscious beings as far as, but only as far as, you are the same with them. Now if we abandon agnosticism, acknowledge identity as something other then tautology, and accept ideas as the fullest form of finite experience, a good deal follows from this.

Both the world and intelligence, we should be able to say, are in principle one. It is possible in various degrees for individuals to contain others, and to be identical with them. This is illustrated in the history of inventions, which so constantly shows independent lives working out to the same conclusion at the same time ; or in the logic of practice applied to the great problems of statesmanship, when an earlier mind will lay down the lines on which all subsequent minds must and will proceed for, say, a century to come. Or more generally, in the relation of great thinkers to those who come after them, or in common life of men who have great capacity to those whose performances are wholly covered by theirs. Or ultimately, in so far as we can conceive the relation of the individual to God in religion as one of identity and inclusion, the supposed difficulty of foreknowledge falls away.

It may be said that this sort of inclusion or covering, as when a minor philosopher moves wholly within the orbit of a greater thinker, is not the " prediction " which forms the difficulty. It does not tell us whether or whom a man will marry or how long he will live, or what he will die of. I leave these two latter instances, although they are not in point, because the fact that they occur to one so naturally is in itself significant. They are not matters of conduct but of

[1] This would hardly apply to irrational prediction, if such a thing were possible. See Mr. Bradley's interesting remark in *Ethical Studies*, p. 17.

natural causation, and therefore they do not illustrate the prediction of conduct. They do not. But are they not just typical of the incidents which most readily spring to mind when we pronounce prediction impossible ? Is not the obvious suggestion, when we review our attitude to such incidents, that lines of conduct are capable of being known and entered into from without in proportion to their magnitude and importance, and that it is really the physical and the comparatively trivial which we cannot enter into by way of knowledge or foreknowledge ? If a statesman is going to take the Secretaryship for India, it may well be possible for some persons to foresee what line of policy he will adopt, and surely this is a more important point, entering deeper into his personality, than even the question whether or whom he will marry, not to say what he will die of.

And this is not merely the case, admitted above, of probable prediction from character. It is a form of knowledge depending on the profound study of a difficult problem, and involving the identity which intelligence, being in principle one, is capable of developing in what are called different minds. There is no doubt, in principle, that one mind can include another, or share its content with another, though, of course, with finite minds, the inclusion or participation cannot extend to every detail.

I conclude then by repeating : the important principle is that not foreknowledge, but reduction, is the impossible and objectionable thing. You can predict for others in as far as you are the same with them. And, contrary to Bergson's agnosticism, we can be and are the same with others in a considerable degree.

# XIII

## THE RELATION OF SOCIOLOGY TO PHILOSOPHY

1. NOTHING could be more startling prima facie to the philosophical student than the proposition that the science of society is a creation of strictly modern thought ; of thought that is, not merely recent in time, but determined by distinctively modern conditions and owning no continuity with the central tradition of European philosophy. Yet this was undoubtedly the view of Auguste Comte ; it was implied by Mill in the sixth book of the *Logic* ; and the same standpoint reveals itself in the independence and isolation which Sociology, or *la Science Sociale*, maintains to-day as against Plato and Aristotle on the one hand and their modern representatives—e.g. Spinoza and Hegel—on the other.

It is not my intention, in the following observations, to challenge the claims of Sociology to an origin and existence independent of Ethical or Social Philosophy ; my purpose is rather to suggest an analogy in accordance with which this independence may be justified on the basis of a definite relation between the two types of theory. Certain traits of parallelism and even of convergence will, however, necessarily disclose themselves as between lines of investigation so closely akin. And each, it will appear probable, may have something to learn from the other.

2. What is the essence of the new science, as Comte repeatedly and emphatically calls it, which he regarded as Social Physics, and for which he invented the name of Sociology ? The philosophical principle of the science is " that social phenomena are subject to natural laws, admitting of rational prevision." [1] The essential novelty of the conception in its author's eyes was, in short, that there could

[1] Martineau's *Positive Philosophy*, ii, p. 62.

be, in the strict sense, a general science of social phenomena ; that natural laws of progress could be ascertained, and that the science of society could thus take its place as part, and the most important part, of the indivisible organism of real and natural knowledge. The present is big with the future.[1] This enunciation of the principle of continuity, drawn from Leibniz, is adopted by Comte as expressing the true spirit of social dynamics ; and is interpreted by him as involving the idea that the social movement is subject to invariable natural laws rather than to any will whatever. A general theory of the co-existence and succession of social phenomena according to " natural " laws—such is the ideal, the need and the aspiration to which Comte gave form and currency under the name of Social Science, Social Physics, or Sociology.

Philosophy has entered upon the study of man in society from a different point of view. According to the simile of Plato, which has never ceased to be applicable, the philosopher has tried to read in society the larger expression of what man—the individual man—has it in him to become, and therefore of what he really is. He has investigated the State, or the social whole, as he has investigated other achievements and expressions of the human mind, in order to learn in its doings what that mind really is and what are its powers of self-assertion or its necessities of self-surrender in face of its human and its natural environment. There is always a bias in his research, or at least a definite problem before him. He tests the life of man by its relation to reality, by its harmony, comprehensiveness and coherence. He wants to ascertain how the highest life exhibits itself in the social organization, or what elements have been contributed by the great nations of history to the fullness of human nature, or how the natural surroundings of a race have stimulated its expressive or constructive activity. The philosopher has dealt, by preference, with what have commonly been accepted as the highest types of civilization, and has drawn in the less mature phases of evolution and the action of material and economic influences mainly as accessory considerations. It is needless to labour the contrast further. I proceed to point out its consequence.

[1] Martineau's *Positive Philosophy*, ii, p. 69.

3. Sociology, as contrasted with those branches of Philosophy proper which deal in any way with the facts of society, pretends to the width and impartiality of a natural science. The laws of aggregation and of the behaviour of aggregates as such, though restricted by limitation to social aggregates, under whatever definition of the term " social " commends itself to the investigator, are the problems with which it deals. It has no primary reason for taking a greater interest in the Greek city or the nation of modern Europe than in the varied and unfamiliar phases of savage or barbarian life. It does not confine its investigations to the State or the civic society, but wherever two or three are gathered together there is a problem such as may be proposed to sociological analysis. The employment of comparison between human society and relations found to exist in groups of the lower animals is, as we might expect, vigorously defended by Comte, and in the hands of Mr. Herbert Spencer has formed the bulk of sociological inquiry. So far, indeed, as impartiality or neutrality is really observed we have no right to impute to Sociology as such the tendency to explain what are commonly held to be the higher forms of life by reducing them to the level of those which are commonly held to be the lower. But some result of the kind has undoubtedly characterized the social science so far as it has hitherto been developed ; and the reason is not far to seek. An impartial science dealing with very general forms of behaviour—we might take chemistry as an example—will give a more complete account of objects in which those forms of behaviour are presented *per se* than of those in which they assume complications subservient to some further type of unity. Chemistry can say something of all material substances ; but it can say less, in proportion, of those which have biological significance. And so the most general treatment of the laws of grouping of living creatures has more in proportion to say of groupings in which no very complex self-realization of the human mind is manifested than of those which involve all the functions of the human spirit at its best. And thus, quite apart from any set purpose of dragging down what pass as the higher manifestations of humanity, it results *ipso facto* that an account is given of them in terms which,

while adequate to certain simpler phenomena, are not adequate to them. One can hardly get over Mr. Herbert Spencer's characterization of a human society as a local variety of the species, a description which appears to disregard all the elements by which it is made social and human.

But the wise application of such an impartial theory to problems which tend to become isolated in their dignity has very great advantages. The mere fact signalized above, that for Sociology the State ceases to be the sole form of social unity, is typical of these advantages. For the State is nothing but an expression of certain needs and aspirations of mankind ; it is itself capable of many degrees of existence, and if it is the highest revelation of social unity it can only be known as such when duly correlated with all others. A general or indifferent theory is a solvent which destroys the rigid limitations of traditional thought and sets us free to contemplate the unity of life in its continuous endeavour after self-expression.

Whether the impartiality or indifference which has hitherto characterized Sociological analysis is really essential to it appears to depend on the question whether the general laws of social behaviour differ in kind or only in degree from the characteristics which give interest to the object-matter of political, historical, ethical, and religious philosophy. The point of view taken by M. Bernès [1] seems to recognize a double tendency in the body of science, such that the purely speculative—or, in our language, the indifferent—nature of mathematics finds its complement at the other extreme of the series in what for him is the practical spirit of Sociology ; the intermediate group of the " natural " sciences being, as I understand him, the chief meeting-ground of these two tendencies, neither of which can be wholly absent in any scientific endeavour. It is a detail of terminology that M. Bernès's phrase " practical " seems to me to approach in actual significance the philosophical expression " speculative." It means, as I read him, not the spirit of an art devoted to immediate action, but rather the spirit of a philosophy which divines, through the will no less than through the intellect, the impulse and the indications of a partially

[1] *Revue de Morale et de Métaphysique*, March 1895.

unrealized unity in the world, which demands realization. If Sociology admits to itself the scientific validity of such an impulse and the demands of such a unity, and applies itself to the discovery of laws and forms which shall be capable of doing justice to this recognition in the comparative treatment of social aggregates and functions, then the course which it has hitherto pursued will have been considerably modified, and the distinctions which separated it from Philosophy will in all essentials have been done away.

It is possible, I think, to exhibit this distinction, and its vanishing quality, in a striking light, by what is something more than a mere illustration. Not only may Sociology be compared with Psychology in its relation to Philosophy proper, but in a great measure, as we shall see, the relation in the two cases is actually the same. For Sociology, in its later developments, seems likely to be regarded as a psychological science.

Thus the relation of Psychology to Philosophy reproduces in many respects that of " Social Science " to the Philosophy of Society. Like Sociology proper, Psychology in the strict sense is a science of modern origin. Like Sociology, it assumed at first the position of an extension of the natural sciences to a field hitherto denied to them, and proclaimed itself to deal, not with the value or significance of special intellectual phenomena, but with the general and causal laws which governed the operations of mind. The impartiality or speculative neutrality which we observed in early Sociology is claimed with startling emphasis even by the most recent Psychology. All revelations of mind, we are told, are of equal interest and importance for Psychology as such. It is not their grade in reality, but their exemplification of psychical laws and causes, which entitles them to psychological consideration.

And the very terminology of Psychological Science appears to confirm the comparison here suggested, both in respect of the primary relation of Sociology to Philosophy and in respect of the possibility of a further one. The Laws of Association, with which modern psychology began, and in which, for a great part of its course, it has principally consisted, might serve for a designation of the general problem of abstract Sociology no less than of the general problem of abstract Psychology. So long as either science restricts itself to the consideration of the abstract conditions of any cohesion whatever, so long as the simplest connection of units is as good an object for it as the great organized structures of civilization, the indifference which belongs to it as a purely natural investigation remains unimpaired. And the strict definition of Psychology undoubtedly demands this indifference. In dealing with the mere course of psychical events, it makes abstraction from the relations to reality which constitute the essence of Logic or Ethics, or other branches of Philosophy. Just so, as we have noted, Sociology as such is indifferent whether the grouping, with which its Laws of Association are concerned, consists of a civilized State or a savage horde, of a Christian family or a polygamous community.

But the further tendency which has suggested itself in Sociology has already taken shape in Psychology. It has been found possible, by a recognition of the more definite facts of mental organization, to come closer to the operations of developed intelligence than could be effected by the Laws of Association alone. The Theory of Apperception, in its modern form, is to the Laws of Association what an explanation of special machines is to a general account of the working of mechanical parts. It still, indeed, remains ostensibly within the province of Psychology ; but it recognizes that though the reality which we think of may not fall within the mind, yet the mind is very different according to the reality which it thinks of.[1] The science, then, may still claim to maintain its speculative impartiality ; but this is no longer to be understood as more than the universal justice of reason. For it cannot any longer be said that the terms in which the highest phenomena are explained are such, without modification, as sufficed for the analysis of the lower. No doubt, indeed, it will always be convenient that Psychology as such should not pretend to absorb into itself the whole range of philosophical sciences, and therefore that it should maintain on the whole the peculiar abstraction which excludes the relation to reality from its view. But the line of this abstraction will always tend to be a vanishing one ; and Psychology, armed with the theory of Apperception,

[1] Mr. F. H. Bradley has somewhere a sentence to this effect.

will tend to be the science, not merely of any and every mind, but of mind where it is most mind, because best and most typical.

The same relation may be predicted for Sociology. There will always no doubt be a difference in point of view, according as we approach the study of " association " from the side of anthropology or of zoology, or from any member of the linked circle of philosophical sciences, which attempt to bring together what is most profoundly real in the world. But as social science acquires command over its material and its conceptions, and as the mere unity of all phases of social existence ceases to be a novelty worth insisting on, it will recognize a gradation and a tendency, and find means to distinguish, on its own ground, the social forms in which development is fullest from those in which it is most meagre. In as far as it succeeds in this, it will assume towards the Philosophy of Society the same general attitude which Psychology holds towards Logic, Ethics, and Æsthetic ; and will be able to render services of the same class.

4. In the present condition of Sociology it appears needless to insist on that difference of method between Social Science and Philosophy which has arisen from a confusion between the claims of intelligence to deal rationally with social phenomena, and the idea that " subjection to natural law " or rational coherence implied causation of the same type as natural causation. It is worth while, however, to point out that on this aspect of social problems—the relation of man to his environment, or the degree in which man is the creature of circumstance—the new social science had much to learn from the ethical and political philosophy of Plato and Aristotle. The distinction between determination by law and determination by the presentation of law, and the relation of the conscious motive embodied in a political order to the facts and modes of behaviour existent in natural surroundings and economic arrangements, are stated with perfect balance and clearness by Plato and Aristotle. Many one-sided constructions of social causation might never have been attempted had due attention been paid to their ideas.

On the other hand, it is of interest to note that the force of facts appears to be determining Sociology to the position of a psychological science, as indeed Mill, in the sixth book of the *Logic*, fully intended it to be. The Psychology of Crowds, the idea of Imitation as the ultimate characteristic of Social Wholes, or the conception of the Consciousness of Kind as the central attribute of Society, bring us into contact with ideas with which political or social philosophy has long been accustomed to work. But while we recognize in these notions an approximation to philosophical thoughts, we cannot but wonder that so little use should be made by Social Science of the resources to which it now seems to hold the key. The psychology of a crowd is not even the psychology of a committee, much less of a representative assembly or of a great State. The working of an organized psychical unity of this kind has at least been more suggestively sketched by Plato in his commonwealth or by Aristotle in his idea of the thinker's function, than by any modern Sociologist. Yet M. Bernès, I observe, rests altogether on the commonplace and popular view of Aristotle's notion of the thinker's life.

Imitation, again, is a bald and partial rendering of that complex reciprocal reference which constitutes social co-opera-tion. To say that imitation is the characteristic of society is like saying that repetition is the soul of design, whereas even symmetry is incompatible with a principle so elementary as repetition. If one man holds a hammer on a rivet and another strikes it, that is conscious reciprocal reference, but not imitation ; and this doing of different things, as parts in a single plan, is the type of social co-operation. The whole idea of function, of structure and organization—in short, of true identity in difference—seems to be absent where such a suggestion is made. It seems probable that Sociology has arrived at these conceptions by re-traversing on its own account the track which leads from the apparent individual mind to the real identity of the universal self ; a track long familiar to philosophy, but one on which " social science " *par excellence* is only now arriving at the earliest halting-places. The same observation might be made with regard to the " Consciousness of Kind,"[1] which appears to be a faint and generalized counterpart of that recognition of oneself in another, to which Hegel long ago gave an explicit rank in

[1] Giddings, *Principles of Sociology.*

the development of self-consciousness, thus laying down the place of social relations in the growth of mind.

And in conclusion, while welcoming the unity of science as proclaimed by Comte and the conception of a probable influence of Sociology on scientific method as suggested by M. Bernès, one is amazed to find any such conception announced (as Comte more especially announces it) to be new in principle.

We seem to have forgotten that for Plato, e.g. *Laws*, 967 E, it was an essential principle that politics was a science ; that political forms corresponded to types of mind ; that the central light of all science, including the mathematical sciences, was the idea of the good, and that no one who had not mastered the connection that runs through the order of the universe, and its bearing on society and institutions, was fit, in his view, to be a ruler of men.

It hardly seems possible that, at the point which has now been attained, a distinction between Sociologists and Philosophers can any more justify itself than a distinction between Philosophers and Psychologists. It does not follow that the retention of a more general analysis and a more indifferent point of view may not be of service in the actual treatment of the sciences in question. We have seen that such a general analysis is a valuable solvent of distinctions which impede the perception of continuity ; but while retaining for this purpose the modern and naturalistic spirit of his science, the true Sociologist, like every great Psychologist, will recognize, indirectly if not directly, the grades of value and of reality, the logical and ideal structure, which belong to certain cases and complications of the very general laws with which he primarily deals.

# XIV

## SOCIAL AUTOMATISM AND THE IMITATION THEORY

1. In applying the psychological conception of Automatism to a human community, I have in mind such cases of secondary Automatism as dressing oneself, walking, reading, and writing. It is an analogy drawn from habits of this type that seems to throw light on a fundamental problem of political philosophy.

In the individual life-history, such habits as these, we are told, subserve the end of an economy of attention. The greater part of our life depends upon actions which we have "learnt" with pains and exclusive preoccupation; but which, when once learnt, we can carry on while giving the bulk of our attention to something more worthy of a mature consciousness. Growth and progress of the mind depend on this relation. If we had never done learning to read and write, we should never be able to spare the attention needed to master a science or to compose a treatise. What can be done by machinery is progressively handed over to machinery, while attention busies itself with the organization of fresh experience.

If the analogy is sound, which suggests itself between the individual and the community in this respect, the ideal of political nihilism is exploded. For our conception would indicate that social life is necessarily and increasingly constituted by adjustments which have become automatic, and are in a large measure withdrawn from public attention. The formation of such adjustments would then appear to be the condition of social progress. A definite habit of orderly action, which receives the *imprimatur* of the State, and is thus put beyond the range of discussion, effects an economy of attention. The public mind is no longer preoccupied with it; it becomes part of the rationalized substructure of conscious life, and subserves the social end, while, so far as it is concerned, setting free the social mind for new ideas.

Now it might be urged that the character of automatism is even more natural and necessary in social activities than in those which we primarily regard as individual. For the condition of automatism is a considerable degree of routine. And while routine is useful to individual life, in so far as it takes a definite shape, with activities which repeat themselves, it is absolutely essential to co-operative existence. At every point, in the complicated work of a civilized society, we have to reckon infallibly upon the actions of others without conscious arrangement or special agreement. Once people walking in the streets fought for the " crown of the causeway "; then they turned out of each other's way as chance might dictate; and then, as Dr. Johnson tells us, the habit grew up that the pedestrian kept to the right. This habit has not passed into law in England, but it easily might do so as foot-passengers over the bridge at Dresden find that it has done and as the rule of the road for vehicles has done. The same account may be given of all the daily conduct of a law-abiding citizen. It moves in certain routines, determined by habit and sanctioned by law; and it is this characteristic alone which enables the enormously complex life of a modern community to be carried on in such a way that, so far from absorbing, it progressively liberates the attention of its members from the maintenance of its necessary conditions.

It is noticeable that in these habits the work of the best minds may be embodied; so that while we economize our attention we are actually better guided than our own best attention could have guided us.

When we speak of the State using force or coercion upon individuals, by far the greater part of what we mean consists in the fact that each private mind is rooted in the common life by interlocking adjustments which have become automatic to all. By being thus rooted, its capacities and faculties are immeasurably extended; and this extension of the private mind, which is a consolidation of it with the social fabric, must inevitably in certain cases act upon it as force. We are necessarily under certain circumstances dragged along with the vast machine whose powers we use as our own. The intentional and deliberate coercion used by the State through law and punishment is only a recognition and regulation of this inevitable situation, on which, as we have seen, the possibility of progress depends.

And we are in agreement with the best theory of punishment if we regard it from a point of view in harmony with this analogy. It is not the furnishing of a new motive to make us do or omit, by the weighing of pains against pleasures, what otherwise we should have violently objected to doing or omitting. It is not essentially directed against intentional rebellion, and would not be rendered superfluous if all men became well-meaning. It is much more analogous to the start of pain which recalls us to ourselves when an automatic activity has failed to be self-regulating. We stumble in walking and hurt our foot ; we pull ourself together, give full attention for a moment, and see that we were off the path ; we take care to get on to it again, and give more heed to our steps in the future. As long as an imperfect mind has to meet progressive requirements, and to maintain a complex activity in excess of its powers of attention, a system of such reminders will be essential to society.

It must be noted that in a society a great deal of individual consciousness may be devoted to activities which are in the social sense automatic. That is to say, when anything has been reduced to routine by the public will, and handed over to a special class to carry out, then, as a matter of principle, it is in most cases withdrawn from the active attention of the community as such and of the bulk of its members, although a certain class are continuously occupied with it. The functions of the police are a case in point. It is plain that a difference exists between functions to which on the whole the maximum attention of the community is due, and functions which demand no attention, so to speak, for their own sake, but only in as far as is necessary to maintain order and freedom.

2. With reference to the rank or quality of these automatic activities a suggestion may be made in connection with the

biological principle of " short cuts," bearing on the problem of character and circumstance.

It seems to be an accepted principle [1] that " animals may perform movements which seem to be voluntary, with a nervous apparatus which would be inadequate to their performance by the child or man." The apparatus which represents a higher stage of mind has so encroached upon the independence of that which represents a lower stage, that the latter, in man, can no longer carry out the work which in the dog, for example, it will be able to take upon itself. A man, we are informed, can never recover his sight after the lesion of a certain higher brain centre ; in the dog a lower brain centre still retains the power of taking over the work of vision, and the dog, after the same operation, may recover his sight. [2]

It is not, perhaps, altogether fanciful to trace a transformation of this kind in the world of volition. It is often maintained that the simple and sensuous conditions which, as stimuli to actions, determine the life of primitive societies, and differentiate the hunter from the shepherd and the shepherd from the tiller of the soil, continue to be the essential determinants of action—the true causal factors of the moral world—throughout the life of higher societies. But development follows a subtler course than this, and the unity of mind is more thorough than such a doctrine admits. The simplest life-maintaining activities of civilized man are conditioned by far-reaching ideas, and if the capacity for these ideas perishes, the simpler stimuli which might have sufficed in an earlier phase are unable to carry out the task of providing for existence. The maintenance of material conditions has been transferred to the higher moral powers—the co-operative qualities demanded by a complex society. But by this transference the simple impulses of love and hunger have become unable to govern the world, as once, perhaps, they did. An objection may be made to the precise nerve of the analogy, on the ground that it is one thing to say that a simple impulse is inadequate to a more complex problem, and another to say that the simple impulse has lost even the

[1] See Baldwin, *Mental Development in the Child and the Race*, p. 20 ff.
[2] *Ibid.*

power which it previously possessed. But the two cases are not really separable. The transference has taken place because the work to be done came to be beyond the reach of the lower capacity ; and the disabling reaction upon the lower capacity itself is a matter of degree, and is always in such cases more or less evident. It would be easy to show that the motor effectiveness of the simpler impulses has been greatly impaired by the transference of their function to completer forms of volition. The phenomena of stationary populations are a case in point.

3. I may now say something of the antithesis of Imitation and Invention, which, under the form of Habit and Accommodation, is alleged to permeate man's social being.

It is clear that in analysing the mind or minds of men in society, with reference to their social character, we have to deal at once with phenomena of identity and with phenomena of difference. The minds which form the mind of a given community have certain features in common as unquestionably as they have certain features which are individual. And it is an elementary fact of psychology that ideas, habits, and actions tend to propagate themselves by suggestion through a number of minds which have the opportunity of acting upon each other. We are not therefore surprised to be told that imitation—the tendency to reproduction of suggestion —is a notable fact in the working of social intelligence. There is an aspect in which one individual may be regarded as a similar repetition of another, and the propagation of fashions or impulses throughout a multitude may be regarded as the imitation of one by others, and the repetition by others of the suggestion presented by one.

Nevertheless, upon a scrutiny of the true operative nature of social unity, we find that repetition and similarity are but superficial characteristics of it. What hold society together, we find, are its correlative differences ; the relation which expresses itself on a large scale in the division of labour, or in Aristotle's axiom " No State can be composed of similars." And we look to our social psychologists for a recognition of the element of adapted difference apart from which co-operation and co-existence are impossibilities. But here, it would almost seem, a technical difficulty bars the way.

Imitation, or the propagation of similarities among similars, holds the field as an account of the common features of a society. But no differentiation can be got out of the tendency to reproduce a copy *per se*; and we seem none the less brought to a deadlock that we are supplied with the word " invention," to indicate the desired well-spring of novelty and individuality. Somehow, we are given to understand, the individual invents, and then, as we can easily imagine, his invention is generalized by the universal tendency to " take suggestion as a cat laps milk."

But here we seem to have an awkward dualism. Imitation and similarity divide the province of mind unequally with invention and difference; and instead of operating throughout with the same indivisible nature, intelligence appears to have an inexplicable preference for creation in some cases and for propagation in others. And the results are unsatisfying. The theory of a social mind is reduced by M. Le Bon to the explanation of impulsive emotion in a mob—the mere propagation of similitudes, as if critical discussion and the collation of points of view were a thing unknown in the formation of the social will. Even for M. Durkheim the spheres of similitude and of difference are wholly disparate; and the force put upon facts in order to demonstrate that penal and industrial law (corresponding to similitude and difference respectively) occupy different regions of the social territory is enough to show that some fundamental assumption is leading us astray.

If we turn to Professor Baldwin's analysis, we find, as we might expect, a resolute repudiation of dualism. " We [1] cannot divide the child into two parts, two realities coming up to the facts of life with different capabilities, one fitted only to imitate, and the other fitted to invent. Of course, it is the same child whatever he does; and if he be gifted with the power of invention at all, this power should show itself in all that he does—even in his imitations." He recognizes that frequently in discussion " the two types of function are as far removed from each other as the letters *vs* put between them would suggest."

But we have seen protests of this kind before, and we

[1] *Social and Ethical Interpretations in Mental Development*, p. 90.

know that they decide nothing. For, only too often, they herald no comprehensive principle of unity, but a resolution of one thing into terms of another, the other being a mere fragment of the whole in which both should be complementary aspects. Have we not, I ask with diffidence in presence of Professor Baldwin's suggestive and laborious researches—have we not, in principle, got a case of this kind here ? I have heard it said, perhaps too curtly, that Professor Baldwin explains invention as the failure to imitate. He does not use the phrase ; but does not the theory and description of the child's invention bear it out ? [1] If the criticism is justified, his theory will remind us of the famous definition of mythology as a disease of language—the work of poetic imagination being regarded as a degeneration of the meanings of words. In some degree, indeed, as I understand him, " the valuable variations of thoughts are clearly more or less determined in their direction by reason of the particular system in which they occur." [2] But yet, it would seem, in the main they have to be picked out by selection,[3] and therefore are conceived as after all mere variations, generated in an attempted imitation, and presented for a choice of survivors to be made from them, not thought-products with an inherent rule and direction which govern the adapted difference with which they come into being. In as far as the pregnant passages just alluded to can be shown to contain the essentials of the view to which I am about to refer, I shall admit my criticism to have been unjustified.

Subject to this reservation, it appears to me that the whole tradition of the sociological psychology in question is vitiated by a fallacy which has its roots in the atomic doctrine of Association. The importance attached to repetition of similar units, as an analysis of society, and as an analysis of habit, betrays this origin. If the unity of the social mind is primarily a repetition or multiplication of resemblances, and if the *modus operandi* of mind as such is primarily the reinstatement of a perception or idea similar to a copy which has been previously presented to the mind from without, we see the ground of the difficulty which has been felt in locating

[1] *Social and Ethical Interpretations in Mental Development*, pp. 105, 107.
[2] *Ibid.*, p. 96.                    [3] *Ibid.*, p. 120.

the origin of difference,[1] which is introduced under the names of accommodation or invention as against the typical processes of habit and imitation. As I read the story, Professor Baldwin, having started like others with this impossible point of view, is working with immense ingenuity to remould it. In doing so, he strains the idea of imitation, in two degrees, beyond its normal meaning. Its normal meaning I take to be the reproduction by a sensitive or conscious subject of some trait presented to it from without, because of its being presented. The typical meaning which Professor Baldwin assigns to it is, however, already an extension of this, including any reaction by which in consequence of a certain stimulus an organism secures to itself more of the same stimulus, as e.g. when an organism approaches a source of light or warmth. It is plain that here we are beyond the limits of the repetition of a trait or movement presented as a copy ; and we are taken one more remove beyond this normal meaning of imitation, when it is suggested that we are essentially imitating in every act of will. " What are we really bringing about in willing anything ? Are we not hoping that through us a kind of experience, object, thing, in the world, may be brought about after the pattern of our idea or purpose ? "[2] Here the origin of our operative idea is wholly lost sight of, and the imitation lies in the passing of the idea into fact.

In all this, then, we have got far beyond the reproduction of a given copy in our operative ideas ; and in being extended to cover volition—the passing of idea into fact—imitation has lost its differentia, and ceases to offer any account of the relation of action or ideas to previous actions or ideas of ourselves or of others. For the origin of difference, therefore, we must look not to this extended account of imitation, but to the passage in which imitation and invention are explained and reconciled. And there, as we said above, it

---

[1] This suggestion is confirmed by the passage quoted from Professor Royce, *Social and Ethical Interpretations*, p. 233, note. The tendency to find a special and separate explanation for phenomena of difference really seems to indicate something fundamentally imperfect in the writer's conception of unity and identity. I repeat a hackneyed illustration. The type of co-operative unity is not to be found in such a relation as that between two similar screws, but only in that between a screw and its nut.

[2] *Mental Development*, etc., p. 382.

is unquestionable that a strong effort is being made to weld
the two together, but it seems no less unquestionable that
the welding is artificial, and must be so, so long as we start
from the point of view of similarity and imitation, which as
such have no essential aspect of difference. The process of
imitation is to reproduce a copy. In this reproduction we
are told a variation may arise from accessory circumstances,
which may be selected as valuable, and that is an invention.
Can there be a doubt that we are here working with the
machinery of Association by Similarity, and the old notion
of a rack full of photograph slides stored in the mind, each
of which is in the normal case reproduced without modification ? Additional stimuli, it appears to be intended,
may produce additional reactions, which form variations
which have to be reconciled with the imitation-reaction, as
parts of a system ; but this is quite different from saying that
the reaction to stimulus is *ipso facto* proportional to the place
of the stimulus in a system. I can find in the whole theory
absolutely no suggestion, unless there was some hint of it in
the brief passage referred to above, that the mind can appropriate as law or principle the scheme of a whole, and naturally
and necessarily differentiate its reactions in accordance with
the bearing of such a principle on the new situation presented.

And yet to the student of social philosophy such a doctrine
is an absolutely fundamental necessity. Nothing of serious
importance happens by genuine imitation. There is no grain
of truth in the restriction of invention to the individual, as
opposed to generalization which takes place by a plurality of
individuals copying the one. All the business of society goes
on by differentiated reactions. We never do simply what
another person does. We do something different, which has
a definite reference to it. I do not build my house. I give
instructions and I pay for it ; and of all the persons concerned,
no one simply reproduces the action of another ; but all do
different things as determined by the scheme or law of action
which is the universal working in their minds. The house
is an invention, and a joint invention, a universal in which
many minds have met. Pure imitation is an extreme sub-
case of this principle, a sub-case in which differentiation is
at a minimum. But strictly speaking, differentiation is

always there. Even if I buy a straw hat because my neighbour has one, I buy one that fits me, and not one that fits him. Every man in society is what he is through a law or scheme which assigns him an individual position, differing from all others, and identified with them precisely through these differences, by which alone he can co-operate with them. Similarities are superficial consequences of the relations which identity in difference prescribes.

The error, then, if I am right, springs from working with Similarity instead of Identity. Directly we introduce Identity, Difference falls into its place as an inherent aspect of the principle, and we understand that no reconciliation is needed, but the universal is unity manifested in difference from the beginning and throughout.

In the laws of habit, thought and action, Identity exhibits itself in the shape of Relative Suggestion ; the point of which is that the mind is reproductive not *of* a similarity, but *according to* a universal, the more or less systematic scheme of a whole. I need not enlarge on the conception in question, which is familiar to readers of Mr. Stout's *Analytic Psychology*. I will only insist on two points ; first, that it follows immediately from the substitution of Identity for Similarity in the theory of Association ; and, secondly, that it at once satisfies the absolute demand of social experience for a doctrine that will show why we never do simply what others do, but always something different from what they do and definitely related to it. The whole idea of the social mind has, in my view, been narrowed and distorted by the failure to grasp the importance of this principle, and it has not been understood that all social co-operation necessarily involves a unity of intelligence and habit which is in its nature logical and inventive ; the invention not being confined within individual minds, but being simply an aspect of the differentiated reactions, by which a co-operative body taken as a whole endeavours to be equal to the situation at a given moment. Every action, without any exception, is in principle a difference within an identity. The use of language is a familiar example. Every application of a word has an element of originality, and when the slightest difficulty of expression occurs the aspect of invention becomes emphatic, and is

ttended with noticeable pleasure. I have taken this oppor-
unity of explaining my position towards the Imitation theory,
artly because in a forthcoming work, which afforded me no
pace for psychological discussion, I have been obliged to
efer very briefly to the views of Professor Baldwin and
thers.[1]

[1] I regret that Professor Baldwin's Presidential Address on " Selective
hinking," delivered in December 1897, only came into my hands at the
oment when the present paper was being sent to press. So far as I can
dge, it confirms my view that Professor Baldwin occupies a position inter-
ediate between that of Associationism and that of Relative Suggestion,
ith a tendency towards the latter.

## XV

## THE REALITY OF THE GENERAL WILL

" There is often a great difference between the will of all and th
general will; the latter looks only to the common interest : the form
looks to private interest, and is nothing but a sum of individual wills
but take away from these same wills the plus and minus, that canc
one another, and there remains, as the sum of the difference
the general will." " Sovereignty is only the exercise of the gener
will." [1]

THIS celebrated antithesis, the statement of which I hav
translated from Rousseau's own words, has the effect of se
ting a problem to which Rousseau himself scarcely finds a
answer. The problem is emphasized by the various reason
and indications which make it difficult to believe that th
action of any community is a mere sum of the effects of wholl
independent causes operating on a number of separate ind
vidual minds. No doubt, the action of a community some
times is, and often appears to be, the sum of effects of such
independent causes. One man gives a certain vote because h
hates Mr. A.; another man gives the same vote because h
thinks Mr. B. will do something for his trade; and a thir
gives the same vote because of some one out of a thousan
possible social reforms which he thinks the man he is votin
for will help or will hinder, as the case may be. Now, assumin
these causes to be independent of one another, the directio
in which they will sum up is a question of chance. Of cours
it is determined by causation, but it is not determined by an
general cause, corresponding to a general element in th
result which takes place. As related to the separate caus
in operation, the general character of that result is a coinciden
or matter of chance.

[1] Rousseau, *Contrat Social*, Book II, chap. i and chap. iii.

And this is, in fact, how Rousseau seems to regard it, and he therefore suggests what is practically, I should imagine, just the wrong method for eliminating private interest and getting at the general will.   Let the citizens all vote as independent units, not organizing themselves in groups or adjusting their views by private communication, and then, he thinks, as I understand him, the general interest will assert itself, as any general cause does in the elimination of chance among a great number of counteracting independent causes; that is, as he says, the independent causes, if present in sufficient numbers, may be expected to cancel, and the general cause will have a visible effect in deciding the question.   If private interests are equally balanced, the public interest will affect some minds on both sides enough to turn the scale.   This element of regard to the public interest is what he calls the general will, as distinct from the will of all.

I do not think that this view is false ; but it is not adequate to the action of a very complex society with elaborate constructive tasks before it.   It is rather adapted to a plebiscite on a single question, in which the general will is represented by a conscious though feeble inclination to what is admittedly the public interest.   The discouragement of discussion and of organization in groups, which he insists on in order to keep the chances fair, i.e. to keep all the private interests independent of one another, would make all complicated legislation impossible, and is quite incompatible with the method which I shall maintain that necessity prescribes for the formation of the general will.   He so far admits this, that the ideal legislator is for him a person outside the community, who interprets the general will into a system of laws.

What we have got then, so far, is a problem or a paradox : the idea of a will whose sole aim is the common interest, although it can exist as a will only in the minds of the human individuals who make up the community, and all of whom are for the most part occupied with their own individual interests.   There is no social brain other than and separate from the brain of individuals, and because we seldom face this difficulty fairly, our great modern gospel, that society is an organism, is becoming a little stale before it has rendered us the one service which it might perhaps be able to render ; that is,

to make us ask ourselves in what properties or relations of
individuals in society there resides anything corresponding on
behalf of society to the brain or mind of each separate
individual. We know that many not contemptible people
speak of the individual members of any community as mostly
fools, and say that the wise and those who are in the right are
always in the minority, and that the ordinary man picks up
his opinions out of a newspaper, and adjusts them by conversation with two or three other persons no better informed than
himself. The expressions, more or less in this sense, of so
eminent a writer as Mr. Bryce, in his discussion of Public
Opinion in the third volume of the work on the *American
Commonwealth*, were what I had chiefly in my mind when
I resolved to try and examine this paradox, which in that
discussion Mr. Bryce fully recognizes. No candid man can
altogether, I think, deny the judgments to which I am referring,
so far as they deal with the general capacity for intellectual
processes in unfamiliar matter. Mr. Bryce indeed tries
to blunt the paradox by pointing out that the so-called
educated classes are *not* especially fitted, by the training which
has hitherto been customary, for dealing with important
practical questions ; but this does not help us to see how the
bulk of the community *are* able and willing to deal rightly
with such questions in the common interest. If the majority
of separate individuals are, on any question immediately put
before them, more likely to miss the common interest than to
hit it, both from blindness and from selfishness, which cannot
practically be distinguished, why does not society come to
grief ? Aristotle says that all the citizens taken together may
have more wisdom than any one. Is there any meaning in
this ?

Is it true that the intelligent pursuit by the individual of
his private interests necessarily in the system of things con-
duces to the preservation of the community ? Not if we mean
by his private interests merely certain aims which are definitely
before his mind, which he might tell you are the ruling objects
of his life. On the other hand, if we say that the pursuit of
his private interests *as*, on the whole, he pursues them, con-
duces to the preservation of the community, that is pretty
much a tautology.

What necessity is there that this mode of action and judgment should have in it any general reference whatever ? When and why is the general will a reality within individual wills ?

I have taken some time to state the paradox, because I think that the facts which it indicates are of extreme importance, even if the explanation offered is inadequate. I will now attempt an explanation, borrowing in some degree the ideas of modern psychology.

By an individual will I mean a human mind considered as a machine, of which the parts are ideas or groups of ideas, all tending to pass into action but liable to be counteracted or again to be reinforced by each other. The groups of ideas are connected with each other by associations of all degrees of intimacy, but each is for the most part capable of being awakened into action by the appropriate stimulus without awakening more remotely associated groups, and the will, for the time being, consists of those ideas which are guiding attention and action. The ideas are not thrown together anyhow, but are more or less organized ; some being of a nature which enables them to serve as a clue or plan in which others find their places, and in a sense every group of ideas might be called a single idea, and all that there is in the mind has the character of a single idea—that is to say, all its parts are connected in various degrees, and more or less subordinated to some dominant ideas which, as a rule, dictate the place and importance of the others. We know what a ruling idea is : it is one that has got the control of the mind, and subordinates all the other ideas to itself. This mental system, with its dominant ideas in relation to external action, is the individual will.

Now, at first sight all these individual wills, or minds in action, are separate machines, locked up in separate boxes, each with its indicator outside, and the response which each of them will make to a stimulus from without is determined by its own structure, which is again determined by its own private history. If we go no farther than this we seem not to get any hint of a general will, but only a sum of individual wills, which need not have any reference to each other's ideas.

But we can perhaps go behind this. The individual will is shaped by its dominant ideas. What, on the whole, determines which ideas get the upper hand ? The answer seems to be that the ideas which tend to be victorious are those distinguished by logical capacity ; because they are especially able to marshal the content of consciousness in a way suitable to themselves, checking and defeating the ideas that cannot be brought into their system, and reinforcing themselves by those that can. All practical action tends to give victory to such ideas as these, while modifying and extending them. Any suggestion which enables you to deal with matter that you have to arrange is maintained in your mind and reinforced by the successful action to which it leads, and receives new content, which it embodies in itself, from the combinations which arise in carrying it out. Other suggestions, that " would not do," as we say, are driven out and disappear. Still, all this is a play of ideas within the individual mind locked up in its separate box.

But now, does the quality which makes certain ideas dominant in one individual mind ensure their having any relation to the ideas which are dominant in other individual minds ? Under certain conditions, clearly this is the case. These conditions are, in brief, community of life and of experience. Ideas do not spring from nowhere ; they are the inside which reflects the material action and real conditions that form the outside. So that the common life shared by the members of a community involves a common element in their ideas, not merely in their notions of things about them, though this is very important, but more especially in the dominant or organizing ideas which rule their minds. For the matter which is before their minds to be organized consists in great measure of connections between persons, and life simply cannot go on unless the organizing ideas in different people's minds with reference to these connections correspond definitely to one another. This is, of course, a truism, except that it is not always driven home with reference to the actual shape and content which it implies in individual minds.

It may be said this only means that different persons' minds in the same country have a good deal in common ; it does not mean that they participate in any conception of a common interest, but merely that they are influenced in the same way by the same appeal, with a certain general result, which is no more *in* each of them than the waving of a field of corn before the wind is in each separate stalk of corn. Well, this comparison is just for some cases; for the case of a mob, for instance, when they act as one man, under the influence of an identical sentiment of anger or cupidity. This is an irrational form of the general will, as a burst of feeling is of the individual will; but it is definitely general in so far as it is owing to the operation of the same sentiment in all the minds at once.

But there are stronger cases than this. Just as the material working of any industry or institution is not complete in a single person, but consists in corresponding though different actions of different persons, so it is with the dominating ideas which in different individual minds represent this working. Therefore, if we could see these minds, which are locked up in boxes tolerably like each other on the outside, we should perceive that each of them bears quite a definite reference to the others outside itself; in short, it is not really a complete machine, as the body, though to some degree marked and moulded by its habitual occupation, appears to be, but is only part of a machine, of which the other parts are the minds of other persons with whom the first is in connection. The proof of this lies in the fact that external life is organized, which organization again consists in the fact that the dominant ideas of the persons who participate in this life constitute, when taken together, a machine whose parts play into one another.

Then we may identify the general will of any community with the whole working system of dominant ideas which determines the places and functions of its members, and of the community as a whole among other communities. The system is never quite harmonious; readjustment is always going on, but the direction of this readjustment is determined by the forces in collision together with the other forces of the machine. Both the more important workings of the machine, and especially the direction of its readjustment, are the most familiar *expression* of the general will. But the general will itself is the whole assemblage of individual minds, considered as a working system, with parts corresponding to one another, and producing as a result a certain life for all these parts themselves.

Such a conception seems illusory, because it is hard to define exactly where the thing which it describes begins and ends; but really in modern philosophy nothing can be parted sharply at the point of transition; it is enough if the central phenomena in each region are clear and distinguishable.

I will mark it off by three negatives.

The general will cannot be identified with the decision of a community by vote upon any single issue. Every such decision is an expression or consequence of the general will, but needs interpretation in order to say what direction of movement it really represents. In short, the general will is a system in motion, and cannot be expressed in a single proposition. And no system of voting can secure its expression, because it does not exist in a form that can be embodied in a vote.

Again, the general will is not identical with public opinion, considered as a set of judgments which form the currently expressed reflection upon the course of affairs. It may include these current notions or part of them, but it certainly includes much more, because the ideas that dominate the will do not always appear in reflection, or at least not with the importance which they have in life. The general will is more a system of wills than a system of reflections, and appears in action quite as much as in discussion.

Again, it is not merely the *de facto* tendency of all that is done by members of the community, though it is much more like this than like a vote or a set of opinions. It *is* to a great extent a *de facto* tendency, but only in so far as this tendency reveals active ideas with reference to the connection of persons or groups of persons. Other tendencies than these do not directly concern the organization of life, and therefore do not directly form part of the active scheme of society.

Take two examples from opposite extremes in mental development. An agricultural labourer thinks, I suppose, chiefly about making his living and supporting his family. His choice of where he will work and what kind of farm work

pays him best does not greatly affect the nature of his con
nection with other people, being all within the same general
scheme. But, although he does not reflect—or even if he
does not reflect—on this general scheme, yet it is represented
in the shape of his mind ; that is, in his customary active
ideas, and in their limitations. Now, these active ideas of
his in their general character—i.e. the general character and
limits of what he is prepared to do and to expect with reference to other persons—this is the factor of the general will
operative in his mind. It is acted on by his daily life, and
rests upon that life ; but it is rather the outline or scheme of
that life than the everyday details of it.

A dramatic poet, again, will exercise his conscious choice
about his subjects and his form of writing, and so forth. All
this makes no direct difference to other people, and they
cannot directly help him in it. Society cannot write a play.
But if, for example, a school of really great dramatists were to
arise in England to-day, the result might be to remould the
working ideas in their own and other minds. The theatre
would force itself as a matter to be taken account of into the
mental systems of individuals, and in doing so would modify
their dominant notions as to the place of art in national life,
and so there would be a tendency of one kind or another which
would enter into the active scheme or logical machine of social
relations as a factor in the general will.

After these three negatives, I will say affirmatively that we
may identify the general will with public opinion in a pregnant
sense ; not as consisting in the things said in the newspapers,
but as the *actual* tendency of the whole process in which the
necessary organizing ideas of all individual minds in the
community are factors.

The corollary from these suggestions, which is chiefly of
interest to us, concerns the process of formation of the general
will, or of public opinion in this pregnant sense.

It is not essentially superficial nor sentimental. It is
essentially logical.

What is the root of the whole matter ? It is nothing less
than the correspondence with each other of the shapes taken
by separate minds, each under the stress of its particular
experience giving the victory to those ideas which are able

to grapple with the matter pressed upon it.   If the external life of the community works as a system, then this internal life must work as a system also ;  the one reflects the other.

Therefore, though it seems, as we said, as though most people are wrong when they express their opinions, and as if they pick them up from hearsay or from newspapers by sheer chance, this is to a great extent a *mere* appearance. Every person who does anything which is a necessary function in the community has in virtue of this function, which is mirrored in the shape of his leading active ideas, a definite position in the logical system of the community.   So far as his mind reflects the real necessities of his active life he is on solid ground, and his will is so far a factor in the general will, because his life—which is his will seen from the outside— is a factor in the general life.   If we all understood our own active ideas completely and rightly in relation to those of others, then we should have the whole general will in our explicit consciousness.

But, as it is, no individual ever can have this, for two principal reasons :

First, we are never thoroughly aware even of our own practical ideas.   The will is a great mass of associated ideas guiding attention and action, of which very different portions come into play in different contexts, and our description of which in general language, however honest we are, is not infallibly true, but, just like our description of any compli- cated phenomenon outside us, depends on our skill, patience, and truthfulness.   Nothing is commoner than to succeed in telling a man something about his own conscious action which he really did not know till you told him.  Especially, the nature of practical ideas consists very much in their limita- tions, and of these, except by intellectual self-criticism, we are not aware.   A man may honestly believe that he has no prejudice against perfect social equality, and a short cross- examination will often show him that he has a strong prejudice of the kind.   We are not conscious either of all the influences active in our will or of its limitations.

Secondly, no one, not the greatest statesman or historical philosopher, has in his mind, even in theory, much less as a practical object, the real development in which his community is moving. In modern philosophy the contrast between man and nature is apt to be far too sharply drawn at this point, as if the whole moral world was consciously constructed by man. In very great men the relation of conscious purpose to historical result seems sometimes—as in Cavour, for example—to be considerable ; but, on the whole, we are to the structure of legal, political, and economic organization like coral insects to a coral reef. All these things, and the body of science itself, are on one side natural products—that is to say, that, although conscious purpose works in them, the effect it produces is always part of a system which is more than any particular agent intended. The process always needs the future to explain its real tendency.

Thus the general will is only in part self-conscious, and in as far as an attempt is made to formulate it in judgments it seems to become fallible. For then it ceases to be fact, and becomes interpretation of fact.

Still, it is important, in thinking of the formation of the general will with a view to its interpretation, to remember what kind of facts it consists of. The solid basis for every one is in his own practical will determined by the real necessities of his life in discharging a function in society. The process of interpretation and rationalization of this will is then technically a process of criticism—that is to say, of adjusting the bearings of our whole view of life to the solid data of our own necessary working ideas in relation to those of others.

Now, this process again is not entirely conscious. It has two forms—practical organization and reflective discussion. In practical organization, ideas adjust themselves to each other without consciousness of anything beyond an immediate daily purpose, and it is only after a long interval that people wake up and find perhaps the entire relations of classes and of industry changed as it were in their sleep. This practical organization is probably the most important phase in the formation of the general will. Of course it includes conflict within the law. And the second phase, discussion, if it is to be of any service, ought really to be the same thing in a reflective form—that is, contrivance, organization, ascertainment by criticism of solid data, consisting in reasonable necessities, and their adjustment in a working system, such as to satisfy them all.

Now, of course these two processes pass into one another, and will more and more do so. And the two together really make up a very great part of life, so far as the persons concerned participate in a common experience. Every person is thus always being moulded into a logical unit much more than he is aware, and the casual opinions which he expresses do not really represent the content of his will or the process by which it is formed.

We must modify the theory to admit of our belonging to more than one community. The different ideas which rule us in different relations allow easily of this. The communities to which we belong are now like a nest of boxes inside one another ; but we cannot effectively share the general will of any community with which we have no common life and experience. Whether humanity can yet be said to have a general will is at least doubtful.

I do not think I am trenching on practical politics if I illustrate the importance which I attach to the unconscious or semi-conscious logic of life in contact with our neighbours by a reference to Mr. Hare's election scheme, the essence of which is that the constituency is de-localized. I once spoke of this to the late Professor Green, being myself much fascinated by its ingenuity, and he replied, " I rather despise all those schemes for detaching people from their locality." Mill, on the other hand, in the *Autobiography*, speaks of it, we remember, as a real triumph of political contrivance.

What I desire to point out is merely that, for good or evil, I think men would judge quite differently, acting under such a scheme, from the way in which they judge when they act in their locality. Everything depends on the context to which one's views and action have to be adjusted. If you have to fight out a set of opinions in practice and in discussion among your neighbours, that is quite a different process from letting the returning officer look out a few thousand people in Great Britain who happen to agree with you on a single point. In the one case your whole life is really an argument, both unconscious and conscious, with reference to the general working scheme of society. In the other case you simply pronounce a single casual reflective judgment.  It appears to me an apt illustration of the general or organic will as contrasted with the will of all as a number of units.

I do not say that locality is a necessary condition.  I only say that it is a simple case of the necessary condition, of which there may be other cases.

Well, then, how does all this apply to matters of very special information either about distant countries or about the technique of management in difficult concerns, which the community as a whole undertakes ?  Here, no doubt, Mr. Bryce's account becomes much more true.  We know what sort of life we want for ourselves and others, but we are not generally competent to construct it *in unfamiliar relations*.  In our own life, as I have tried to explain, the thing works itself out by a self-adjusting process, because, whether we *know* what is wanted or not, we ourselves *are* the want, and behave accordingly.

The result is, then, that the general will is a process continuously emerging from the relatively unconscious into reflective consciousness.  And the reflective consciousness does its work best when it as nearly as possible carries on, in self-criticism and adjustment of purposes, the same moulding of the individual mental system, as part of a machine in which other mental systems correspond to it, as goes on unconsciously in the formation of the everyday practical will.

Is the view which I have suggested hostile to the theoretical study of social conditions ?  I should be very sorry if anything that I have said appeared to have such a tendency.  But it is not a bad thing to bear in mind that all knowledge, whether practically or theoretically employed, is only real and vital when it is the extension of a process like that which I have been describing.  Books cannot contain knowledge in a perfectly vital form ; they are rather instruments or materials of knowledge than knowledge itself.  In this science differs from fine art ; poetry, for example, is destroyed if we destroy the particular form which it has in a book ; but knowledge hardly exists for us till we have destroyed the form which it has in a book.  It must be recast in the intelligence—that is, interpreted and criticized bit by bit till we have made it all of one tissue with our own vital experience—our experience of the matter in question in its most real form, whatever that may be, whether given in observation only, or in practice as well. When this is accomplished, and not before, the knowledge is really knowledge—that is, it is present as intelligence in our view of life or nature, and not as a recollection of something printed in a book. Such intelligence, however wide-reaching, always begins at home, both in social matter and in abstract science ; there is always some point where we are more especially in contact with reality, and from which we extend our ideas by analogy. In all social matters this point is furnished by our own necessarily dominant ideas prescribed by our individual life. Therefore, I say that all vital speculation is a process analogous to that which I have described as the formation of the general will, and speculation upon social matters is actually an extension of this process, ultimately radiating from the same centre. The end of the whole inquiry is to understand life, and we are not likely to understand any other life until after we have understood that which is at our doors.

# XVI

## THE DUTIES OF CITIZENSHIP [1]

### I

I HAVE been considering how most usefully to deal with so vast a subject as the Duties of Citizenship. And it has occurred to me that a certain amount of theory may be the most practically valuable contribution which I in particular am able to offer to you. It is agreed, I believe, among authorities on technical education that no reading or lecturing can be a substitute for workshop training. And therefore I shall avoid every attempt to instruct you what in particular you are to do. For that you need workshop training, and your presence here shows that you know where to go for it. Nor again would it be useful that I should attempt to give even general advice as to the line of life and of work which it is most expedient to take up. Individual lives must be moulded by individual judgment.

But perhaps there is some use in trying to throw light on the connection between our several lives and the society in which we find ourselves. It may be possible to exhibit some perfectly simple conceptions which may be capable of serving as clues to the unity of life underlying the confusion of purposes and opinions by which we are surrounded.

### 1. *The Ancient City*

Many of you will think that I am beginning far away from the subject if I take the idea of citizenship first in its simplest form—as we see it in the ancient Greek world—in the little sovereign state with its central town and surrounding

[1] Lectures delivered at the Women's University Settlement, Nelson Square, Southwark.

territory, the whole being equal in extent to a small county, and in population to an English city of the second rank. And to-day we will not scrutinize the numerous defects of these little commonwealths, but will try to gain inspiration from their positive ideas. And in order to grasp these ideas, and to apprehend the pure and simple nature of citizenship, we must forget a great part of what surrounds us to-day. We must forget our divisions and estrangements, our "interests," as we call them, the claims of birth and of wealth, the regimented and incorporated forces of labour and of capital, of industry and of commerce, of agriculture and of manufactures ; we must forget the distinction of town and country, so deep that half the nation hardly knows how the other half lives ; we must forget the vast and powerful organizations and traditions of the Church, the Army, the Civil Service and the Law ; and more than all, we must learn to forget the daily contrast of the executive and official staff which we vaguely call the Government, with the mass of unofficial persons who practically regard themselves as mere units among millions of their like, living indifferently under the protection of the law. In place of all this, let us call up a different picture. Let us think of an independent sovereign community of some 20,000 men, the whole free population amounting to 100,000 souls, more or less. There is free inter-communication between the town and the rural territory which immediately surrounds it ; the freeman, as a rule, has at least a small landed property, and is able to enjoy a fair proportion of leisure from manual toil. Industries indeed exist, giving brightness and variety to life, but heavy and monotonous labour is little in amount, and chiefly devolves upon slaves, who were to the Greeks what machinery, kept in its place, might be to us.

What was it that the citizens of such a city chiefly thought of ? What filled their minds from day to day ?

First, we may suppose as with us, the care of their family, their property, and their livelihood. But probably this was less often than with us an all-absorbing anxiety, and never a cause of absolute isolation. It was a source, no doubt, of occupation and eagerness in life, but it did not shut a man up within the walls of a great industry or profession, with its routine and traditions, so as to put all else out of sight. One would be doing, on the whole, what others did, and their work would bring them into contact mentally as well as physically.

Secondly, the need of civic self-defence, and perhaps the desire of aggression, would be ever present to their minds. The citizens were their own army ; they had to be, and always were, ready to fight ; their very livelihood was bound up with the gain or loss of their city as a whole. To return without your shield—the heavy shield which could hardly be carried in flight—involved disfranchisement not at Sparta only but probably in every Greek commonwealth. The Athenian confirmation vow, as we might call it, began with the words, " I will not disgrace my shield nor desert my fellow-soldier." The leading states were almost always at war by sea or land, and whatever may have been the other consequences of this state of things, this much is certain, that the simplest form of citizen duty, which is also the ultimate form, could hardly be absent from the mind of a Greek of the great time. His life, he knew, was at the disposal of his country.

But, thirdly, in a typical leading state of Greece there would be a good chance of any individual having to think about government and justice. They worked much by large boards and commissions, and by huge juries ; every citizen would have to serve in some administrative capacity now and again. The sovereign power, moreover, and, indeed, the actual executive responsibility, rested with the *primary* assembly of all the citizens ; there was no throwing off the decision on the shoulders of elected representatives. Your personal vote helped to decide, and, in voting, you knew that you must stand to the decision of the majority with purse and person. " We who stand here to-day have in a large measure created our country's greatness " ; that is how an Athenian spoke. No modern assemblage of persons can unite in words like those.

Fourthly, they were bent on enjoyment and distinction ; first, perhaps, bodily, but secondly, intellectual. Distinction for a Greek citizen was to be the best man in Greece in battle, or at running or wrestling ; to be the most beautiful man ; to have the best horses ; to possess and to appreciate in your city the most beautiful things—the stage-plays, the singing and dancing, the statues, the pictures, the temples.

Thus the meaning of citizenship was plain. Nothing stood between you and your fellows in the community. Citizenship was obviously and visibly a life, your whole life, with common dangers, common responsibilities, common enjoyments, and common ambitions. Your education, your character, your religion, came direct from the written and unwritten laws of your city. Your happiness was to fill satisfactorily a recognized place, to be acknowledged by your fellows as doing so, and to appreciate in common with your city and your race what Pindar emphatically calls " the pleasant things of Greece."

And so Socrates and his followers, the teachers to whom we owe our definite scheme of virtue and of duty, were only insisting upon the essence of the life around them, when they told us that man's excellence was to do that which in the system of citizenship it belonged to him to do ; that the true citizen was he who knew both how to govern and how to be governed ; that man was naturally a social being ; that society was not artificial, but the outcome of human nature and the condition of human morality ; and that though, historically speaking, it originated out of the needs and impulses of bare living, yet, nevertheless, its abiding purpose was that all its members should live well. And to live well meant for him to live that life in which the separate human animal feels and knows himself to have his true being in an " end "—as philosophers call it—an aim or purpose or will which is at once in the deepest sense his own, and also real and permanent and greater than his separate self, having actual existence in a social group with its sense of community, its spirit and its laws. And such a life is called living well, because only in it, and not without it, can the nature of a human individual unfold its capacities and become the most and highest that it has in it to be.

Now, under Greek conditions, this relation of the individual to the community was tolerably easy to see. The commonest Greek citizen could never altogether forget that his actual existence was bound up with his discharge of civic duty. He would not be allowed to forget it. If he and others were careless of bodily training, or neglected their drill by sea or land, their city might be defeated in its next battle with the people over the way, and terrible losses or worse might happen in consequence to his family or to himself. And so the mind was not distracted ; the path of duty was plain ; the soldier was a citizen soldier, the poet a citizen poet, the artist a citizen artist, and the philosopher a citizen philosopher. Even the rebel, the bad citizen, did not in his rebellion lose the civic character ; on the contrary, the frightful bitterness of the civil wars of Greece was due to the fact that both sides were fighting (as in the Florence of Dante) for the very centre of their existence—for that which was the whole world to them.

## 2. *The Modern Wilderness of Interests*

In modern life it is very much harder to see our way. According to our birth, our education, and our profession, we fall into a groove, and some one or two huge incorporated " interests " fill our horizon. We are very much let alone by the general community, very *free* in that sense ; but this does not seem to develop in us either character or originality— there is always a cry that national character is decaying. Perhaps this is so far true, that character is not developed by being let alone nor yet by mere mechanical pressure of circumstances, but only in as far as we succeed in detecting some plan or value in the circumstances that press upon us, in relation to which we can assert ourselves.

But it is very hard to detect such a plan or value in our surroundings to-day, compared with those of the citizen of a small ancient commonwealth. We have not their definite set of duties *on which the common good visibly depended*. We common folk do not realize that many people are going to be much the worse or much the better for the way in which we spend our lives. The interests which fill the horizon for each of us are very different, and many of us never think of trying to connect them together. We have our ideas of right and wrong, and the little drama of our own character and destiny plays itself out on its tiny little stage, but we do not see how our fate and character is the fate and character of our nation. One of our little stages on which our life is enacted is the family. It is one great root of morality. But it takes divergent forms as a purpose in the modern world. Family selfishness has two main directions—to the inside and to the outside. The family may be sacrificed to the world of business and pleasure, or the claims of the community may be sacrificed to the family. In either case, both sides of life are distorted, and the selfish self-complacent family is a symptom of the same disease which preys on the household in which no one but its head is treated as existent. How often family pride obscures and narrows the view, and distorts our idea of the society around us. And the same is true of " society " in the narrower sense. Many of us do not grasp the idea of belonging to a human community at all ; we judge everything by the standard of a class or clique ; we make no serious attempt to see any connection between the life of this small minority and the life of the nation. Those whom we call the educated, the cultured, the distinguished, have very frequently, owing in great part to their disadvantages of birth and education within a narrow circle, no germ of a genuine idea as to the relative importance of their own lives and those of the general mass of the community, nor any capacity of judging what is or is not socially mischievous. There is not much to suggest such a connection in many homes and circles. It needs a considerable effort to realize. People are born into a certain life and sphere, and there is so much isolation in the modern world that they can simply go on in their routine without feeling any difficulty. Education does not mean, as it should, the victory over idols of the class.

So with the industrial class interest. One can observe that men born into it think that no other exists. Of course they have one great advantage in point of truth—viz. that their life is more typical than ours. There are few who live as we do, there are many who live as they do. Against that we have nothing to set but our power of acquiring knowledge. Still, industry, especially a single industry, is not all that makes up the national life.

Then there is the characteristic modern contrast of Church and State. I think we all feel how difficult in practice this is to handle—I do not mean with an established church in particular, but with all visible churches—the temporal power always comes up in one form or another, and I think I may say that any one brought up with an exclusive feeling for any visible church has a great difficulty in grasping a spiritual connection with the community as such. Where a church is concerned there is apt to be a side issue in all handling of practical questions, just as with every other strong association ; only a body of this kind is very strong and very important as a rival to the civil community. It is the most bewildering of all the schisms which the ancients had not to deal with and we have. If we could regard the Church as the intensification of our civic sentiment and not as its antagonist we might manage better than we do. So, again, the modern soldier is hardly a citizen soldier. He thinks of his regiment, his Queen, and his flag, but he hardly knows what he fights for. His courage would not satisfy the conditions of valour as laid down by Plato or Aristotle.

Thus, and in many other ways, the idea of citizenship, which was the first thing to a Greek, has almost ceased to be a controlling conception for us. It is apt to be narrowed down to what concerns the parliamentary election, and the burning question of the hour, or sometimes it includes the municipal elections in a very intelligent town, or at a striking crisis. We know our family, our neighbourhood, our trade, our church ; but our citizenship we are only just beginning to recognize, except in the parliamentary franchise, which women, more than half the community, do not possess.[1]

### 3. *Citizenship as a Clue to the Adjustment of Duties*

Before saying a word on the question *How* we should recognize our citizenship, it may be well to ask ourselves, " Is it really necessary to recognize it at all ? " Perhaps, you may think, citizenship was indeed the form which duty took in the ancient world, but as it does not seem to press upon us now, it may have been superseded by something else— the family, for instance, and the workshop and the European federation, not forgetting our duties to the human race as a whole, which the ancients, as we are somewhat erroneously informed, hardly thought of. If citizenship actually plays so

[1] [Printed in 1895.—ED.]

small part in life, as we say, why should we try and make it
play a greater part ? Perhaps " playing a greater part " is
not the right way of describing what we want it to do for us.
It is not, so to speak, one among other things, as we shall
see directly. But the reason why we should recognize our
position as citizens is, in short, that it alone includes all the
other interests and associations, and makes them possible.
The association to which we belong as citizens is the only
one to which we ascribe the right of compulsion, i.e. the only
one which we accept as having natural authority—that is,
again, as fully representing our own greater self, or our whole
conception of a common good. All the others are partial,
and leave out whole provinces of our lives and whole masses
of our fellow-countrymen, and the sign of this is that they are
voluntary, except in as far as the State delegates authority
to them. Thus it is the State or civic community, in which
alone society is focused as a whole, that represents the
connection and adjustment, the criticism, of all the other
interests and relationships so as to form parts in a many-
sided good life. Even our duty to humanity in general is
chiefly possible through and by the community ; it receives
its form from our social ideas, and has to be adjusted to the
demands of citizenship. Humanity does not exist as a whole
in the same real way that the community does. It is true
for us, as it was for the Greek, that the organized society which
we recognize as sovereign is the field and sphere of good life
for each of us.

Then how is this recognition to be worked out in our
lives ? Are we all to throw ourselves into municipal or imperial
politics, to spend our days in reading up about Egypt and
Uganda or Home Rule, in organizing Liberal associations or
yellow flowering leagues ? Well, there must be politics, and
some people must take part in them, and a healthy political
interest is one mark of a good citizen. But, as I said, we do
not rightly indicate the duties of citizenship by demanding
that politics—that some separate concern to be called citizenship—should play a great part in our lives.

That is not the point. We must begin at the other end.
Our aim is not to expand direct public or political action
over our whole lives—that would narrow our lives, not widen

them—but to understand our whole lives in the light of citizen ideas, in the light of a common good. This, as I said, is hard in the modern world. And the fact that it is hard is the reason why it is necessary.

The very solid and special interests and institutions of modern society, if misunderstood, are limits which confine and narrow each one of us, but, if rightly understood, are incomparably effective instruments of our good will. Take, for example, the family as inherited by us from Roman law and interpreted by Christianity. It is much stronger, more exclusive, than the Greek family. No Greek citizen could be wholly absorbed in his domestic relations. The position of women forbade it. They were not equal mates for men, and the true life of the Greek lay outside his home. An Englishman or Englishwoman to-day *may* be absorbed in the family. It is a real danger. What do we ask of them in the name of citizenship ? To neglect their family for local or parliamentary politics ? No. Just the reverse—that is, to deepen their family sentiment by remembering that the home is after all an element in the common good of the community; that the wife and children are not playthings, nor animals to be fed, nor instruments of social or industrial advancement, but are members of a great nation, that has a past and a future, and relations of duty and participation in a common good, binding together all its citizens. Thus the family will stand between its members and the community, not as a blank wall may stand between the eye and the sun, but as the half-way house may stand between the beginning and the goal of a journey. For thus our English homes will be nurseries of citizenship and the symbols of the social will, and become something more, not something less, than they are to-day. So too with the workshop, the neighbourhood, the Trade Union, the profession. It is not that people ought to jump out of the circumstances which put them in these conditions, but that, while remaining in some recognized groove, some accepted form of duty, they should bear in mind that their little life only has value as embodying some element of a common good. Therefore, while faithfully working in their groove, they must apply to it the best conception of human welfare that they can. They must *criticize* it, as we say in philosophy. Starting from this idea they will find improvements to make—simple little daily improvements. They will be pressed and coerced by moral necessity to this and that piece of work which their position and place brings to their hand, falling well within conditions which they are familiar with in practice, and which they will make it their duty to understand theoretically as much as they are able. How far they busy themselves with philanthropy or politics of any kind will be a question of aptitude and opportunity. They will not be neglectful of local and municipal life, but yet will always attempt to confine themselves to what they understand, and to understand thoroughly whatever they touch. They will avoid the illusion that duties which deal with public matters are the only public duties. All duties are public, or at least take us beyond the ordinary self. Better probably than any philanthropy or politics is the work of a successful employer of labour who has a decently human relation to his employees.

But, no doubt, many people, especially women, have not what may be called natural duties to fill their lives. And also those who are engaged in a domestic or professional capacity may still have spare energy for public work, and are in many ways the best qualified of all. Now, in order to give some real detail to the sense of a common good, and to make it a genuine force, whether one is in an everyday groove or trying to do something of a public or philanthropic kind, every one should try to understand at least the outline of our system of local government, of our Poor Law in relation to character, and something of the history and conditions of industrial life. That comes across us in every station and vocation. The busiest professional people need such knowledge, because they are apt, out of hurry and good-nature, to interfere at random with other people's lives. The idle people need it terribly. The least they could do would be to cease from working mischief ; and what a revolution that would make ! We all spend money. We all employ labour. The least wealthy of us, as an aggregate, employ most. How we spend our money and what labour we employ determines nothing less than this : on what things the working people of this and other countries have to spend their lives, and under what conditions their lives are to be spent. If we will have nasty things, shoddy things, vulgar things, ugly things, we are condemning somebody to make them. If we will have impossibly cheap things, we are condemning somebody to work without proper pay. But I am beginning to trench on workshop training. General rules are dangerous, though principles ought to be thoroughly grasped. For any kind of reform, the thing is to understand your particular business and the life of your district. All depends on how you go to work. I have been hearing about a northern town where it is alleged that bad sanitary conditions prevail. The philanthropic people seem to have got hysterical, and raised a public hue and cry, quoting some cases in quite exaggerated language. The health department has become exasperated. There is friction. They cannot get things put right. They do not seem—I speak at second-hand—to be able to find half a dozen simple-minded people who will inform themselves quite precisely of what nuisances exist in particular cases, and then report them quietly but persistently to the health department, adopting a friendly tone to the health officials ; and yet I do not doubt there is the usual charitable crowd going to and fro in the city. If I am rightly informed, this seems like want of understanding. Of course, in social matters, you must keep your powder dry ; it is always possible that you may have to fight—I mean, to enter upon public controversy. But as a rule, accurate knowledge, perseverance, and gentleness, confining yourself closely to the matter in hand, and working out your principles rather than flourishing them, are the way to do business.

Then, in conclusion, the duties of citizenship will not necessarily drag us out of private life into politics, administration, or philanthropy, though it may well be that every one ought at least to be prepared to participate in such functions if occasion should arise. But they emphatically call upon us never to forget that every duty of life is ultimately a duty to develop the capacities of that human nature which finds its fundamental condition and expression in the many-sided whole of the organized community. They call upon us, therefore, whether or no we undertake what are known as public functions, at least to understand our life as something which concerns the neighbourhood and the nation in which it is spent. To "criticize" is to adjust a part of its due and harmonious relations with a whole. In this sense the conception of citizenship is a standard by which our life—whether in the family, in the urban or rural neighbourhood, in trade or industry, in the Church, or in the work of charity—may be, and must be, criticized if it is to be in the full sense human. If we were bedridden our whole life long, it would still make a difference to others whether we spread around us a sensible and unselfish or a selfish and frivolous atmosphere. If we were scholars or astronomers, it would still concern our fellow-countrymen and the world that our work should be a type of sincerity, liberality, and devotion. But the issue at stake is more than this, and cannot be exhausted by one or two extreme illustrations. The shape and colour, so to speak, the spirit, tone, and energy of life, throughout and within every special sphere, will be altogether different according as we have or have not striven to understand its bearing, and the interlacing tissue of causation which makes us materially, as also spiritually, members one of another. And in such a criticism or adjustment we shall recover the unity of principle which, at first sight, may appear to have deserted the modern world.

## II

Let us recall to begin with the conceptions suggested in the previous Lecture.

We examined, in the first place, the pure or simple case of citizenship, as it presented itself in the typical communities of ancient Greece. Here we observed that the path was plain, the interconnection of lives was obvious, the oneness of purpose and of spirit throughout the society of freemen was unmistakable. No subordinate "bodies," "interests," or "worlds," so strong as to be practically isolated, barred off the individual from the state. What for us is hard to discover, and perhaps impossible always to remember—the relation of our lives to a common good—was for him, in one form or another, impossible to forget.

In the second place, we cast a glance at the wilderness of "interests" which constitutes the intricate texture of modern society. We noted the difficulty of finding any clue to a unity between our surroundings, in which we are imprisoned from birth, and the life and well-being of our fellow-countrymen as a whole. "What is he?" we ask about any of our neighbours, wishing to ascertain the relation between his aims or interests and our own. The answer may be given by naming his rank, his industry, his profession, or, again, by naming any one of a hundred social, political, or religious movements with which he has identified himself. And for distinction's sake such a selection is necessary. But how confidently we draw the conclusion that we shall find him a prisoner within the limitations thus assigned, and that the adjustment of his isolated "world" to the national life has never really presented itself to him as a serious problem for study and for criticism ! Is citizenship, we asked in effect, some department of affairs outside and narrowed down by all these ranks and interests and institutions, or does it rather permeate them all as the lifeblood of the organism, and if it does, what does it demand of us, and where are we to find it as a reality ?

And, in the third place, we returned to the idea of citizenship as a clue to the criticism or adjustment or unification of these separate "worlds" through a spirit which takes account of social purpose as a whole. Not for this,[1] we suggested, is society organized, that any single element should be wrapped up in its own purposes, and seek its fulfilment in isolation, but that, as an organism into which human nature unfolds itself, society throughout every subordinate function and institution should assert and maintain a harmonious principle of life. Therefore, we urged, in every sphere or institution we must find not a limit to our life, but an instrument of it ; not a barrier, but a half-way house. The strength and specialization of these subordinate worlds is a gain and not a loss, *if*, in deepening and enlarging some special organ of our consciousness—the family affections, for example, or

---

[1] Plato, *Republic*, Book IV, 420 B : " Not with this view are we constructing our commonwealth, that any one body within it shall be supereminently prosperous."

the tradition of law, or the sense of religion, or the habit of discipline and chivalrous courage—they can be prevented from absolutely swallowing us up, or cutting us off from the many-sided social self—the community as sovereign in virtue of the general will—which is the condition and the expression of our human nature as an organized whole.

Before proceeding with the illustrations of this principle which were to occupy us to-day, I will say a word on the supposed moral difficulty of the choice of our work, which arises as a moral problem when we find ourselves lost, as it were, in the wilderness of private and public relations and interests.

If, for example, we start from the conception that " my station and its duties " are the root of morality, the question may immediately be hurled at us, " But what *is* my station ? " Even the Church Catechism, on this point usually misquoted, leaves our vocation to be determined by the course of life : " To do my duty in that state of life to which it *shall* please God to call me." In its full extent this difficulty can only exist for those who do not make their own living, or who, from exceptional ability or versatility, have an unusually free hand in selecting their vocation. Nor is it *necessarily* a social abuse that the majority have but a restricted choice of callings. As a matter of principle, true freedom consists in making the best of what we have—our parentage and our birthplace, for example, involving our whole initial outfit, both physical and moral, are unalterably given facts—rather than in an indefinite range of possible selection. Provision for adapting vocation to capacity is of course desirable, but in the end, whatever variety may be attainable, capacity must after all in a great degree adapt itself to vocation. But even those— the vast majority—whose lives are to a great extent externally determined, remain responsible for the spirit and temper of their work, and for the private duties on the one hand, and the public or semi-public on the other, which lie round its margin. A workman of my acquaintance, a painter by trade, has hardly an evening in the week free from the claims of working-class clubs and societies, in the management of which he, like so many of his fellows, displays a wonderful administrative energy and devotion. There is scope for choice in every life, and not merely in the life of the leisure class ; but undoubtedly it is to the latter, and especially to women who have no need to support themselves, that the problem of selection presents itself like a pathless desert.

Now I am speaking not of the practical question of the most appropriate choice, but only of the moral question raised by the *idea* of a conflict of duties, and the consequent perturbing impression that whatever you do, something must be neglected, and therefore every course must in some degree be wrong. And here I think that a simple distinction may really give relief. We are to distinguish between a true conflict of duties and a conflict of duty and selfishness. In the former, which we profess to constitute our difficulty, there is no cause for scruple or for remorse, although there may be a just and natural regret at our inability to undertake some branch of useful work. For a conflict of *duties* presupposes that the conflicting alternatives urge themselves *as duties only*, and so long as this is truly the case, our selfishness has no say in the matter, and we have no cause for moral anxiety and perturbation. It is as though I were entrusted with a sum of money with which to meet a variety of obligations, but insufficient to defray them all. The weighing of obligations against each other in order to determine which ought first to be discharged may be a nice and delicate task ; but no ground arises for a case of conscience, unless I have reason to suspect that, in the perplexity of the situation, my own selfishness is taking occasion to influence me. It is undoubtedly possible that a man setting out to discharge two disagreeable duties may so deceive himself as to the difficulty of combining them, or of selecting the one in preference to the other, that he may return having achieved neither. Then is the just occasion for genuine remorse and the acutest self-contempt. But the moral emergency as such is adequately dealt with if we honestly bear in mind that only a duty can justify the avoidance of a duty. Then, if we are sincere, we have drawn the sting of self-accusation, and may confidently proceed to judge and to act according to our lights. I am inclined to think that for highly conscientious minds it is unwholesome to dwell on the customary idea that there is always one right course and one only. If we knew everything, this might be so ; the one right course might then present itself as the one course possible. But in human life it is untrue that there is only one right course open to us ; it is truer to think that every course is right which, presenting itself as a genuine path of duty—though not the only one possible—is followed with the full force of our nature, and with the determination to make it effective to the common good. In preference to the maxim, " Search out the one right course before you choose," I should suggest as a deeper and a truer principle, " Begin anywhere, if you know of no plainer duty unfulfilled ; but bear in mind that the course which you adopt can only justify itself if pursued as a duty ; seriously, devotedly, and with eagerness to learn and criticize its bearing on the common good. The unpardonable sin is not in choosing the wrong duty, but in shirking all." Whatever clue you fasten upon will lead you to the centre, if followed whole-heartedly and with an open mind.

And now let us illustrate these principles from one or two branches of work or modes of life which may be interesting to the members of this settlement. In the first place, speaking generally, all women of the leisure class should especially study the probable effects of their working for pocket-money wages on their poorer rivals in the labour market. The question is a difficult one, but it seems plainly a cruel thing for ladies whose livelihood is secure to accept less than the market price for any kind of work in which they really compete with those who have their whole living to earn.

Passing from this general consideration, let us look at one or two examples of the evils which may arise if we fail to scrutinize our particular vocation with reference to the welfare of society, to modify our isolated " world " by the spirit of citizenship.

No one can value more than I do the work of those women who, being trained nurses, devote themselves to attendance on the poor at their own homes. Especially, perhaps, the indirect results of their exertions are of permanent social value. They bring light into dark places ; they make known sanitary defects and cause them to be remedied ; they educate those on whom they attend in the management of a sick-room, and in numberless details of cleanliness and household economy.

But in one aspect of their vocation there is apt to occur a certain collision of duties which has long become a matter of friendly discussion and adjustment between some of their ablest workers and other persons engaged in a more general endeavour to improve the condition of the poor. A person who is ill needs food—often comparatively expensive food—and fire and house-room, as well as nursing and medicine. Now let us suppose that a case on which a nurse is in attendance is one in which the family has not resources even to provide adequately for all its members, not to speak of diet for the sick. If the nature of the illness, and the general circumstances of the case, are such as to give reasonable hope that the family may by attention and perseverance be restored in the future to a self-supporting condition, then no objection will probably be made by persons interested in sound charitable work against finding some friends to provide the nourishment required, and to do what is necessary for the whole family with a view to ultimate re-establishment on a self-supporting basis. But if all the circumstances point in an opposite direction, if the condition of the family appears hopeless, if character is bad, if the illness has been caused or seriously aggravated by drink, if the absence of work is not due to sickness, but the sickness is a mere incident in a life of continued unemployment, so that its cure is no remedy for the evil, then it will be held advisable in the interest of society, and indeed of the family itself, especially if it includes young children, that the case should be dealt with by the Poor Law, the patient should be received into the infirmary, and the children, instead of dragging on in semi-starvation, should make a fresh start in the Poor Law schools. But recourse to the Poor Law is voluntary, and is shunned by the worse among the poor because of the loss of freedom and submission to rules which life in an institution demands, as by the more independent, owing to the confession of failure implied in an appeal for public relief. It is therefore probable that for mixed reasons, by no means necessarily discreditable, the sick person or the family will display the greatest repugnance to appeal to the Poor Law, especially if outdoor relief is not likely to be granted, which would not be done in the case described under any moderate relief policy. The nurse is then, no doubt, in a dilemma. Her duty, she will say—and who can deny it?—is to bring the patient through his sickness. Obviously it is idle for her to give attendance and medicine to a sick person who has insufficient nourishment, and perhaps inadequate house-room, and a difficulty in providing fire. If, therefore, the case is rejected by those with whom she commonly works on the ground that no permanent good can be done to the family, while by assisting it much harm will be caused perhaps to the children themselves and certainly to the *morale* of the neighbourhood, then she is of course very strongly tempted to assist the case out of her own resources or by appealing to other private friends, whose aid is given entirely because of her request. And, in fact, she cannot possibly do otherwise unless she is prepared to refuse further attendance, or unless an arrangement exists by which she can attend as the agent of the Poor Law authorities —a case which we are not at present discussing.

But now let us look at the matter from the point of view of those who have banded themselves together to improve the condition of the poor in a certain district by a definite and intelligent policy in the administration of charitable relief. Their aim and desire is to bring to bear the resources of their neighbourhood effectively and thoroughly where substantial good can be achieved by strengthening and supporting those sufferers whom it appears reasonably possible to restore to independent life; but, for a thousand reasons, to discountenance the scattering of relief among hopeless cases in which no permanent good can be done to the sufferer, for whom institutional treatment is as a rule far more adequate, while infinite harm is caused by the precedent and example of lavish help to the characterless or incompetent held up before a whole street or district. To these charitable workers the action of the nurse in the case supposed cannot but seem to be in frustration of their whole policy; and they feel it all the harder, because to whatever extent they habitually labour to assist her with cases which in their judgment demand assistance, precisely to that extent they are made to stultify themselves through the course adopted by her in perfect good faith with regard to " unhelpable " cases. For it is plain that the amount of assistance procured by their means for those cases, brought to their knowledge by the nurse, which are suitable to be completely and continuously relieved, is the amount to which it may be supposed the private resources of the nurse and her immediate friends are set free to help those who in the judgment of the experts ought not to be relieved by charity. "Had we never helped at all," such workers must feel, "then presumably the resources which are now taxed to help these hopeless cases would by preference have been drawn upon to benefit those in which assistance can do real good ; so that our endeavours to aid, though themselves strictly limited to cases which we approve of, have the direct result of setting free a large amount of charitable relief for the cases which, in our judgment, could be for every reason better dealt with by the Poor Law." And thus they cannot but see that their co-operation for good is so far converted into co-operation for harm. It may be mentioned in passing that throughout the charitable world, in so far as organization is imperfect, the same radical difficulty prevails, a curious symptom of the indissoluble connection of lives within the social tissue. In as far as fresh financial resources are called into play by those who strain every nerve thoroughly to remedy all remediable causes of distress, there is no doubt that the resources previously and on the average devoted to relief work are set free to be more and more widely expended by methods which can do nothing but mischief.[1] The terrible problems and wide-reaching responsibilities which arise from this state of things can readily be inferred.

The importance of a thorough insight and of breaking down the barriers of traditional routine by help of the citizen spirit could not be more strikingly illustrated. Except in so far as we can break down this moral and intellectual isolation, the extension of wise methods in the charitable world appears to involve a corresponding extension of foolish ones.

But returning to the example of the nurses, what is it that we ask them to do ? Their position, as I have said, is difficult. It cannot be expected, I have often heard the most experienced charitable workers say, that a nurse should

[1] Almost all old-fashioned charitable societies, including too often the clergy and the District Visiting Societies, avowedly send all " good " and " heavy " cases to the Charity Organization Society, thus retaining their own funds to be expended in the less costly " doles."

maintain the point of view which commends itself to those who are dealing with the problem of poverty as a whole. And I do not wish to dogmatize. It seems clear indeed that if the nurse universally gives way to the threat of the patient, " You may abandon the case, but I will not apply to the Poor Law," [1] all possibility of distinguishing between hopeful and hopeless cases is radically cut away, and owing to the fact that the needs of sickness presuppose the needs of life, and that a patient can hardly be kept in comfort with a starving family beside him, it would become necessary to maintain by charity for long periods the most improvident and character-less families, many of whose members would thus be confirmed in idle and vicious habits. In various degrees the rule, I believe, is already adopted that when the medical attendant recommends the Poor Law infirmary, and the patient refuses, the nurse should abandon the case. But it is not for me to lay down rules on practical points of workshop training. What can do nothing but good is that a lady, who is exercising such a vocation, should have learned or should learn to appreciate the bearing of her work, not only on the immediate sufferer (and that in the largest sense, including his future and that of the other members of the family), but also on progress or retrogression in the whole condition of the poor, and consequently in the welfare and good life of society as a whole. Then, in the particular case, her trained wisdom will suggest to her what measures to adopt, and she will be an educating influence not only as regards the conditions of health, but as regards those of character.

Analogous conclusions are obviously applicable to the work of the district visitor, and above all, to that of the minister of religion. It appears almost inconceivable, when we remember that every minister with a cure of souls is practically the head of a powerful relief society, that candidates for orders should pass through no systematic training on a subject in which more than in any other naïve impressions

[1] It should be borne in mind that the Poor Law authorities are absolutely responsible for the relief of destitution when application has been made to them ; and that, therefore, if a patient who applies to them is too ill to be moved to the infirmary, they must attend to him to the best of their power in his own home. It is therefore possible for the voluntary nurse to abandon any case which is not fit for charitable assistance, care being taken if extreme need exists to notify the Poor Law authorities.

are revolutionized by education, and the treatment of which is all but decisive for moral and material good and evil in the lives of large sections of the poor.

Let us apply our conceptions for a moment in conclusion to that which has brought us together here to-day—the social settlement movement.

I take it that the natural basis of the settlement idea is to be found in that which Edward Denison had in view when he took up his residence in the East End of London. The notion was simply, I presume, that persons with some degree of leisure and education should become residents in districts where such residents are rare, and thus do something to destroy the isolation of classes, and supply a force of volunteers well qualified to lead in the more public kind of civic duties. The change of residence was thus intended simply to overcome the physical difficulty of remoteness, and not to imply any radical change in mode of life, nor necessarily, an exceptional self-consecration or self-devotion incompatible with the pursuit of a profession or the life of a man of the world. Many men of comparatively leisure class do live in the East End to-day apart from any settlement, and then take up what work comes to their hand, as they would it they lived in the West End. The late Canon Bradby was a notable example. He lived with his wife and family in the St. Katharine's Dock House, and worked at his several occupations, and mingled with his neighbours as he would have done in any other vicinity. And this appears to me to be a very healthy and sound type of life. It remains practical and ordinary. The natural points of contact between a lodger or householder and servants, shopkeepers, workmen, and other neighbours are not minimized. There is no risk of waste ; no collegiate buildings ; if you die or are compelled to leave, the house is there, like other houses in the same district, only perhaps in better sanitary condition, and it is useful for any inhabitant.

But as the powerful modern spirit of association has seized upon this movement, its nature has been unconsciously transformed. This forced itself upon my observation especially in the United States of America, and is becoming more and more noticeable in London. It is a special form of associated enterprise, a movement in which the collegiate, if not monastic or conventual aspect, is becoming exceedingly prominent. The subject is a very large one, and the few observations which I can make must not be taken as a complete estimate of the movement, which would however be well worth attempting. If we look at the addresses of able and experienced settlement workers in the United States, we see that beyond a question the movement is regarded as a good in itself and as eliciting a new type of self-consecration and self-devotion.[1] Now the idea of methodic training and study, under skilled direction, with reference to social work and social problems, as a preparation for the duties of the clergyman or district visitor, or indeed for those of ordinary home life in any neighbourhood, and especially for the theoretical study of social phenomena, appears to be a most desirable application and development of the principle of association. But this is an ideal which is not realized without resolution, experience, and wisdom. Bad method grows up of itself, especially under the artificial conditions of a settlement, if no special provision is made for skilled instruction and criticism. I confess to a certain feeling of terror, when I think of the increasing number of centres where groups of inexperienced young men or young women have come together, burning " to do good," and, so far as I am aware, without any special provision for acquainting themselves with the conditions of their task. Rumours which come to my ears both from the United States and from parts of London justify some disquietude. In this settlement, indeed, I know how skilfully and resolutely a curriculum of practice and theory is planned and executed. I believe that conferences occasionally take place at least among the women's settlements. Could not this question of a definite training for workers be brought up at such a conference, the practice of different settlements be compared, and some attempt be made to arrive at a clearness as to the methods and objects of settlement work ?

I am jealous—I frankly admit it—of any movement which appears to disparage by comparison the life of the citizen who lives at home and works among his neighbours. This

[1] *Philanthropy and Social Progress*, New York, Crowell and Company. Miss Addams (head of Chicago Settlement), pp. 6, 49. Mr. Woods (head of Boston Settlement), p. 95

and not the other, appears to me to be the ideal. For systematic training of workers the settlement is good, and also, perhaps, to supply a centre of residence in districts where the leisure class are few. I should further distinguish the special value of settlements which provide the buildings and other facilities essential to university extension work and similar undertakings. Halls and public rooms are hard to come by in London, and the provision of them in certain proportions for educational purposes may be taken as supplying a definite need in a poor district. Thus, from all that I can hear, I cordially welcome the work of Toynbee Hall as a poor man's university.

But apart from these special needs and functions, I do not believe that a monastic or conventual movement is to-day a movement towards a higher life. The higher life lies in the opposite direction—in the home, the family, the commonplace neighbourly acquaintance. It occurs to me forcibly that within the walls of a large settlement the young men or young women must have actually less habitual contact with poorer neighbours, of an unconstrained and spontaneous kind, than where each has his or her own centre of richer and poorer acquaintances and dependents. Is not, for example, the marketing done for a collegiate settlement, and the repairs seen to on a large scale by some steward or housekeeper, so that the little daily courtesies and reciprocal interests which establish themselves in ordinary household life between us and our tradespeople, and their workmen, must in a great degree be abolished? One who has lived for many years in a college would be apt to reflect that a more inhuman form of existence could hardly be conceived.

These suggestions, I repeat, are not aimed against settlements, of which I recognize the value, but against the glorification of the settlement life as one specially set apart for the service of man. Here as throughout we must demand that the specialization which is an indispensable feature of modern life shall not isolate us from the citizen spirit, the pulse-beat of the social heart. We shall feel with Browning—

> If we have souls, know how to see and use,
> One place performs like any other place
> The proper service every place on earth

Was framed to furnish man with ; serve alike
To give him note that, through the place he sees,
A place is signified he never saw,
But, if he lack not soul, may learn to know.

I have deliberately abstained from trying to map out the different provinces of citizen duty. I am sure that any one who with good heart sets himself or herself to understand a neighbourhood with its local life, or the family, or a trade, or profession, as an element in the welfare of the community, will do so more vitally for not having a tabular form to start from. The point is to gain such an insight as may make our particular place transparent to us, and may make it a symbol which we understand more thoroughly itself because we see how it affects the welfare of our whole organized society. To do this, there is no cast-iron formula that will help us. Whenever we have grasped a clue, either an interest or a difficulty, we must follow it up into the best thought and experience of the day, and if possible become practically acquainted with the facts that bear on it.

Of course such a settlement as this considered as a " training school " is an immense facility for learning at least how much there is to learn. On every charity organization committee, again, we shall find interests that ramify in all directions, into educational and industrial problems, into local government, very likely into national art and its true conditions.

Do not suppose that at first we can see things as they are. For this—to know and feel things as they are—is the goal of all science and practice, and the goal is at the end. It is always true that to grasp things as they are—that is, in their spirit and movement—we must grasp them in their connection as a whole, and the duties of citizenship form no exception to the rule.

# XVII

## " LADIES AND GENTLEMEN "

. THE occasion of these remarks was a correspondence in
he *Daily Chronicle* a few months back. I refer to it only from
memory, and I believe that it contained some good letters ; but
aken as a whole, it impressed me painfully. I thought that
here was little if any attempt to go below the purely conven-
ional point of view, and to ask what these symbols—the terms
Lady and Gentleman—really mean, and whether or no they
arry a tradition of value to mankind.

The discussion appeared to me to go off into considerations
bout the ratio between the cubic content of the front hall in a
man's house, and his gentlemanly qualities. It is a kind of
alculation in which I have no skill.

According to my recollection, no one definitely asked the
question : " Is there anything, precious to humanity, repre-
ented by these titles ; and if so, what is it ? "

I believe in Ladies and Gentlemen, and this ignoring the
oint at issue seemed to me very sad.

2. There is a difficulty or paradox threatening every
pproach to this subject ; and in a blundering way even that
orrespondence showed it to have been felt.

It springs, perhaps, from the very ardour of our Christianity,
ur democratic spirit, and our Teutonic gospel of work. We
ave learned to say, What *really matters* in human nature
—goodness, perhaps, or ability, or " backbone " ; all that we
all " character." And having said this, we really do not know
here to put certain other human qualities ; we have, in our
ough working theory, simply no place left for them.

And so we get our puzzle. The man who has the root of
ae matter in him (say, in religion, character, courage, dis-
terestedness) is any man's equal. " A man's a man for a'

that." "The honest man's the noblest work of God.'
Nothing can be better than the best, and a strong inner life
or a great definite achievement, a great mind or heart or will,
*is* the best. To be Lady or Gentleman adds nothing. How
can any qualities add anything to the best ?

And yet, "the quality"—what a significant phrase—is
valued. There is something in it which appeals to man
wherever he is civilized in any degree worth mentioning
The very efforts made to explain it away are proofs of it
"Nature's gentlemen," "true" ladies and gentlemen, we are
told, may be found in any rank or country. Very likely
but the suggestion shows that they have a quality which is
valued, and which is not possessed by all.

Thus we are in a contradiction ; and because in a contradiction we are also in an uneasy sensitive frame of mind. We
admit that the quality exists—the quality of being a lady or
gentleman—and we show in practice that we value it. But
still not really knowing what to make of it, we turn round and
disparage it, and grumble that the distinction indicated has
no real basis, and would be better away.

We want some intelligible account of the relation of these
qualities to the recognized sterling attributes of human
character.

3. Let us take some examples of defect in these qualities
from which we may form a rough judgment of their nature
And for our purpose, we may omit what in some respects is
the most important case. That is to say, we need not give
examples of acknowledged badness of mind or character
making people unladylike or ungentlemanlike. They would
give us too much for our purpose. Our puzzle is, in brief, the
question what is added to a *good* man or woman by being a
gentleman or lady. In the case of a bad man or woman the
basis of excellence is lacking, and the absence of the super
structure is no paradox. The paradox would be if it were
present : if bad people could be real ladies and gentlemen
Something like this can happen ; and we will say a brief word
on it below.

But our examples, to solve our main paradox, must show
us the difference, the addendum by which one who has sterling
worth, and is a lady or gentleman, excels one who has sterling

worth and is not. If a thoroughly good man or woman can fail in these qualities, what do they lose by it ? What does humanity lose by it ?

We begin from the outside, with examples which may perhaps be thought wholly irrelevant, and work inwards to mind and character.

I. Some of us need not go far to find a man who cannot raise his hat to a lady while he is riding a bicycle. Here we have a little failure in a matter of bodily training, and consequently a little failure to be equal to a certain trivial situation. Take another trivial case. It is noticeable nowadays, that in travelling by rail, especially in cold weather, a man who has lowered the carriage window to let himself out will usually replace it before closing the door. This is one of the little democratic courtesies which we learn in the train and the omnibus, and which it is so pleasant to see making progress amongst us. But to replace the window when the door is open, and often with only one hand free, is just a little difficult, and one envies the people who can jerk it into place with a motion of their left hand. If you fumble with it, the little act of courtesy is spoilt ; the people for whom it is being done are more put out than if you had let it alone. There are many other little instances where bodily skill makes life easier ; a whole tableful of people may be disconcerted because you cannot carve properly at dinner. From these cases we naturally pass to dancing and athletic exercises, riding, skating, rowing. Without suggesting that it is a serious duty for every one to be good at all these things, we see quite plainly that each one of them is a means of being equal to a certain set of situations, in other words, of being pleasant and serviceable in certain ways and on certain occasions. An old gentleman in a novel by Wilkie Collins says that when he was young, people were expected to bring social qualities with them on social occasions, and now, as he sees that a croquet mallet and ball are the social qualities in demand, he will not fail to employ them. Some people, who detest croquet, may feel a little rebuked by this old gentleman.

In short, as we have been told that all Fine Art is athletic it would seem that the same is true of some qualities of the lady or gentleman. This was a Greek and mediæval idea, an

idea powerful among ourselves almost down to the last generation, and probably, *mutatis mutandis*, it ought not to be lost.

II. Let us turn to another set of defects, still half bodily,
and, as I think, highly suggestive for our subject ; defects in
expression by language.  The simplest and typical case is being
in a foreign country, and either unable, or very imperfectly
able, to speak the language. Under such conditions one is
apt to feel oneself simply a brute beast ; one cannot explain,
nor apologize, nor thank any one for a courtesy. If conversation is attempted, the sentences are certain to be awkward and
abrupt, and very likely take a shape which, according to the
idiom of the country, is imperative or rude.  I remember a
German who had really assisted me in explaining my ticket
coupon to the guard of the train, saying to me when the
explanation was ended, " You can retain your seat." To an
English ear the form of that sentence implies a permission
which might have been refused ; and as I was in the right
throughout, I was half annoyed, though in fact the speaker had
rendered me a great service.  Or again, when we made use of
the club hut on a hill in Norway, and some Norwegians, apparently club members, were there, we could not say a word of
thanks for the courtesy by which English travellers were
allowed to lunch in the room.  The Norwegians, indeed, were
cleverer than we, for as there was a schoolboy in our party,
and also one in theirs, they sent their schoolboy to ours to
offer him a piece of cake, a pleasant courtesy, which we had
no way of returning.  Here, too, is a comic incident, with a
serious side.  A friend of mine, bold, but not strong, in the
French language, was staying somewhere in Brittany, and at
table d'hôte the conversation turned on French and English
bathing fashions.  My friend did his best to explain that in
England we do not commonly wear costumes, but that men
and women have separate bathing places.  An elderly French-
man regarded him with a horrified gaze, and then turned to
his own party and reported to them in French that the Englishman had just told him how in England bathers do not wear
costumes, and the men and women have the same bathing
place.  My friend was at the end of his French, and was forced
to let the impression remain.  This is bad enough, but in even
more serious matters what an impression of brutality such a

misunderstanding might produce ! It seems hardly too much to say that if we really knew each other's language half the international complications would disappear. The same is obviously true, in the most literal as well as the most metaphorical sense, of intercourse between different classes, professions, political parties, and other distinct elements within the same country. Offence, given and taken, depends very largely upon defects of language.

III. Following the same clue we may now come closer to intelligence and will. In passing, we should once more note the instance of games, speaking now of those which demand some little attention and mental effort, but are in no way athletic. The principle is the same as before. For want of a modicum of skill and practice, in the present case not involving any special bodily gifts, we are unable to be pleasant and useful in certain ways. We may have good reason for the line we take, but the fact remains. One has heard a saying, " If the Queen asked you to play whist with her, and you could not, you would have to be a great philosopher not to feel a fool." Or we may put it more strongly by saying, " If any old person or invalid desired you to play with him———" Then we come to a set of defects almost affecting morality and intelligence, but yet on the whole compatible with " sterling worth." Of these is slowness in recognizing people whom you meet, owing frequently to preoccupation or again to what may be called student's paralysis—the tendency to hesitate too long when some simple thing is to be done suddenly. This may of course give most serious annoyance absolutely without intention. The same result may be produced by strictly physical drawbacks—short sight, for example. It has been said of Lord Sherbrooke (Mr. Lowe) that he simply could not see to find the people by talking to whom he might have made friends and become more popular than he was ; so that a wholly false impression of him became current. Shyness, impatience, the flurry which prevents one from attending to others, may all be pretty much of this type, and are quite compatible with real readiness to do service. A very young and nervous lecturer, having been conscious of a bustle in the middle of his lecture, observed afterwards to a friend that he feared people had found him dull and gone out. On being answered that Miss X. had fainted from the heat, he exclaimed cheerfully, " Oh, that is all right then." " Except for Miss X.," his friend replied. But the lecturer was not a bad man. There is one opportunity which I should very much like to have over again. After lecturing at Plymouth, in New England, I was going down to the station on my way West, when a gentleman who had been among my audience met me and offered me some flowers. They were some specimens of the Sabbatia, which is a striking feature of the wet woods near Plymouth, and which would have been a pleasant memorial of the place. But I was fretted about my journey, and was carrying, I suppose, my bag and coat, and had, or thought I had, no hand to spare for the flowers, and declined to take them with me. It was not bad intention ; it was quite unnecessary flurry. My action, however, distresses me when I recall it.

Closely akin to these is lack of conversation, a more inward phase corresponding to ignorance of another's language. It is a good old ideal that a gentleman should be able to talk properly to any one. Inability to do so is bad in any case, but worst of all as a class barrier. It may be urged that this is a symptom of a deeper want and not in itself a cause. But that is only half true. Even if you argue that learning to talk means acquiring sympathy and intelligence which you had not before, still it is the case that they can be acquired in this way ; but, really, to say that unexpressed sympathy is non-existent is pressing a good idea too far. You may have a true sympathy and understanding, and yet, from comparatively minor causes, fail to give it effect. This inarticulateness is like not knowing the language ; and like it, makes you *pro tanto* inhuman.

Another defect closely connected with this is " saying the wrong thing." It is the greatest of errors to suppose that the first thing a man blurts out is what he really meant to say. To say what we mean needs training. What Ruskin says of telling truth applies to it. " Telling truth is like writing fair ; it comes only by practice."

Always excluding malicious intention, we may treat inconsiderateness from this same point of view. It means want of facility in picking up a new context. The persons we meet are more or less " unseen pieces " whom we have to construe. If we have no gift or no practice, we construe them all wrong ;

we fail, that is, to piece together their real thought and wish out of the acts and words which we have to go by.

All these latter and more intimate defects might be brought under the general heading of want of presence of mind. We are supposing that the man or woman has sterling worth ; but there is, so to speak, an " uncultivated " margin all round his centre of thought and conduct. It is a margin which his mind has never thoroughly " cultivated " ; has never worked over or been worked into, and therefore is not readily present in.

Of course there are people who have a quality which is an opposite of this, and yet is also a defect—the defect of " having all their money in small change," of being equal to small and everyday situations, and to no others. There is no difficulty of principle in this fact. All defects have false opposites which are as much defects as themselves. That is why people are half proud of certain faults ; because they seem opposed to faults which are even worse. All sound characters, then, have their caricatures—the false opposites of those faults to which the sound characters are the true opposites. We are looking for the nature of the sound character, and the existence of the caricature does not trouble us.

IV. We are now ready to throw out one or two suggestions for a conclusion. If we review these groups of examples, they all seem to be obstructions or impediments ; failures, by reason of external or comparatively external incompetence, to express or display the intelligence or good will that we really have. Either the body, or the mind in some special phase of activity— and we have plainly seen that these two regions are continuous—has not been successfully made instrumental to working out the great ends of life in details, in the sphere of little things or of daily routine.

But these terms " obstructions " or " impediments " are metaphors, and in this reference are a little dangerous. They favour unduly the popular view from which we started. They suggest the notion of " sterling worth " which is really and completely there, but somehow screened off, like the sun behind a cloud.

But we should bear in mind what the " obstruction " in these cases really means. It is this, that a certain margin of positive work, of the same kind as all moral growth and will-formation, has been left undone. Morality, we know, is a *second* nature. All that is good and human in us means that a work has been accomplished; mind and body have been disciplined, impulses have been harmonized, the power of intelligence has asserted itself, right through and in our habits of thought and action. At the beginning of our development we are not a moral self, perhaps not a self at all. The self, certainly at least the moral self, is not born but made. Obstruction of the kind we have indicated means that this work has been left imperfect.

Thus it is only a first approximation to say in the ordinary sense of the words, that the qualities of ladies and gentlemen are *expressions* of humanity and goodness, and the defect of them is a mere obstruction, a cloud which prevents us from seeing a humanity and goodness which are really there. If we say this, we have to remember that expression gives perfection and existence to what it expresses, and if there were no expression there could be nothing to express. The " obstruction " in these cases does not leave the soul and its qualities intact behind it like a fire behind a screen. It means that the process of making the soul actual, of making the man or woman, has never been completed. A quality may be real, though unexpressed in minor ways, if it is expressed in great ones. But for all that it is the less real in as far as it is not expressed.

The idea that goodness or sterling worth is somehow and in some way real, when it seems not to be actual at all, is sometimes a very touching self-deception. We remember Dickens's Joe Gargery, whose father was simply a ruffian, and who always ended any allusion to him by saying, " But my father were that good in his 'art, don't you see."

On a first reading of Aristotle's *Ethics* we are apt to complain that the excellences of social intercourse—agreeableness, true modesty, and wit or the power of saying the right thing, ought hardly to be prominent in a serious treatise on moral qualities. But on further consideration we see how thorough and effective is the Greek moral idea of a life that embodies the right ratio in every situation—the beautiful life. We certainly need to bear it in mind in correction of the more modern ideal of " sterling worth."

Thus I am led to suggest a simple account of the difference

between the " quality " of lady and gentleman, and those solid endowments of intellect, heart, or character, which we have learned chiefly to value to-day. It is a question of nothing other than the degree in which intelligence and good-will have found expression in the detailed behaviour of body and of mind. *In this sense* we may fearlessly say that a lady is higher than a mere woman, and a gentleman than a mere man. For, other things being equal, the lady is more of a woman, and the gentleman more of a man. Humanity is in them more thoroughly achieved ; something is perfected in them which is present, but not perfected, in the others. The human nature, which is a rough sketch in the one, is a finished work in the other. We may say if we like that to be a lady or a gentleman is only an expression or manifestation of " sterling worth," but, in saying it, we have to bear in mind that expression, if not the whole of the reality, is at least something apart from which there is no reality at all.

V. Finally, we must say a word on the troublesome subject of the current usage of these terms in designating social classes.

I am not in the very least degree frightened on behalf of my theory by the existence of sham ladies and gentlemen. No marked type, I should imagine, can exist without giving rise to its caricature. It is as in bad art—the expression of a genuine meaning can in some degree be imitated by a trick, and you can have a thing that looks clever or attractive, and yet has no idea in it, or a bad one. To some extent we are all of us continually playing a trick like this. In trying to be like what we admire we hit off the emphasis wrongly, and reproduce less of its merits than of its defects. The point is too obvious to press, but it is sufficient to account for any quantity of false pretension to qualities which have something admirable in them. And then we may admit that all have defects, and the possession of the qualities is a matter of degree—and of direction. This latter point is highly illustrative of our principle, and the facts seem to me unquestionable, though much everyday prejudice contradicts them. A man who is a gentleman in one direction, in one section of his mind, so to speak, often, if not always, fails to be so in another. And, as a rule, he is a gentleman in what he understands, and less so, or not at all, in what he is ignorant of. I believe it to be merely prejudice which affirms that knowledge and experience generate an overbearing temper. A man who is accustomed to be heard with respect on one subject is often overbearing when he meets with opposition on some other matter, but not, I think, as a rule, in dealing with the matter which he has made his own. It must have struck others besides myself that men unaccustomed to writing seem sometimes to lose all self-restraint when they put pen to paper, and though good enough gentlemen in private life, seem not to know how to behave in the republic of letters. They never were there before, and they do not know the traditions and conventions of the place. So a soldier will become violent in a political discussion, but yet will treat a difference of opinion on a point of military technique with candour and with respect for the views of others. We have long ago condemned the doctrine that virtue is knowledge ; but this is partly because it has depths of meaning which we have never sounded.

But all this makes no difference to the important question which is, not whether there is much of the false and much failure in the world ; but whether there is enough of the true to be recognizable, in the intention which on the whole governs the application of the words Lady and Gentleman.

There is one difficulty in asserting this, on the principle above suggested, which seems to me serious though not fatal. It may be said : " Well, grant that these terms are meant to mean the completest expression of humanity. You will judge, I suppose, where this is to be found, by considering who in fact can be said to make their humanity effectually felt ; who are at home and at ease with the greatest number and variety of mankind. And these surely, are the poor and the manual workers. They are at their ease, comfortable and kindly with a far larger part of mankind than " Ladies and Gentlemen " in the usual sense. On your principle, the application of the term should be reversed, and the qualities usually indicated by them should be condemned as a ground of exclusiveness."

I believe the fact alleged by the supposed objector to be true, and it seems to me very important, and not, as a rule, sufficiently considered. We have to think not merely of the kindness of the poor to one another, but of the freemasonry of the poor and the manual workers generally with one another, both with those of their own country and to a great extent with foreigners. The very definite and direct common experience of work, hardship and simple pleasures, seems to give them a power of being easily at home with one another. It is needless to enlarge on this. I take it to be unquestioned that, unless some special cause of quarrel exists, a workman will be welcomed by others, treated as a friend, and shown what courtesy and hospitality is in their power, pretty nearly all the world over. Of course in laying stress upon this point, I do not mean that this is all that could be said if our object were to form an estimate of their social qualities throughout. But this is the one point in which it might be urged that their life is on an absolutely different footing from that of the more leisured classes. " C'est le peuple qui compose le genre humain," and to be in touch with the people, it may be said, is to have mastered the full expression of humanity.

Still, we must never judge by numbers in a question of completeness. We must consider how far the possibilities of human nature, as experience vouches for them, are realized. And it seems clear that what forms the strength of the life of manual workers is also, for our present purpose, its weakness ; that is, the simplicity of its situations. For this has the result of leaving, as a rule, a great part of human nature in them " uncultivated." We have found that the defects which we passed in review amounted pretty much to forms of inarticulateness ; and inarticulateness [1] is a leading characteristic of manual workers. The frightful language which some of them habitually use, means, I take it, merely this : they feel emphatic about something, and the accustomed epithet presents itself because truer modes of emphasis are not at command. Ultra refinement here joins hands with its opposite. The use of " jolly " in University talk seems a counterpart, for inarticulateness, to the costermonger's most deeply tinted epithet. And the best workmen would themselves, I think, deplore as a misfortune incident to the simplicity of their

[1] It is very striking that workmen, especially in the country, will often show an articulateness in their work, which they are trained in, entirely beyond anything they can express in speech, which they are not trained in. They will execute carefully and precisely a piece of work, which you can't feel at all assured that they have understood when you talk it over beforehand.

training what might be called the passive form of inarticulateness, inability to meet a new point of view or another person's position with sympathetic appreciation. The power to respond in this way is a thing which I believe they are eager to acquire, but no one who observes them in controversy can think that they have attained it.

I have ascribed certain limitations to the hardness and simplicity of the workman's life. But before concluding this article I should like to refer to an utterance which shows the immense importance of training and family tradition quite apart from differences of income. It is contained in the views expressed by the late T. H. Green in consequence of his work as an assistant commissioner of the Endowed Schools Commission of 1864. He found at that time, in the course of his very careful personal investigation, a most remarkable difference between the start in school-life obtained by children of the professional and those of the commercial class, owing entirely to the difference of educational standard between the two classes. The difference need not in the least coincide with a difference of income. It depends on the love of culture, and the habit of using books, and speaking English correctly, and the recognition of knowledge as something worth having. It is to be hoped that things are not now as they were thirty years ago. The Board Schools are changing many things, and this perhaps among them. But if it were true that between any two contiguous social strata there was a difference of this kind, or in as far as there is such a difference, man's natural respect for complete humanity will probably insist on marking it by the use of the terms which we are discussing.

Thus I suggest that the qualities pointed out by the words Lady and Gentleman *are* precious to humanity ; they are its completion by effective utterance ; and, roughly speaking, social usage intends to teach us to look for them in dispositions formed by careful and high-minded education, within families or schools where it has been an object to train the bodily and mental habits to be in detail the efficient expression of human nature at its best.

# XVIII

## SOME REFLECTIONS ON THE IDEA OF DECADENCE

In choosing a colourless title for my address, it was my purpose
to avoid misunderstanding. If I had announced as my
subject " The Praises of Decadence," apart from the explanations which I hope to furnish to-day, I might have incurred
the old imputation of being a corrupter of youth. And I
shrank from the honour of sharing this imputation with my
betters, whether of ancient or of modern times. None the
less, it is my desire to call attention to the debt which we are
under to periods of art and letters and ideas, other than the
great classical epochs ; which latter form, after all, but brief
interruptions in the routine of human affairs. Some consideration of this matter seems at once to be forced upon us
if we adopt in any degree what I take to be the modern standpoint with regard to continuity in history. For if it were
true that for long ages together the human mind is either
manifestly in decay or retrogression, or, at all events, is living
on its capital, and ceasing to be intellectually and artistically
productive, how could such a state of things enable us to
account for the occasional renaissance of brilliant achievement ? I do not suggest that this paradox is at all final or
decisive against the reality of decay and degeneration in
mankind, as we certainly observe them in particular forms
of art, letters, and philosophy. Of course, we may suppose
that new combinations, racial perhaps, or economic, may
disengage latent energies, and that thus, practically, a new
thing may be created and new life arise after what was really
a decay and not merely a transformation of the old. History
is much too complex, I take it, to allow of our pro-
nouncing definitely that the conditions of a totally new
civilization might not come together at some time and place,

practically without inheritance from anything that had gone before.

I only suggest that the conception of continuity in human life makes a prima facie case for anticipating that we shall find some element of positive gain in periods which we have been wont to set down as abandoned to gloom and retrogression. Shakespeare's great saying, " Love speaks with better knowledge, and knowledge with dearer love," will probably justify itself here, as it seldom fails to do. And the course of modern study is showing us, I think, that what we called the decadence was determined in some measure by the point where our college curriculum broke off, and that the darkness of the Dark Ages, for example, was in us at least as much as in them. Not that I would hint a denial of the contrast between classical and decadent periods, taken in a certain sense which we are partly to illustrate to-day. But the interesting and very important question is, how far in such ages new life is stirring in the decay of the old ; how far in fact this decay is itself a symptom or appearance in a new positive development to which the old growth itself or its conditions furnished indispensable factors.

I will put the point afresh by the help of a solution which is likely to be offered as obvious. It might be said to me with some appearance of reason : " You are making a paradox by confusing together facts which are simple but different. Undoubtedly there is real decay in human life ; but life is complex and its different growths or branches are not all decaying at the same time. One thing, say literature, or the drama, may be in decay, while another thing, say politics, or morality, may be gaining new vigour. Philosophy and learning may languish while a new religion is conquering the world. Or the exact sciences and free intellectual speculation may progress by leaps and bounds, while painting and architecture and the drama are dwindling to the shadow of a shade. Then, if you choose to apply such a name as decadence to a whole many-sided epoch of human affairs, you can doubtless appear to prove that elements of growth and of decay are paradoxically intermingled and connected. But the fact is quite simple. One thing is growing and at the same time another thing is dying. But that which is growing is not dying, and that which is dying is not growing. Your paradox, the suggestion that a decadence, as such, may be fertile, is a mere equivocation."

In this objection, no doubt, there would be a certain truth. New emotions and ideas may arise independently of the old. We cannot wholly account for their kindling, and they may find new fuel, so to speak, among classes, populations, and types of mind, which socially or geographically have hitherto been outside the focus of history. Or, in a still more perplexing fashion, the attention of civilized society may be divided ; and an effete literary tradition may continue to preoccupy the cultivated world, while changes and ideas of the deepest import are pressing upon the very society in which that world is included. I am thinking primarily of Mr. Dill's portrayal of the scholar and gentleman during the last centuries of the Western Empire ; but I suppose you might have seen the same thing nearer home in our ancient Universities not a hundred years ago.

I will not argue the matter further in the abstract. I will try to put before you, in the scanty and fragmentary form which my knowledge and the opportunity permit, some illustrations of the fertility of a decadence. I will try in doing so to indicate how, very frequently, it is the actual break-up of great classical traditions—the simplifications, application to life, experimentation, exploration, which naturally go on when the first impression and dominating excitement of the great classical creativeness has passed away—it is, if you like, the reflectiveness of the day after the intoxication, from which strange and new developments, of the greatest importance for humanity, have often sprung. Often, perhaps, it is thus that the material and instruments are prepared, as it were underground, for a new period of classical creation. I will venture to brush aside the formal difficulty that what we learn to treat as great works and ideas we shall no longer set down as decadent. I shall assume in particular that there is justification of some kind for the common feeling which has found a general "decadence"—social, political, and æsthetic—in and after Euripides and throughout the Athenian fourth century and the Hellenistic period ; after, and to some extent in, the later Roman and Byzantine Empire ; and a decadence, more perplexing, because at first sight more exclusively æsthetic, in the age succeeding the classics of the Italian Renaissance or of the Elizabethan drama in England; a decadence obviously extending, in some respects, to our own day.

It is no doubt a very noticeable fact that a change is coming over the judgment of critics upon the art of Euripides, and that of critics and historians upon the Athens of Demosthenes, upon the later Greek literature and philosophy, and upon the Middle Age and the Byzantine Empire. The continuity of thought and of history has during the last fifty years been splendidly asserting itself, and I suppose that the ironical spirit of Gibbon and the caricature of Walter Scott—I speak of the description of the Byzantine court in *Count Robert of Paris*—are now decidedly out of date. Still the difference which has always been felt is there; and we feel that something real is meant, for example, by giving the name of decadence (as Mr. Courthope does) to the change which began with Euripides, and, dare I add in a somewhat similar sense, with Praxiteles, and, it may be, with Plato.

It is obvious that with Euripides a modern spirit breaks into the ancient world; and the fact that the great classical tragic drama comes to an end in him is, we are sure, nothing more than natural. I shall not attempt to characterize his genius in passing, and in the middle of a mere enumeration of suggestive points, which is all that I am aiming at to-day. Those who wish to read about him should go to Professor Gilbert Murray's history of Greek Literature.

But now let us follow up the further beginnings of this modernism in the Hellenistic and Greco-Roman decadence.

In the first place, then, we may note the revival of the Greek epigram, which has a fairly continuous history of sixteen centuries, from the seventh century before Christ to the tenth century after—a golden bridge from the ancient world to the new. But one great gap which occurs in its productiveness almost precisely coincides with the ascendancy of imperial Athens and that extraordinary prime of art and politics which we call the classical period. This is a symptom, and not at all an isolated one, of a certain crushing and overwhelming influence exercised by the imperious excitement of that tremendous age. Before the defeat of the Persians

he epigram—a gem of poetry, but not, like the Latin epigram
n Martial, all sacrificed to a point—the epigram had attained
something like perfection, and with the accession of Alexander
t started again with new life. Thus we may fairly say that
he decadence, the relaxation of spiritual tension in the post-
classical age, not merely coincided with, but actually produced or permitted, the revival of the epigram. Here is a
jewel from the decadence, a poem by the librarian of the
Alexandrian Library in the third century before Christ—
this is a mark of decadence in itself ; you do not hear of
libraries and librarians in classical Greece. Suppose yourself
to have lost by death a friend who was also a fellow-student
and a poet, and you might wish you could have written of
him like this :

> They told me, Heracleitus, they told me you were dead,
> They brought me bitter news to hear and bitter tears to shed ;
> I wept, as I remembered, how often you and I
> Had tired the sun with talking, and sent him down the sky.
> And now that thou art lying, my dear old Carian guest,
> A handful of grey ashes, long, long ago at rest,
> Still are thy pleasant voices, thy nightingales, awake,
> For Death, he taketh all away, but them he cannot take.

This revival of the epigram after the Periclean age suggests
many things to us. The poetry of love, the poetry of the
home and the family, like the epigram, had lacked attention
in the classical age. Before that age, in Sappho the love-
poetess, the former had a marvellous first prime. Now in the
Alexandrian period it rises again, and also the poetry of the
home, with wonderful charm and freshness, and we feel that
the romantic spirit is beginning the long romance of its history.
Here is an epigram of the first century B.C. :

> Ah suffering soul, now thou burnest in the fire, and now thou revivest,
>     and fetchest breath again ; why weepest thou ? When thou didst
>     feed pitiless love in thy bosom, knewest thou not that he was being
>     fed for thy woe ? Knewest thou not ? Know now his repayment, a
>     fair foster hire. Take it, fire and cold snow together. Thou
>     wouldst have it so ; bear the pain ; thou sufferest the wages of
>     thy work, scorched with his burning honey.

You will find greater things in Aeschylus or Sophocles, but
you will find nothing like this.

Closely bound up, as always, with the romantic spirit is the passion for the beauties of Nature. If you were asked where this fateful expression, " the beauties of Nature," so hackneyed to us, so alien from classical Greece, first occurs in literature, I do not know whether it would occur to you to suggest that we owe it to the Greek decadence. " In the house is rest, in the country the charm of nature," the first time the words occur in this precise meaning, is a sentence from an epigram of the third century B.C., the age of Theocritus. And I may mention here that this feeling for the beauty of the external world evidently tended to grow and prosper during the decadence : and it is in the very depths of what we commonly regard as the decay of Paganism, in the third century A.D., that the last of the great Greek thinkers states distinctly for the first time the modern idea—the idea of Ruskin and Wordsworth—of the beauty of material things. The return to nature, the falling back upon human and simple sources of enjoyment, in reaction against the over-refinement of culture and luxury and the crowding and smoke and clamour of huge cities, is one of the happiest features which the world has always owed to a decadence. It begins in the Alexandrian period, and we find it beginning once more in the time of our own Thompson and Cowper, in short, in the age of Rousseau.

Well, we mentioned Theocritus in connection with the third century B.C. ; it is a name which at once symbolizes for us the connection of the return to nature with the romantic spirit. But here we have something more than epigrams and theories ; we have nothing less than the beginning of pastoral poetry. We have, indeed, in the lament over Daphnis, the actual type to which in our English literature alone we owe the *Lycidas*, the *Adonaïs*, and the *Thyrsis*.

One thing more in the present connection. Most of us have heard, through Mrs. Browning's poem, if nowhere else, the name of Heliodorus :

> And we both praised Heliodorus
> For his secret of pure lies,
> Who forged first his linked stories
> In the heat of ladies' eyes.

Heliodorus was a Christian bishop in the fourth century A.D., and he wrote, it would appear, the first, or nearly the first, considerable prose love-romance. His heroine was " Clorinda." Perhaps it would be held that the modern novel of society and the family had a separate origin of its own in Richardson's love-letters (again, I should say, like the return to nature, in a decadence) ; but anyhow the love-romance, as a form of literature, unquestionably dates from the decay of letters under the Roman Empire.

Perhaps we have said enough of this wonderful many-coloured growth of literature which sprang up after the centralized art of Athens had died away. It is poor work talking about poetry instead of reading it. Let me urge those who care for literature, but have not yet come in contact with the later Greek writers, to familiarize themselves at least with Theocritus and the epigrams. There is Mr. Lang's translation of the former, and Mr. Mackail's selection, accompanied by a translation, of the latter. The introductions to these works have furnished me with most of the learning which I have just been displaying to you.

Now let us turn to something else.

When you call a man a Stoic or a Cynic or an Epicure—we do not often call a man an Epicurean, though Shakespeare speaks of a " damned Epicurean rascal "—we bear witness to the influence which the great philosophical creeds of antiquity still exercise on our thought and feeling. So it is when we speak of doing our " duty," or of following our own " nature." Now these great creeds, the language of which is so persistent in our mouths to-day, were not the central or classical philosophies of Greece. They, or the tendencies which they indicate, existed no doubt before and during the time of Socrates and Plato and Aristotle ; but they were repressed and disguised by the force of the central Athenian movement. Being rooted, however, in human nature, they revived in the time of breaking up and reflection, when a man had to look about for himself and find some hold and impulse in his own mind which would help him to live his life. At their best and in their essence these great forms of belief were not so far removed from each other. The Stoic and the Cynic have left a fair impress of themselves upon popular language ; the Epicure has not been so fortunate, unless we restore the

meaning of his name by insisting on the ideas which it might
be held to imply, of a certain daintiness and selection at the
banquet of life, a pursuit of satisfaction, not by greediness,
but by restraint, intelligence, and choice. The common
basis of these creeds is in the conviction that with courage,
sense, and resignation, to which at their best they add devotion
to duty, life, even in a gloomy period, may be made very
fairly liveable. It is a lesson permeated to the core with
decadence, but nevertheless a most precious lesson for the
world. It is symbolized to us all I suppose by the great name
of Marcus Aurelius, with the saying which we know through
Matthew Arnold, " Even in a palace, life may be led well."

*Duty* is a good part of our current morality. Who wrote
the treatise upon duties the name of which is known to every
schoolboy ? Not Plato or Aristotle ; they had ideas which
were higher, perhaps, and fuller, but certainly less sharp in
outline to the popular mind, less fitted for the burden of the
signal flags at Trafalgar. It was Cicero, certainly a decadent
in philosophy, but a man touched with humanity in the modern
sense, and with the instinct of a statesman and a Roman for
the practical and effectual point—it was Cicero, following the
Stoics, who wrote the *De Officiis*, the treatise on our duties
which is almost a household word.

We have spoken of *humanity*. The sense of humanity and
urbanity grew up, it would seem, with the growth of polite
experience, and the habit of intercourse in a large and fairly
peaceful civilization. It is mere ignorance of course to deny
that the Greek Ethics of the great classical philosophy were
founded on the idea of humanity ; but it was then an idea
hidden away in technical definitions and not really operative
in daily feeling. It was the later comedy, Terence or his
Greek model, to which we owe the saying, " I am human,
and I count all that is human my own."

As with duty and humanity, so with nature and freedom.
If you want these ideas in the context of a great philosophy,
criticized, limited, and entangled in reservations, you would
go for them to Plato and Aristotle. But if you want them
as the ferment of popular imagination, as the banner of a
school, or in definite continuity with the gospel of natural
right, you must go for them to the later Greek comedy, to

the Stoic and to Cicero, and to the later Roman jurisprudence
with its echoes in the middle age.   It is the comic poet of the
closing fourth century, after the death of Aristotle, who so
far as I know first definitely says, in a line which he who
runs may read, " no one ever was by nature born a slave."
Like other human instincts which we have referred to, this
conviction existed during the classical time, but did not gain
a hearing in all its simplicity.

I have used more than once this word " simplicity " to
indicate a characteristic of the decadence.   " Simplification,"
" simplify yourself," is a literal rendering of one of the precepts
of Marcus Aurelius.   We commonly think of a decadence as
characterized rather by elaboration than by simplicity ;
and in fact the two are found side by side ;   there is even
such a thing as an elaboration of simplicity ;   you may find
it in Rousseau, perhaps in Marcus Aurelius himself.   But I
mentioned the term for the interest which it has, as at once
the utterance of Marcus Aurelius, and the catchword, in a
much more external sense no doubt, of Tourgenieff's reformers
in *Virgin Soil*, or of Kropotkin's Nihilists.   It suggests one
of the points at which you can verify most readily the connection, as opposed to a mere coincidence, of the elements
of life and death in a decadence.   In this yearning to revert
to the elements, or the inner things of life, and liberate yourself from its accessories, there is undoubtedly something of
impotence.   There is a letting go of much that has been
gained ;   a confession of inability to deal with the intellectual
and ethical inheritance of the world ;   with " the white man's
burden."   It is, on the one side, the spirit of a dying age—

> For this losing is true dying,
> This is lordly man's downlying ;
> This his slow but sure reclining,
> Star by star his world resigning.

On the other hand, it gives a certain evidence of the power
of the naked soul, as it were, which the world would fare
badly without.   It is an embodiment of the feeling which the
most capable of modern workers will own to now and again,
" a recurring need," it has been said, " to get away from society,
and to dispense with the swimming belts of popular habits

and duties, public opinion and the aid of books and friends."
The conviction that institutions were made for man, and not
man for institutions, may be suggested by a sense of failure,
and yet may amount to an inspiration.

And at this point of our treatment of Decadence, when
it is obviously metamorphosing itself under our hands into
the idea of Renaissance, we can hardly avoid some reference
to the coming of Christianity. It seems plain that the great
transformation which began with the Christain era cannot be
wholly dissociated from the movement which we have been
reviewing. If for example we were to take into account the
relation of Christian theology to the Pagan philosophical
schools, or the growth of Christian painting and architecture
out of the tradition of the Greco-Roman world, matters which
are really too vast in their scope for our consideration to-day,
we should unquestionably conclude to a unity of movement,
and not merely to a contemporaneousness of events, in the
growth of the modern consciousness out of the decay of the
ancient world. I may mention simply the date (530 A.D.)
of the Church of St. Sophia in Constantinople, which has been
described as " the most perfect work of art that has yet been
known in organic beauty of design and splendour of ornament,"
because this date shows us clearly, in contrast, I think, with
popular opinion, how close upon and within the decay of
Paganism there arose the true first prime of Christian architecture. In fact, it was the Emperor Justinian, the builder of
St. Sophia, who almost in the same year closed for ever the
philosophical schools of Athens.

Let us return to another side of the decadence. Consider the intellectual origin of University education in Europe.
It dates, I imagine, from the death of Plato, who bequeathed
to his disciples at Athens at once a doctrine and an endowment.
The Platonic Philosophy, of course, was a splendid work of
the close of the classical period ; but the organization of
University teaching at Athens and elsewhere, and the formation
of a curriculum analogous to Plato's ideal draft of a higher
education, are characteristic of the age of decadence ; and
the curriculum thus originated, in some respects a parody of
that really suggested by Plato, descended as the Trivium and
Quadrivium through the middle ages, and was not without

an influence on the working of the modern Universities. It
is thus no mere paradox to say that we owe the idea of University Education to the Greco-Roman decadence. Greece,
in fact, became just in that decadence the paid instructor of
the Roman world in Art and Letters. It is characteristic
for the part played by the decadence that the ideal theory
of the higher education sprang from the greatest genius of the
classical philosophy, while the dwarfing and disfigurement of
it which seemed involved for the time in its application to
life, were the work of generations in which the original doctrine
was no longer understood. The title which still survives for
the old " Greats " school at Oxford, the school of *Literae
Humaniores*, breathes the better spirit of the Greco-Roman
decadence, which came to Oxford, I should suppose, by way
of the Italian Renaissance. We all remember as an example
of this spirit—of this faith in a world the key of which one
has lost, Colonel Newcome's favourite quotation from Ovid,
*ingenuas didicisse fideliter artes Emollit mores nec sinit esse
feros!* The Humanities, I think, is the name they give to
Greek and Latin in Scotland.[1] We are saying nothing depre-
ciatory of this great tradition when we point out that it was
naturally first formulated in an age which felt that something precious had passed away, and that its memory must be
maintained by special institutions, if it was to be maintained
at all.

An interesting example of this tendency on a smaller scale
is the foundation of the Professorship of Poetry in the University of Oxford. Judging from the account given by
Mr. Courthope, the late Professor, in his inaugural lecture recently published, there can be little doubt that Henry Birkhead,
the seventeenth-century founder of the chair, belonged in spirit
to the decadence. Their object was, says Mr. Courthope of
him and his co-workers in poetry, to give distinction to any
theme, however trivial, by adorning it with a multitude of
far-fetched metaphors, similes, and allusions. They published
together a small volume of poems, Birkhead's contribution
to which was " not absolutely the worst " ; but he was the
champion of a losing cause, alike in politics and in poetry.
He came of course after the exhaustion of the Elizabethan

[1] [*Latin* is called Humanity.—ED.]

fount of song, and he must have held, we may suppose, that study and learning were the essentials of poetic art, and yet we owe to the chair which he founded some of the best literary criticism in the English language, and to one of its occupants we owe the *Golden Treasury*.

We may insist a little upon this example, in order to come nearer to something like the essence of our subject. Shakespeare, it was observed the other day by the present Professor of Poetry, was not a conscientious artist. I have little doubt that Henry Birkhead was. Now it would not be safe to say, with the example of Sophocles or Raphael before our eyes, that the artist of a great creative period is never conscientious ; but we might say, perhaps without much danger of going wrong, that a strained and scrupulous conscientiousness is likely to be characteristic of a decadent art and culture. Literary criticism and æsthetic theory almost necessarily prosper in a decadence. How important the treatise *On the Sublime*, of the Augustan Age or later, has been for modern thought ! Mr. Courthope has said that a classical period is universal in its character, and a decadent period is individual. Individuality, perhaps, is too good a name for the thing which is meant ; and it might be better to say that a classical period has a solidarity of faith and spirit, while a decadence is tentative and particularist. But these general names will not help us much ; the bearing of all such observations lies in the application of them. It is, however, so easy to speak in deep-seeming metaphors of the death-birth of a world, or life springing out of corruption, that it does seem worth while to try to express, straightforwardly, what it is that we take to be the paradox of a decadence and its connection with a renaissance.

First, then, it seems essential that the decadence should be relative to a prime. It implies that there has been a very great achievement, whether in art, science, or government, of such a kind as causes and implies a high tension of life on the part of a whole community, or some large section of it. It was really with reference to the decay of the Roman Empire that the term decadence [1] was first used in English.

---

[1] It is a perfectly good English word, with a history on English soil of more than two hundred years.—See *Oxford English Dictionary, sub voce*.

Secondly, it is implied that owing to one or more of very various causes, whether external or internal, this great achievement is no longer sustained, but yet its tradition and its fragments remain, and in some way influence the world.

Then thirdly, it is implied that this tradition and these fragments, although held in reverence, cease to be understood as the thing itself was understood when it existed in all its grandeur.

But fourthly, this ceasing to be understood is a two-sided process. You may illustrate it by Max Müller's idea that imaginative mythology arises through people forgetting the true meaning of words. Well, in a certain sense this is a true account of what happens. People do forget the old meaning of words as they are applied, necessarily, in new experiences and to meet new difficulties, just as I suppose people used catchwords out of the Bible in very new senses in the time of the English Commonwealth. Just so in a decadence words and ideas and forms of art are all dragged off by different minds according to their needs and fancies, the unity of thought and feeling having broken up ; and are applied and elaborated narrowly, practically, intensely, becoming mottoes and creeds and scholastic theories, but for that very reason being worked out, sometimes corruptly, or with frigidity, sometimes again with a certain many-coloured novelty and audacity, the audacity of the specialist. You can see the old language, the old moral notions, and the old beauty echoing on and on, but acquiring a new and original note in their very echoes, echoes from new kinds of substances, one might say, as for example when the Greek beauty was touched with Asiatic richness. The very formation of the Romance languages, I suppose, indicates a process of that kind. French must be in a sense the very debris of Latin, but has acquired of course in its formation new and wonderful powers. This is to me the central interest of a decadence ; to see the mind of man forging ahead, as it were, by the inherent logic of things, in the teeth of circumstances and without the aid of transcendent genius.

This then perhaps is the characteristic note of a decadence ; the meaning of a great past being forgotten, but its tradition respected, and worked out by fragmentary applications which end in new forms, and which produce material for another age of supreme insight and creation. In matters of art and literature this might apply to some phenomena of our own day. I do not think that the whole of social life rises and falls together so immediately to-day as in the little Greek cities or even in the Greco-Roman time. Society is stronger, and the connection of the sides of life, though absolutely real, is subtler and slower in its operation. So in finding decadent features within our life to-day, I am not agreeing with Nordau that we are a decadent society. But the anarchy or particularism of decadence is very observable in our art and letters, every man fighting for his own hand, by the help of some fragment of tradition which he misunderstands in his own way. The absorption of our younger painters in the pure study of light, which our better critics insist upon, is I believe a case strikingly in point. Undoubtedly those are right who contend that such a realism, if it is a realism, or impressionism, if it is an impressionism, involves in itself no narrowing of the imagination, but places a fresh instrument in its hands and opens to it new worlds to conquer. The same thing is ultimately true, I have no doubt, even of that elaborate and conscientious study of the remoter meanings and effects and associations of language—of the actual word—to which has been given the name of symbolism or of decadent style. It is, I repeat, in itself the forging of a new instrument in the hand of imagination. But whether the workmen in these materials are more than the journeymen of a decadence; whether they see and understand the place of their workmanship, their mosaic, so to speak, in the whole fabric of a great imaginative construction, is more than I would venture to determine. Here, however, in this sense of unity and of the whole, of the relation between form and substance, is the "*articulus stantis aut cadentis ecclesiae*," the criterion of life and of decadence in the realm of art and literature.

We have attributed many beautiful things to periods of decadence, and it may be thought that we have blurred the distinction which the term is intended to convey. Even Homer, it has been suggested, belongs to the close of a civilization which the telescope of archæology sees stretching behind him, and is not without his touches that indicate a sense of bygone greatness. It would certainly seem that the Homeric warrior was not possessed by that love of battle for its own sake which we ascribe to our own Northern ancestors in the youth of the modern world. There is, however, one form of art—the true poetical drama—which can hardly be produced except in a classical period ; a period when the creative excitement of some single impulse is shared by at least a large section of the public, making them able and willing to sympathize in the constructive effort of the poet and to live up to the tension of his mind. The Poetical Drama has flourished for very few centuries indeed in the history of the world, and its cessation, when its conditions have ceased to exist, has generally been sharp and definite. Whether it is ever to appear again I will not prophesy ; but its appearance would be the surest, I do not say the sole possible sign, that the world was once more fusing into a splendid unity the anarchic and ambiguous beauties of a decadence.

# XIX

## ON THE TRUE CONCEPTION OF ANOTHER WORLD [1]

' With such barren forms of thought, that are always in a world beyond, Philosophy has nothing to do. Its object is always something concrete, and in the highest sense present."—Hegel's *Logic*, Wallace's translation, p. 150.

IT will surprise many readers to be told that the words which I have quoted above embody the very essence of Hegelian thought. The Infinite, the supra-sensuous, the Divine, are so connected in our minds with futile rackings of the imagination about remote matters which only distract us from our duties, that a philosophy which designates its problems by such terms as these seems self-condemned as cloudy and inane. But, all appearances to the contrary notwithstanding, Hegel is faithful to the present and the concrete. In the study of his philosophy we are always dealing with human experience. "My stress lay," says Mr. Browning,[2] "on the incidents in the development of a soul ; little else is worth study." For "a soul" read "the mind," and you have the subject-matter to which Hegel's eighteen close-printed volumes are devoted. The present remarks are meant to insist on this neglected point of view. I wish to point out, in two or three salient instances, the transformation undergone by speculative notions when sedulously applied to life, and restrained from generating an empty "beyond," or other world, between which and our present life and knowledge there is a great gulf fixed. That the world of mind, or the world above sense, exists as an actual and organized whole, is a truth most easily realized in the study of the beautiful. And to grasp this principle as Hegel applies

[1] This Essay was first published in 1886 as the Introduction to a translation of a fragment from Hegel's *Æsthetic*.
[2] Preface to *Sordello*.

it is nothing less than to acquire a new contact with spiritual life. The spiritual world, which is present, actual, and concrete, contains much besides beauty. But to apprehend one element of such a whole must of course demand a long step towards apprehending the rest. It is for this reason that I propose to explain, by prominent examples, the conception of a spiritual world which is present and actual, in order to make more conceivable Hegel's views on the particular sphere of art. So closely connected, indeed, are all the embodiments of mind, his *Philosophy of Fine Art* may be said to contain the essence of his entire system.

We know, to our cost, the popular conception of the supra-sensuous world. Whatever that world is, it is, as commonly thought of, not here and not now. That is to say, if here and now, it is so by a sort of miracle, at which we are called upon to wonder, as when angels are said to be near us, or the dead to know what we do. Again, it is a counterpart of our present world, and rather imperceptible to *our* senses, than in its nature beyond contact with sense as such. It is peopled by persons who live eternally, which means through endless ages, and to whose actual communion with us, as also to our own with God, we look forward in the future. It even, perhaps, contains a supra-sensuous original corresponding to every thing and movement in this world of ours. And it does *not* necessarily deepen our conception of life, but only reduplicates it.

Such a world, whatever we may think about its actual existence, is *not* the " other world " of philosophy. The " things not seen " of Plato or of Hegel are not a double or a projection of the existing world. Plato, indeed, wavered between the two conceptions in a way that should have warned his interpreters of the divergence in his track of thought. But in Hegel, at least, there is no ambiguity. The world of spirits with him is no world of ghosts. When we study the embodiments of mind or spirit in his pages, and read of law, property, and national unity ; of fine art, the religious community, and the intellect that has attained scientific self-consciousness, we may miss our other world with its obscure " beyond," but we at any rate feel ourselves to be dealing with something real, and with the deepest concerns of life. We may deny to such matters the titles which philosophy bestows upon them; we may say that this is no " other world," no realm of spirits, nothing infinite or Divine; but this matters little, so long as we know what we are talking about, and are talking about the best we know. And what we discuss when Hegel is our guide, will *always* be some great achievement or essential attribute of the human mind. He never asks " Is it ? " but always, " What is it ? " and therefore has instruction, drawn from experience, even for those to whom the titles of his inquiries seem fraudulent or bombastic.

These few remarks are not directed to maintaining any thesis about the reality of nature and of sense. Their object is to enforce a distinction which falls *within* the world which we know, and not *between* the world we know and another which we do not know. The distinction is real, and governs life. I am not denying any other distinction, but I am insisting on this. No really great philosopher, nor religious teacher —neither Plato, nor Kant, nor St. Paul—can be understood, unless we grasp this antithesis in the right way. All of these teachers have pointed men to another world. All of them, perhaps, were led at times by the very force and reality of their own thought into the fatal separation that cancels its meaning. So strong was their sense of the gulf between the trifles and the realities of life, that they gave occasion to the indolent imagination—in themselves and in others—to transmute this gulf from a measure of moral effort into an inaccessibility that defies apprehension. But their purpose was to overcome this inaccessibility, not to heighten it.

The hardest of all lessons in interpretation is to believe that great men mean what they say. We are below their level, and what they actually say seems impossible to us, till we have adulterated it to suit our own imbecility. Especially when they speak of the highest realities, we attach *our* notion of reality to what *they* pronounce to be real. And thus we baffle every attempt to deepen our ideas of the world in which we live. The work of intelligence is hard; that of the sensuous fancy is easy; and so we substitute the latter for the former. We are told, for instance, by Plato, that goodness, beauty, and truth are realities, but not visible or tangible. Instead of responding to the call so made on our intelligence by

scrutinizing the nature and conditions of these intellectual facts
—though we know well how tardily they are produced by the
culture of ages—we apply forthwith our idea of reality as something separate in space and time, and so " refute " Plato with
ease, and remain as wise as we were before. And it is true
that Plato, handling ideas of vast import with the mind and
language of his day, sometimes by a similar error refutes himself.[1] He makes, for instance, the disembodied soul see the
invisible ideas. Thus he travesties his things of the mind as
though they were things of sense, only not of *our* sense—thereby destroying the deeper difference of kind that alone enables
them to find a place in our world. That his doctrine of ideas
was really rooted, not in mysticism, but in scientific enthusiasm, is a truth that is veiled from us partly by his inconsis-
tencies, but far more by our own erroneous preconceptions.[2]

There is, however, a genuine distinction between " this "
world and the " other " world, which is merely parodied by
the vulgar antitheses between natural and supernatural, finite
and infinite, phenomenal and noumenal. We sometimes hear
it said, " The world is quite changed to me since I knew such
a person," or " studied such a subject," or " had suggested
to me such an idea." The expression may be literally true ;
and we do not commonly exaggerate, but vastly underrate its
import. We read, for instance, in a good authority, " These
twenty kinds of birds (which Virgil mentions) do not correspond
so much to our species as to our genera ; for the Greeks and
Romans, I need hardly say, had only very rough-and-ready
methods of classification, just as is the case with uneducated
people at the present day."[3] Any one may verify the same
fact as regards the observation of flowers. Every yellow
ranunculus is called a " buttercup," every large white umbel-
lifer a " hemlock." These, with hundreds of other differences
of perception, affect the surroundings in which men consciously live, at least as much as a considerable degree of
deafness or blindness. It is no metaphor, but literal fact, to

[1] " Endless duration makes good no better, nor white any whiter," is
one of Aristotle's comments on Plato's " eternal " ideas, and is just, unless
" eternal " conveys a difference of kind.

[2] We are apt to misinterpret Plato's language about astronomy in this
sense. Plato is not decrying observation, but demanding a theoretical
treatment of the laws of motion—a remarkable anticipation of modern ideas.

[3] *A Year with the Birds*, by an Oxford Tutor [W. Warde Fowler].

say that man's whole environment is transformed by the training even of his mere apprehension of natural objects. But there is more in the matter than this. Without going into metaphysics, which I wish to avoid, I cannot, indeed, maintain that mind " makes " natural objects, although by enabling us to perceive them, it unquestionably makes our immediate conscious world. My individual consciousness does not make or create the differences between the species of ranunculus, although it does create my knowledge of them. But when we come to speak of the world of morals, or art, or politics, we may venture much farther in our assertions. The actual facts of this world do directly arise out of and are causally sustained by conscious intelligence ; and these facts form the world above sense. The unity of a Christian church or congregation is a governing fact of life ; so is that of a family or a nation ; so, we may hope, will that of humanity come to be. What is this unity ? Is it visible and tangible, like the unity of a human body ? No, the unity is " ideal " ; that is, it exists in the medium of thought only ; it is made up of certain sentiments, purposes, and ideas. What, even of an army ? Here, too, an ideal unity is the mainspring of action. Without mutual intelligence and reciprocal reliance you may have a mob, but you cannot have an army. But all these conditions exist and can exist in the mind only. An army, *qua* army, is not a mere fact of sense ; for not only does it need mind to perceive it—a heap of sand does that—but it also needs mind to *make* it.

The world of these governing facts of life is the world of the things not seen, the object of reason, the world of the truly infinite and Divine. It is, of course, a false antithesis to contrast seeing with the bodily eye and seeing with the mind's eye. The seeing eye is always the mind's eye. The distinction between sense and spirit or intellect is a distinction *within the mind*, just as is St. Paul's opposition between the spirit and the flesh. Nevertheless the mind that only sees colour— sense or sense-perception—is different from the mind that sees beauty, the self-conscious spirit. The latter includes the former, but the former does not include the latter. To the one the colour is the ultimate fact ; to the other it is an element in a thing of beauty. This relation prevails throughout between the world of sense and the world above sense. The " things not seen," philosophically speaking, are no world of existences or of intelligences co-ordinate with and severed from this present world. They are a value, an import, a significance, superadded to the phenomenal world, which may thus be said, though with some risk of misunderstanding, to be degraded into a symbol. The house, the cathedral, the judge's robe, the general's uniform, are ultimate facts for the child or the savage ; but for the civilized man they are symbols of domestic life, of the Church, and of the State. Even where the supra-sensuous world has its purest expression, in the knowledge and will of intelligent beings, it presupposes a sensuous world as the material of ideas and of actions. " This " world and the " other " world are continuous and inseparable, and all men must live in some degree for both. But the completion of the Noumenal world, and the apprehension of its reality and completeness, is the task by fulfilling which humanity advances.

I pass to the interpretation, neither technical nor contro-versial, of one or two of Hegel's most alarming phrases.

The " infinite " seems to practical minds the very opposite of anything real, present, or valuable. As the description of life, it is the mere negation of the life we know ; as the descrip-tion of a purpose, it is the very antithesis of any purpose that we can conceive to be attainable ; as the description of a being, it appears to be formed by denying every predicate which we attach to personality. And I could wish that Hegel had not selected this much-abused term as the distinctive predicate of what is most real and most precious in life. He adhered to it, no doubt, because his infinity, though different in nature to that of common logic, yet rightly fills the place and meets the problem of that conception. I will attempt to explain how this can be, and what we are discussing when we read about infinity in the Hegelian philosophy.

It is an obvious remark, that infinity was a symbol of evil in Hellenic speculation, whereas to Christian and modern thought it is identified with good. Much idle talk has arisen on this account, as to the limitation of the Hellenic mind. For, in fact, the Finite ascribed to Pythagoras, and the idea of limit and proportion in Plato or in Aristotle, are far more nearly akin to true infinity than is the Infinite of modern popular philosophy. Infinite means the negation of limit. Now, common infinity, which may be identified in general with enumeration *ad infinitum*—the *false* infinity of Hegel—is the attempt to negate or transcend a limit which inevitably recurs. It arises from attempting a task or problem in the wrong way, so that we may go on for ever without making any advance towards its achievement. All quantitative infinity—which of course has its definite uses, subject to proper reservations— is of this nature. A process does not change its character by mere continuance, and the aggregate of a million units is no more free from limitation than the aggregate of ten. A defect in kind cannot be compensated by mere quantity. We see the fallacious attempt in savage, barbaric, or vulgar art. Meaningless iteration, objectless labour, enormous size, extravagant costliness, indicate the effort to satisfy man's need of expression by the mere accumulation of work without adequate idea or purpose. But such efforts, however stupendous, never attain their goal. They constitute a recurrent failure to transcend a recurrent limit, precisely analogous to enumeration *ad infinitum*. A hundred thousand pounds' worth of bricks and mortar comes no nearer to the embodiment of mind than a thousand pounds' worth. To attempt adequate expression by mere aggregation of cost or size is therefore to fall into the infinite process or the false infinity.

Another well-known instance is the pursuit of happiness in the form of " pleasure for pleasure's sake." The recurrence of unchanging units leaves us where we were. A process which does not change remains the same, and if it did not bring satisfaction at first, will not do so at last.[1] We might as well go on producing parallels to infinity, in the hope that somehow or somewhere they may meet. An infinite straight line may serve as a type of the kind of infinity we are considering.

Infinity in the Hegelian sense does not partake in any way of this endlessness, or of the unreality which attaches to it. Its root-idea is self-completeness or satisfaction. That which is " infinite " is without boundary, because it does not refer beyond itself for explanation, or for justification ; and therefore, in all human existence or production infinity can only be

[1] See note above, p. 323.

an aspect or element. A picture, for instance, regarded as a work of fine art, justifies itself, gives satisfaction directly and without raising questions of cause or of comparison, and is in this sense—i.e. in respect of its beauty—regarded as " infinite." When, on the other hand, we consider this same work of art as an historical phenomenon, as a link in a chain of causation —e.g. as elucidating the development of a school, or proving the existence of a certain technical process at a certain date— then we go beyond itself for its interest and explanation, and depress it at once into a finite object. The finite is that which presents itself as incomplete ; the infinite, that which presents itself as complete, and which, therefore, does not force upon us the fact of its limitation. This character belongs in the highest degree to self-conscious mind, as realized in the world above sense ; and in some degree to all elements of that world —for instance, to the State—in as far as they represent man's realized self-consciousness. It is the nature of self-conscious-ness to be infinite, because it is its nature to take into itself what was opposed to it, and thus to make itself into an organ-ized sphere that has value and reality within, and not beyond itself. If false infinity was represented by an infinite straight line, true infinity may be compared to a circle or a sphere.

The distinction between true and false infinity is of the profoundest moral import. The sickly yearning that longs only to escape from the real, rooted in the antithesis between the infinite and the actual or concrete, or in the idea of the monotonous " *infini* " which is one with the " *abîme* " or the " *gouffre*," is appraised by this test at its true value. It is seen to rest on a mere pathetic fallacy of thought and senti-ment. So far from the infinite being remote, abstract, unreal, nothing but the infinite can be truly present, concrete, and real. The finite always refers us away and away through an endless series of causes, of effects, or of relations. The infinite is individual, and bears the character of knowledge, achieve-ment, attainment. In short, the actual realities which we have in mind when, in philosophy, we speak of the infinite, are such as a nation that is conscious of its unity and general will, or the realm of fine art as the recognition of man's higher nature, or the religious community with its conviction of an indwelling Deity.

Now, whether we like the term Infinite or not, whether or no we think that man's life can be explained and justified within the limits of these aims and these phenomena, there is no doubt that these matters are real, and are the most momentous of realities. In acquainting ourselves with their structure, evolution, and relation to individual life, we are at least not wasting time, nor treating of matters beyond human intelligence.

There is a very similar contrast in the conception of human Freedom. " Free will " is so old a vexed question, that, though the conflict still rages fitfully round it, the world hardly conceives that much can turn upon its decision. But when in place of the abstract, " Is man free ? " we are confronted with the concrete inquiry, " When, in what, and as what, does man carry out his will with least hindrance and with fullest satisfaction ? " then we have before us the actual phenomena of civilization, instead of an idle and abstract Yes or No.

Man's Freedom, in the sense thus contemplated, lies in the spiritual or supra-sensuous world by which his humanity is realized, and in which his will finds fulfilment. The family, for example, property, and law are the first steps of man's freedom. In them the individual's will obtains and bestows recognition as an agent in a society whose bond of union is ideal—i.e. existing only in consciousness ; and this recognition develops into duties and rights. It is in these that man finds something to live for, something in which and for the sake of which to assert himself. As society develops he lives, on the whole, more in the civilized or spiritual world, and less in the savage or purely natural world. His will, which is himself, expands with the institutions and ideas that form its purpose, and the history of this expansion is the history of human freedom. Nothing is more shallow, more barbarously irrational, than to regard the progress of civilization as the accumulation of restrictions. Laws and rules are a necessary aspect of extended capacities. Every power that we gain has a positive nature, and therefore involves positive conditions, and every positive condition has negative relations. To accomplish a particular purpose you must go to work in a particular way, and in no other way. To complain of this is like complaining of a house because it has a definite shape. If freedom means absence of attributes, empty space is " freer " than any edifice. Of course a house may be so ugly that we may say we would rather have none at all. Civilization may bring such horrors that we may say, " Rather savagery than this " ; but in neither case are we serious. Great as are the vices of civilization, it is only in civilization that man becomes human, spiritual, and free.

The effort to grasp and apply such an idea as this can hardly be barren. It brings us face to face with concrete facts of history, and of man's actual motives and purposes. True philosophy here, as everywhere, plunges into the concrete and the real ; it is the indolent abstract fancy that thrusts problems away into the remote " beyond," or into futile abstraction. Plato, the philosopher, knows well that the mind is free when it achieves what, as a whole, it truly wills. But Plato, the allegorist and imaginative preacher, refers the soul's freedom to a fleeting moment of ante-natal choice, which he vainly strives to exempt from causal influence. Pictorial imagination, with its ready reference to occurrences in past and future, is the great foe to philosophic intelligence.

Finally, it is impossible to omit all reference to the notion of an immanent Deity, which forms the very centre of Hegel's thought. When an unspeculative English reader first meets with Hegel's passionate insistence that God is not unknowable, that He necessarily reveals Himself as a Trinity of persons, and that to deny this is to represent men as " the heathen who know not God," he feels as if he had taken sand into his mouth. He is inclined to ask what these Neo-Platonic or mediæval doctrines are doing in the nineteenth century, and why we should resuscitate dead logomachies that can have no possible value for life or conduct. Now, I must not attempt here to discuss the difficult question of Hegel's ultimate conception of the being of God, and I am bound to warn any one who may read these pages that I only profess to reproduce one—though by far the most prominent—side of that conception. But, subject to this reservation, I have no hesitation in saying that our own prejudices form the only hindrance to our seeing that Hegel's subject-matter is here, as elsewhere, human life. He gives us what he takes to be the literal truth, and we will have it to be metaphor. Verbally contradicting Kant,

he accepts, completes, and enforces Kant's thought. " Revelation can never be the true ground of religion," said Kant ;
" for revelation is an historical accident, and religion is a
rational necessity of man's intelligent nature." " Revelation
is the only true knowledge of God and ground of religion,"
says Hegel, " because *revelation consists in the realization of
God in man's intelligent nature.*" We are, however, not unaccustomed to such phrases, and our imagination is equal to its
habitual task of evading their meaning. We take them to be
a strong metaphor, meaning that God, who is a sort of ghostly
being a long way off, is, notwithstanding, more or less within
the knowledge of our minds, and so is " in " them, as a book
which is actually in London may be in my memory when I
am in Scotland. Now, right or wrong, this is not what Hegel
means. He means what he says ; that God is spirit or mind,[1]
and exists in the medium of mind, *which is actual as intelligence, for us at any rate, only in the human self-consciousness.*
The thought is hard from its very simplicity, and we struggle,
as always, to avoid grasping it. We imagine spirits as made
of a sort of thin matter, and so as existing just like bodies,
although we call them disembodied. And then we think of
this disembodied form as an alternative to human form, and
suppose spirit to have somehow a purer existence apart from
human body. This error really springs from imagining the
two as existences of the same kind, and so conflicting, and
from not realizing the notion of spirit as mind or self-consciousness, which is the only way of conceiving its actual presence
in our world. Mind uses sensuous existence as its symbol ;
perhaps even needs it. The poet who has hit Hegel's thought
so nearly,[2] fails here :

> This weight of body and limb,
> Are they not sign and symbol of thy division from Him ?

Here we leave the track of the higher Pantheism for that of
vulgar mysticism. Spiritual being is conceived as somehow

---

[1] The fusion of these meanings in the German " Geist " gives a force to
his pleading which English cannot render. He appeals, e.g., triumphantly
to *God is a Spirit*, i.e. not " a ghost," but " mind."

[2] See Tennyson's *Higher Pantheism*, especially the fine lines :

> Speak to Him thou, for He hears, and Spirit with spirit can meet,
> Closer is He than breathing, and nearer than hands and feet.

incompatible with bodily shape, either because incapable of any concrete embodiment, or because it has a quasi-material shape of its own. Now, this is just the reverse of the Hegelian idea. According to Hegel, it is only in the human form that intelligence can for us find its full expression. The notion of a spiritual body other than and incompatible with the natural body does not arise. Spirit exists in the medium of consciousness, not in a peculiar kind of matter. The spiritualization of the natural body is not to be looked for in an astral or angel body, but in the gait and gesture, the significance and dignity, that make the body of the civilized man the outward image of his soul, and distinguish him from the savage as from the animal. The human soul becomes actual itself, and visible to others, only by moulding the body into its symbol and instrument. It ought to have been an axiom of physiology, Hegel says, that the series of animated forms must necessarily lead up to that of man. For this is the only sensuous form in which mind could attain adequate manifestation. Thus anthropomorphism in fine art is no accident, nor an unworthy portrayal of Divinity. If the Deity is to be symbolized to sense, it must be in the image of man. The symbol is not, indeed, the reality, as the sensuous image is not conscious thought ; but this is a defect inherent in artistic presentation, and not attributable to anthropomorphism in particular.

It is obvious that, in the light of such a conception, a speculative import can be attached to the doctrine of the Incarnation, and Hegel's reading of Christian ideas is, in fact, to be interpreted entirely in this sense. This is not the place to go deeper into such views, which, however profound, may perhaps continue to seem non-natural expositions of Christian dogma. I am only concerned to show how here, also, the speculative idea, operating upon the concrete and actual, generates a fresh and inspiring insight into life and conduct. Few chapters of anthropology are more thorough, profound, and suggestive than Hegel's account of the " actual soul " ; i.e. of the habits and attributes which make the body distinctively human by stamping it with the impress of mind. Nor has philosophic insight ever done better service to the history of religion than in grasping the essence of Christianity as the *unity* (not merely the *union*) of the Divine and human nature.

Among the things which are spiritually discerned, an important place belongs to beauty. As a boundary and transition between sense and thought, it is peculiarly fitted to illustrate the reality which we claim, in contradistinction to mere sensuous appearance, for what is best in life. Many who distrust Hegelian formulæ are convinced that beauty at least is real. They will admit that fine art and the recognition of beauty are not trifles, not amusements, but rank high among the interests that give life its value. All such will find themselves in sympathy with the purpose of a great philosopher who has bent all the power of his genius and his industry to vindicating a place for art as an embodiment of the Divine nature, that is to say, of the fundamental purpose which reveals itself in the history of the human spirit.

## XX

## THE KINGDOM OF GOD ON EARTH [1]

MUCH is said in the New Testament, with very various meanings, about the Kingdom of Christ or the Kingdom of God. I want to consider, this evening, some of the forms which this idea has taken in the New Testament and elsewhere, and what meaning it can have for us to-day.

I. " Sell all that thou hast, and give to the poor, and thou shalt have treasure in heaven." " Grant that we may sit, the one on Thy right hand, and the other on Thy left, in Thy kingdom." " Now he is comforted, and thou art tormented." In such passages as these we think that we find two ideas which have had enormous influence on the world.

1. Heaven is to right the wrongs and to compensate the injustices of this world. " Thou in thy lifetime receivedst thy good things, and likewise Lazarus evil things ; but now he is comforted, and thou art tormented." Part of this natural conception has been a comfort to those for whom the world seemed to have nothing but misery, and part has rudely represented a wild feeling of justice. But at all times, and especially in modern times, it has had another and a very mischievous influence. It can be turned round the other way. God, we think, will look after those who are ill-off on earth, and therefore we need not trouble ourselves about them. Heaven becomes a sort of Poor Law, to which we refer the cases of distress that we do not know how to deal with. We even feel very virtuous in doing this. It is so humble of us to be content with this world's goods, and to leave the next world to our poorer neighbours. And it makes everything easy ; it cuts the knot of all those troublesome questions, how every member of a great nation can have a man's share in the

[1] An address given for the Ethical Society.

work and knowledge of the world. Let him read his Bible and believe what he is told, and then, after a few years, which do not much matter, he will be as well off as an emperor ; or perhaps better, for he will go to heaven, and many emperors will not.

This belief has great power for good and for evil. It has raised men's estimate of their dignity, and has made them feel the value of a soul. But it has made them careless of the world in which they live, and has narrowed their notions of duty and of manliness. Life must not be split up into a present of endurance, and a future of enjoyment. Injustice must be redressed, beauty enjoyed, knowledge won, and goodness attained, here on this earth of ours.

2. Then there is the other common idea, very like the last. " Great is your *reward* in heaven." " Thy Father which seeth in secret shall reward thee openly." This is the notion, not very marked, I think, in the New Testament, of a moral government of the world by rewards and punishments. The Churchmen who write about religion have made a fatal delusion out of this conception too. But I do not think that sensible people have taken it very seriously. We all know that we are not to do good for the sake of what we expect to get by it ; and if a preacher tells us that we are to be good Christians in order to go to heaven and keep out of hell, we think that he does not quite understand what he is saying. A man who tells you that is mixing up two notions. One notion is that you are to obey God's will in order to gain the pleasure of heaven and escape the pains of hell. And the other notion is that you are to obey God's will, because in doing that you get rid of the bad in your own heart, and make your will rest or repose in the good will. This hope of finding peace, of resting your will in something greater than yourself, of being at one with the good purpose of humanity, is the very mainspring of life. But it is here on earth that we want our will to be good, and to get rid of the bad in our own hearts. There is no reason in putting it off to a future life, of which we know nothing. If we must have something future to hope for, let us put our hopes on our children, and do something to carry them out. However, this desire to be good and to be at one with a society of good people is the root of our life.

But that other notion, that we are to be good in order to gain the pleasures of heaven, is very wrong, or rather, it is absolute nonsense. I should like to explain why I say that it is absolute nonsense.

A man is good when his will is good, and bad when his will is bad. It all depends upon what kind of thing he really has at heart when he acts. It does not depend on what he does, if you look at it from the outside. If a man says he meant well, when he did not, then he is a hypocrite. But we all know that a man may really mean well, and yet may make a mistake and do great harm. Then we do not call him a bad man, though we may call him a fool. This shows that it is the will which makes a man good or bad, and a man's will is his choice ; it is what his heart is really set on when he acts. So, when we talk of being good or doing good, for the sake of what we can get by it, this can only be a pretence of being or doing good. You may do, for reward, something that on the outside looks like doing good, but it is not doing good, because the will is selfish—your heart is set on your own pleasure or comfort, and not on a substantial good for its own sake. A man who really thought of nothing but getting safe to heaven would be as bad as a man in a shipwreck who thought of nothing but getting himself safe into a boat. There are a few such people, I dare say. But of course most people are better than they make out. When they speak of reward and punishment, they do not mean merely pleasures and pains ; they mean, in part at least, the goodness which causes the pleasure, and the badness which causes the pain. We can see that true Christians have never thought the reward the chief thing. St. Paul was ready to give up his own reward, to be accursed from Christ, if that would save the souls he loved. And to go from great things to small, there is a fine scene in a novel which I once read. A young man is afraid to go to the rescue of some people in a flood, because he has a conviction that if he is drowned then, he will go to hell. And the old man, an old Scotsman, to whom he tells this, shouts out to him in reply, " Better be damned doing the will of God than saved doing nothing." This is the instinct of true religion revolting against the false doctrine of rewards ; and I believe that this revolt has the sympathy of all true Christians.

Of course this fancy of rewards and punishments has had its uses. It has enabled people to believe against appearances that good was stronger than evil. And it has helped to *make* good stronger than evil. We cannot judge these old beliefs fairly, unless we think of the power they had and the way in which they were used. In rough ages it was a gain that men should recognize anything as above themselves. There is a striking picture in a poem of Longfellow's of a monk forcing a Norman Baron in England, on his death-bed, to set his serfs free.

> In his chamber, weak and dying,
> Was the Norman Baron lying ;
>
> \*　　\*　　\*　　\*
>
> And, as on the sacred missal,
> He recorded their dismissal,
> Death relaxed his iron features,
> And the Monk replied, " Amen."

I do not say that this picture represents a fact ; but no one can doubt that the thought of heaven and hell must often have reinforced the appeal of conscience, and kept alive the persuasion that there was a power higher than the sword.

These were the old convictions about heaven and the kingdom of God—that it was an invisible future world, in which wrong was to be righted, and good and bad men rewarded and punished. These fancies have not in reality a great place in the New Testament ; but they were known to the Greeks and to many other nations. Plato speaks with scorn of the priests and charlatans of his time, four centuries before Christ, who go about telling men that they can make it all safe for them in the next world by their prayers and ceremonies. So these notions are as old as civilized mankind ; and the right way to look at them is to see that people naturally came upon them when they felt sure that there was a right somewhere, and that it was better to be good. The last thing people understand is what is before their eyes. It is so much easier just to fancy that something used to be, or that something will be, instead of looking patiently at what actually is. Men look round them and see that the world seems very bad, but they feel sure that there is a real good somewhere ; and so they make up a story that it was all very good once, and then the devil put it wrong ; but God will put it all right again some day—at least for some of us. It is just as people say, " How do there come to be so many kinds of plants and animals ? " And they answer that God created them a long time ago, and Adam gave them names. Well, of course, if we look carefully at what is under our eyes, we see that this is a fantastic idea. The kinds of plants and animals are always changing now, precisely as they always have been changing since they began.

Just in the same way, when you look patiently and carefully at the world we live in, you see that those ideas of another world are nothing but imperfect explanations or reflections of the good that is being worked out in this world, and are of no value, excepting as they contribute to the furtherance of this real good. Good is not a thing which can be made up by deferred payments.

3. In the same way, again, God has been thought of as a king or master, somewhere outside the world we live in, and the Bible as the book of His decrees ; as if God could make anything right by choosing to command it. This is the old meaning of revelation ; that man had no way of knowing God's will, and so God had this book written to tell us what His will was, and we have to do everything that is commanded in this book. Of course this idea turns things upside down. Things are not right because the Bible says them, but the Bible says them, *if it does say them*, because they are right. And when we say now that anything is God's command, we ought to know that we are using a figure of speech, which means something quite different from the command of a person outside ourselves and having power over us.

4. And this makes an enormous difference ; because, if you have a master in heaven, whose orders you must obey, and if he has had a book written to tell you what to do, then the most important people in the world are the people who spend their lives in interpreting this book. And in fact, as you and I have not time to be studying a book written in Hebrew and Greek all our lives, we should be under the thumb of these gentlemen, who say they know all about it, and some of them even say they have a special commission from God to tell us

about it, and we are not to listen to any one else. This is plainly a mere dream. There is no great harm in talking of a revelation, but it means nothing in the world but our own common sense and reason, dealing with the circumstances of our lives.

All these ideas—compensation, rewards and punishments, God's commands in the Bible, the authority of the clergy—are closely connected together. They are all fancies that men have had, just as though they were children, and being children knew that they must be treated like children. Children do things because they are told, until they have learnt to behave themselves. And so men had to learn to behave themselves, only they had to fancy that there was a parent or schoolmaster looking after them. They naturally invented the only sort of instruction they could receive.

II. But then, in the New Testament we find yet other ideas mixed with those which we have been speaking of. The kingdom of God is within you (or perhaps " among you ") ; it is like leaven ; it is like a seed ; it is not of this world. This might mean it is in heaven, but I do not think it does ; I think it means that the kingdom of God is not what people in this world call a kingdom. The New Testament writers did, in fact, think that the next world was to be on earth, and that it was to begin soon, and had in truth begun already. But we must not count this altogether on our side, because there was to be a miraculous end to the old earth, and a new one was to be made. Still, we may fairly say that they thought the kingdom of God was a moral kingdom ; that it was to come on earth ; that it was something quite close to them ; and that it had partly begun with Christ's life. The idea of the Church grew up in place of this conviction, when the belief in Christ's coming gave way.

This moral kingdom of God is what is meant in the prayer, " Thy kingdom come," which is explained by the next petition, " Thy will be done on earth as it is in heaven." Most of the New Testament writers, and, it would seem, Christ Himself, expected this kingdom to come within a man's lifetime. We may leave out these words, " as in heaven," which belong to the fancies of which we have been speaking, fancies that the good which we do not see here is real somewhere else.

But the kingdom of God on earth is here, as the Lord's prayer implies, in as far as what we call God's will is done on earth. But now there is a question which stares us in the face.

What have we men to do with God's will ? The question has two forms :

1. How are we to know what is God's will ? and

2. Why should we do God's will when we do know it ?

We have destroyed the vulgar answers to these two questions. I will repeat briefly how we have destroyed them. They were : " We are to know God's will from His inspired revelation in the Bible," or " from the Catholic Church "—a very mischievous doctrine ; and " we are to do God's will because He will reward or punish us according as we do it or not." The first of these answers is a mistake, because books and men are just books and men, and they cannot have authority except by convincing our own minds. And the second is an absurdity, because the nature of what we do depends upon our will in doing it ; and if what we will is to get a reward, then our action is not good. Rewards and punishments are legal sanctions and not moral influences.

There is only one true way of answering these questions. We must know what is right, what we call God's will, by finding it in our own will. And we must do what is right, what we call God's will, because we find that it is our own will. We must look at it in this way.

If we come to think over our lives, and to ask ourselves what fills up the greater part of our thoughts and purposes, we shall find, if we are decent people, that it mostly comes back to our station in life,[1] and the duties that are recognized by ourselves and by others as belonging to it ; and also in certain duties and interests, usually connected with our station, which we have taken up and made our own. A man can hardly live without something or other which is required of him by others, and which he requires of himself. Those whom we call idle people have their duties, but partly they are mistaken about them, partly they neglect them. In judging morally you must

---

[1] This portion of the address consists in the main of an attempt to popularize the ideas contained in Mr. F. H. Bradley's *Ethical Studies*, and especially in Essay V of that work, " My Station and its Duties."

take a man's own point of view, at least in part. You and I may think fox-hunting a waste of time and money; but a master of foxhounds does not think himself an idle or useless man. He does what he and all his friends believe to be a social duty; and it is very necessary that we should recognize this, because it helps us to see that man really does not exist as man without *some* station and duties. Our station and its duties are the greatest part and the simplest part of the right will or the good will, which is also our own will. Without this object and interest in life, a man is like a boat without sail or helm. This sounds rather commonplace, and it *is* rather commonplace. If it were not, in a sense, known to every one, I do not see how it could be imagined to be every one's guide through life. If a preacher should come here and tell us that he had a brand-new set of duties, which we never heard of before, that we ought to do, I should myself be inclined to vote for sending him away again. Still, most things that we know have a good deal in them that we do not notice. And I will try to point out some truths about our station and its duties which we are apt to forget.

Our station and its duties:

1. Tells us what to do, for it is the very heart and spirit of our little individual life; and

2. It gives the reason for doing what we ought to do; for, just because it is the heart of our individual life, it raises our weak and ignorant will into the good will, which is the *real* will that unites mankind together.

1. Our station and its duties is the heart and spirit of our own little life. I may say that I make no distinction, morally, between rights and duties. That which our station demands of us is a duty, if the difficulty in doing it is in ourselves, and a right if the difficulty is in some one else. Suppose you are the head of a family. That is part of your station. It is the *duty* of the head of a family to rule and educate his children; and it is the *right* of the head of the family that his children should obey him, and that they should attend to their schooling; and it is his *right*, moreover, that society should provide, somehow, that there shall be schools and teachers. Then, again, it is the *right* of the *children* to be properly ruled and taught to behave, and to be educated; and it is the *duty* of

the children to obey the head of the family, and to make the best use of their schooling. It is the *duty* of society to see that there shall be schools and teachers, and it is the *right* of society that both the head of the family and the children shall do their part in making proper use of the schools and teachers. The same social good or social purpose is a right or a duty, according to the source of the opposition it meets with.

Now these requirements or demands, which are recognized by society, and which we recognize in our turn, make us what we are. Apart from them we should be nothing at all. Suppose a man has a brain fever, and all these ideas and purposes are wiped out of his mind. Suppose he forgets that he has a wife and children, forgets how to do his daily work, and does not know his friends when he meets them, does not remember the kindnesses which have been done him, nor the services which he owes to others ; the man may still be alive, and you may know his face, but his own self, all that made up his individual life, is lost and has vanished. I have heard of some one to whose wife this happened ; and when, two years after the loss of her mind, the poor lady died, her husband said, " In fact, I lost my dear wife two years ago."

This helps to show how we ourselves are really made up of all these ties and relationships, all these rights and duties, purposes, feelings, and hopes. We spoke about people's ideas of the invisible world. Here is the invisible world which really does concern us, which is our own very self, which we and all others recognize, and which has its existence simply in this invisible fact, that it is so recognized. And this, our own self, is what makes up our own will, by giving us something definite to do, which is the particular purpose of our own particular self. This is the chief thing that tells us what to do.

Perhaps this seems too simple, and it may be said, " Every decent man does the duties of his station ; cannot something be suggested which is higher and harder than that ? " I shall try to answer this question in part, presently, but first I must confess that the whole principle of what I am saying is against overmuch dictating and giving moral advice. I know well enough what *I* ought to do ; but it is very difficult to talk about what other people ought to do, because one does not know the ins and outs of their station. But if any one says that he habitually does all the duties of his station, thoroughly, with good heart and good sense, one would be inclined to suspect in one's own mind that his standard is rather low. A few points may be enumerated, by way of illustrating what one's station really means. There are the simple duties of honesty and thoroughness in all work ; there is education ; there is wise and painstaking help of our neighbours ; there is wise management of societies or clubs which we have to do with ; there is forming an enlightened judgment on trade questions and on questions that concern us as citizens ; and there is the attempt to make the tone of our society a little higher, more full of real interests, more free from vice and vulgarity. Every man is responsible for the tone of the society in which he moves, and for the influence which he spreads round him, hour by hour.

I do not know whether all this is really so simple, *when you come to act upon it.* Plato wrote an account of an imaginary commonwealth, in which goodness was to be the ruling principle. And the one great root of all virtue in this commonwealth was simply this, that in it every one was to mind his own business. Plato thus thought one's station and its duties the root of all the virtues. And he was right. But Plato's commonwealth, in which every one was to mind his own business, has become a by-word for an impossible imagination.

2. Then, again, I said our station and its duties give the reason for doing right. It not only gives us something to do, but it makes us feel that what we do is right. This is the very root of the matter.

There are two ways of doing what you have to do. You may do it like a machine, or you may do it like a man. If you do it like a machine, that is not really doing the duties of your station, for our station is, above all things, to be men. He who is a machine has no heart in his work. His family and his country mean nothing to him. Most likely it is not his own fault, but all the same this is very sad. But now I want to speak of the other way of working. We all know what it is to feel that we are not alone in our work ; that we are working together with others for a common good, and each doing the best he can. One who feels this about the duties of his station is a man, and not a machine. He knows, indeed, that he can do very little with his single arm. Even a great statesman or a great poet is merely guiding the forces or uttering the feelings of mankind. If a man thinks of the common purpose, of the good cause, and knows his will and effort are devoted to it, then he will not complain because he can do so little. The great thing is that his will is at one with the real will or the right will; and because it is so, he is content in the common work, and knows he is doing right. Think of a family all working hard to make their living. One of the children will earn only a little compared with the father; but if the child does his best, and puts his heart into it for the common good, then he has a right to be satisfied in the happiness of the family as the achievement of his purpose. A man who does the duties of an undistinguished station with good will is just the same in society as such a child is in a family. He is not a wheel in a machine, nor an animal trying to get food; but he is a man whose will is inspired by the common purpose of mankind, and whose little private piece of work is a pledge to him that the general purpose is *his* purpose.

This, then, is why we should do God's will, that is, why we should do our duty. If " why " meant a reason outside the duty, like a reward or punishment, then it would be nonsense, as we saw, to ask *why* we should do our duty. But the reason why we do it is that we find the good will to be really and at bottom our own will. That is to say, it is through our station and its duties that we take hold of our humanity and bring it home to our particular selves. On the one hand, the good will is ourself; and on the other hand, it is the common aim and spirit of society and of mankind. The goodness of our own particular private will consists in grasping this common aim and spirit, and applying it in the particular duties of our daily life, which gains all its reality and vigour from its particular form of this aim or purpose, and vanishes, as we saw, if the common purpose is entirely destroyed in us—if a man forgets his family, and his work, and his friends.

All that we mean by the kingdom of God on earth is the society of human beings who have a common life and are working for a common social good. The kingdom of God has come on earth in every civilized society where men live and work together, doing their best for the whole society and for mankind. When two or three are gathered together, co-operating for a social good, there is the Divine Spirit in the midst of them.

And there is something more, which may meet a difficulty that I mentioned just now. A man may be a good doctor, or a good painter, or a good engine-driver, and yet he may be a brute, or a liar, or a cheat. How will the duties of his station prevent this? First, we saw just now that there is a good deal belonging to our station which we are apt to forget. A man's station is not merely his trade. His family and his neighbours and the commonwealth are part of it. If he does his duty to all of these with sense and good will, there will not be room for very much vice. But then, secondly, we must bear in mind that he is to make his own particular will harmonize with the purpose of society; now any vice or sin would so far cut him off from that, and make a contradiction between the spirit in which he seeks his own particular pleasure and the spirit in which he seeks the common good. No man can serve two masters. The bad will is our own particular will, when it rebels against the moral spirit of society.

And this common spirit or conviction of society explains another difficulty. It may be asked, Are we to stand still for ever? Are we not to try to be better than people are now? Are we to obey society, and never to reform it? I do not think that this difficulty really perplexes any one, though it sounds very formidable. Of course every society is moving, and has a spirit of reform in it, and an ideal before it. We can only live by striving after an ideal; but our ideal must not be a whim of our own vanity, not something all for ourself and by ourself. It must be a social ideal, rooted in and founded upon what is real. Every sound ideal grows out of something real. For we saw that our very self, our life, is a purpose; and this purpose *is* the ideal which is in great part real as well as ideal. Thus a great nation, such as England, is a living real purpose, which exists, and prescribes our ideal to us. To-day is real and to-morrow is ideal, but you cannot draw a line between them. Our own life, and still more the life of a nation, is something that goes beyond the present moment; and so, in trying to be better and to do better, we are only carrying out the higher mind of society. We are born into our ideal, just as we are into our actual life. Of course the reformer does not in truth *invent* his ideal; it is " in the air."

I do not think it matters whether we call the community in which we have our station a Christian community. If we keep the substance of Christianity, we may let the shadow, the name, take care of itself.

III. Is the kingdom of God on earth a *Church* ? I will say a very few words about this. Wherever there is a community of persons working together for a social good, there is a portion of the kingdom of God on earth. A visible Church, like the Church of England, or of Rome, if it is useful for good life, may be a part of the kingdom of God on earth. But a family, or a nation like the English nation, is a far more sacred thing than any Church, because these are what prescribe our duty and educate our will.

What we are to remember about a visible Church, like the Church of England, is this. It is a good thing if it makes our wills good, and points out, or helps us to feel, duties which form a part of the good will. We judge whether a Church is a useful society just as we judge any other society. " By their fruits ye shall know them." But we must remember that no visible Church, Christian or Comtist, has any authority ; and no church service is a duty, except in as far as it makes us better.

On the other hand we may say if we like that the kingdom of God on earth is the same thing as the invisible Church ; " the blessed company of all faithful people." I will explain directly what I mean by faithful. The invisible Church, like true religion, is wide enough for all mankind. It is invisible, not because it is in heaven—for it is on earth—but because it extends so far in past and future, and is bound together not by such symbols as buildings, or creeds, or books, but by the great achievements and purposes which form the life of mankind.

IV. I wish, before I conclude, to say something of what we mean by religion. I have been speaking about the duties of our station and the spirit in which we ought to do them. I said that we ought to feel that we are not alone in our work, and that the good purpose which others achieve is ours just as our good purpose is theirs. This is, so far, morality.

Even this morality requires some faith. It is not possible to act, unless you believe that what you are trying to do can be done. In everyday life we do not trouble ourselves with a general belief; but we never doubt that the particular aim which we have in view is possible in the nature of things. If we did not believe this, we should be paralysed. We should not even eat, if we did not believe that food would sustain life.

Thus, in everyday life we need the belief that the good is a reality. If we hold this belief more distinctly and more intensely, it amounts to this, that *nothing but good is* a reality.

This faith is what people mean by religion. Of course it is a faith in spite of appearances. But it does not recognize the appearances against it as worth noticing. A man, in as far as he has this faith, does not admit that the bad in his own heart is his real self at all, and so he does not admit that the bad in the world is the reality of the world. This has been twisted like everything, as if religion could mean that you were to be indifferent to sin, because you say, " It really does not belong to me." That is sham religion. The truth is that nothing gives such force in getting rid of evil as this belief that the good is the only reality. Nothing gives such confidence in a battle as thinking that your enemy is only a sham. Stopping short of the good seems something mad and incredible, when you believe that nothing else is real. Yet, on the other hand, the man who has this faith is not worried or uneasy. He knows that he is on the side of the reality, and his heart is one with it, and he is not afraid of anything. Even his own wickedness is like something that comes to nothing, and is sure to fade away, as long as his heart is really and truly set right.

The difference between morality and religion seems then to be that in morality we know that the good purpose is real, in religion we believe that nothing else is real. It is the same faith, differently held.

An all-important truth follows from this—from religion and morality being the same in principle. The *duties of religion are the same as the duties of morality*. If we speak of duties to God, we mean the same duties as duties to man. Worship or prayer, in the sense of meditation, are good things if they help us to do our real duties. But it is a sad degradation of words to speak of a ceremony in a church as Divine Service.

And it follows from this that there is only one religion ; though there are many creeds, and for every creed a particular book and tradition. All these creeds and Churches and ecclesiastical precepts are mere vehicles of one religion, and what each of them superadds in forms, ceremonies, and doctrines are mere historical accident, and belong to the childhood of humanity.

These ideas are not new. It would be ridiculous to try to invent new ideas about what men are to find in their inmost hearts. European morality, in all its essentials, was built up in life and expressed in language more than two thousand years ago, by men who lived and spoke and wrote in the cities of ancient Greece. One of such men, the story goes, being asked by another, " How shall I educate my son ? " replied, " Make him a citizen of a city that has good laws." And when three hundred citizens of Sparta had fallen before overwhelming numbers in a battle that largely contributed to save Europe from an Asiatic despotism, a great Greek poet could devise for their grave no better epitaph than the two simple lines which say, " Go, you who pass by, and tell the Spartans that we lie here in obedience to their commands."

And the citizen of Athens, when he attained the age of eighteen, and his name was entered on the civic register, received in an ancient temple the shield and spear which symbolized his entrance into the citizen army, and publicly made oath to the following effect : " I will not dishonour my sacred shield. I will not abandon my fellow-soldier in the ranks. I will do battle for our altars and our homes, whether aided or unaided. I will leave our country not less but greater and nobler than she is now entrusted to me. I will reverently obey the citizens who shall act as judges. I will obey the laws which have been ordained, and which in time to come shall be ordained, by the national will. And whoever would subvert the laws, or would disobey them, I will not suffer him, but I will do battle for them, whether aided or unaided. And I will reverence our ancestral temples. Of which things the gods are my witness." This formula errs, to our minds, both by omission and commission,[1] yet the root of the

[1] The word translated " greater " means in the first instance " larger," and I fear that this meaning was realized in the Athenian disposition

matter is in it, and I have always regarded it with reverence as, to the best of my knowledge, the earliest European creed.

The Christian religion deepened and widened these convictions, and proclaimed that the freedom of living well was the birthright of humanity, and not merely of the noble, the citizen, the wealthy, or the wise. For Divinity, the Christian religion said, was to be looked for in the spirit of man, implying, as we now see, that it need be looked for *nowhere else*. This was the distinct announcement of what had really been working in the mind of Greece and Rome. I should like to read you a paraphrase of some verses by Lucan, written, I suppose, a few years before the date at which the Gospel of Matthew was composed. The hero of his poem, Cato, had been asked by a friend to make some inquiry of the oracle of Jupiter Ammon in Africa, which they passed in their march. And Cato, in the poem, answers thus :

> What wouldst, my friend, that Cato should inquire ?
> Needs he be told what conscience bids desire ?
> Whether 'twere better die in arms, and free,
> Than see Rome sink into a tyranny ?
> If man's mere life be nought that merits praise,
> And to live long but lengthens out his days ? [1]
> If that the just can fear no violence,
> Nor fortune against virtue do offence ?
> If 'tis enough that men will what they should,
> And triumph adds no lustre to the good ?
> All this we know, nor is our certain sense
> One jot more sure for Ammon's evidence.
> Heaven lies about us, and we do its will,
> Not uninspired, though all the shrines be still ;
> God needs no language, for at birth he taught
> All man can know, and that is all he ought :
> Nor has Jove willed in Afric's burning zone
> To preach his truth to wandering tribes alone ;
> Nor buried here, amid the shifting sands,
> That revelation all the world demands ;
> For where is God, but in the earth and sea,
> And clouds and sky—and truth and purity ?
> Why blindly seek we other gods to know ?
> God is where'er we look, where'er we go.

[1] He implies that life is desirable not for its length, but only for its nobleness.

And if I may conclude with a further quotation—for I think that it strengthens us to feel that we are not alone—I will read an extract from a work written one hundred years ago by a man whose name is honoured wherever the great thinkers of Europe are known. By this work, the philosopher Kant sounded the death-knell of European superstition in a deeper strain than his contemporaries Hume or Voltaire. And the new reformation which began in that springtime of genius has advanced steadily during the present century, which it will undoubtedly characterize in history. Kant wrote as follows in his work entitled *Religion within the Limits of Pure Reason*:

" The moral capacity of man is the foundation and the interpreter of all religion. Religion, for this reason, must come to be gradually liberated from all arbitrary ordinances, from all commands which rest merely on history, and which unite men in the advancement of the good for a time only, and by means of the creed of a Church. . . . The leading-strings of sacred tradition, with its appurtenance of rules and obser- vances, which did good service in their time, gradually become superfluous, and even become a bondage when man approaches years of discretion. When he was a child he understood as a child, and he found that scriptural learning and even a sort of church-philosophy agreed very well with commands imposed upon him from without. But when he becomes a man, he puts away childish things. The degrading distinction between layman and priest disappears. True freedom demands equal- ity. But equality is not anarchy, because every one obeys the law—not a command imposed upon him, but the law which he dictates to himself. This law he cannot but regard at the same time as the will of the Ruler of the world, pre- sented to man by his own reason. And this will unites all men invisibly into a community, which before was very meagrely represented and foreshadowed by the visible Church." (The conception of a Ruler of the world, apparently external to the spirit of man, and of a future life, continued in Kant's philosophy as survivals, though they are, in my judgment, quite unessential to it.) " All this is not to be expected from an external revolution " (Kant was writing during the French Revolution), " which is attended with storm and violenec.

and yet has an effect largely dependent upon chance. In a new constitution thus created, any maladaptation has to be reluctantly borne with for centuries, because it could not be altered without another equally dangerous revolution.

" The transition to a new order of things ought rather to be effected by the principle of a pure religion according to reason, considered as a Divine revelation constantly being made to all men through their reason only. Such a principle, when once grasped by mature consideration, will be realized by gradually progressive reform, in so far as its realization depends upon human intelligence ; revolutions are providential, and you cannot reckon on their results.

" But we may reasonably say that the kingdom of God is come on earth, as soon as ever the principle has taken root generally, and in the public mind, that the creeds of the Churches have gradually to pass into the universal religion of reason, and so into a moral, that is, a Divine community on earth ; although the establishment of such a community may still be infinitely remote from us. For this principle, because it contains the motive-force of a continual approach to perfection, is like a seed which grows up, and scatters other seed such as itself ; and it bears within it invisibly the whole fabric which will one day illuminate and rule the world. Truth and goodness have their basis in the natural disposition of every human being, both in his reason and in his heart. And because of this affinity with the moral nature of rational beings, truth and goodness will not fail to spread in every direction. Hindrances arising from political and social causes, which may from time to time interfere with this expansion, serve rather to draw closer the union of hearts in the good. For the good, when once it has been clearly perceived, never abandons the mind.

" This, then, though invisible to the human eye, is the constantly progressive operation of the good principle. It works towards erecting in the human race, as a community under moral laws, a power and a kingdom which shall maintain the victory over evil, and secure to the world under its dominion an eternal peace."

These words were published in 1793, and in consequence of the book which contained them the veteran philosopher, then in his seventieth year, received a warning from the Prussian Government, and had to undertake to teach no more about religion. And we may be glad that they now appear to us to be no dangerous speculation, but the utterance of the most sober common sense ; for it is none the less true that they contain the essence of European civilization—a hard-won inheritance, which it is our duty, in the words of the Athenian oath, to leave to others, " not less, but greater and nobler than it is now entrusted to us "

# XXI

## THE PLACE OF LEISURE IN LIFE [1]

I PROPOSE to throw my remarks into a form which may not quite correspond with what was expected from my choice of a subject. But I do believe my treatment will touch the essence of the matter, and it will attempt to bring home to us the inner meaning of a great book, to which it seems to me that even expert scholars hardly as a rule do justice.

I want, then, to lay before you a popular account of the unity, or what I love to call the plot, of Aristotle's *Ethics*; the great work in which he studied, not individual morality as contrasted with politics, but the nature of the true aim of life for man, as contrasted with the methods of statesmanship, by which it might be impressed upon and embodied in the civic organism. To me the subject is fascinating. The gradual development of the great teacher's thought, the depth of meaning which reveals itself in formulæ which taken unintelligently by themselves seem the very type of abstractions and emptiness, and are so considered by critics of repute—all this is to me a never-ceasing delight. Whether I can in any degree impart my feeling of the matter remains to be seen. Of course, I omit technicality and tell you things as I understand them. I owe my leading conception to Professor Burnet's edition of the *Ethics* and certain points also to that of Professor Stewart; and the former has himself stated an idea of the same type in his book on *Aristotle's Theory of Education*.

1. Every soul of every creature, such is Aristotle's starting-point, has a form or possible perfection, which the universe is striving in it to bring to completion through its life.

In the human soul every stage toward this completion may be called an excellence or virtue; and of these excellences or

[1] An address to the Cardiff Educational Society.

virtues there are two general divisions. There are first the excellences of man's compound nature, in which feeling and desire are learning submission to the law of reason. These he calls the "ethical" virtues; a term which we, somewhat unfortunately, have taken up and rendered as if equivalent to all that we understand by moral excellence. They derive their name, for him, from their connection with habit; they are qualities or rather attitudes of soul which we acquire in society, and in the main through assimilating the social tradition. Temperance, courage, gentleness, generosity, with many like them, are Aristotle's excellences of man's compound nature, or excellences of habituation, *ethical* excellences.

The other set of excellences are the excellences of the intellectual part, the so-called intellectual virtues. But I will say at once that we commit a mere misconstruction if we take them to be excellences of intellectual capacity; as we might say, memory, or mathematical talent, or the power of learning languages. The dominant ones at least are nothing of this kind; they are clearly, as we shall see, the excellences of good life and habit, exalted, reinforced, and reinterpreted by passing into the region of principle and of great ideas. Intelligence is not an exclusive part, but is the form of the whole.

Now let us begin to sketch the nature of a single act of duty, as Aristotle conceives it, and trace from that point the expansion of the moral horizon, till time and place fall away or rather are rounded into a whole and morality passes into religion.

2. The simplest moral duty has for Aristotle a double aspect. The motive of the citizen who gives his life for his country, for example, is described in a curious twofold language, the significance of which is not difficult to see. He does the act of duty for its own sake. There is in it something absolute. If it were done for the sake of something beyond, of praise or gain, it would no longer be the act it seemed to be. This we can see at once. But again; this and every act of duty is performed for the sake of the beautiful—for in all virtue this is the motive. And here again we have no doubt what is meant. The duty is done for its own sake, for the sake of what it is. But the conception of what it is is capable of

expansion. " For the sake of the beautiful "—a widening horizon is set before us by this description of the moral motive. What is the moral beautiful ? If we fully understood the simplest act of duty, what is it that according to Aristotle we should see there ?

Let me illustrate further by the famous doctrine of the mean, the definition of an ethical excellence. An ethical virtue or excellence of man's compound nature is an attitude of will, " being in a relative mean defined by a ratio, and by whatever the man of practical wisdom would define it by."

I will not trouble you with negative criticism, I shall say at once what I think it signifies, having just pointed out that once more it refers us to something on ahead—to the man of practical wisdom.

We must have observed in any such form of conduct as an act of beneficence, or munificence, how infallibly the churl in spirit betrays himself, to use Aristotle's phrase, in the quantity or degree or time or place or manner or personal relations of his action. Only the true motive gives you the perfect act. The brave man again ; how hard it is to be brave, and gentle, and modest, and calm, and wise. The brave and noble soul, and it alone, will ring true in every side and aspect of its act ; time, place, manner, degree, behaviour to persons ; all the characters which make up an act whose quality takes form in quantity, and is adapted to the situation with a beautiful adequateness, in every detail just right, neither too little nor yet too much, like the petals of a rose. Such an action is a manifestation of an excellence, a soul rightly tempered and attuned, a disposition or attitude of mind that is the " mean " or adjusted condition relative to or demanded by the situation.

So far, then, the horizon has expanded. The excellent action, done for its own sake, which is for the sake of the beautiful, is now understood to be an act expressive of a state of soul rightly attuned so that in every detail and quantitative particular its utterance hits what is appropriate and adequate.

But there is something more ; this temper or attitude does not explain itself, and the phrase which described it at the same moment beckoned us forward to a further standard. The mean adjustment or ratio which was the characteristic of the excellent attitude of soul was not yet, we say, thoroughly defined. It is an adjustment to circumstances; but an adjustment in the interests of what ? The answer was given by a reference to something not yet stated. The mean is determined by a further standard ; and the standard is the right ratio, and whatever the man of practical wisdom would determine.

3. This is a reference forward from the first half of the treatise to the second half. Let us recapitulate. Every act of the compound nature of man—his combined reason and desire —which is excellent, or an act of virtue, is done, we saw, at once for its own sake, and for the sake of the beautiful. That is to say, its own nature, being more fully understood, is one with the nature of the beautiful. Wishing to know to what this points us forward, we found that such an act, as an expression of virtue, is something perfectly adequate and adjusted to the situation, right in every particular, in every detail. If the motive or attitude of soul were in any way wrong or imperfect, the act would betray it at once by passing over into exaggeration or deficiency at some one of its innumerable aspects and peculiarities. What should be courage, for example, would be vulgar or ostentatious, or rash, or false, or wanting to itself in resolution or in tranquillity or in gentleness.

> The churl in spirit, howe'er he veil
> His want in forms for fashion's sake,
> Will let his coltish nature break
> At seasons through the gilded pale,
> For who can always act ?

We can understand that a moral perfection which results in a reliably perfect expression may be called beautiful, but still we have not learned in the interest of what central principle our adjustments are to be determined, and we have been referred to something that lies ahead.

The standard, we are told, lies in what is determined by the man of practical wisdom. What is practical wisdom, and where does it obtain its standard ?

We said that besides the excellences of man's compound nature, Aristotle ascribes to him what he calls the intellectual excellences ; not, we said, such capacities as memory, or scientific acumen, or creative genius, but rather the content of good life, when raised to a level of principle and systematic insight, as opposed to mere habituation and customary self-control.

According to Aristotle, the two intellectual excellences are practical and theoretical wisdom. About theoretical wisdom we will speak later. It is practical wisdom to which we have been referred ; and which, in approaching its discussion, Aristotle implies to possess " the standard of the means or adjustments."

Practical wisdom for Aristotle is one with something which is present in all the animal creation and different for every kind of creature. It is the group-instinct, or the group-intelligence, or the consciousness of kind. In humanity it is the statesman's knowledge and perception ; the gift and ability of the man who, having trained insight into the distinctively human good or evil of life, based on his own excellence of character in which it is up to a certain point realized, is able to guide the organization, habituation, and education of the group (for the statesman's business is more especially education) in the direction which will lead them to it.

But here once more the horizon expands. The statesman knows what is the end of human life, and has skill and insight to govern society and direct the educational habituation which instills the ethical or current social virtues in the right direction and to the right adjustments and adaptations—the ratios or means in conduct.

But still our quest is not ended. *What* is the end of human life in view of which the statesman organizes both politics and education ? The answer is to be found in the relation of practical wisdom to theoretical wisdom. Practical wisdom, we have seen, is different for every organic group, and in a measure may be said to be distributed throughout creation. Theoretical wisdom is always one and the same, and strictly speaking, it is divine ; it studies no production of instruments for the good of mankind ; it cannot strictly be said to aim at the special good of mankind ; it does not specially concern itself with man, or at all with one group of creatures rather than with another. Its object of study or contemplation is rather what is above and beyond man ; there are many things in the universe more divine than man, Aristotle emphatically observes ; more especially, it occupies itself with the nature of God. But though it is not an *efficient* cause of attaining the end of man, the name for which in Aristotle is happiness, it is the formal cause, or at least part of the formal cause ; that is to say, it does not produce human happiness as a cause may produce an effect other than itself ; but it *is* human happiness or the end of man, or at least a considerable constituent of that end.

Now the precise relation of practical to theoretical wisdom according to Aristotle is an interesting point. Practical wisdom, we said, is the wisdom of the statesman, and so far must be assumed to be supreme in society. On the other hand, theoretical wisdom is the higher activity, and is identical, or identical so far as human nature can attain it, with that activity of the soul which is happiness and the end of human life. Now how can the lower activity of practical wisdom be supreme over the higher, which is theoretical wisdom ? Which of the two is really superior and the guide of life ? Aristotle puts the contradiction plainly, and his answer is clear. Practical wisdom rules society in the interests of theoretical wisdom, but does not rule over theoretical wisdom itself. Expanding the answer, a follower of Aristotle compares the statesman's art to the house-steward or head of the servants, and theoretical wisdom to the master of the house. The house-steward rules the house with a view to the master's leisure, his σχολή. The master has his duties of magistrate or thinker or soldier to perform ; the household is organized to give him leisure for them. Just such is the statesman's duty, let us say, toward art, or the life of thought or religion.

The relation is expanded by an Aristotelian writer : " So whatever choice or distribution of worldly resources, whether of bodily qualities or of wealth or of friends or of other goods, will be most helpful toward the contemplation of God, that is the best, and that is the most beautiful standard or organization ; and whatever arrangement, whether by defect or by excess, hinders men from glorifying God and enjoying him, that arrangement is bad." (Stewart, II, 4, E. E. Θ., 3, 1249 a21–b25.) The final standard of the means or adjustments of conduct, then, is the highest life of the soul.   The habituation of the young and the moral education of society are to be so guided and framed by the statesman that art and learning and religion shall always hold the highest place and so far as humanly possible shall have the lead in, and form the inspiration of, his country.   The simplest act of duty, we may say, in its twofold scope, points forward to the knowledge of God. The act of duty, we saw, in being for its own sake, is for the sake of the beautiful ;  and in being for the sake of the beautiful it is a perfecting of the soul by a fine and delicate adjustment and adaptation to the social order ;  and further, in being an adaptation to the social order, it is finally instrumental to that which inspires and justifies and resumes the meaning of the social order, namely, to the activity in which the soul finds its perfection in laying hold of the divine.   You do not, in the view of Plato and Aristotle, in aspiring to intellectual excellence and to religious contemplation, tread a separate and diverging path from that of the ordinary good citizen.   You follow his path, but pursue it farther, and what the saint or the poet or the thinker may attain at the end is only the quintessence of what all of you have been practising from the beginning.

4. The true relation of theoretical wisdom to moral development receives a remarkable illumination from the theory of friendship, which shows how practical wisdom must in its highest form actually pass into that which is theoretical.

Practical wisdom, we saw, is the human form of the group instinct or consciousness of kind.   In Aristotle's view there is, all through creation, a certain feeling of affection corresponding to every form of this consciousness of kind.   He illustrates it by the different levels of parental care which attend upon the different levels of intelligence in the animal world.   This is so in man as in other species.   Every form of human association has its characteristic type of group-sentiment or liking, or " friendship," as he terms it, corresponding to the form of group-intelligence which it implies.

This being so, you have only to consider the case of the highest form of human association to see how the group-intelligence or sense of group-welfare (practical wisdom) must transform itself into theoretical wisdom.   For the highest form of human association is that in which human beings have come to care for that in each other which is the best and consequently the most real thing in them, namely, the highest goodness and intelligence. When this is so, the group-consciousness has become the consciousness of a response in the other person to what is highest and best in the self. This response is a heightening of life, by the extension of the awareness of our life to the life of the friend who shares our consciousness of the best things. We feel our life intensified in his. Therefore the consciousness which we share with him is *ipso facto* the consciousness of the highest activity of the soul. Any other common consciousness would be comparatively external and accidental, and would not give us the same community of feeling.

Therefore practical wisdom or the instinct toward group-welfare, not only, in directing human society, aims at adjusting it to the presence of the highest activities ; but, in so far as men become all they might become, actually passes into those activities.

Thus we have followed the expanding horizon of the great moralist's account of the end of human life, or of the activity of the soul, which is the provisional definition of that end, also called by the name of happiness.

What we have found is that the simplest act of social duty taught by habituation to the growing citizen, say courage or soberness, has in it a motive, or we may say really implies an awakening and a yearning of the soul, which first expresses itself in loyalty to society and in good citizenship, but which can find no final satisfaction till it completes itself in the knowledge and thought of God, in union with whom alone the individual comes to be that which he really is.

5. How, we may ask, can these ideas be translated into characteristics of any actual society ? Are we to draw a picture of a social life sharply divided between pleasure and industry on the one hand and a monastic quietism on the other ? Or again, are we to think of a futile and pedantic effort to make philosophy and theology the common occupation of men, in place of the healthy activities of living ? What the Greek idea of the social mind suggests to us is neither of these things.

We have to remember that the social mind is to be thought

of as a single spirit, though pouring itself into different channels according to the differences involved in social organization. The form of the individual soul is perfected in this way. The importance of this is that every individual mind, while attending especially to its private functions, is at the same time a microcosm which lends to, and borrows from, every other mind, or factor of the social spirit. The ruler learns from the workman, the scholar from the soldier, just as the workman is guided by the ruler, or the soldier can only apply himself rightly to his profession by borrowing the spirit of the scholar. What Aristotle wishes, then, is to see States so organized that the lamp of religion and fine art and high thinking may always be kept burning, and that this fact may have its fair and proper influence on the spirit and ideals of the people as a whole. " I assume," says Miss Kingsley, in one of her delightful books on West African experiences, " that the whole desire of every man is to know God." This is one of those sayings that fill us with delight. But it is, of course, a matter of implication and not of conscious wish. Yet it illustrates the point that all persons are capable of religion and knowledge, and that the tone and worthiness of their life is very different according as they are or are not, in their degree, conscious of an inspiration and an ideal pervading their society. The servant who sweeps a minister's study, having respect for his office, shares in his spiritual work, and is the better even for that amount of sharing in it. The minister, of course, as Plato's *Republic* should imply to us, has also to learn from the servant. We have to think of the tone of a society in which saintliness and intelligence and science or, again, fine art and poetry are respected, compared with one in which all things of that kind go to the wall. The two are different, not merely in including a few individuals of different types, but in the whole mind and spirit of every person, right down to the simplest and the least fortunate citizens. The contrast of Scotland and probably Wales with some other countries might illustrate what is meant. Or take, with all their defects, the case of Athens under Pericles, or of Geneva under Calvin. Such societies are the salt of the earth. That is a general example of what Aristotle meant, as we can see to-day ; though it is possible that local and national feeling and a severe political judgment prevented him from entertaining an unmingled respect for the Athens which we admire.

6. How is this glorification of *theoria* to be reconciled with what we take to be the needs of practical life, and the necessity that education should prepare us for it ? In the first place, let us understand distinctly of what we are speaking. Theoria for a Greek is not what we mean by theory ; and the theoretic life is not what we call a theoretical pursuit. Theory for us comes near to an intellectual fiction ; a way of grasping and comprehending a complex of observations. Theoria for a Greek meant the vision of what is most real ; the mind of one who sees life steadily and sees it whole. Theoretical considerations for us mean mostly what is abstract and hypothetical : " if this change, then that consequence." Theoretic life for the Greek meant the life of insight, a man's hold and grasp of the central realities of what is most valuable and most divine, and therefore also most human.

I have ventured to suggest elsewhere [1] that not only in conception, but in actual fact there is no inconsistency between the theoretic activity thus understood and the most practical activities in the ordinary sense of the term. Is it not a striking thing apart from all satire and from all jesting that among the world's leaders of business activity we should always find the Jew, the Quaker, and the Scotsman ? Is not, perhaps, a certain security and sagacity of judgment conferred by a habit of mind in which everything is referred to a centre, and which is capable of a superior view permitting the details of life to drop into a subordinate place ?

But as to the idea of theoria in the sense we have spoken of, in connection with the practical aim of life, we may hear Aristotle himself. " The practical life need not, as some think, be a life of action toward others ; nor are those thoughts alone practical which are cherished for the sake of the results of the action. The name practical belongs much more truly to the thoughts of intrinsic value, thoughts which are ends in themselves ; for to attain the end is necessarily a kind of action, and even in external action we give the title of agent *par excellence* to those to whom the constructive thought belongs."

7. There are three kindred ideas which for Aristotle express

[1] [See p. 143 above.—ED.]

attainment of the end of human life : Theoretical Wisdom, Leisure, Happiness. (It is interesting that so strict is Aristotle in affirming his idea of happiness as the fullness of human life and capacity that he denies it to the child, as to the brute creation.) Leisure is especially to be distinguished from recreation and amusement. Both are alike, in that they appear to be chosen for their own sake only, but it is only an appearance. Recreation and amusement are in truth means, not ends. Their value is to make work possible, not in any worth of their own. Leisure is different ; it is the expression or condition of the attainment of the end ; or, as we might say, it is the satisfaction of a disinterested interest. We all know that " school " = " leisure " ; to have leisure for a thing means to devote yourself to it as an interest. So much in earnest is Aristotle with this distinction that he modifies Plato's judgment upon music with a view to it, and says that the labourer must be allowed his music, oddly enough of an elaborate and artificial type, by way of amusement and recreation ; while the educated man will require for the right use of leisure his own music of a more classical kind. And the main object of education is to teach the right use of leisure ; the devotion of the mind to what it feels to fill its need.

All this comes to saying that the object of education for Aristotle was to communicate disinterested interests. But perhaps nothing could, to-day, be more practical or of a higher social importance. What could be more practical than to rescue some large proportion of the one hundred and sixty million pounds that in this country go every year in drink ? And was not Dr. Johnson fundamentally right when he said, " Sir, the reason why a man drinks is that he is not interesting enough to himself to pass his leisure time without it ? "

As we have seen, it is an error to suppose that these interests are only for a cloistered caste, distinct and divided from society at large. They are implied in and permeate all social life and are its quintessence. They are not artificial, or imposed upon the social whole *ab extra*, but spring out of its nature. Take the mere phrase, " Learning to read." How many meanings it may bear ! I remember a severe critic once observing that our circulating libraries act as middlemen between writers who do not know how to write and readers who do not know how to read.  What a thing it would be if the children who pass through our schools had " learned *to read*," in the sense in which the critic meant that our novel-reading public had not.  To read, that is, for their own enjoyment, things worth reading.  Grant, if we like, that Aristotle throws his *desideratum* too much into the form of philosophy and theology. Both of these exist, and Aristotle knew it well, in the more accessible forms of poetry and religion.  And these at least are universal possessions, and no class in a modern State need be excluded from participating through them in the supreme spiritual activity.

# C.—ÆSTHETICS

# XXII

# THE PART PLAYED BY ÆSTHETIC IN THE DEVELOPMENT OF MODERN PHILOSOPHY

IF I assert that a decisive impulse was, as a matter of fact, imparted to the course of modern philosophy by æsthetic reflection at a critical moment, I do not intend to deny that thought was already inclining in the direction in which this new influence peremptorily urged it. I am content to explain, if I can, how, historically speaking, a definite philosophical effect was produced in Germany by reflection upon the nature of fine art, about a century ago ; and to point out the characteristics which enabled æsthetic science to exercise such an influence at that epoch, and which invest it with the capacity to produce a somewhat analogous result whenever it obtains a prominent place in culture.

Of course in a discussion which is partly historical we must always begin at the wrong place, because the right place to begin at would be the beginning, and that is out of reach. Thus, in the present case, it would be no more than right to trace far back into the ancient world the factors which embodied themselves in the Kantian philosophy, but even if my knowledge permitted such an analysis, time would forbid it. I must accept the Kantian system as a historical datum, and point out that for the present purpose it must be taken as formulating, with extraordinary penetration and audacity, the chief paradoxes or contradictions known to philosophy. Kant seems to have been a centre or point of transition to which the ideas of the age converged, and from which they diverged again. And the part which I attribute to æsthetic reflection is that of having intervened at the moment of divergence, and having then impressed upon the main branch of the post-Kantian philosophy the character which it still retains, and which, being deeply engrained in the development of our time, is gradually revealing itself in all nineteenth-century ideas. This character is commonly indicated by such phrases as "reconciliation of opposites," "concreteness," "organic synthesis," "identification of the real and ideal," "the idea of humanity," "the spirit of modern civilization." I repeat that the tendency thus designated is predominant throughout modern life and intelligence in all its departments, and that æsthetic or the philosophy of fine art is merely a striking case of this tendency, which case, because it is so striking, is apt to be the first that attracts philosophical attention.

I will now attempt first (1) very briefly to indicate the problem of modern thought as presented by Kant, then (2) to sketch, as a study in the history of philosophy, the function of æsthetic in the partial solution of this problem, and finally (3) to compare this solution with the latter course of thought in our own country, including in the comparison some factors of English culture which lie outside professional philosophy.

(1) If I possessed the knowledge which I have admitted to be wanting, then it would be my duty at the very least to trace back to the Renaissance and beyond it the varying attitudes of European culture towards the sensuous and the supra-sensuous worlds. I suppose that such an inquiry would reveal a perpetual alternation and confusion between the influences of the actual and the ideal, but also a growing apprehension of their unity, always most marked in the greatest epochs and among the greatest men. Even Dante, for example, who might be thought of as completely absorbed in the contemplation of a world beyond the present, seems rather to expand the actual into the ideal than to sever the actual from the ideal. If he is specially bent upon discriminating precisely between things temporal and things spiritual, we must remember that right distinction is the first foundation of unity, and that synthesis has no worse enemy than confusion. If Dante condemned the temporal encroachments of the spiritual power, this was because he considered that the spiritual power as organized for religious purposes could not but cease to be spiritual by assuming functions for which it was not adapted ; but there can be no doubt, I should imagine, that the true temporal power in doing the work of government which

properly fell to its share appeared to him, by this discharge of duty, to fill a place in the spiritual world.

I suppose, further, that in and after the time of Dante, religious idealism was attacked or rather undermined by a sensuous semi-pagan realism, and that the profound intellectual idealism which followed upon the Reformation was in its turn finally challenged by eighteenth-century scepticism in France and Great Britain. Yet we cannot rightly estimate these historical abstractions unless we bear in mind that from other points of view their places might well be reversed ; that the faith in the unseen world of Dante or Giotto was rooted in a far firmer grasp of present reality than belonged to the easy humanism of the later career of Raphael, and that the mathematical researches of Descartes or Leibnitz indicated a far more profound interest in the phenomena of nature than did the abstract idealism of Berkeley or of Hume.

Thus the reality of sense and the ideal of thought were struggling together and displacing one another, not merely in the whole movement in the modern world, but, as is always the case with intellectual matters, in every particular wave of that movement. It is not surprising, therefore, that Kant felt this contradiction and applied himself with wonderful courage and persistency to drag it into the light of day. Hegel has said,[1] and, I think, not unjustly, that before Kant's time the receptacle of all contradictions was God, but that Kant located them in the human self-consciousness. Thus Kant speaks [2] of the two worlds, the sensuous world of nature, and the suprasensuous world of freedom, between which there is a gulf that you cannot even see across. Now, if we ask the question suggested by our present subject, namely, which if either of these two worlds, according to Kant's account, can be said to have actual and real existence, it is not easy to give an answer.

The suprasensuous world would, I take it, be the more real of the two, if you could know anything in particular about it, which you cannot ; the sensuous world would be the more knowable of the two, if it could be said to be objective, which it is not. I assume that what is nothing in particular for us is not real for us, and that what is not objective is not an object of knowledge.

[1] *History of Philos.*, iii, 526.    [2] *Krit. d. Urtheilskraft*, p. 14.

All that can be said, then, to be real for us and accessible to us, according to the conception which we are discussing, appears to be a nature and a life which make themselves for us, or which we make, by a constant finding or bringing together of these two worlds, each of which in itself is a mere unreality, the operative elements in this fusion being rational perception and rational will. I give a single startling example. We are to act the moral law as if it were the will of an invisible Ruler of the world, but we must not say that there is such a Ruler, because that we cannot prove. He is a sort of illustration, not drawn from fact, of how we ought to behave. The reality is only in the actual moral life. As Hegel says, the God thus postulated is like a scarecrow that children set up, and agree together that they mean to be frightened at it.

Of course this sketch is only a selection of the features that bear upon the development which I am discussing, but I do not think it is substantially false.

If it may pass, then we have here three very remarkable things. We have, first, a single reality consisting in the union or concrete cohesion of two worlds, which had previously been envisaged, as indeed they were by Kant himself, as two separate systems of existences, although he saw that, as separate, each must be practically unreal. We have, secondly, this concrete reality in the shape of that which exists for rational perception and rational will, the concreteness depending on the rationality. And we find, thirdly, that this concrete rational reality, although theoretically subjective, that is to say, relative to the human individual, is on the other hand also practically objective, that is universally valid because relative to something which is the universal nature of the individual. Thus we have the real as concrete, the real as rational, and the real as subjective objectivity.

But Kant does not seem, so far as I am aware, to be at all deeply impressed by this aspect of the matter, or by the unreality of his separate worlds as separate. He writes down the paradoxes which he takes to gather up the elements of truth, with a peculiar *sangfroid*, and it is largely for this reason that his views have had such enormous influence. For they are not at all completely built up into a symmetrical theory, and perhaps for that reason do not arouse the suspicion that their parts have been tampered with. They are a sort of *media axiomata*, carried through all aspects of experience, largely in the form of flat self-contradictions which it is exceedingly difficult to deny.

He will tell you, for example, that that is beautiful which is universally and necessarily pleasant, without the intervention of an idea. But necessity usually involves an explicit or ideal relation of antecedent to consequent. Or again, he will say that is beautiful which has the form of adaptation to an end, in so far as this is perceived without the idea of an end. This sounds, in ordinary language, like a contradiction in terms. Yet, in fact, the more these statements are tested, the harder it is to deny them, and the suggestion presses itself upon the reader that, as has been said, probably a great many times, Kant has really hit upon a new departure by basing his philosophy upon an objective subjectivity, or concrete of rational perception, and that the chasm between the two worlds, which his philosophy inherited, and which, at first sight it appears to perpetuate, is thus in principle overcome.

But in principle only. For Kant was very shy about venturing beyond formal abstractions, and he shuns giving a positive development or content to the unity which his principles suggest. He was a pioneer in all directions, but a builder in none. Even in æsthetic, where his new departure is exceedingly marked, he is so afraid of admitting a concrete emotion, that he is inclined to reject the interest in beauty along with the interest in sensuous satisfaction, and to shrink back from the idea of a significant content in art to that of its correspondence with a psychological balance between our faculties.

Thus Kant left much open to his successors. Would they have the force to maintain the grasp by which he had for a moment united two unreal worlds into one reality, and would this real meeting-point develop, in their hands, into an organized whole, capable of including the movement of human experience? Everything depended on the possibility of showing some justification for the pretension to find the ideal world in the movements and principles of that which we touch, and about which we will, by demonstrating that such an identification could be made good in science and history, and driven home throughout the daily facts and requirements of human life.

(2) I think it probable that the essential answer to the question was practically determined within ten years after the publication, in 1790, of Kant's epoch-making treatise on Æsthetic, *The Critique of the Power of Judgment.* But a much longer interval elapsed before the new philosophy was elaborated in books and lectures and acquired extended influence.

An essential step in its determination was no doubt the philosophy of Fichte. I merely accept the judgment of history, in saying that the ideas of this great man were not, in themselves, an adequate theory of concrete existing reality. And further, not professing to make an original criticism, I suppose I may take it as admitted, that the nature of their inadequacy consisted in laying stress on the form of thought at the expense of its content. For any such view is lacking in solidity, and is incapable of assimilating the movement of experience. It is most instructive that the work which committed Fichte to the central importance of thought in its abstract activity should have appeared the year *before* Schiller's Æsthetic Letters.

Great minds, however, not only discover truths, but by their inexorable logic force others into the track of truths outside the course they have themselves adopted. And it would be curious to consider how far Schelling and Hegel owe their more concrete ideas to the very slight priority in time [1] which caused Fichte's doctrine to be laid before them while they were still uncommitted by any important writings.

But although Kant's *Kritik d. Urtheilskraft* was the foundation, and Fichte's *Grundlage* the negative suggestion of their views, there was, as I have just hinted, a more positive influence at work besides.

Down to the publication of Kant's *Critique of the Power of Judgment*, the living movement of æsthetic speculation in Germany had not been concentrated into a branch of technical philosophy. Baumgarten had indeed in 1750 made a new departure of immense importance, by applying, for the first time, the name " Æsthetica " to a treatise upon beauty in

[1] Fichte was thirteen years older than Schelling and eight years older than Hegel.

thought and feeling ; and Kant himself had, at an early date in his life, set down observations upon the nature of beauty.

But it was not from sources like these, not from Leibnizian rationalism, or even from the abstractions of the critical. philosophy, that the later German idealism acquired its unique depth of insight and sympathy for the idea within the reality. Allowing, as I must always be understood to allow, that every mind in some way reflects the influences of its time, we may nevertheless say, so far as such a thing can ever be said at all, that the peculiar assimilative vitality of the new Renaissance in Germany is primarily owing to the initiative of a single man. Take away the life-work of Winckelmann from its place in the lives of Schiller and Goethe, and it is impossible to form an idea what those lives could have been. We need not trace his individual influence beyond this point. It was through these two men of genius that Winckelmann chiefly acted on philosophy, and apart from this specific result, to have modified the thoughts of Goethe is almost as important an achievement as it would have been to have modified the acts of Napoleon. Winckelmann, in spite of all his defects as a theorist, endowed the human mind with a new organ in the sphere of fine art. This judgment is Hegel's, evidently based upon Goethe's opinion, and has been repeated with emphasis in our own day by Mr. Walter Pater. And it was this new organ or capacity, awakened in the first instance by enthusiasm for the ideal realism of Hellas, which, when brought to bear in the province of technical philosophy, had the effect of focusing attention on living realities, and of suggesting for the first time a really profound conception of history, as the evolution of man's spirit in civilization.

It has been said by a critic whose attitude is eminently judicial, that the philosophy of history and the history of philosophy may almost be said to have been discovered by Hegel, and that he has thrown greater light upon Greek thought than all other thinkers put together.[1] But if Winckelmann had not first discovered the history of fine art, if Schiller had not insisted on the real synthesis embodied in beauty, and if Goethe had not pointed out the evolutionist principle of Winckelmann's historical conception, I do not see how Schelling

[1] Jowett, *Dialogues of Plato*, iv, 424, Introduction to the *Sophist*.

and Hegel could have arrived at their concrete treatment of the self-realizing idea.

In order to take the separate æsthetic movement down to the time at which it affected philosophy, I will mention two or three significant dates :

> Baumgarten's *Æsthetica*, which gave the inquiry its name, but showed no special insight into concrete beauty, 1750.
>
> Winckelmann's first work *On the Imitation of Greek Art*, 1755 ;  his second work, the *History of Ancient Art*, 1764.
>
> Lessing's *Laocoon*, 1766 ;  and, a really more sympathetic and appreciative work, his *How the Ancients Depicted Death*, 1769 ;  and his *Education of the Human Race*, which shows the evolutionist idea, 1780.
>
> Goethe's *Iphigenie*, the finest quasi-classical play in existence, 1787.
>
> Kant's *Critique of the Power of Judgment*, 1790.
>
> Fichte's *Foundation of all Science*, 1794.
>
> Schiller's *Letters on Æsthetic Education*, 1795.
>
> Goethe's *Study of Winckelmann*, 1805.

Now down to the year 1795 Hegel, born in 1770, had published nothing. Schelling had only written one or two short works completely on Fichte's lines. In this year (1795) the two friends were corresponding, partly about Fichte's mode of thought, the startling results of which Hegel was welcoming with great enthusiasm, conceiving them as in close connection with the ideas of Kant's *Critique of Practical Reason*. At this moment Schiller's " Æsthetic Letters " were published in the *Horen* for 1795, and are referred to by Hegel, writing to Schelling, as being a masterpiece.

Bearing in mind this influence of Kant, Fichte, and Schiller, in the order here given, on the early philosophical development of Schelling and Hegel, before the divergence, that is to say, before the definite formation of their characteristic modes of thought, let us now turn to Hegel's lectures on Æsthetic, which belong to his mature period from 1818 onwards.

In the introductory portion of this course, Hegel takes occasion to trace the genesis of the post-Kantian philosophical movement, which is in his view intimately connected with the advance in æsthetic science, and he speaks in one place of the general reawakening of philosophy as having been the condition of a new kind and degree of insight into the significance of fine art, and in another place of the deeper conception of the beautiful as having paved the way for the great transition in which strictly modern thought had taken its rise. This double account of the matter is not hard to understand. The deeper appreciation of the import of fine art preceded the philosophic revival, but the intellectual formulation of æsthetic philosophy could only accompany or succeed it.

In this sketch Hegel starts from Kant, more particularly from the *Critique of the Power of Judgment*. He then points out that Schiller, especially in the letters on Æsthetic Education, was beforehand with philosophy proper in indicating the true direction in which a reconciliation of the Kantian antitheses should be sought, and after speaking of Schiller, he passes on to Schelling as the thinker with whom modern or complete philosophy originates, and with whom also the science of fine art for the first time attains its true intellectual position. He takes occasion, however, to observe that the true nature and dignity of art in relation to the highest human interest had begun to be appreciated, though not philosophically formulated, some time before. The subsequent sentences make it plain that he is referring to Winckelmann's life and influence. Winckelmann, he continues, created a new art perception, aroused his age to the task of searching for the idea of fine art in its historical growth, endowed the mind in this province with a new organ, and suggested a treatment of the subject which was a wholly new departure. Here, I think, Hegel clearly has in his mind the judgment of Goethe in the sketch of Winckelmann published in 1805.

From this point Hegel goes on to discuss the Schlegels, Tieck, and others, with reference to the critical doctrine of irony, and in doing so treats their opinions as being, like Schelling's, determined by Fichte's system, but unlike Schelling's, devoid of any further and objective principle of synthesis.

Now, comparing this sketch with the letters of 1795, we can hardly doubt that Schiller's work on *Æsthetic Education* was the first immediate point of contact between technical philosophy and the deeper estimate of fine art which Winckelmann had created. For Lessing, with all his critical skill, had hardly entered into Winckelmann's historical spirit.[1] It was Schiller, then, who first not merely suggested, but impressed upon the age with all his force, the idea that in beauty, and in the mind which is perceptive of beauty, there is an actual and existing reconciliation of such opposites as sense and thought, natural necessity and moral freedom, matter and form.

The concrete ideal reality on which both Schelling and Hegel base their philosophical conceptions appears to be an enlarged transcription of the import thus attributed to beauty, coming, as it did, in face of the problems which Kant embodied in his antitheses, and which Fichte, apparently for want of some such suggestion, had failed to meet. The place occupied by fine art in the systems of the two great objective idealists is a very remarkable fact, which coincides with this explanation of its essential significance to them. We may notice in passing that the distinctive peculiarity of Hegelianism originated—if this analysis is in any degree correct—in that very recognition of the reality and value of individual feeling and action for which, as we are sometimes told, it fails to find a place. And for this reason, what von Hartmann rightly calls " concrete idealism " in Æsthetic begins with Hegel, and, as von Hartmann remarks, is founded upon Schiller. Schelling, though not a mere formalist, inclined more and more throughout his life to abstract idealism, that is to say, to treat actual beauty as a secondary incorporation of an ideal or suprasensuous beauty, which to a concrete idealist is a contradiction in terms. And thus he more and more lost his hold of the principle by which he himself had been the founder of modern philosophy ; for nothing less than this is the position which his great rival assigns him. In the places to which I have already alluded, Hegel gives a short analysis of the main positions of Schiller's Æsthetic Letters, and then goes on to say that the unity of sense and thought, and of other opposites, which Schiller scientifically apprehended and laboured to embody in actual life, was recognized by Schelling as the idea or principle of knowledge and existence, and that by this recognition, philosophy, in Schelling, attained its " absolute standpoint." Hegel, no doubt, has also his own contemporary

[1] Hegel, Æsthetics, ii, 439.

development in his mind, though he does not think right to allude to it.

Now I propose to say something of the fundamental nature of the absolute standpoint, showing how its character corresponds to its genesis, and then to explain how the needs which it dealt with in Germany have been provided for in the culture of our own country.

For the phrase, " absolute standpoint " we may not incorrectly substitute the apparently more simple phrase, " modern standpoint." I do not say that the word " modern " has a technical signification in philosophy; but the spirit or conviction embodied in the word " modern " does correspond to the idea conveyed by the word " absolute." When, for example, we speak of modern science, modern enterprise, modern civilization, what is the fundamental feeling which the expression is intended to convey ? I believe that we may safely answer, " a sense of rational freedom," that is to say, the conviction that man can meet with nothing that is outside himself, in the sense of being necessarily and fundamentally superior to his rational nature and incapable of being faced or dealt with by it. We know that the individual may be cowed by superstition, degraded by vice, or destroyed by physical agencies, but we do not believe that man, as such, is beset with any necessary inferiority in face of any power or of any phenomena in the universe. It is the " Si fractus illabatur orbis," or Campbell's *Last Man*, reasserted in terms of a reality greater than the individual. It would take me away from my subject to argue this point, but I do not think that the fact of this conviction being characteristic of the progressive civilization of Christendom can well be denied.

It is this conviction which took philosophical form at the time of the French Revolution in the doctrine of the absolute or the objective idea. Admitting, as every sane man must admit, that the difference between contact *with* the whole, and comprehension *of* the whole, must always subtract something from the absoluteness of any human attainment, I still maintain that this doctrine does embody the great and vital conviction of modern life, and of modern life alone. However narrowly limited the individual may be, however far beyond his reach the whole of reality may extend, still we are now convinced that, as this doctrine tells us, contact with the only reality is ours here and now. The world, which is accessible through morality and science and art, is not dwarfed by anything else of a more real kind that remains beyond it and incapable of assimilation, although, of course, we cannot precisely say to what extent, within its continuous totality, the accessible world may be capable of modification. We can only say that we are not going to believe in the discontinuous or in the irrational.

This, then, Reality, as accepted by the modern spirit, is the meaning of the Absolute. It bears this name because it does not permit of being referred to or put in relation with anything other than itself, that is to say, of being treated as dependent on anything other than itself. Within itself, of course, its parts, among which we are, depend upon and are relative to one another. Thus it is worth noticing, as against a common misapprehension, that no underlying reality, no purely supersensuous will or idea, could be reasonably called Absolute, because, as our perceived world would be in external relations with it, both terms would by the fact of this relation become merely relative and dependent. No abstraction can be absolute.

The connection between the meanings of Absolute and Modern is therefore quite plain. Both of them fundamentally signify " freedom from the beyond," or " the concrete unity of life." And so when Hegel speaks of philosophy attaining its absolute standpoint in Schelling's time he may be not unfairly paraphrased by saying that the chief underlying conviction of the modern civilized world, which was no doubt immanent in Christianity, was then for the first time explicitly formulated in philosophy.

If we now look at the shape which this mode of genesis has impressed upon objective idealism as formulated by Schelling in his first systematic treatise published in 1800, and by Hegel in the *Phenomenology of the Mind*, published 1807 (the dates are worth observing in connection with what has been said), we shall at once be struck by a peculiarity obviously connected with the conditions of which we have been speaking. I wish mainly to *draw attention* to this peculiar feature, which forms the weakness and the strength of all Idealism which has its

roots in Hellas, though I do not pledge myself to withhold my
judgment of its value.

I. If we ask, approaching the question from that side which
admits of least mistake or controversy, what is the *denotation*
of the reality thus pointed to as concrete mind, or as the union
of freedom and necessity, of subject and object, of thought
and sense, the first answer that occurs to us on the basis of
this philosophy is undoubtedly furnished by referring to what
an Englishman would call the artificial as opposed to the
natural world. Objective mind with Hegel, taken in the
technical sense, does not mean Nature, as might be thought by
those who are careless about terminology, but indicates actually
existent although consciously constructed human organizations and institutions, such as the family, law, the concrete
moral will, Society, and the State. Absolute mind, again,
does not mean the same thing as " the Absolute " or " the
Idea," but is the term which designates human activities,
which, being objectively real in persons and things, involve
also a thorough consciousness of their own ideal nature. That
is to say, the denotation of absolute mind consists of Fine Art,
as a connected whole consisting of minds by which certain
actual things are regarded in a certain way, and of Religion as
a particular kind of consciousness in actual individuals forming
actual communities, and of the philosophic intelligence as a
common recognition existing in human minds of a common
nature and development.

Now it is plain that both the objective and absolute mind
thus described presuppose and rest upon the actual properties
and laws of natural bodies ; and, therefore, if philosophy fails
to include the reality of nature, its basis is completely swept
away. But, subject to this reservation, it appears to me to
be an invaluable gain to culture that the objective reality of
the artificial world should be forced upon our attention. It
may be said that this attitude is a repetition of the error committed by Socrates in disregarding the study of natural science.
And, undoubtedly, there is an essential relation between these
two points of view. I shall endeavour to show, however, in
the right place, that ultimately this mode of consideration,
in its modern development, is that which does fullest justice
even to the importance of nature and of natural research.

And it must be remembered, as one of the facts to which history, aided by modern science, has not long opened its eyes, that where the natural real world passes into the artificial real world, there is a territory of enormous extent and importance which is the reflex, in what we call nature, of our progressive civilization.  The history of man is at the same time the history of the habitable surface of our globe, and of all that lives and grows upon it.  No animal, no plant, no square inch of soil, except in a few mountains and deserts, has been left unaffected by the practical idealization which human purpose introduces.  And if we take further into consideration that whole second nature which exists in the shape of machinery and buildings, and all the instruments of life, we shall see that the artificial real world, although founded throughout on the laws and properties of the natural real world, is yet a phenomenon of existence which, as the body of the objective mind, may well claim the peculiar attention of philosophy.  Infinitely less than nature in quantitative extent, it is no less objectively actual, and is perhaps even more significant.  I may add that a consciousness of the historical importance of the transformation of the earth's surface was one of the few points in which the Hellenic mind possessed a historical sense almost more penetrating than our own.  The Æschylean contrast between the tamed and the untamed earth recurs constantly in Hellenic ideas.

It was when attention was thus called, for the first time I believe in the modern world, to the ideal objectivity of human works, relations, and institutions, that the actuality of civilization was thoroughly brought home to consciousness, with the double result of creating the historical sense and of investing with imperative urgency the claims of human society as something not less real than the perceptible individual.

2. But, secondly, the whole basis of life is laid in Nature, although the environment of our terrestrial existence is mainly a second nature which has been practically idealized by mind. Philosophy must therefore include nature in its scheme on pain of omitting the essential necessity in which all life is rooted, and some of the greatest ideas which can be presented to the intellect.  Now it appears to me to be characteristic of objective Idealism, for good or evil, that it approaches the natural

real world from the side of the artificial real world, and extends to the former that kind of consideration which has been suggested by the latter. This course, as a procedure from the better known to the less known, has much to recommend it in logic, and it is strikingly analogous to Darwin's luminous treatment of the natural variations of species by comparing them with the variations of species under domestication. And Mr. Case's brilliant work on *Physical Realism* furnishes a somewhat less closely analogous example of a similar argument. Fine Art, or machinery, is Nature made easy ; Nature is, for this treatment, a harder example of the ideal objectivity which is actual in the works of man. Nature is therefore set down as a phase of the Idea, but as a phase neither containing nor presupposing consciousness, and one therefore in which the Idea is hard to disentangle. In every sense, therefore, Nature is below mind [1] ; the essential [2] process of Nature is the struggle towards the manifestation of life and of intelligence. This language points directly to Darwinism, but truth requires me to admit that Hegel at least did not believe in the evolution of species as a historical fact, though I am quite unable to see why he should have denied it. If Nature is called, as by Schelling and others, petrified or frozen intelligence, we must not forget, so Hegel insists, that the stones cry out and exhibit a movement towards life and mind.

I will only comment upon this mode of approaching the natural real world, as a historical phenomenon, and not from a metaphysical point of view.

The form of the conception was deeply conditioned by the circumstances of the age. Men's minds, in the time of Napoleon and of Goethe, were busy with such realities as man and his works ; with history, law, politics, art, and civilization. The influence of æsthetic on the conception of nature—which in Goethe's hands helped to found the science of morphology— is a natural focus of the culture of that age.

Again, this view of Nature is modern or absolute. Nature is necessary, is the unconscious idea, is potentially mind. Therefore, it is the legitimate prey of physical science and of fine art. The understanding is to have its rights ; understanding without reason is something ; reason without understanding

[1] Hegel, Introduction to *Æsthetic*.        [2] *Id.*, *Naturphil*. p. 24.

is nothing. Nature is indeed chance, as indifferent to particular human purpose ; but has no inner and outer,[1] no essence, no latent remainder ; and therefore there is no miracle and no supernatural. This is the bearing of the modern or absolute standpoint when Nature is in question, and as I shall try to show by reference to later English culture was a prophecy 100 years ago which has since been magnificently fulfilled.

Lastly, these conceptions do, as has already been observed, definitely rank Nature below mind. A straw, it has been said, suffices to prove the existence of God ; but Hegel retorts that the weakest word or thought of subjective mind shows more of God than any single natural object.

Great heart-searchings, and as it appears to me entirely idle ones, have been caused by this last feature on its æsthetic side, according to which Æsthetic, as the science of beauty, is identified with the philosophy of Fine Art, the beauty of Nature thus appearing to be omitted in theory, and being also to some extent neglected in the detailed criticism of the subject.

This matter seems to me almost too simple to need discussion. Beauty, however objective, is necessarily and unquestionably subjective. That is to say, it exists for a particular mood and perceptive capacity, and except as relative to these cannot be judged or apprehended at all. That in discussing the beauty of nature we presuppose a normal civilized appreciative capacity is as much a matter of course as that in discussing effects of colour we presuppose a normal eye. Therefore, the ordinary person's perception of natural beauty is essentially the same thing as the perception which the artist embodies in a work of art, the only difference being in degree of appreciativeness, and in presence or absence of plastic skill. And therefore, once more, the spectator's perception of beauty in nature is a perception of precisely the same kind as his perception of beauty in a work of fine art ; the only difference being that the work of fine art lends him the guidance and assistance of the artist's mind and perceptive mood, " lending our minds out," as Browning says, and is therefore more easily appreciated than the unmodified nature in which the artist's work has to be done by the spectator himself. The appreciation of natural

[1] Goethe's lines : *Ins Innere der Natur*, etc.

beauty by the public mind is in fact conditioned by and historically sequent upon the revelations made by great painters
and poets ; though no doubt the tendencies of these men are
themselves controlled by deep-seated influences in the state
of culture and society. In short, natural beauty is that
beauty in respect of which every man is his own artist ; and
the consideration of natural beauty is usually and most conveniently conducted with reference to its representation by
fine art, in which case the distinction is no longer between the
beauty of nature and the beauty of fine art ; but between
the beauty *of nature* (that is, not human beauty) *in art*, and
the beauty *of man* or *history in art*. This is the attitude which
all consideration of nature practically takes, for instance, in
Ruskin's works. In speaking of natural scenes which cannot
be fixed on canvas, for instance of the actual sunset colours,
we treat them by description and memory precisely as *if they
were* pictures. If nature is really to be opposed, not to man,
but to fine art, it is plain that the whole world of reality would
have to be considered in respect of its beauty twice over, once
as natural, and once as represented in fine art. The distinction
is utterly untenable, and is never maintained for a page of
good criticism.

There was no doubt at the end of last century [1] very little
conception of pure natural beauty in the former sense, because
nature, as opposed to man and history, had not successfully or
completely been made the object of art or of art criticism. If
Hegel had had the *Modern Painters* before him he would no
longer have been able to say that the realm of nature had never
been systematically criticized with reference to the attribute of
beauty, as it is in the *materia medica* with reference to utility.

Thus the inclusion of natural beauty within the beauty of
fine art presents no philosophical difficulty whatever.

The subsequent history of objective idealism in Germany,
with its offshoots and the reactions which it has provoked,
would almost be the history of German if not of continental
culture during the present century. The concrete grasp of
life, which gave it its force, has been widened and deepened
by critical and sympathetic research into the whole actual
evolution of the human spirit, from theology to economics, from

[1] [The eighteenth century.—ED.]

Strauss and Baur to Lassalle and Karl Marx ; and the seven-league strides of physical science, whatever may be its explicit attitude to philosophy, are performing, as Schelling distinctly foresaw, the definite demonstration of the idea in nature.

The centenary, next year,[1] of the *Critique of the Power of Judgment*, will see the formal and abstract paradoxes in which Kant first expressed the fusion of reason and of sense developed into the self-consciousness of an immense many-sided movement in which the modern spirit recognizes actual reality. And of this distinctively modern consciousness one obviously traceable source or root—it would be rash in so complicated a matter to say more than this—was the profound conception of the significance and history of fine art initiated by Winckelmann, and developed by Schiller, Goethe, and the philosophers who inherited their ideas.

(3) If we now turn, as our subject demands, to the consideration of British culture and reflection, through which modern philosophy more especially appeals to us, it cannot be denied that we find ourselves in a different atmosphere. If we recall the names of the writers of greatest repute in British philosophy during the present century down to the publication, say, of Jevons' *Principles of Science* in 1874, we find that with one great exception, in Herbert Spencer, they are chiefly writers on abstract moral philosophy, or on psychology, or on logic ; or indeed, and here no doubt they touch the concrete, on the theory of legislation as Bentham, and on political and economical subjects as Mill. The history of philosophy, of religion, of fine art, of civilization, is conspicuous by its absence, even allowing Mr. Lewes's and Mr. Buckle's works to be solitary exceptions. All reflective thought must, I think, have its definite stimulus or nutriment or material, and it is plain that the nutriment of English philosophy has not been the same as that of continental thought. It has touched the concrete works of man chiefly in the theory of legislation, in political philosophy, and in the procedure of physical science, which latter came to the rescue of British logic just in time to save it from death by inanition. The conception of evolution has come to it not from history but from physical science, and is, through Mr. Herbert Spencer and others like him, making its

[1] [Written in 1889.—ED.]

influence felt in all regions of inquiry. The entrance of English philosophy into a concrete and constructive direction during the last thirty years, not counting the Germanized movement, is quite unmistakable. But on the whole, by a contrast that will surprise no student, the reflective thought of our most practical and concretely active of races is singularly abstract, introspective, and unorganized, and, till lately, wanting in constructive purpose.

Now I hold it to be both unseemly and unjust to assume a tone of mere disparagement towards the eminent philosophers of our country through three generations. Philosophy, I take it, is an expression of national life, and our business is to understand and appreciate, not to depreciate. One of Shakespeare's grandest sayings should never be forgotten by the historian of thought : " love speaks with better knowledge, and knowledge with dearer love."

I would venture from a historical point of view merely to suggest the consideration, which is to my mind anything but disparaging, that nineteenth-century philosophy in Great Britain has borne perhaps to some extent the character of an opposition to all that vainly pretended to be the national culture and institutions.

In England, at least as distinct from Scotland, where better social conditions prevailed, we observe a marked divorce —I speak of the time before 1860—between philosophy and the older universities, and we perceive in the arguments of the Associationist Psychology and in the new logic based upon scientific inference, a feeling that there is a predominant superstitious tradition, adverse to free explanation and bound up with a kind of orthodoxy, which ought to be overthrown. No one can read the very clear and powerful writings of Mr. G. H. Lewes without being struck by this attitude. The life of this rebellion was supplied by the unconquerable spirit of natural science, hostile to the dominant embodiment of so-called religion, and closely allied, for reasons obvious under the circumstances, with a spirit of political reform. And there was, in the culture which ought to have satisfied these new demands, no surviving intelligence adequate to cope with them or to transform them. Sir W. Hamilton's philosophy fell before Mill's attack, not so much because what Hamilton said was false, as because, supposing it ever so true, there was nothing in it. Thus it is not surprising, nor blameworthy, that there should be something schismatic or one-sided about the new philosophy, which has at all events the credit of having carried the nation with it, by high courage and energy, by what seemed a direct appeal to facts, and, in many cases, by splendid literary gifts. A nation must think in its own language, and must reach the truth by its own road, and if the Mills and John Grote, and Lewes, and Clifford had never written—I do not speak of living writers—then those who now wish to build further upon the present state of philosophy would have no public to address, and no philosophy to discuss.

What I have said makes it clear, however, that in British technical philosophy of the nineteenth century there is no æsthetic, and no part played by æsthetic. In Mr. Lewes's history of German thought from Kant to Hegel inclusive, you will hardly find six lines dealing with the epoch-making treatment of this subject by the writers of that day. Darwin here, as everywhere, made suggestions of great interest, and the problem has now begun to affect abstract inquiry, but the enormous, solid output of German research in this direction during the last 100 years, which, with all its faults and awkwardness, is a gigantic contribution to the history of the world, finds no parallel whatever in English reflection.

In passing to culture outside professional philosophy, I may mention two great works in the province of pure history which are really, I think, not exceptions to what I have said, but confirmatory negative instances. Could Germany show, it may be asked, any historical labours that for grasp and interest and insight could compare with Gibbon's *Decline and Fall*, and with Grote's *History of Greece* ? Perhaps not. But both of these splendid works distinctly bear that mark of antagonism to which I have referred, of antagonism in religion, or of antagonism in politics. In both, therefore, there is something contentious, something unappreciative, which has debarred them from their full legitimate effect on the speculative consciousness, in spite of their position as monumental works of historical research.

If we now look at other sides of the higher culture of the people of these islands, we are struck by the existence during the present century of a succession of great writers who, without being professional or systematic philosophers, have occupied a sort of prophetic position in Great Britain, and have been, man for man, at least equally influential with the great logicians, psychologists, and ethical writers. I ought not to include among such leaders men who have simply worked as great poets, because we are speaking only of reflective culture ; but it is the case that two or three of our poets have had a distinct intention or effect beyond the usual influence which belongs to an artist as such, and these have a right to be considered. I will now briefly explain the philosophical import which I ascribe to the work of some among these great men, and its probable bearing in the future upon technical philosophy.

It would seem, perhaps, absurd to fix upon the most unreflective of writers, Sir Walter Scott, as the chief initiator of a philosophical influence ; but I believe there is little doubt that historical humanism in England, as on the Continent, received an epoch-making impulse from his writings. Wordsworth, too, and Shelley, must be mentioned, the former if only for his incalculably important influence on Mr. Ruskin, and on the public to which Mr. Ruskin addressed himself ; and the latter for his profound and literally accurate judgment on our debt to the ancient Greeks, which sounded a note quite new to England in historical criticism. Then came Carlyle as a philosophic historian and student of great literature ; and then Mr. Ruskin, whose influence appears to me to mark a revolution in general culture as great as, and in many ways corresponding to, that produced by Darwin in scientific conceptions. With him, allowing as always for the surroundings of the times, and especially for the kindred influence of physical science itself, there awakes on the one side the appreciation of the idea in nature, and on the other side the profounder appreciation of the idea in history.

In speaking of the idea in nature, I assume, what I believe I may safely assume, that the main contentions of Mr. Ruskin's *Modern Painters* [1] with reference to the natural truth of modern landscape painting, are, on the whole, established.

[1] Cf. Ruskin's *Elements of Drawing*, pp. 116 and 262.

They amount, as I understand them, to two assertions :

(i) That a completely new departure in the appreciation of natural beauty—meaning by this, non-human beauty—has been made by the great English landscape painters of the present century ; and

(ii) In spite of Mr. Ruskin's own occasional protests against the heedless *identification* of beauty and truth, that this appreciation mainly consists in a wholly new grasp of the actual governing facts and tendencies apparent to reason in the natural world.

It is plain that this artistic perception of the idea in nature not only has a parallel result to that which so rapidly opened upon natural science in the same generation, but it is very largely interwoven with the latter, and dependent upon a similar intellectual aspiration. And the name of this intellectual aspiration is, once more, the modern standpoint. It is the spirit which refuses to believe that there is anything without significance, or any irrational remainder. Mr. Ruskin's account of the true or penetrative imagination, as opposed to the false or fantastic imagination, shows the profound underlying unity between modern fine art and modern natural science. By these two characteristic achievements of the nineteenth century, the discovery of the idea in nature, which was a mere dream in the natural philosophy of Schelling or Hegel, is becoming, to a daily increasing extent, an accomplished fact.

And the same with history. I have not the literary knowledge which would justify me in asserting that the chapter on " The Nature of Gothic Architecture " [1] in the *Stones of Venice* actually *caused* a revolution in England, though as to its representing one there can hardly be two opinions. Here, it seems to me, we recognize once more, as in Shelley's isolated saying, the new and unmistakable note of philosophic history, the history which sees the works of men as instinct with the human reality of the life from which they spring with all its necessities and purposes.

Many of Mr. William Morris's writings on art represent this tendency of æsthetic reflection in its noblest form ; and his

[1] Cf. Goethe in *Wahrheit und Dichtung*. The interest in Gothic architecture was what he desired in his youth, and saw in his old age.

estimate of the historical and social significance of architecture
and the architectural handicrafts illustrates the philosophical
thesis on which I am endeavouring to insist, viz. : the peculiar
force of æsthetic reflection as an exponent of ideal reality.  It
owes this force to the fact that it irresistibly lays the grasp of
objectivity on that individual region of fancy and feeling which
is commonly held to be the kingdom of caprice, and which is
inaccessible both to abstract reasoning and, as a rule, to the
categorical imperative of duty.  I do not mean that æsthetic
can supply formal principles by which taste and feeling may
be directed and deduced ; I mean that by analysis *a posteriori*
it is able to interpret with vital significance all man's artificial
surroundings, especially in as far as they express his tendencies
to enjoyment, or to imaginative emotion, or to display.  We
may observe this new insight in our sympathy for the history
of peoples, rather than of dynasties, and of industrial conditions
rather than of political disputes ; or again in the whole mode
of thought which now presides over archæology, anthropology,
and the history of architecture.  Thus, for the first time
perhaps, man's life is rounded into a totality of which no part
can escape the grasp of reason ; and here again we recognize
in one of its bearings the absolute or modern standpoint.
I may add that this development of English æsthetic, with
that outburst of artistic idealization of nature in which it
arose, forces me to differ fundamentally from one of the conclusions at which its great leaders seem sometimes to be
pointing.  I do not believe in the artistic degeneracy of the
modern mind as a whole.  If our everyday surroundings
reflect a vulgarized social life, a degraded taste, and a blunted
sense of form, we must hold this together with the fact that
natural beauty has, in this century, for the first time, been
thoroughly drawn into the focus of consciousness.  Modern
life is stronger than any that has existed before, and can bear
deeper contradictions.   It is plain that the one of these extremes
was the condition of the other, which of course does not hinder
that the other, when obtained, should have power to rectify
the one.

If I further allude to such writers as Robert Browning,
Matthew Arnold, and Walter Pater, I do not think it can be
doubted that the series of thinkers mentioned in this context,

with the addition perhaps of George Eliot, have supplied a reflective and intellectual element in English thought, without which all English-speaking men and women who care for the higher life would have been deprived of half or more than half their philosophical and rational nutriment. All the sciences of civilization, as they might be called, from æsthetic to economics, which two extremes have naturally met in our greatest æsthetic writers—all these sciences of civilization have assumed a wholly new complexion under the influences represented by these names. Our professional philosophers, illustrious men as I have admitted that they are, have not as yet occupied the whole place in English life which has been held by Kant, Hegel, Schopenhauer, Schleiermacher, von Hartmann in the life of Germany. An element has been wanting, which those whom I have called the prophetic writers have supplied. And the missing element is not, as we English are apt to pride ourselves on supposing, the element of ontological superstition, but it is the element of intelligent and sympathetic history, that is, of self-conscious civilization.

Now it may of course be replied, " The dualism which you deprecate in English culture is a proof of English common sense : philosophy ought to be scientific ; and reflection upon history and religion and fine art should be kept separate from philosophy, in the mere province of taste and polite letters."

I believe that this states the fundamental question as between objective idealism and English empiricism ; and I should like to point out what it amounts to. It seems to mean that man and his works, after the point at which he ceases to be merely animal, are not included in the object of philosophical analysis. I do not know that such a view has ever been explicitly maintained. English philosophy has not been unmindful of law, politics, and the intellectual operations revealed by physical science. Herbert Spencer has, at any rate, what I must consider the great merit of having struck out boldly into the ocean of historical evolution, and there is absolutely no doubt that the positive and constructive tendency, which is heralded by his life-work, will be more and more imperatively felt, and will bring with it a fusion between abstract science and philosophic history. I have tried to show how æsthetic reflection is paving the way for this fusion in England, as it did in Germany a century ago.

I have not in any way alluded to the work of Professor Edward Caird or of Professor T. H. Green, or of others who have sympathized with them. It was my task to point out those indigenous [1] conditions of English culture which established, in my judgment, the fact of a recognized imperative necessity for deeper and more human theories of life in England, as elsewhere. The English revival does not primarily spring from Hellas, as did that of Winckelmann and Goethe. If I were forced to name two out of many great men as its chief authors, I should be inclined to select Turner, the landscape painter, and Darwin, the biologist. But though thus original and indigenous, yet being fundamentally an expression of the same necessity, it must ultimately include the material with which the parallel movement began ; and therefore I have tried to show, not that German idealism has introduced into English thought an element wholly exotic and unknown, but rather that it has suggested certain intellectual forms and presented certain organized regions of experience, drawn from the analogous, though distinct, development of a kindred nation, which may aid in the systematic expression of that many-sided ideal reality which our national mind also has been grappling with and gradually comprehending throughout the nineteenth century.

[1] I do not suppose that the points of contact between Wordsworth and Kant, or Ruskin and Carlyle, have been cardinal points in the English development. Ruskin detests all he understands of Schiller.

# XXIII

## ON THE NATURE OF ÆSTHETIC EMOTION

IN raising the question, " What is Beauty ? " we are admittedly dealing with very various phenomena. Some elements, it may be, are obviously given as common throughout the whole range of the beautiful ; such, it might be alleged, are the formal feelings, those states of pleasure and pain which accompany ease or obstruction in the flow of ideas. But it will hardly be proposed to-day to restrict the feeling of beauty and the reverse to those simple elements ; and I may rely on the support of Mr. Bain and other British psychologists for the view that in considering the nature of beauty it is necessary to examine a " circle of effects." [1] But while accepting this as a starting-point, I cannot but think it a self-contradiction for any science to acquiesce in a " plurality of causes " [2] as ultimate. " Plurality of causes " in Mill's sense, which I assume that Mr. Bain intends to adopt, means of course the recognition not of " a plurality of constituent factors " [3] or co-operating conditions resulting in a certain effect, but of a number of alternative causes from any one of which the same effect may spring.

But in the full scientific sense it is a contradiction to say that $a$ and $b$ are alternative causes of the effect $c$. Either a common element must be detected in $a$ and $b$, or $c$ must be divided into $d$ and $e$. To surrender this postulate as a matter of principle is to abandon scientific method, although an incomplete analysis must of course pass through the stage

---

[1] Bain, *Mental and Moral Science*, p. 292 ; cf. Sully, *Encycl. Brit.*, art. " Æsthetics," *Outlines of Psychology*, 538, or *Human Mind*, ii, 142 and 361. A comparison of these passages suggests that under pressure of the facts Mr. Sully has greatly modified his assent to Dugald Stewart's view.

[2] Bain, loc. cit.

[3] Sully, *Human Mind*, ii, 361.

of tracing alternative causes. It is quite possible that much which has been included in the object-matter of æsthetic science does not really belong to it. Many matters have been banished from it by the self-criticism of the science, and I admit, or rather maintain, that alien considerations are still improperly introduced. Nevertheless, within the science, and in considering a common element which somehow attaches to the circle of effects that are its data, there can be no ultimate plurality of causes as such. This is not postulating an unreal unity. It is only requiring that if we fail to establish a coherent principle we shall admit the failure.

I now desire to suggest that the central characteristic of æsthetic emotion is an aspect of the central characteristic of æsthetic presentation.

The above admission of a prima facie diversity in the species of beauty releases me from the attempt to identify any simple given feeling or intuition as one and the same throughout all of them. In every example of æsthetic emotion we are to go behind the first undiscriminating impression, if such there be, which finds utterance in the exclamation, " How beautiful ! " and we are to attempt to trace a common root in phenomena of admitted variety.

This point of view, so far from being a difficulty to me, is all-important for my argument. It is possible, in considering the data of beauty, to start from a passive or from an active attitude. We may take a presentation more as it affects us, and ask what enjoyable feeling it awakens in us, when we regard ourselves as spectators or auditors to whom a perception comes *ab extra*. This has, as I think, been to a great extent the attitude of British psychologists. Or we may start from a more active frame of mind, such as without special gifts we may all experience in simple or familiar regions of beauty, while in its higher forms it is the productive or creative state which we attribute to the poet or artist. The commonest and most homely experience, together with attention to the moods demanded by the greatest and most genuine art, bear strongly in favour of the contention that this latter is the natural and normal condition of the mind in enjoying beauty. Empirical facts have been neglected, I should maintain, not by those who support this view, but by those who oppose it. Wherever the mind of the work-man has been appreciatively considered, wherever the simplest phases of art and their connection with natural impulses of the ordinary human being have been drawn into account, there the explanation of beauty has tended to start from an active rather than a passive attitude of mind.[1]

The " plurality of causes," as a datum of æsthetic theory at starting, is in favour of this view. We do not, at the first feeling of a charm or pleasure in a beautiful thing, fully enter into its peculiar and individual character. And in the same degree we remain, no doubt, passive or receptive. But in proportion as through continued attention we are seized by the special delight or emotion which the perception in question has power to produce, so far, that is, as we appreciate the diversity of the beautiful in all the depth of its individuality, we depart from the attitude of the mere spectator, and assume that of the mind which is impelled to expression and utterance, the mind of the " maker." That is to say, we no longer feel ourselves in face of the presentation as something given *ab extra*, but rather enter into it as something which embodies for us the emotion that craves utterance. This emotion, of course, the presentation has itself in the commonest instances occasioned. But none the less, when we enjoy it fully, we seem to have made the presentation transparent or organic through and through, as the vehicle of our emotion. The simple facts of rhythm, metre, the dance and song, in their continuity with the formative impulse in all its phases, seem to me a mass of experience strongly favourable to this point of view. And I grant that any one impressed by experience of this kind is greatly influenced by it in his whole treatment of æsthetic science. Those who lean to regarding the mind as mainly receptive [2] in æsthetic enjoyment naturally tend to think of æsthetic science as an analysis of given pleasur-able effects. They are therefore apt to explain a beautiful presentation by a congeries of pleasurable suggestions in a

---

[1] It is impossible not to observe that the theories of the British psycho-logical school date from just about the low-water mark of the æsthetic con-sciousness in this country. In saying this, of course I do not refer to living writers. The endurance of a theory is quite a different problem from that of its origin.

[2] Mr. Sully's insistence on this is noticeable, *Human Mind*, ii, 135–6.

way which impresses others as hostile to the purity and coherence of æsthetic emotion. In as far as this danger is avoided, I think that every explanation of beauty reduces itself to expressiveness.

I may point out also the serious dualism between beauty and fine art which arises from regarding the former as coincident in principle with pleasurable effect as such. For a good observer will hardly admit that fine art, of the greater periods at any rate, makes any effect of this kind its purpose, and though it may be said with plausibility that beauty is the result but not the aim of art, still it is a serious matter to define the beautiful in a way that wholly neglects the essence of the artist's impulse.[1]

I suggest therefore as the most fundamental and universal feature, from which all the common characteristics of æsthetic emotion may be deduced, the simple fact that it is expressed. And I propose to consider what consequences affecting its nature may be derived from this condition.

An ambiguity meets us at once. All emotion is expressed ; perhaps indeed emotion may be found to consist in little more than the psychical side of the movement or organic changes which in part constitute its expression. For plainly there is no distinction of principle between an inward physical effect and one which happens to be visible or audible. So, if all emotion is expressed, in virtue of effects which either are external or differ in no essentials from external effects, it would seem that expression is no differentia of æsthetic emotion.

Here no doubt we must admit a gradation, and the true nature of expression may be very conveniently taken up from this point of junction. There is plainly a distinction of principle between the mere physical side of the bodily resonance by which an emotion discharges itself, and any forms of action that aim at prolonging the resonance of the emotion for the sake of the enjoyment it affords. " Jumping for joy " may pass into the dance ; the manifestation

---

[1] See Volkmann, *Lehrbuch d. Psych.*, ii, 359. Volkmann accepts this dualism, and thinks that it is confirmed by Greek æsthetic, finding, e.g., a complete severance between beauty and art in Plato. But the truth is the other way. The art which Plato *rejected* was that which he could *not* bring under an expressive theory of beauty.

of anger may pass into poetical invective; love and admiration, at first displayed by look and attitude, constantly lead up to a graphical or poetical representation of their object. An interesting remark arises at this point. Expression in the form of an object (including a definite action) seems to be the only healthy means by which feeling can be purposely dwelt upon. To brood over feelings because we enjoy doing so, without trying to embody them, is the note of sentimentalism. In making the distinction, however, between mere discharge of feeling, and its expression as such, we must not lay exclusive stress on the involuntary or voluntary nature of the means adopted. When rhythmical, musical, or metrical form begins to qualify the utterance of joy, grief, or anger, it is plain that new elements of presentation are being employed as a way of dwelling upon the emotion, whether the agent is conscious of any such purpose or no. Emotion in such a case is not merely discharged but expressed; that is to say, the original feeling is prolonged and accentuated by help of positive symbols and presentations, so that the mind may dwell upon it, not merely brooding over it, but portraying its nature in more or less definite actions and perceptions. Here we may fairly say that we no longer have mere discharge, or accidental expression through mere discharge, but expression as such, or expression for expression's sake.

Now in such expression or embodiment of an emotion, how is the expression related to the emotion? How are the presentative elements of rhythm, metre, and musical sound related to the emotion of joy or anger which finds utterance through them? The primary answer appears to be that the two sides cannot be separated; the emotion simply is the whole presentation, including both its sensuous and its ideal elements, in so far as it qualifies the pleasure or pure feeling which accompanies it. The individual action or object and the emotion which is expressed or embodied in it are psychologically speaking precise correlatives, and no question can intelligibly be asked which implies that the one could be given to a normal mind without the other. This is an important point, because it saves us from a dualism which has very absurd results. We speak in general terms of a content of presentation as if it, the same content—death, for example—could be treated or embodied so as to be the object of different emotions. This is true if we mean to contrast the abstraction "death" with the various ways in which it may be concretely brought before us, but not otherwise. In being differently "treated," sadly, humorously, indignantly, the content is differently filled in, is itself modified by the manner of presentation, and, as object of different emotions, does not remain the same content. We cannot say, "Here is the content, and now we will add the 'expression,' or elements which more particularly correspond to the emotion": the content, so far as it goes, actually in that degree is or constitutes the expression of emotion, being simply that which is felt, because it must be felt, in a certain way. Even an abstract idea, death, ruin, fate, triumph, has no doubt its correlative element of emotion, a way in which it is felt; but so far as the idea is indeterminate, the feeling, considered as qualified only by that idea, is also indeterminate, while if the idea is individualized the feeling which it qualifies is *ipso facto* individualized along with it.

Feeling, then, is only articulate through that of which it is the feeling, viz. a presentation more or less individual, and every presentation has its correlative emotions (pure feeling as qualified by the presentation itself), and if this emotion appears to be indeterminate this is merely because the presentation in question, being highly abstract, is not sufficient to determine the character of an entire psychosis, and is in fact variously filled in by the accidental content of the mind from moment to moment. None but a highly individual presentation, it would therefore seem, can be the expression of such an emotion as constitutes a principal or dominant element in any entire psychosis. Yet there is no complete contrast between an abstract idea and the expression of emotion, but only between an abstract idea as an expression of slightly determinate emotion, and an individual idea as an expression of highly determinate emotion. The nexus between presentation and emotion is then, speaking generally, that such and such a presentation must be felt, by a normal mind, in such and such a way. All that we can do by analysis to explain a nexus of this kind would seem to consist in drawing out the content which is implied in the more individual among the presented elements—say a " springing curve," or a certain sequence of notes—and showing how this content is related to larger ideal characters which it modifies and reinforces. When this has been done, so far as it can be done, it will be found that the pure feeling accompanying the whole—its degree of pleasure or pain—has also, in the same measure, been accounted for. Whether we start from emotion or from content, what we are analysing is in the last resort the same matter, the relation of context, as expressed, to life ; this of course including the success or failure of expression which constitutes, as we have seen, a modification of the content expressed.

If this is so, if would seem that every emotion exists only as correlative to its expression ; or that strictly speaking we do not first have an emotion and then proceed to express it ; but that an emotion assumes its character, or becomes what it is, through the mode and degree of its expression ; and therefore that æsthetic emotion first arises in and is essentially constituted by, expression for expression's sake, or in other words, when its discharge takes the form of a positive production or action which has no purpose beyond that of uttering the content of our feeling.

The modification which a feeling necessarily goes through in being " expressed " in the sense thus suggested, has never, if I am right, been more fruitfully analysed than in Aristotle's account of tragic emotion, as explained and expanded by Lessing and Bernays. This interpretation, with unessential modifications, is accepted, so far as I know, by the best judges to-day.[1] Omitting detail, the principle comes to this. There is a form of art called Tragedy which produces pleasure by means of two painful emotions, pity and fear. How this is possible is a problem that answers itself when we consider the conditions of artistic expression or representation. By a typical portrayal of human life in some story that forms an individual whole, the feelings in question are divested of their personal reference, and acquire a content drawn from what is serious and noteworthy in humanity, and thus alone, it seems clearly to be Aristotle's view, can their quintessence be fully

[1] See Professor S. H. Butcher's *Aspects of the Greek Genius*, 1st ed. ; and Susemihl, *Aristotle's Poetics*, Introduction.

uttered and drawn out and find its pleasurable discharge free from morbid elements of mere shock and personal sensibility. The connection of pity and fear, which is the centre of his doctrine, really indicates that fear, for art, is a fear idealized by expression or objective embodiment, while free utterance is not aided but lamed and obstructed by any intrusion of the dumb shock of personal terror. Thus then, and thus alone, can fear be made an æsthetic emotion, a source of artistic enjoyment or the pleasure of tragedy. It is not, and this is a fundamental point, it is not merely that the emotion is " refined," in the sense that its bodily resonance is rendered less intense. A modified resonance will attend a modified emotion but the intensity of feeling is not a question of principle in relation to its æsthetic character. The æsthetic character lies in the dwelling on and drawing out the feeling, in its fullest reference, by help of a definite presentation which accents its *nature*. Refinement, in the sense of mere diminution of intensity, cannot make an unæsthetic emotion into one which is æsthetic. Sensuous pleasure as such, however remotely suggested, is no more æsthetic than personal terror.

The accepted distinctions between the æsthetic and other points of view might be easily read off from the foregoing account. That which is " expression for expression's sake " is *ex hypothesi* secured from subservience to other ends whether ethical, intellectual, or sensual.

But a word remains to be said about the limit imposed on the factors of æsthetic emotion by the demand that it shall be expressed. " How much," it may be asked, " is in fact expressed by any given presentation ? Is there any limit ? Does it express whatever any one feels when it comes before him ? " Here we must recur to the contrast of abstract contents and contents individualized by concrete presentation.

" Two bits of wood nailed crosswise " (Browning) may suggest anything from the spokes of a wheel to the usual associations of a cross. Such a presentation, it may be urged, is capable of calling up any conceivable emotion. And no doubt this is so, but only because it is capable of calling up any conceivable presentation. It is not that the same presented content may call up different emotions, but that a content indeterminate in itself may be differently determined in the context of the mind. The emotions which may pass through the mind on seeing so bare a symbol, are not, in relation to it as it stands, "expressed" or "embodied" emotions, and therefore cannot qualify it æsthetically, and are not, so far as their suggestion by it is concerned, æsthetic emotions. Of course if they come into the mind with poetical or other imaginative matter, of the nature of expressive embodiment, that is accidental relatively to the seeing of the wooden cross, which alone was in question. Emotion brought up by mere associated content, irrelevant to a real or universal connection with presented elements, is not æsthetic emotion.

A more individualized presentation than that just taken as an example has more power to ensure a determinate mode of feeling, in other words, is more nearly such as by a normal mind must necessarily be felt in a particular way. Therefore, although no presentation can be so imperiously dominant as wholly to exclude accidents of feeling in different persons, yet as a matter of principle plurality of causes—the production of the same emotion by different contents—is impossible. Cause and effect are shown to be, as strictly they always must be, precisely correlative ; and although, or because, individual consequents correspond to individual causes, there can be no common property residing in or attendant on the " circle of effects " which is not matched by a common property pervading the diversity of causes. Thus it is not true that presentations, sharing no identical property, can be alike qualified as beautiful by emotions the identical element of which in that case would be accidental, or independent of the definite presentative elements which really make them what they are.

The attempt to determine the sources of beauty by examining the pleasurable feelings liable to be suggested by beautiful objects or actions, has, of course, led to many valuable observations respecting the connection of expression with feeling. As a method of æsthetic science, however, I cannot but think it disabled by the general defect of associationism, that is to say, the attempt to explain general connections of content by the chance conjunction of particular experiences. This leads, if I am right, to two errors of principle.

The first of these errors is the obliteration of the line between what is beautiful and what interests me personally. Though undoubtedly difficult to draw in practice, this distinction must surely be maintained in principle and on the whole. No doubt I may have associated experiences which cause me to enjoy the croaking of frogs [1] or the cawing of rooks,[2] but does that make them beautiful? Are there elements within the sounds themselves which in any sense or by any kind of analysis can be said to be symbolic of country life? My old travelling trunk reminds me delightfully of many pleasant experiences, but does that make it beautiful? Surely even the "ideal" element of beauty must be founded in some universal connection, indicated within the four corners of the beautiful object, and not on a wholly unanalysed conjunction which, as taken, is an accident of my personal history.

This first error, however, though as I am convinced a matter of principle, is also, just round the margin of the beautiful, a matter of degree. But the second, which is an aggravated case of the first, seems to me an absolute reversal of the æsthetic point of view. It arises when among the pleasurable feelings brought up by association are counted, however indirectly, the dumb gratifications of sense.

Refinement of allusion, as I tried to show above, does not help the matter so long as it merely means disguised or remote suggestion. The view which Bain [3] for example finds himself obliged to take of the range of art in these respects, restricting it, as I understand, by mere convention, and by no principle,[4] is a very serious matter indeed. "But," it may be retorted, "if these gratifications can be expressed in art, according to your own conceptions they are æsthetic; while if they cannot be expressed, *cadit quaestio*." Here, however, we must bear in mind that there is such a thing as

---

[1] Cf. Ward in *Encycl. Brit.*, art. "Psychology."

[2] Sully, *Human Mind*, ii, 78. This enjoyment is not ranked under the head "Æsthetic," but I do not see how it is differentiated.

[3] *Emotions and Will*, 3rd ed., p. 227. "The ideal representation of the sensual pleasures comes strictly under the province of Art, but, for prudential and moral reasons, is kept within narrow limits, varying in different ages and countries."

[4] For, as Bain points out, the mere requirement of universality (construed as generality) does not exclude sensuous *suggestion* in art or nature.

bad art, and that this largely consists of art which leans over and strains to do that which it cannot, by the law of its existence, really achieve. In presenting the pure sensuous gratifications art cannot indeed achieve expression; but it may, and thoroughly vicious art most frequently does, attain suggestion. Let us think of the mere sensuous gratification of drinking to intoxication. No artistic presentation will reproduce the taste and the peculiar excitement which constitute this sensuous enjoyment. Nothing will do this but the process itself. But it can of course be easily suggested or recalled in painting or poetry through its accompaniments or its effects. Now to treat such reference as a suggestion of an associated pleasure, and therefore as an element in beauty, seems to me not a blunder of taste but a contradiction in principle. It is a sin against the independence or purity (of course not meant in a moral sense) of æsthetic form, which is stated (e.g. by Schiller) as the law that æsthetic pleasure as such is incapable of enhancement by the real existence of the object represented. This is involved in the formula of "expression for expression's sake" and on this or other grounds commonly accepted. On the other hand, it is quite in accordance with this law that those elements in passion or intoxication, which are emphasized when the emotion has been made objective in a presentation, form that quintessence of feeling which finds utterance in the true poetry of love or wine. This is wholly different in principle from something which draws its pleasurableness from a faint reproduction of stronger actual pleasures. It is better and greater and deeper than the ordinary feelings of the normal man, and is not a mere suggestion of them. And it is noteworthy that though the art or poetry of passion is not to be judged by ethical standards, yet in practice morality has little to fear from it. But this is not at all the case with the art which depends on refined suggestion.

The theory which relies on expressiveness is no doubt confronted with a certain difficulty in dealing with the splendours of colour or tone when wholly isolated (if this is ever true), or at any rate very slightly moulded by arrangement and combination. The inquiry at this point is one of extreme interest and difficulty, involving a good deal of criticism upon alleged facts of æsthetic perception. It is impossible to go into it in detail on the present occasion ; but I will indicate the class of considerations which induce me to think that this region of phenomena is capable of furnishing a signal example in favour of the point of view which I have been urging. In the first place, I do not think that difficulties of distinction which meet us in tracing a certain element to its admitted vanishing-point are ever very strong arguments against a continuity well established in clearer phases. The lower limit of morality or of judgment shows closely parallel uncertainties. Does beauty, traced down to single colours or tones, suddenly become mere pleasantness to sense ? Does morality, traced down to the actions of a savage, suddenly become mere impulse or mere dread of a superior ? There is always the possibility that the element which is being tracked tends to vanish in something else, but that in as far as it survives at all, it retains the essential nature which it displayed throughout. Secondly then, starting from this idea, I should point to the improbability that sensations of the æsthetic senses are devoid of the pleasurable element, whatever it is, which characterizes all the sensations acknowledged to be unæsthetic—taste, warmth, touch, and the like. It is therefore extremely likely, prima facie, that the higher sensations have in some sort a double aspect, adding to the pleasurable quality of the " lower " sensations a source of pleasure in which as a rule those lower sensations do not share. It might further be pointed out that this higher or, at least, peculiar pleasure does not seem to attend the sensations of eye and ear in proportion as they give the gratification which is most analogous to what we roughly call a " physical pleasure," but seems rather to increase as they leave this character aside, and assume degrees and combinations which are not of interest to untrained perception. Again, by a correlative set of instances it might be shown that when, by exception, something which recalls æsthetic pleasure attaches to sensations of the " lower " senses, this does not consist in their " physical " pleasantness or any modification of it, but in some chance relation by which they are enabled to mimic the expressive power of the æsthetic sensations. And lastly, if I am attacked with direct instances and challenged to say whether my æsthetic enjoyment does not actually depend in many prominent cases on the purely sensuous quality of a yellow or a red, a trumpet-note or violin-tone, I reply with absolute conviction, so far as my own experience goes, that the mind undoubtedly revels in the splendours of the sensation, but always in the way of plunging into its peculiarity, of dwelling on and drawing out that which makes it what it is, so as very soon to pass into the beauty of combination, even if this is not, owing to constant experience (and, in sound, to its composite nature,) really inherent in the whole process from the first. I maintain, then, that even an enjoyable colour is not a mute gratification of sense, but is felt as an utterance. We dwell on its nature, but it is its *nature*, positive though not definable, on which we dwell. As Mr. Gurney felt with melodies, I feel with colours ; they say something to me, though if I could know what they say instead of seeing it they would be colours no longer. The difference between the lower sensations and the " æsthetic " sensations is so universally accepted that I think I am entitled to press it home as I have done, although I am not prepared with a rationale of it if I am bound to consider both as sensations pure and simple. My suggestions rather point to the conception that it is not *as* sensations that sounds or sights can have æsthetic value ; and any one who affirms that the whole pleasurable effect of bright light on a young child is of a nature truly continuous with æsthetic feeling proper, is bound, I think, to show the difference at that early stage between pleasure in light and pleasure in warmth or softness. I should not shrink, on the other hand, from admitting that in the sensations which are commonly classed as unæsthetic there is a vanishing element of æsthetic feeling in so far as pleasure in them arises from appreciation of a distinct individual quality which leads us to dwell upon its nature with a more or less genuine interest.[1]

Inherited associations need hardly be discussed until they are shown to be a *vera causa* in the definite form which alone could make them serviceable in explaining æsthetic emotion. We are born with many predispositions ; and a few more, unless singularly positive and definite, would

　　　　　[1] Cp. Dr. Middleton's remarks on wines in *The Egoist*.

merely be an addition to the general stock of material out of which our mind organizes itself. A definite inherited forest-emotion is imaginable, but could it ever be verifiable among the strong and various components which are easily seen to enter into our feeling for woodland scenery and surroundings ? Would it not necessarily be so overlaid and defined by other matter as to be of little more explanatory value than our primitive sensitiveness to light or to musical sound in general ? A superfluous hypothesis, not shown to rest on a *vera causa*, can hardly claim attention.

Much of the foregoing argument, it may be thought, could be summed up by saying that æsthetic emotion is " impersonal." But the word is a dangerous one, and gives rise, I think, to serious fallacies in art-theory to-day. I should prefer to borrow the expression of a recent writer on a different subject, and call it " super-personal." In becoming æsthetic, emotion does not become something less but something more ; it does not forfeit the depth of personality, but only throws off its narrowness, and modifies it by an enlargement which is also a reinforcement. The impersonality of art has recently come to be thought of as approaching a critical or intellectual attitude. This I take to be a grave error, having its root in a confusion between the existence of feeling in a person— which is necessary to its existence at all—and the restriction of its content to his narrowest self, which the nature of feeling or of its qualifying accompaniments does not in any way demand.

I suggest, then, that æsthetic emotion is emotion which in creating, or adapting itself to, its pure expression—" pure " as expression for expression's sake—has undergone a definite change of character. It has become " objective " in the sense of being attached to presentations which are as a rule highly individualized and are related to entire psychoses much as abstract language is related to abstract thought. Its impersonal or super-personal character is deducible from these conditions ; while the typical aspect of the pleasure which attends it must be looked for within the general field of that enjoyment which accompanies the discharge of any and every emotion. It is however, as æsthetic, confined to cases where, in the discharge, there suggest themselves presentative elements ideal or sensuous, or in perfect examples both together in complete fusion, such as sustain and justify and individualize the main emotion by charging it with the deeper and wider ideal contents of the self. I start from such simple comparisons as that of the anger of a common man, which in serious cases may impart a certain dignity to his bearing and sometimes a certain nobility to his expressions, with the indignation of Burns when he wrote the epigrams on the Earl of Galloway, or, at a higher level, with Milton's sonnet on the Vaudois or Dante's satire on Florence in the *Inferno*. If we follow such instances into detail, noting how passion tends to purify and harmonize its utterance as its content more deeply involves the issues of human life, we shall, I believe, be on the right track of æsthetic analysis. All modes of pleasurable suggestion which truly fall within æsthetic limits can be shown, I think, to be organic to such self-utterance as this, and we begin at the wrong end when we reckon them up as æsthetic elements because *per se* suggestions of pleasure.[1] On the contrary, their pleasurableness will be found to centre in some property or condition—as, for example, in the condition of " efficient attention "— which makes them conducive to expressiveness.

[1] See this point trenchantly stated by Ward, *Encycl. Brit.*, art. " Psychology," p. 70, col. 1 [of the ninth edition, corresponding to vol. xxii, p. 584. col. 1 of the eleventh edition.—Ed.].

# XXIV

## CROCE'S ÆSTHETIC

ART and Beauty are one and the same thing, and that thing is an experience of the human spirit. We might even say that it is the simplest of all such experiences, and the earliest. Whenever a human being concentrates his total feeling into an image which is at once its essence and its utterance, the spirit of art is awakened. Beauty, in other words, lives in the creative imagination, and there alone ; and art is nothing more and nothing less than the experience which we call beauty. All else is irrelevant. True and false, real and unreal, good and bad, have no place in the æsthetic world. Here nothing counts but the perfection of the imaginative act in itself, and by its own standard. And this is in principle all that we need to know about the beautiful. It has no subdivisions within itself, and its manifestations array them-selves in no kind of series. Æsthetic philosophy lies in explaining the rank of beauty among the experiences of the spirit, and in defending the simplicity of the principle against traditional but unjustified intrusions.

This is the meaning of Croce's doctrine that beauty is expression. And that doctrine is sound. It does justice to the essential qualities of the beautiful ; to its spirituality and its simplicity. Wherever, it says, you find vision and utterance, there you have art and beauty. They may be on a great scale or a small, but they have one quality throughout.

It is a real service for a man to have thrown the whole weight of his conviction into this principle, and through it to have asserted æsthetic theory as a plain and human thing, disembarrassed of traditional lumber, and addressed directly to the central interest of all who care for beauty. This service it appears to us that Croce has rendered, and it should not and will not be forgotten when the exaggerations by which he has endeavoured to emphasize it have gone the way they will go.

For here, as elsewhere in his philosophy, it is impossible not to ask why the thinker who has given us so much has also taken so much away; why, to set off his true and spirited outline, he has thought it necessary to erase the whole supporting system.

To understand this necessity, we must follow his argument step by step.

The conceptions of Art and Beauty, which are for him coincident, are developed in his system by two constantly recurring terms, which are coincident both with the two former and with each other. These are Intuition and Expression.

The term Intuition insists mainly on the simplicity of the artistic experience, and on its priority in the scheme of the spiritual forms, which two characteristics intimately involve one another. The term Expression insists on the distinctive quality of the constructive imagination by which *ex*pressive activity is distinguished from the passivity which marks the *im*pression.

The two terms, being conjoined throughout as descriptive of the same experience, convey the conception that man's primary attitude to the world, before in the judgment of perception he discriminates the real from the unreal, is that of an intuition which is at once and inherently an imaginative expression. He does not judge; he pictures, focuses, apprehends ideally in an image the matter presented to his mind. Ideally, or imaginatively—for apprehension is ideal or imaginative when it portrays and does not affirm. This intuition-expression, as he calls it, this primary self-concentration of the mind in something which without any intellectual character is none the less a determinate spiritual utterance—think, Croce would say, of the simplest imaginable phrase of love or song—this intuition-expression is the elementary type of art and beauty. Let it swell to a five-act tragedy, and include all the sayings of Hamlet and Polonius, yet the constituents take their characters from the whole, and the primary intuition is a primary intuition-expression still. The mind gathers up in it the state and the material which it feels driven to portray as a whole, but it makes no judgment of reality, and simply looks before it at the expression it has created. Here is a passage which emphasizes in connection the simplicity and priority of the intuition :

" I observe in myself—that, in presence of any sensation whatever, if I do not abandon myself to the attractions and repulsions of instinct and feeling, if I do not permit myself to be distracted by reflections and reasonings, if I persist in the intuitive attitude, I am in that very disposition by means of which I enjoy what is commonly called a work of art. I live the sensation, but as a pure contemplative spirit. In ordinary life, reflections and volitions follow like lightning on the sensations, and then follow other sensations and reflections and volitions. But however lightning quick that succession may be, it does not abolish the first instant, which must be one of pure intuition. That first instant, multiplying and expanding itself, forms the region of the life of art. Without that first instant, without the little spark, the great flame could not follow. Artists in the pre-eminent sense are those who have the power of persisting longer than others in the moment of pure sensation or intuition,[1] and of inducing others to persist in it. Artists (as has been imaginatively observed) preserve the ingenuous and intent regard of the child ; remain remote and undistracted by practical preoccupations." [2]

This conception of the artistic intuition as something essentially primitive and prior in nature to intelligence and practice, while communicating a welcome emphasis to Croce's view of the simplicity and universality of art, is yet, in the systematic exaggeration which he imposes on it, the source of serious defects in his doctrine, which we must now consider.

Intuition in Croce's theory is the primitive form of knowledge, the higher form of which is philosophy. To call it knowledge seems strange to us, as it is in its proper nature free from conceptual affirmation and so prior to the judgment of perception, and unconcerned with discrimination between real and unreal. On the other hand, it is inherent in Croce's

[1] As a rule Croce ranks pure sensation with impressions as a condition precedent of intuition or expression.
[2] *Problemi di Estetica*, p. 484.

whole theory that language, conceived as an expressive flux of tone and gesture, belongs to the primitive stage, and is in fact a thing identical with intuition. Its conceptual and conventional side belongs to logic and the judgment, and by dwelling on this we are led to misconceive the nature of speech, which is in truth far nearer akin to poetry than to logic.

Art then, as prior and single, is independent. Art does not need the concept nor philosophy, but philosophy and the concept depend upon art, without which they would not possess the original flow of language—the poetry natural to man—on which their structure of universal meanings has to be erected.

These, then, art and philosophy, are the two theoretical phases of the spirit. Above or beyond these, in the sense of employing and depending upon them, are the two practical phases, the economic, that in which the particular person wills his particular end ; and the ethical, in which the parti-cular is expanded into the universal end of man and dominated by it. The practical forms depend on the theoretical, because will depends on knowledge ; the ethical on the economic, because you must have a will before you can have a good will.

These four forms constitute the complete cycle of reality, of the spirit's phases, which are not united in any complete experience, but are traversed by the human mind in spirals,[1] so to speak, in which every cycle recommences at the point of experience to which the race has been raised by that previously completed.

Thus Croce by no means denies that art can absorb and include the products of conceptual thinking. It precedes all other experience, he would maintain, in a logical but not in a temporal sense. Nevertheless, the idea of temporal prece-dence is influential in furnishing his theory with its primary type and ideal, as the passage which has been cited suffices to show. And from this idea there arises a series of conceptions, which, while they rhetorically reinforce his leading contention, really undermine and empty its substance. These conceptions draw out the consequences of reducing art and language to a common measure, the depth of which is prescribed by the

[1] This phrase is not to my knowledge used by Croce.

conviction which we have already observed in Croce, regarding the primitive intuition.

The origin of this conviction, to which Croce continually recurs, and which he holds with extreme intensity, we find apparently in Vico's influence. In the spring of 1900 Croce communicated his first paper on Æsthetic theory to the Accademia Pontiana at Naples, and in April 1901 he published his first contribution to the history of the subject under the title "Giambattista Vico primo scopritore della scienza estetica," which twelve years later he developed into a complete study of Vico's philosophy. What concerns us here is Vico's fundamental attitude to poetry in its connection with primitive language and primitive imagination. He adopts, or rediscovers, what our own Blackwell, an Aberdeen professor and late contemporary of Vico, speaks of as the "Ancient Opinion that Poetry was before Prose." But he intensifies it into a general theory of the origin of language in Song [1] and of the vast and profound imagination belonging to primitive men. "The men of the world's childhood were by nature sublime poets." [2] "These two common errors of the grammarians, that prose-writers' language is proper, and that of Poets improper, and that speech in prose came first, and verse afterwards." [3] Croce is thoroughly permeated with the ideas here suggested, the former of which he insists on in his rejection of the rhetorical distinction between bare and ornate language, and expands, as we shall see, into a general condemnation of doctrines which establish laws and classes in art and literature.

Now we cannot venture to say that these suggestions of Vico determined the whole form of Croce's philosophy of the spirit, the theory, that is, of the successive grades of reality, related as we have described. But obviously this doctrine harmonizes with Vico's attitude, and is reinforced by it; and we have now to consider the consequences which this fundamental orientation of his philosophy imposes upon Croce's æsthetic.

---

[1] So Blackwell (*Life of Homer*, A.D. 1735), αὐδᾶν = ἀείδειν. Vico points out that men who stammer can often sing without impediment, which reminds us of an incident in one of Marryat's novels.

[2] Vico, *Scienza Nuova : Degnità*, (axiom) xxxvii, cf. lxii.

[3] Op. cit. ii.

It is a fundamental principle with him, embodied in the attitude which we have seen that he shares with Vico, that language is identical with expression in the whole pregnancy of the term, that is, with intuition, art, and beauty. This reduction of art and language to a common measure depends on the idea of a phase of linguistic utterance in which logical meaning and assertion have not yet appeared ; in which parts of speech are not distinguished, and words are not discriminated as signs for objects, each to each, but the dramatic flow of tone and gesture springs from the total state of mind like a song or an imaginative vision. That there is much truth in a view which insists upon such an aspect of language need not be questioned. It is familiar ground to us to-day that the sentence and not the word is the linguistic unit.

But to enable ourselves to say all that Croce says, not merely " all language is expression " but " all expression is language," it is obvious that we must not only insist upon this aspect of speech but must exclude every other. If language is to be intuition and expression in a sense level with that in which these terms apply to all the utterances of art and embodiments of beauty, then logical affirmation and conceptual or conventional meaning must necessarily be banished from it. And this, we see at once, is the point in which Croce's scheme of degrees and Vico's equation of poetry and primitive speech converge and agree.

We may put it thus. We are quite accustomed to say that all art and beauty are expression and " speak a language." We are then adopting a phraseology which has for us a strong and unmistakable significance derived from our familiarity with the definite and conventional usage by which the spoken or written sentence " means " to us something definite, other than itself. When we say that the music or the picture speaks a language to us, we allude to this familiar quality with a modification distinctly understood. It speaks to us, we say, but we cannot put in words what it tells us. What it tells us cannot be told except by the music or the picture itself. It is not something outside them and separate. Even of a poem, which is in explicit words, we say the same. And we say it because the words of the poem

have undergone a tiansformation, and no longer are mere
words.  They have been made part of a new whole, and have
acquired a quality peculiar to them.

But the general truth we are urging is this.  When we
say that the music or the picture speaks to us, but we cannot
put in words what it says, we are referring to the significance
of language, not in any partial value, but in its completeness.
We employ the full conception of definite meaning, modified
by a reservation which we believe ourselves clearly to understand, to help in explaining what it is that we experience in
the intuition which we call art or beauty.  Something, something of supreme value, we are sure, is communicated to us,
though what it is we can only indicate by retraversing
the actual communication, which differs in this respect
from " language," that is, from the articulate discourse of
ordinary life.

Now when language is despoiled of its full capacity for
significance, in order to equate it, to level it, with expression
in general, the manœuvre is self-destructive.  Language has
become a gesture or a tune, and to compare a tune or a gesture
to language is now to compare a thing to itself.  If expression,
beauty, and language are taken in principle as prior to thought
and explicit meaning, then the problem of beauty is treated
as if it were solved, when in truth it has not yet been raised.
Beauty is not a datum but a transformation ;  not a gift at
birth, but the achievement of an adult.

We can see, however, the advantage which to Croce's
masterful and, I had almost said, unscrupulous genius appeared
to be offered by Vico's attitude.  Singleness was the gain ;
the absolute annihilation of everything that could in the
slightest degree appear to dictate from without to the self-
creating expression which is beauty.  To be rid of alien aims ;
of instructiveness, moral or intellectual ; of pleasurableness ;
of rank, dignity, and appropriateness in the subjects selected
for artistic expression ;  to banish technical rules and the laws
of stereotyped kinds ;  to shake off even the dictatorship
of well-authenticated physical beauty considered as located in
actual works of art or of nature—we can imagine the relief
which came to so uncompromising a spirit from the idea that
all this was to go, and that nothing was to matter any more

but the intuition of a mind that in a coherent imagination had found and satisfied itself. It is evident to an English reader that there must have been a struggle with traditions of rhetorical and literary criticism with which we are less familiar, and which imparted a zest and keenness to the work of repudiation. And this together with Croce's proneness to sweeping and unmodified conclusions goes far to account for the exaggerations and distortions, as they seem to us, into which his systematic doctrine impelled him.

Singleness, we said, was the lure. Not even content, we add to our former statements, was to dictate to expression. You cannot lay it down that this theme must be treated thus, and that other in that other way. For apart from the expression the content does not exist. You cannot take the content as a burden or a trust, to which in some way justice has to be done or appropriate treatment meted out by a method and form to be contrived. Content and form are created *pari passu* ; the intuition or expression is the two in one. And this true doctrine I hope is not unfamiliar to us ; our great English students of fine art and poetry have shown, I believe, no disposition to ignore it.

And yet, when we speak of expression, it is plain that sheer singleness, the singleness of priority and primitiveness, of the initial moment of sensation as it was portrayed for us above, cannot be the last word. Expression after all is an empty name, unless there is a something to be expressed, in an utterance which bears a definite quality and character. We cannot here pursue at length a profound misinterpretation of which Croce has been guilty, because he will not admit that you may so much as say that art and beauty are the sensuous reflex of the spirit that lives in the world-life. If you have called it the reflex or semblance of anything, he seems to say, you have made it the vehicle of an idea, and then, because such a vehicle can be nothing but an inferior philosophy, it must vanish and be absorbed when knowledge comes to its own.[1] But this is the very madness of method. In all vision of beauty of course there is present and concentrated a shape and revelation of life, and though to dissolve it into sides of burden and utterance is to falsify it, yet to study its

[1] See Appendix, " Croce's view of ' the death of art ' in Hegel."

coherence as a whole and the mode and self-congruence of
its harmony is both inevitable and desirable.  Art is in truth
the perpetual union of body and spirit, and to refuse to study
the body in which it clothes itself betrays a bias which indicates
a one-sided philosophy.  Croce, in fact, denies the reality of
the external world, and we shall see how this denial, advocated
with vehement conviction, converges with the influences we
have mentioned in his attitude to art.

Now whether or no Croce's philosophical scheme was
moulded initially by the impulse of Vico, there can be no
doubt that, to go no further, the position which the latter
assigns to art and intuition and with them to language in its
simplest form is exaggerated by Croce into self-contradiction.
The impulse to look to the primitive for the type of perfection
is natural and recurrent, and is not without a certain rough
justification.  There are obvious obsessions of advancing
civilization from which all that is nearer to the primitive
seems relatively free, and it is a natural suggestion that by
pursuing a regressive inquiry we shall come upon a phase of
experience which shall be single, utterly expressive, and wholly
free from alien preoccupation and from analytic thought.

But it cannot be so.  The whole conception of antedating
intuition and language by comparison with the logical affirmation and the concept or category is a nest of contradictions.
Intuitions, we are told, are things, concepts are universals or
relations.[1]  Things !  We can have intuitions of things, then,
without concepts or categories, without the *de facto* working
in our minds—questions of reflective recognition are here quite
irrelevant—of the thoughts of identity, distinction, substance,
whole and part.  It is a complete absurdity.

And so with language.  We can have language, the poetry
which is primitive speech, without the agreement upon the
reference of signs—agreement with ourselves and with others—
upon which the definite interpretation of language depends.
Signs cannot be conventional in origin, because you must
understand their reference before you can agree upon their
significance.  And so we are told the belief in a conventional
aspect of language drives you necessarily back to an original
gift of God.  The solution of this problem by the development

[1] *Estetica*, p. 27.

of natural signs into conventional meanings, the inevitable result of co-operation in practice, seems not to have attracted Croce's attention. In fact, apart from an aspect of definite analysis by which meanings are broken up and reconstituted out of simpler meanings, the primary function of language, to communicate to a mind what it does not know in terms of what it already knows, could not possibly be achieved.[1] The primitive mind, so far from being purely contemplative and imaginative, is immersed in practice ; and at every moment it must demand communication through definite and separable elements of speech. " Cross two rivers and turn upstream by the third." How could primitive life be carried on without such communications as this ? And how could such a sentence convey useful advice if the points at which error is possible were not distinct and recognizable references ? The mood of art is a victory and an advance, a divergence which contemplates from a new and happier standpoint the determinate taskwork with which life begins. It is an extraordinary contradiction to appeal, as Croce does more than once, to the contrast, already remarked by Aristotle, between the logical assertion or proposition and the sentence which utters a wish or command. Croce takes this to mean that the former alone had a significance according to agreement, while the latter could be a type of the primitive poetry which he thinks of as free from such meaning and prior to it. But both kinds of sentence alike, though one of them is not assertory, have of course " conventional " or logical significance, and it was to clench this point that I used an imperative as my illustration. Language, in short, is not language without its conceptual side ; and to equate language with intuition, and treat intuition as prior to thinking, is to shatter and overthrow the whole conception of a unity of the human mind.

The exaggeration which we have been criticizing is summed up in Croce's favourite identification of Æsthetic Philosophy with the general science of language. The problems of linguistic, so far as they are philosophical, are the same, he continually urges, with the problems of Æsthetic. Language is truncated by the rejection of its logical aspect, and its name is reduced to an indication that somehow, when the

[1] Stout, *Manual of Psychology*, pp. 595 ff.

mind finds relief and completeness in an utterance, an intuition, or an expression—we may hardly say, a communication—is achieved. The problems of the acquisition of definite meaning, or of the degree in which affirmation asserts reality, are set aside. All problems, on the other hand, which concern the theory of art—for example, we must suppose the question whether the human imagination reveals a progress in its creation of beauty—are swept into the province of " general linguistic." Many matters which we should consider to be problems of æsthetic—the nature and relations, for instance, of comedy and tragedy—are indeed excluded from the philosophy of art by the limitations which Croce imposes on it. But enough remain, it would seem, to make it a serious paradox that they should be assigned to the philosophy of language. The moment we look at language in its full significance we see that to identify its problems with those of the theory of art is an absurdity.

Croce rejects, we said, the reality of the external world. With this rejection, the singleness of the intuition-expression is forcibly intensified. In art, it is usually felt and held, there is in some sense an inner and outer. True, beauty lies in imagination and not in physical character, but yet the striving for expression seems to be a striving to give outward reality to something from within. To any such feeling of an inner and an outer in art or beauty Croce will not yield a hair's-breadth. The external world is not real at all; art is the most real of things. How then can art become a part of the external world, or be in any way concerned with physical processes or media ?

The " work of art " then, picture, statue, musical performance, printed or spoken poem, is called so only by a metaphor. It belongs to the practical (economic) and not to the æsthetic phase of the spirit, and consists merely in expedients adopted by the artist as a practical man, to ensure preservation and a permanent possibility of reproduction for his imaginative intuition. The art and beauty lie primarily in his imagination and secondarily in the imagination of those to whom his own may communicate its experience. The picture or the music are by themselves neither art nor beauty nor intuition-expression.[1]

[1] See account of stages of expression and externalization. *Estetica*, p. 113.

Thus all embodiment in special kinds of physical objects by help of special media and special processes is wholly foreign to the nature of art and beauty. Every expression is single and individual. There is nothing to be learned from the practical means by help of which intuitions of beauty receive permanence and communicability. The whole of Lessing's line of inquiry is futile. Expression does not fall into classes and types ; neither according to the media employed in externalizing it, nor according to any other principle of division. There are no limits of the arts.[1] There are indeed no arts distinguishable in accordance with the philosophy of beauty. The distinction, for example, of sound and colour is purely empirical. The inner vision, the intuition which is expression, *is* the experience of beauty. Or better, there is no question of inner or outer. The outer world is an abstract construction of physicists in order to explain and deal practically with our experiences. You cannot translate intuitions into terms of it.

We see how this philosophy reinforces Croce's devotedness to the undivided expression. But the contention seems on the way to become ridiculous. It has destroyed our meeting-point with ourselves and others in linguistic significance, and now it offers to destroy our medium of intercourse through the body and through natural objects. True, an object not experienced cannot be the experience of beauty. True, we hope and believe that all which we call body is in some sense an incarnation of the spirit. Nevertheless, it is an incarnation, and is not a mere state of mind. We experience natural objects as full concrete existences, with real qualities of colour and sound and splendour. Externality is a character of the world and a sign and vehicle of spiritual achievement, and there can be no doubt that the creative imagination yearns towards externality, and externality in some special medium.

Indeed, as we have seen, Croce's whole heart is set on insisting that there is no jot or tittle of content in our imagination beyond what has passed into expressive form, and that it is self-deception to suppose that we possess a mental store of

[1] There is some laudatory criticism of writers whose prose is like verse or like painting in *Scritti di storia letteraria*, x, 342.

beauty which only a lack of physical skill prevents us from translating into outwardness. " If you really had the thoughts, you would have coined them into as many beautiful ringing words." [1] " You are confronted with the reality of your imagination, when you are set to traverse the asses' bridge of expression—speak, or, here is a pencil, draw, we shall say to you." [2] Now on this side all is clear, and we claim no imagination which is not fused with expressive form. But has not Croce here committed himself also on the other side ? Is not, in this latter sentence, externalization at least the test, if not the essence, of expression ? Can the art-impulse, which is complete only in lines, colours, words, and tones,[3] be content before it has realized them in determinate objects of sense ? The external object, certainly, is not imagination ; but can imagination complete itself without the external object ? Croce tells us himself, " When our music is really music, it quavers in the throat and thrills along the fingers, as they run over an ideal keyboard." [4] Is this yearning of soul and body for complete determinateness in the world of sense-perception nothing but the practical man's precaution that his expression may not be lost ? Surely the simple fact is that the external world of sense-perception, though we may call it a form of the spirit, is yet a peculiar and distinctive form, with a function which nothing can replace ; and the noblest part of this function is to be the medium to ourselves and to others of the special discipline and determination with and by which the artistic imagination is formed. We may consider the art of music. Apart from the special discipline and experience which the instrument affords, the special world of purified sound in which the musical imagination is exercised and educated could hardly have existence for it at all. To reject the function of the body—our own and nature's—is not to honour but to bereave the spirit.

The truth is, surely, that different inclinations of the spirit have affinities with different qualities and actions of body—meaning by body that which a sane philosophy accepts as concretely and completely actual in the world

[1] *Estetica*, p. 12.                [2] *Ibid.*, p. 14.
[3] *Ibid.*, p. 11.                [4] *Breviario di Estetica*, p. 56.

of sense-perception. The imagination of the particular artist is

> like the dyer's hand,
> Subdued to what it works in,

and its intuition and expression assume a special type in accordance with the medium it delights in, and necessarily develop certain capacities, and acknowledge, however tacitly, certain limitations. Croce has remarked indeed that painting, for example, is not solely concerned with visual expression, but can raise softness, coolness, or keenness to the level of beauty. But this is irrelevant. What has beauty may concentrate in itself all the qualities of life; but it is not every quality of life that can form the vehicle of beauty; nor can everything that is capable of beauty present the spirit of life in the same aspect and mood.

After all, then, it is necessary for philosophy to study the specialities and limits of the arts; for in considering them we are considering the qualities and aspects of the human spirit; nay more, of the spirit which is in the world. If you know or can feel how the beauty of bronze—that is, its expressive capacity—differs from the beauty of marble, you are on the way to understand the diverging beauties of the arts; and if you insist on neglecting these affinities of the spirit, your theory remains abstract, and has no illuminating power.

And one thing more you lose, almost the greatest thing of all. You lose all sympathy with the spirit which is in nature. For you have forbidden yourself to think of it as a real revelation of the heart of things, though needing to be apprehended by man's appreciative imagination. And you come to account for it as a reproduction, by association with a physical stimulus, of some expression which you have experienced before. You impose yourself on nature, and do not submit your spirit to hers; and so you condemn yourself to say that " she is stupid in comparison with art, and is dumb if man does not make her speak." [1]

If indeed the properties of what is " outer " were separable and distinct from what is " inner," the repudiation of the former would be plausible. But Croce's passionate insistence

[1] *Breviario*, pp. 60-1.

on the inner determinate expression recoils upon him, as we have amply seen, when he comes to reject the necessity of outer determinateness. For it is perfectly plain that the inner— the imaginative vision—depends upon the outer, and that the human spirit, as is just and right, attains its greatness and its clearness only by going to school to the spirit of the universe in all its manifestations. In music we saw a decisive example of this ; and in visual art the " innocence of the eye " may be indeed a second childhood, but probably there never was a first corresponding to it. Practical necessities have taught us to see things " as they are," before we have had leisure and interest to see them as they genuinely appear. Here again the ideal of singleness and priority leads us astray. To love and to see the semblance is a victory and not a beginning. The spirit of the universe may be revealed in the spirit of man, but certainly not apart from man's intercourse with his surroundings ; and his imagination, already fashioned by discipline under the spirit that is in the outer world, feels itself incomplete until in union with the most perfect bodily effort it has created an example of complete self-determination in one of the vehicles which that world supplies. We have merely to think of the effort of song or of passionate speech to realize this creative outward pressure of soul and body as a whole. We may set against each other no doubt the saying of Leonardo, " The more of bodily labour any art demands, the less is it honourable," and the words of Mr. Ruskin, " All art is athletic." It is not difficult to interpret the balance of body and mind—the fine adjustment and intense concentration —which taken together they suggest.

The beauty of physical objects, we agree, is the experience which they suggest to a human imagination. But where Croce argues at length [1] that such beauty, because relative to variety of cases, is subjective and unreal, we are confronted with the hoariest of fallacies. If anything is certain in philo-sophy it is that an experience varying relatively with the variation of conditions is an experience that indicates a reality. By such an argument, as we have seen, we shut our souls against the world spirit, and refuse to submit to his teaching.

Thus the ideal of pure singleness in expression and intuition

[1] *Estetica*, c. xiv.

has led us to the point that, because there is in beauty no
content distinct from the expression, there is therefore in the
whole expressed, and in the total gamut of expressive forms,
no life or spirit whose character concentrates itself in their
quality and shaping.   We have abandoned all regard for the
respective affinities which fuse the spirit's utterance with the
several splendours of sense-perception.   And we are now to
see, further, how we lose all interest in the ordered variations
of the expressive quality itself—the subdivisions of the
beautiful and the transition which connects it with the ugly—
and the shapes and patterns of poetry which the various
visions of life have forged for themselves and are for ever
forging anew.

An overstrained emphasis on the distinction, in principle
obsolete, between what is philosophical and what is empirical,
will always bring us into peril of nominalism and particularism.
And so we find it here.  " Sublime " (and comic, tragic,
humoristic, etc.)  " is all that which has been or shall be so
*named* [1] by those who have employed or who shall employ
these words." [2]  These distinctions, that is to say, are not
philosophical.   They are *only* what we find essential to apprehending the special and characteristic values in which beautiful expression arrays itself.   So again :  " He who speaks of
tragedies, comedies, dramas, romances, genre paintings, battle
pieces, landscapes, sea pieces, poems, idylls, lyrics, and so
forth—certainly says nothing scientifically erroneous, because
he is employing names and phrases, not establishing definitions."  (The " laws " of kinds of literature, considered as
rigid imperative rules, are his great *bête noire*, which shows,
as I noted above, that he is partly incensed by the prevalence
of traditions which have become unfamiliar to us.)  These
distinctions he goes on to compare with the arrangements of
books in bookcases according to their format or publisher's
series—a useful arrangement, but without literary significance !
We will say a word upon each of these classifications.

First it is to be noted that the doctrine of sheer simplicity
in expression destroys what a philosopher might call the
dialectic of expressiveness ; that is to say, the tendency of
distinctions of quality to arise through the presence of some-

[1] Croce's italics.                    [2] *Estetica*, p. 106.

thing which is felt as entering into, breaking through, or breaking down, the unity of the imaginative utterance.

Thus the difference between the merely beautiful and the sublime is for Croce no question of æsthetic, but a verbal and fallacious distinction, arising from what he classes under the heresy of æsthetic hedonism, namely the restriction of beauty as such to the sympathetic or what is immediately pleasing. The beautiful being for him coextensive with expression, and equated with the æsthetically excellent, admits of no sub-division into more facile and more difficult types, such as beauty *par excellence*, the sublime, the terrible, and the gro-tesque. And this extension of the term " beauty " to the whole province of the æsthetically excellent is in harmony, I believr with the best artistic feeling, and if this were all that he mair, tained, Croce's position, as is often the case with him in the advocacy of very general truths, would be exceedingly strong. But when he denies all æsthetic value to the distinction, within the general region of beauty, between the simply beautiful and the sublime, he is influenced by the ideal which destroys for him the dialectic of expression. There can be little question that in some intuitions of beauty there is a felt or threatened interruption to the perfectness of the harmony, such as itself to be expressive of a presence which no vehicle of manifestation can altogether contain.[1] We cannot here go further into the theory of the sublime, but it is easy to see that it is a variation of the beautiful dependent on a negative factor in the expression demanded in some experiences by the spirit of the whole.

An analogous dialectic connects the beautiful with the ugly, and here it is interesting to note how an imperfect recognition of the particular mode in which the one is negative towards the other introduces confusion into Croce's account of both.

The question about ugliness which stares a student of æsthetic in the face is whether or no it is an æsthetic quality—whether it is to beauty as evil to good, or merely a vacancy and an absence. Croce's primary position is laid down thus : " It is idle to speak, as does the doctrine which confines beauty to the sympathetic, of ugliness in art. For us there is no

[1] E.g. A. C. Bradley, *Oxford Lectures on Poetry*, p. 58.

ugliness but the anti-æsthetic or the inexpressive, which can
never form part of the æsthetic fact, being on the other hand
its contrary and antithesis." [1]   Now it is difficult for a contrary
and antithesis not to be something of an invader ; it is not
quite the same as a contradictory and privation.   And so we
are not surprised to find that where you have the spiritual
fact of expression you have a bipartition between the poles of
the beautiful and the ugly,[2] which thus, I take it, *is* after all
held to be an æsthetic quality.   And we further find that
ugliness implies the presence of some element of beauty ;
for if no such element were present the ugly would lose the
self-contradictory quality which is its essence, and falling
outside the æsthetic frontier (so I understand the passage)
would cease to be ugly.[3]   A clearer case of ugliness and one
which seems to us best to elucidate its nature as an aggres-
sive contrary within æsthetic territory—" æsthetic ugliness "
Croce himself calls it—is that in which the would-be artist
has " nothing of his own to express, but attempts to cover his
inward emptiness with a flux of words, with sonorous verse,
with deafening polyphony, with dazzling colour—all without
meaning.   The ugly is the arbitrary, the charlatanesque—it
is due to the intervention of the practical will in the theoretic
function, and without this you might have absence of beauty,
but you could never have anything effective which should
merit the name of the ugly." [4]   You create, that is, a something
which both is and *is not* æsthetic.   One other case will complete the account.   " There are uglinesses and beastlinesses
(*turpitudini*) in the world, and as long as this is so they will
impose themselves on the artist and the correlative expressions
will arise.   But these expressions a true critic, in opposition
to the vulgar, will recognize as beautiful." [5]   It is clear that
in these various cases of the ugly, as in the sublime, and, we
shall further see, in comedy and tragedy, we are dealing with
a connection between expression and something to be expressed.
The cases can only be brought into intelligible order if we
recognize the conception of conflicts and collisions within the
life which takes shape in art, giving rise, in the expressions
which it creates, to intuitions in which conflict is explicit but

[1] *Estetica*, p. 104.     [2] *Ibid.*, pp. 112–13.     [3] *Ibid.*, p. 93.
[4] *Ibid.*, p. 115.     [5] *Ibid.*, p. 99.

wholly reconciled, or announces itself through a hinted restraint or check in the artistic structure, or dominates with its falsehood the entire utterance, fashioning it into an involuntary caricature—a tawdry imitation—of something which truly expressed would have been great or strong. Some such relations as these obviously subsist between the tragic along with other types of difficult beauty, the sublime, and the ugliness which, disguised as an æsthetic quality, or entangled with one, invades the æsthetic province.

And finally we may test the doctrine which expels from æsthetic philosophy the consideration of literary genera, by some reference to the recent discussions of tragedy, comedy, and the distinction between poetry and prose.

To begin with the latter. " In fact," Croce tells us, " the two expressions (poetry and prose), *qua* expressions, are of the same nature, and they both have the same æsthetic value ; because, if the poet is the lyrical singer (lirico) of his own feelings, the prose writer is no less the lyrical singer (lirico) of his own, that is to say, a poet, though it be with reference to feelings which rise in him from the research of the idea (as opposed to the intuition). There is no reason to concede the quality of poet to the composer of a sonnet and to deny it to the composer of the *Metaphysic*, the *Summa Theologica*, the *Phenomenology of Mind*," or to Thucydides and Tacitus,[1] etc. All this springs from the doctrine we have noted throughout. Expression is individual and indivisible ; there is nothing to observe of its correlation or adapted variation in view of anything to be expressed. It would be an injustice to the subject if we were here to reproduce imperfectly the study which one of our finest critics devoted not long ago to the meaning of verse as returning or repeating language, as opposed to the language of prose, which moves on without any such return or repeat.[2] " The essence of poetry is that it is patterned language." It is the repeating and yet continuous pattern in language which makes it technically poetry, and its substantial and vital function is to make patterns out of life. And with this mere reference we may leave the subject ; only pointing out that here as everywhere to the philosophical critic the study of expression in correlation with what is

[1] *Breviario*, p. 93.        [2] Mackail, *Lectures on Poetry*, pp. 12 ff.

expressed is endlessly fruitful in the revelation of organic and inherent variations, and a doctrine which demands its rejection stands self-condemned. A word on the ideas which emerge from the consideration of Tragedy and Comedy will lead us to a suggestive conclusion, bearing upon yet another aspect of Croce's æsthetic conceptions.

Tragedy and comedy correspond to a certain type of pattern which art in their case finds in or weaves out of life. They work in a certain medium, which is the stage, and their action is what can be acted. They have in common a certain tension and concentration ; " a problem, we may say, is in each case set and solved." These characters are inherent and essential ; they spring from the relation of the art-function to certain characters of life.[1] Other modes of pattern-making are possible *ad infinitum*, who can doubt it ? It is in contrast with such another mode that in the study I am referring to these characters are emphasized. But we repeat—relative variation is no proof of arbitrariness ; to a philosophy that knows its business, it is the sure indication of reality.

About tragedy, where it differs from comedy, there is also much to be said which has essential truth. Where Aristotle and Hegel have given us of their best, and recent criticism has pursued the study on the highest level,[2] it seems an impoverishment of life to argue that in principle the distinction of these forms is valueless.

But there is an essential distinction between Comedy and Tragedy. " When Dante (in speaking of the *Divina Commedia*) wrote *Subiectum operis est homo*, one can hardly doubt that he had in his mind, consciously or subconsciously, the famous line of the Terentian comedy, the *Homo sum, humani nihil a me alienum puto* of Chremes, which is the complete and permanent motto of comedy itself." " Comedia," the same writer quotes from John of Salisbury, " est vita hominis super terram," and after further quotations he continues : " The great truth upheld in, latent in, these fragmentary but illuminating sentences is that in the evolution of poetry, comedy tends to displace tragedy, or tragedy to merge in a higher and wider Tragi-comedy. Only in that larger and wider scope

[1] Mackail, op. cit., p. 211.
[2] A. C. Bradley, *Oxford Lectures on Poetry, Shakesperian Tragedy.*

can the expression of life be given, the pattern and interpretation of life be found. All the more tense and exclusive forms of poetry gradually translate themselves into a larger pattern and looser texture." [1]

And finally, we are to feel that in the *Aeneid* itself " there is a something which transcends art, properly so called,[2] for the function of art is to create and embody some image of perfection ; and the image which Virgil finally sets before us is of imperfection ; the wistfulness, the haunting trouble of its poetry, is of its inmost quality." " That transcendence, that continued search further and further after what cannot be found, that stretching out of the hands (to use his own words rather than those of any later appreciation) in love of a further shore, is not consistent with the requirements of a complete and finished work of art."

The evolution from tragedy in the direction of the larger and looser texture which is characteristic of comedy in the widest sense, or of romance ; the transcendence of the limits of art just when the summit appears to have been attained— who that is familiar with the theory of Hegel will fail to recognize, in the finer and subtler design of the critic of to-day, the impulse of transformation which the philosopher's insight detected ? Here is what Hegel intended when he portrayed the longdrawn dissolution or resolution of art, as it passed from the age and habit of classical tradition to the freedom and fullness, on the constant verge of self-transcendence, which belongs to the modern artist.

As Mr. Mackail applies to the Shakespeare of the romantic plays Virgil's crowning address to Dante, so we might apply it to the free and modern artist as Hegel portrays him.[3] And in Croce's misconception, which has fatally obscured for him Hegel's great work of insight, and has reiteratedly impeached the profoundest student of beauty with teaching as a truth and necessity that art's life has reached its term, and the hour of its dissolution, which is its death, has come,[4] we see

[1] Mackail, op. cit., pp. 176 ff.
[2] *Ibid.*, p. 90.
[3] *Æsthetik*, ii. 232.
[4] Croce, *Scritti di storia letteraria*, x, 306 and *passim*. The phrase " death of art," which Croce constantly cites as if verbatim from Hegel, does not, so far as I know, occur in his writings. It is, I presume, a mistranslation of *Auflösung der Kunst*.

the reaction of the fatal pursuit of singleness, which insists that to assign a meaning to expression is to turn it into bare philosophy.

The truth is surely other. Schiller was right, and to love and look at the appearance for its own sake, which is for the sake of its meaning, is not a primitive gift, but perhaps man's most typical self-conquest on the path to civilization. It is well to proclaim the unity of beauty and the autonomy of the shaping imagination ; but it is not well to disregard the fact which forms the glory of art, that in it alone the body of man and of nature rushes to meet the soul in a splendour which springs from both, and every particle of which is charged with significance.

## APPENDIX ON CROCE'S CONCEPTION OF THE " DEATH OF ART " IN HEGEL

Considerable interest attaches to the problem raised by a hostile criticism of Hegel's æsthetic theory, which Croce repeats, so to speak, at the top of his voice, throughout the whole range of his writings. The statement has passed unchallenged in English critical literature, although it concerns no mere question of technical philosophy, but the appreciation of a whole aspect of beauty, in his vision of which Hegel was right, and profound, and in harmony with what our best recent critics have taught us. Here is the statement in its fullest form.[1]

(For Hegel) the artistic activity is distinguished from the philosophical solely by its imperfection, solely because it grasps the Absolute in sensible and immediate form, whereas philosophy grasps it in the pure element of thought. Which implies, logically, that it is not distinguished at all, and that art, for Hegel, reduces itself substantially, whether he will or no, to a philosophical error, an illusory philosophy. The true art, then, must be philosophy, which re-proposes to itself the same problem on which the other [art] labours in vain, and resolves it in a perfect manner.

That such is Hegel's genuine thought is proved by the fact that he does not repudiate the extreme consequence of this theory ; when

---

[1] Croce, *Saggio sullo Hegel*, p. 89.

philosophy is completely developed, art must disappear, as a super-fluity ; art must die, and, moreover, is to-day stark dead (*bella e morta*). If it is an error, it is not necessary and eternal.  The history of art, as Hegel traces it, is directed to exhibit the progressive dissolution of artistic form, which, in modern times, no longer pertains to our true and profound interest ; it is a past, or a survival of the past.  This immense paradox illuminates Hegel's æsthetic error in all its detail ; and better perhaps than any other example, elucidates the error of the logical presupposition itself.  It has been said, in defence of Hegel, that the death of art, of which he speaks, is that eternal dying which is an eternal rebirth ; as it is observed in the spirit of man, when from poetry it makes a transition to philosophy, from intuition exalts itself to the universal, and thereupon the world of intuitions loses its visible hues.  But contradicting this interpretation there is the fact that Hegel speaks of a death of art, not perpetually renewing itself, but, strictly, as happening and having happened ; of a death of art in the world of history.  And this is fully in agreement with his treatment of the grades of reality as if they were a series of opposites,[1] infelicitously abstracted and dissevered.  Given this application which he made of the dialectic, Hegel was left no choice but either to suppress art by that immense paradox, or to preserve it by an inconsistency no less immense.[2]

This and many similar passages raise two questions, one of logical necessity, one of historical judgment.  I believe that it can be shown briefly and finally that the author is wrong in his answer to both.  Hegel was under no logical necessity to infer the death of fine art ; and in his historical judgment he affirmed not that, but something very different, which is still of interest.

1.  Croce himself has formulated an unanswerable criticism on the inference which he here asserts that Hegel is logically compelled to draw.  " On the assumption that art is a necessary grade of the spirit, to question whether art is eliminable would be neither more nor less than like asking whether sensation or intelligence is eliminable." [3]  Now why does he launch this as a criticism against Hegel, instead of advancing it as an

---

[1]  " Opposite " concepts are for Croce such as " true " and " false " ; " distinct " concepts are such as " true " and " beautiful."  His technical criticism is that Hegel treats the latter just like the former, and therefore as inadequate on one side at least.  Croce's own doctrine is difficult to reconcile with his account of the stimulus to progress from phase to phase of the spirit. *Breviario di Estetica*, p. 82.

[2]  Compare *Estetica*, p. 76.

[3]  *Estetica*, p. 76.  The passage is directed, I take it, against Hegel's and kindred views, though his name is not there mentioned.  [See below, p. 431.—ED.]

interpretation of Hegel's view? The answer is indicated in
my quotation. It is because, in theory, Hegel treats the
phases of experience as degrees of completeness in the characterization of reality, and because, in fact, as we shall see directly,
Croce mistranslates and misreads Hegel's historical judgment upon " the dissolution of art." The former point could
only be explained with completeness in a logical discussion.[1]
But the net result is this. Croce thinks that if you treat the
forms of experience as terms in a logical progress towards
perfection, you have committed yourself to regard them as
no more than logical abstractions, of which every earlier is
absorbed and included without remainder in every later term.
He seems unable to employ the conception of a system whose
members, just because each implies a logical progress to some
other, are constituent factors of it, as well as degrees of its
perfection. Croce's own " grades of the spirit " are not
" degrees of reality," although he makes use of this expression.
They are successive and alternative phases of spiritual
activity, and each contains in itself no logical demand for
advance or completion beyond itself and towards any other.

Thus when Hegel exhibits fine art as continuous with
religion, which is its complement, and both of them together
as experiences which demand a fuller understanding in philosophy, and apart from which philosophy would itself be
incomplete, Croce holds himself entitled to infer that when
philosophy comes on the scene the other two are taken to be
*ipso facto* swallowed up and annulled, as the Ptolemaic by
the Newtonian astronomy.

But this whole reading of Hegel's logical method is
erroneous. The phases of experience which reveal relative
approximations to completeness are not successive in time
nor vanishing in logic. Croce's own observation above cited
shows the absurdity in trying to take them so. As factors
implying the whole system and implied in it they are grades
of the spirit in the fullest sense. The absolute is the whole
which they constitute, and if any of them were eliminated
would be the absolute no longer.[2] If art finds its completion

---

[1] See *Mind*, October, 1918, review of Croce's logic.
[2] On the absolute as the inclusive whole of its stages, cf. Hegel, *Encyclo-
paedia*, sect. 237.

in philosophy, then a philosophy lacking the peculiar experience of art is an incomplete philosophy. One might as well argue that philosophy must be taken to supersede and become a substitute for life or being.

Thus the defence of Hegel's view, to which Croce refers in the passage quoted above, has a sound logical basis, which in his version is sufficiently explained. The terms of a logical progression whose mainspring is the spirit of an immanent whole, must necessarily tend each to pass beyond itself, into the more complete terms which succeed it, while each nevertheless retains its being as in itself an irreplaceable experience. Croce knows no immanent whole, no systematic unity which is the mainspring of a logical advance towards the definition of an inclusive perfection. And therefore he can understand no logical advance which does not supersede whatever came before it.

2. On the question of Hegel's *de facto* historical judgment the evidence leaves no room for doubt. The points can be stated very shortly.

(i) The phrase " the death of art," which Croce reiterates as if a verbal quotation, does not occur in the sixteen hundred pages of Hegel's *Lectures on Æsthetic* and I do not believe that it occurs anywhere in his works. It probably represents a mistranslation of the term " Auflösung " encouraged by the logical misunderstanding elucidated above. This word has a pregnant meaning of great interest, which we will examine below.

(ii) The general relation of philosophy to life in Hegel's theory excludes the possibility of an historical judgment which involves a prediction, such as that of the non-persistence of art in human life. All students are aware that for Hegel philosophy explains but does not predict. It is needless to labour this point further.

It is, however, interesting to note that as a mere illustration Hegel does at one point permit himself to speak of the future of epic poetry, and expresses the opinion that the necessary national contrast for a great war epic of the future could only be found in the relations between America and Europe, and not within the European complex of peoples.[1] It is

---

[1] *Æsthetik*, iii, 355.

plain that the disappearance of art from human experience has never occurred to his mind. The same ridiculous mistake is frequently made, by neglect of the same principle, about his view of the historical succession of peoples in the leadership of the world. Philosophy for him deals with the past and present. He actually mentions America as the country of the future, and as, being so regarded, no subject for philosophy.[1]

(iii) The citation of texts almost weakens an argument which depends on the appreciation of a philosopher's entire attitude and systematic convictions; but so far as any expression can be decisive, the following words, the authenticity of which there is no reason to doubt, forming the close of the Introduction prefixed to his posthumous *Lectures on Æsthetic*, appear to settle the question of his *de facto* belief and opinion. "What, therefore, the particular arts bring into being in individual works of art are according to their notion only the universal forms of the self-developing idea of beauty, as whose external realization there is rising the immense Pantheon of art, whose architect and director is the self-recognizing spirit of the beautiful, but which to complete, the world-history will require its evolution of millennia."[2]

(iv) And the question is set at rest finally and in detail, as it seems to me, by the elaborate and most interesting discussion devoted by Hegel to the function and position of "the modern artist," the artist "of our own day,"[3] considered with reference to the situation which existed *after* the period of "romantic" art had come to an end, and therefore *after* the final Auflösung of classical and romantic art, to which as a rule, and not to art in general, he attaches the term Auflösung.[4] In a word, after all the Auflösung had taken place, art and the artist survived in a new attitude and a new world. On the main point at issue this is enough. But the interest of the question will justify a brief examination of what Hegel meant by the Auflösung or any similar term as applied to art or to any form of it; and what was this function and position which he recognized as that of the "modern artist," the "artist of our own day."

[1] *Philosophie der Geschichte*, pp. 107–8.
[2] *Æsth.*, i, 114.
[3] *Ibid.*, ii, 233–5.
[4] On a rare example to the contrary, see below.

(v) The word " Auflösung," like the English word " dissolution," may of course in certain contexts be equivalent to " death." But its natural usage rather follows the suggestion of loosening a knot, as in a tragic complication (*dénouement*), resolving a contradiction or a dissonance, solving a problem or difficulty, elucidating by analysis. In Hegel we find it once at least in the *Logic* bearing such a meaning, where the contradiction embodied in an infinite series is said to be " resolved " into the end or terminus.[1] Of course this does not imply that the contradiction so resolved ceases to be experienced. It is used in the extra-logical works in a sense akin to that of the familiar logical verb " aufheben " or " sich aufheben," which expressly involves the persistence of the element so " set aside." And it is noticeable that in a crucial passage of the Æsthetic lectures [2] Hegel applies the term " sich aufhebt " (transcends itself) to the process which he mostly describes as the Auflösung of art in some special form. What Hegel means by the dissolution of art is the course of development which transformed the art of classical Greece into the art of Christian Europe, and ultimately into the art of the world in the early nineteenth century. It divides itself primarily in his rubrics into the dissolution of classical art and the classical ideal, and the dissolution and the close of romantic art. But this matters little for the general problem, since what he means by romantic art *is* [3] for him, in its several stages, one and the same thing with the dissolution of classical art, with its own dissolution, and with the dissolution of art as such, in so far as he intended to speak of any such thing.

The meaning of the term is double, logical and æsthetic. Art is being dissolved or set aside, as any logical form is dissolved or set aside, which becomes by its inadequacy a source of contradiction demanding resolution and explanation by larger points of view. Undoubtedly the whole world of art, as addressing itself to sensuous intuition, was in his eyes tending to become a spring of such contradiction and transcendence when compared with the full resources of the human spirit in religion and philosophy. And art is within itself in a

[1] *Encyol.*, sect. 242. Cf. *Wiss. d. Logik*, p. 7.
[2] *Æsth.*, ii, 136.
[3] *Ibid.*, i, 217, where this is very definitely stated.

parallel way being dissolved, resolved, or disintegrated in abandoning the relative narrowness and fixity of early traditional vision, and expanding from the relatively rigid and inherited basis of Greek and of Christian art into nothing less than the love and imaginative penetration of any and every feature by which man or the world can touch in the region of sense man's own heart and mind. This *is* " Dissolution," if we will have it so ; after all, it is Browning's metaphor

> That one face, far from vanish, rather grows,
> Or decomposes but to recompose,
> Become my universe that feels and knows.

Necessarily in this " resolution " a change has come about not only within art, but in the relation of art to our whole experience. " One may hope that art will continue to ascend and to perfect itself ; but its form has ceased to be the highest demand of the spirit. How excellent soever we find the Greek statues, however nobly and perfectly we see portrayed God the Father, Christ, and Mary, it makes no difference, our knees no longer bend." [1] The observation is surely a simple truism, and even of the most modern and most comprehensive art it holds good in spirit. There are more things in heaven and earth than are dreamed of even in beauty. The " dissolution " of art is both into an altered art, and also into an altered status in life.

It is an obvious case of such transcendence and displacement, both logical and æsthetic, when Hegel speaks definitely of comedy as " leading to the dissolution of art in general." [2] It is a truth akin to that which recent criticism has recognized in agreement with Hegel to the effect that " in the evolution of poetry, comedy tends to displace tragedy." [3] " All the more tense and exclusive forms of poetry gradually translate themselves into a larger pattern and looser texture." When " Dante meant to include everything in his poem," he called it a Comedy. And to include everything would be to transcend the limits of art. There is always a world which art cannot include. So even with the *Aeneid* ; there is in it, the same

---

[1] *Æsth.*, i, 132.
[2] *Ibid.*, iii, 580.
[3] Mackail, *Lectures on Poetry*, pp. 176–7.

critic has pointed out,[1] a transmutation and spiritualization of poetry which transcends art properly so called, " a continued search further and further after what cannot be found."

But that art, like every experience, has in it the spirit which leads it at a certain point to pass beyond itself, tells no more, as we saw, against its persistent vitality than the same characteristic tells against the vitality of sensation or of science.

The whole 143 pages [2] of Hegel's Æsthetic lectures which deal with the Auflösung of the special art-forms and of art bear out the above account, which is a very brief and unworthy summary of them. The Auflösung, the dissolution or resolution, goes hand in hand, for example, with the Versöhnung [3]—the reconciliation, or union of inward feeling and the complex actual world, with the Aufschliessung [4]—the unfolding or self-manifestation of the divine, and the infinite Erweiterung [5]—expansion of the range of art, obtained by a correlative concentration in the focus of the human soul.

(vi) Enough has really been said. But a word may be added on the decisive climax, which comes in Hegel's explicit attitude to the modern artist, the artist of his own day, whom he regards as living and working *after* the Auflösung of art in general has fully come into play. Here one or two quotations will be in place and will suffice.

" In contrast with the time in which the artist, owing to his nationality and his age, stands essentially within a definite view of the world and type of artistic production, we now find an absolutely opposite standpoint, which in its complete development has become important only in the most recent period. In our day, among almost all nations, reflective culture and the critical spirit, and with us Germans freedom of thought, have extended their domination to the artists themselves, and have made them so to speak a *tabula rasa* with regard to the matter and form of their production, *after* [6] even the inevitable particular stages of the romantic form of art have been traversed. For the artist of to-day it is a feature of the past to be bound to a particular content and a

---

[1] Mackail, *Lectures on Poetry*, p. 90. [Cf. p. 426 above.—ED.]
[2] *Æsth.*, ii, 100–243.                    [3] *Ibid.*, p. 118.
[4] *Ibid.*, p. 123.         [5] *Ibid.*, p. 281.         [6] My italics.

mode of representation appropriate to it, and art has become a free instrument by the fact that he can operate in accordance with his subjective ability in relation to any content of what-soever kind. Hence the artist stands above the determinate traditional forms and shapes, and moves freely in his own mind, independently of the content and mode of intuition in which consciousness in former ages envisaged the holy and the eternal." [1]

" In this latter form of art (the romantic), as in those before it, the divine was essentially and definitely the object of art. But this divine element had to take objective shape, to particularize itself, and thereby to advance out of itself into the secular import of subjectivity. To begin with " (as Hegel has described) " the infinite value of personality lay in honour, love, and loyalty, then in the peculiar individ-uality, the determinate character, which fused itself with the special substance of a man's existence. The amalgamation with such a specific limitation of content was finally set aside again by humour, which had the power of rendering unstable and resolving every specification, and thus caused art to transcend itself. Yet in this self-transcendence, it is none the less a withdrawal of man into himself, a descent into his own breast, whereby art strips off from itself every rigid limitation to a definite sphere of content and of apprehension, and adopts as its modern saint the human man,[2] with the deeps and heights of the human heart as such, with universal humanity in its joys and griefs, its aspirations, acts, and destinies. Here-by the artist receives his content within himself, and is one with the human mind as it actually specifies itself, as it con-templates, creates, and expresses the infinity of its feelings and situations, the mind to which nothing now is alien, which can live in the human breast. This is a subject-matter which is no longer essentially and definitely determined as artistic,[3] but surrenders the choice of content and of creative shaping to original invention, but yet excludes no particular source of interest. For art no longer needs only to represent that

[1] *Æsth.*, ii, p. 232.
[2] " den *humanus*," a reference probably to the famous line, " Homo sum, humani nihil a me alienum puto." See five lines below.
[3] i.e. We do not now say " these and these subjects are the subjects of art ; those and those are not."

which is absolutely at home in some one of its particularized
stages, but has everything open to it which man in general
has capacity to make his own." [1]

" The artist need feel no special necessity, with a view to
his work, of settling his own conviction and caring for his
own salvation ; his great and free soul must, fundamentally,
and before he enters upon production, know and possess the
basis on which it is to stand, and be sure and confident within
itself ; and more particularly the great artist of to-day [2] is
in need of the free development of mind, in which all superstition and belief such as is permanently limited by determinate
forms of intuition and representation, are set aside as mere
parts and aspects, over which the free mind has made itself
sovereign. For he sees in them no consecrated conditions of
his exposition and imaginative shaping, but assigns value to
them only in virtue of the higher import with which, in his
re-creation of them, he endows them as their true belonging." [3]

In a word, art, after passing through phases determined
by the conditions of relatively early mind, has achieved
its freedom, as thought after a similar apprenticeship has
achieved its own.[4] What the necessary evolution of the
art-forms, in Hegel's view, here says to the modern artist,
inasmuch as the dissolution of art was concurrently its libera-
tion, is in the tone of what Virgil said to Dante : [5]

> Tratto t' ho qui con ingegno e con arte,
> Lo tuo piacere omai prendi per duce :
> Fuor sei dell' erte vie, fuor sei dell' arte.

> Non aspettar mio dir più, nè mio cenno.
> Libero, dritto e sano è tuo arbitrio,
> E fallo fora non fare a suo senno :
> Perch' io te sopra te corono e mitrio.

This I hold to be the truth about " the death of art " in Hegel.

[1] *Æsth.*, ii, 234–5. This passage, besides indicating Hegel's view of modern
art, is a brief epitome of the Auflösung and self-transcendence of art, setting
in relation its positive and negative sides.
[2] *heutige* : cf. p. 234, *Der moderne Künstler.*
[3] *Ibid.*, 233.
[4] See the *Phenomenology of Mind.*
[5] Mackail, op. cit., p. 216. This application of Dante's lines, analogous to
that made by Mr. Mackail in speaking of Shakespeare's romantic plays,
suggested itself to the writer, he believes, independently.

# INDEX TO PERSONS

# INDEX TO PERSONS

441

Schleiermacher, F. D. E., 390
Schopenhauer, 143, 390
Scott, Sir Walter, 308, 387
Shakespeare, 306, 311, 316, 385
Shelley, 387 f.
Sherbrooke, Lord, 297
Sidgwick, Henry, 41
Sigwart, 49
Socrates, 272, 311, 379
Spencer, 38, 42, 46, 148, 157, 238 f., 384, 390
Spinoza, 141, 154, 164, 236
Stewart, J. A., 352
Stout, G. F., 70, 90 f., 94, 96 f., 152, 254, 416
Strauss, D. F., 384
Sully, James, 41, 392, 394, 401
Swift, 59
Swinburne 108

Tarde, Gabriel, 65, 227
Taylor, A. E., 150 ff., 182, 197
Tennyson, 330
Terence, 426
Theocritus, 310 f.
Tieck, J. L., 375
Tourgenieff, 313
Turner, J. M. W., 391

Vico, G., 411 ff.
Virgil, 427, 437
Volkmann, W. F., 395
Voltaire, 349

Wallace, William, 15–16
Ward, James, 41, 401
Winckelmann, 373 f., 384
Woods, R. A., 290
Wordsworth, 159, 227, 310, 387 f.

# INDEX TO SUBJECTS